MW01611720

ALISON INGLEBY

Liberators

The Wall Series Book 4

First published by Windswept Writing 2020

Copyright © 2020 by Alison Ingleby

All rights reserved. No part of this publication may be reproduced, stored or transmitted in any form or by any means, electronic, mechanical, photocopying, recording, scanning, or otherwise without written permission from the publisher. It is illegal to copy this book, post it to a website, or distribute it by any other means without permission.

This novel is entirely a work of fiction. The names, characters and incidents portrayed in it are the work of the author's imagination. Any resemblance to actual persons, living or dead, events or localities is entirely coincidental.

Alison Ingleby asserts the moral right to be identified as the author of this work.

First edition

ISBN: 978-1-9999022-3-0

This book was professionally typeset on Reedsy.
Find out more at reedsy.com

Dedication

For Skye. You taught me a lot about grief but more about love.
Love you to the moon and back.

A Note on Language

This story is set in a future London and is written in British English. For my readers who are more accustomed to U.S. English spellings and terms, I hope you don't find this too distracting.

1

Aleesha

The small, bare room is blindingly white. A narrow strip light bounces light into every corner, and the bleached tiles I lie on have been polished to a gleam that no Outsider could achieve, even with a hundred years of scrubbing. My head feels fuzzy, and there's a sour, vaguely familiar aftertaste in my mouth.

I don't want to think about where I am.

I sit up with a moan, pressing my back against the wall. The door opposite me has a square of reflective glass set into it, a quarter of the way down from the top – too high to catch my reflection. A shiver runs through me, though the room is not cold. Quite the opposite.

Memories rush back. The note, signed by Ella, saying Trey was in trouble. Running through the Wall to Milicent's house. Finding it empty and deserted. The Metz arriving – four officers to take down one girl. It was a trap, and I had run straight into it.

You've stayed free twelve years, then you let your guard down for one moment, and it's all for nothing.

My first thought may be for me, but my second is for Trey. Was he taken captive, too? He could be on the other side of the wall and I wouldn't know. Had that note really been from Ella? I thought she was on our side, but deep down, I know Trey's family wouldn't approve of his relationship with me, an Outsider. And not just any Outsider, but an illegal girl from the streets of Area Four.

Realizing I'm clenching my teeth, I stretch my jaw to relieve the tension. I don't think Ella would have betrayed me, and even if the government had discovered Milicent was working for the Chain, captured her, then laid the trap for me, they wouldn't have known anything about Ella.

No. All the evidence points to one person. Milicent.

I lick my lips, trying to get enough moisture into my mouth to be able to swallow. My stomach is tight with hunger, adding to the aches in the rest of my body. Mika's medic pod had healed me, almost like magic, but there was a price to pay. She'd said my body needed food, water and rest to recover from the fight with Primo.

My left arm falls to my side, the bone healer encasing it from shoulder to wrist landing with a *thunk* on the floor. With this on my arm, I hadn't stood a chance against the Metz officers.

I look around the room again. If I'm to believe the rumours, there are only two places the Metz take you – the Farms or the Labs. The only thing I know for certain about both places is that no one ever leaves them.

The sound of faint footsteps breaks the silence. There's a click, then the door opens. A pair of female guards walk in and haul me to my feet. Their hair is cropped close to their heads, and they wear skin-tight navy suits, similar to those the Metz officers wear under their armour. I try to yank myself from their grip, but I can barely stand on my own, let alone fight. They half pull, half drag me down a short corridor and into another white-tiled room. This one has a table in the centre and a glass door set into the far wall.

One of the guards tugs off the elastic band securing my braid and orders me to strip. I turn my back to them and do as they say, though

I can feel their eyes on me. My cheeks warm as I stand there, naked, my hair hanging loose down my back. I leave the amulet tied around my ankle, offering up a silent prayer that they will let me keep this one thing. It's a cheap piece of jewellery, just a bronze triquetra encircled by a ring of green glass, but it's all I have left of my mother. It also reminds me of my father.

Just thinking of him sends conflicting emotions racing through me. *I wanted to prove that I could be a leader, yet my first act as Phoenix leader was to get myself captured. Good job, Aleesha.*

The blonde-haired guard barks an order, and reluctantly, I untie the amulet and place it on top of the pile of clothes. She walks over and picks it up, turning it over before pocketing it.

"Hey! What are y—"

She jabs me in the stomach with her baton. I stumble back, my bare feet slipping on the tiled floor. I resist the temptation to cross my legs and cover my chest. They want me to feel ashamed, humiliated. This is to remind me that I am the lowest of the low, that I have no rights. Not the right to dignity. Not even the right to life.

With a gloved hand, the guard picks up my clothes and drops them into a chute marked "Incinerator".

I straighten my shoulders and meet the stare of the other guard, who stands by the door. She looks me up and down, smirking.

Heat courses through my body, making my toes curl. I eye the blonde guard's baton, wondering how hard it would be to take it from her. But the woman moves like a fighter, and I'm still weak from whatever drug the Metz gave me.

"Go through the decontamination chamber." She motions to the glass door behind me. "It'll lock behind you. Keep your arms above your head and walk forward slowly. The door at the far end will open once you're done."

Decontamination chamber?

"What is this place?"

"You'll find out soon enough."

Something about the glass door and mention of "decontamination" makes my skin crawl. I turn back to the door we entered through, but the dark-haired guard moves in front of it, one hand resting on her taser.

"Come on. We haven't got all day."

Blondie's baton prods me in my back. Reluctantly, I cross the room and pull open the glass door. There's a narrow passageway, about ten paces long, a second glass door at the far end.

Another jab in my spine makes me stagger forward. The door clicks shut behind me, and when I try to pull it open, it doesn't budge.

There's a hissing sound, and the air around me changes, sucking at my skin until all the hair on my body rises. The pressure intensifies until I can barely breathe, my skin feeling like it might burst like a balloon.

Keep your arms above your head and walk forward slowly.

Raising my arms, I step forward into a wave of water. It cascades over my head, soaking me. I splutter when some gets into my mouth. It tastes medicinal. The water shuts off, then I'm surrounded by a dense mist. I keep walking. Hot air blasts from all sides, causing me to reel back. It soon cools, and I feel that suction again, not as intense this time, as my body dries.

Finally, I reach the second door. It opens on its own, and I emerge into another room, almost identical to the first. A young woman in a white tunic and trousers waits.

"Please dress." She gestures to a small pile of folded clothes on the table. Underwear, thin trousers and a tunic similar to hers, except grey. The fabric feels rough against my skin, but I don't care. It's better than being naked. I strap the flat sandals to my feet and wonder if I'll ever see my beloved boots again.

"Your right hand, please."

I hold it out obediently, then jerk back when the woman presses a grey box against it. Her grasp is firm. There's a *clunk* and a small stab of pain.

"There. All done." She releases my hand.

I raise it in front of my face, noticing a small, raised, reddish area between my thumb and first finger. It feels numb, but I can see a tiny light flashing underneath my skin.

"It's a monitoring chip. Let's see what's going on in your body." The woman indicates a screen up on the wall where various lines track across the display. "See? Your rapid heart rate and spiked adrenaline tell me you are nervous, which is to be expected. Please, try to relax."

I lick my lips to moisten them, but they're cracked and sore. The woman walks over to a machine on the wall and presses a button. A cup of liquid appears, and she hands it to me with a smile.

"Here. You must be thirsty. Drink up. Your body needs water."

I gulp down the liquid, my throat craving the soothing wetness. It's only when the last drop trickles into my mouth that I realize it's not water. I stare down at the pink-rimmed cup, the sweetness lingering on my tongue.

"What …" A wave of dizziness washes over me. I reach out to the table to steady myself.

An arm wraps around my waist and pulls me forward. "This way."

My legs begin to buckle. I sense a door opening and the presence of other people, but my vision blurs. "Where am I?" I croak out.

Just before I succumb to the whirlpool pulling me down, the woman's words break through my consciousness.

"This is Laboratory Two. One of the government's testing facilities."

* * * *

I stand in front of the Wall. Shades of yellow swirl above me, as if guided by an invisible painter's brush. It's beautiful. But despite the warm sun beating down on my back and the faint chatter of birds around me, something is wrong.

I glance down at my hands. They are smooth and unlined, my fingernails rounded into perfect arcs. They don't look like my hands at all.

When I look up again, the Wall seems different. I can see shapes moving around on the other side. People. At first, they're just outlines, then they coalesce into familiar faces as the colours in the Wall fade and become transparent. Trey is there, dressed in his posh blue Insider suit. He looks happy but tired. Bryn and Abby stand behind him, heads bent together, laughing about something. Trey turns to talk to a willowy woman with long, dark hair.

Megan. I frown. *But they don't know each other.*

Tommy runs up to them, pulling Rogue along by the hand. As I watch, Rogue picks him up and spins him around. Tommy screams in delight.

My eyes scan left along the line, and for a second, my heart stops.

Jay appears on the other side of Trey, Lily beside him, the hole still in her forehead. Behind her, one hand resting lightly on her small shoulder, stands my mother.

I close my eyes, but when I open them, they are all still there.

A pit opens in my stomach.

Finally, Trey seems to notice me. He smiles and waves, saying something I can't hear. I step forward and reach out to the Wall. But rather than the tingling sensation I usually get when I walk through it, my fingers buckle against a hard, unyielding surface.

I run my hands up and down, colours swirling, as if my touch controls the patterns on its surface. "Trey!" I bang on the Wall, but he just shrugs, as if he can't hear what I'm saying.

Dread seeps through my body, flowing through my veins like liquid ice. My stomach is frozen tight.

Something bad is coming.

I catch Trey's attention and wave my hands, trying to indicate that they should move, but he just smiles and waves back at me.

Then everyone's expressions change. Rogue sets Tommy down and glances over his shoulder at something outside my field of vision. His face tightens as he pushes Tommy behind him. The smile falls from Bryn's face as he exchanges a glance with Trey, and Abby pales. Only Jay, Lily and my mother stand unmoving and expressionless.

Dark shadows build behind them, taking the shape of gigantic Metz officers. They are all helmeted, except one. Primo looks down on the figures cowering below him and smiles a cold, twisted smile that I know can mean only one thing.

"No!" I pound my fists against the Wall, then kick the barrier, pain shooting from my toes. "You're dead!"

Primo's face melts and changes into that of the President – slicked-back, black hair, hard eyes, chiselled jaw. It changes again. This time, Samson stares down at me, his face impassive. The face changes one final time and I stare into my father's blue eyes.

What does it mean?

My throat closes up as I claw at the Wall, my perfect fingernails turning ragged and bloody.

Then the shadowy figures attack.

Tommy is the first to fall, Rogue unable to protect him. Tears stream down my face as I watch, helpless, while my friends die, one by one. Under my fingers, the swirls of colour change from yellow to red, until bright crimson and dark red pour down the Wall, as if blood runs from the sky. The colours thicken, hiding the carnage

7

in front of me. As Trey crumples to the ground, the Wall finally becomes completely opaque, hiding everything from sight.

I turn, panting, and look around for the first time. The sun still shines. A small bird dips and dives on the breeze, chirping. Pristine buildings, neat gardens and trees rise up in front of me.

I'm Inside.

I look down at my hands again, so smooth and perfect. It's only then that I realize I'm not wearing my trusty boots or black Outsider clothing. I'm dressed head to toe in red.

I am an Insider.

My legs wobble and I fall to my knees, slamming my clenched fists on the ground. Throwing my head back to the sky, I howl, letting the anger, frustration and grief rush out of me.

It is all I can do.

My eyes fly open and I sit bolt upright, disorientated, heart pounding in my ears. Sweat trickles between my breasts, the rough tunic sticking to my back.

I hold out my shaking hands. The usual traces of dirt and grime are gone from the creases in my skin, but the lines are still there, my fingernails cracked and uneven. Relief rushes through me.

It *was* just a dream.

"Bad dream, huh? Those drugs are a bitch."

The voice is familiar. I look around, but I'm alone in a small room.

Not a room. A cage, but one with no bars, just transparent walls.

Curiosity cuts through the fog in my brain as I take in my surroundings. What I'd taken to be a bed is more like a long, white box inlaid with some strange, spongy material. I poke it. It gives slightly under my finger, springing back when I release the pressure. At least it's more comfortable than the hard floors I'm used to.

I have to swing my legs up and over the side of the box to get out. When lying down, my body must have been completely below the surface, invisible to anyone looking in.

The cage is a perfect cube, as wide as it is high. On one wall, there's a door-shaped outline with a palm access pad on the outside.

I cross to the door and push it, but nothing happens. Outside, there's a metal staircase, a narrow corridor of space separating it from a tall, brick wall. I turn around. Two metal chutes run into the far wall of the cell. The top one looks like some kind of ventilation system. The lower chute ends in a silver hatch, perhaps a foot across. Next to the hatch, a small tap extends from the wall, a shallow, curved dish underneath. I run my hand underneath the tap, and a few drops of water fall onto my fingers. I lift them to my nose and sniff, then touch them with the tip of my tongue. Water. The fresh, clean, tasteless water that pours from the fountains Inside. Not the water we get Outside that tastes of rust, dirt and mould. There's just enough room to twist my head under the tap, and I gulp greedily, letting the water dribble out of my mouth and down my chin.

"Don't drink too much! It's rationed."

The alarm in the voice causes me to jerk back. The flow of water stops. I look around again, this time staring through the transparent walls of my cell. There's an identical cube next to it, another behind that. Most contain a single person dressed in a grey tunic and pants. Others appear to be empty.

My pulse quickens as I whirl around. The sight is almost identical – a line of cubes stretching into the distance. Looking down, I jump. I can see through the floor to the top of a woman's head below. She's slumped in one corner of her cell. Above me, bare feet pace the transparent floor of another cube. I can make out the lines on the man's feet and the pale, cracked skin around his heels.

I stumble backward and sit down, hard, on a square panel at the end of the bed. "What is this place?"

"Subject quarters at the London Compound, also known as Lab

Two. Or, to those of us who live here, Hell."

I twist to look behind me. Dark eyes meet mine. The man looks to be in his thirties, his face weathered by the sun, though his skin has a dull, greyish tinge and his cheeks are hollow. He sits with his arms folded, hands crisscrossed with scars.

"Mitch?" I stare at him in disbelief. "What are you doing here?"

The man scowls. "Got caught in the Metz raid just after you visited. Wish they had shot me like the rest of 'em, but they brought me here instead."

I close my eyes and swallow, his words dragging up the taste of tronk and my memories of that day. I'd been so desperate for the drug that I'd dragged Lily down to the roughest part of Area Four and made her wait outside while I went to get some tronk from Mitch. When the Metz came, I hadn't been there to protect her.

Guilt squeezes my chest. I failed to protect Lily, failed to rescue Trey. And in getting captured, I have failed my gang. My Phoenixes.

I gave them hope, promised them a different future.

"How did they catch you?"

I don't answer.

Mitch huffs impatiently. "Well, however they got your sorry little arse, I bet you had the same experience as the rest of us. You came out of the decontamination chamber super thirsty and gulped down the 'water' they gave you. Then you fell asleep and had the worst dream of your life, right?"

I nod. "What did you mean about the water being rationed?"

Mitch grimaces. "Just that. We get a daily allocation, which isn't much. I suspect you drank most of yours already."

I look at the tap longingly. *And here I was, thinking there was something good about being in this place.*

"Not enough for washing then?" I pluck at the tunic to pull it from my sweaty body.

10

"Nah. They take you to the cleaning chambers once a week." His face twists into a cold smile. "If you're still alive."

The drug dealer has lost some of his cockiness, but his eyes are still calculating.

I hug my knees to my chest and tap the wall experimentally. It's as hard and unyielding as the Wall was in my dream. "What do they do to you?"

"Experiments. Drug testing. The guy on your other side looks like he's been tortured every day since he came in. Don't think he'll last much longer. Reckon I've survived the longest out of everyone here, and it must be about six weeks since they got me."

I glance over my shoulder, but the cube on the other side of mine appears to be empty. He must be in his bed.

I tap the wall again. It feels like Plexiglas. "How can I hear you?

Mitch points up. There's a small, circular opening, about as wide as a Chaz bottle, in the top of the wall, a transparent tube connecting it to an identical opening in the wall of Mitch's cell. "You can only talk with the people on either side of you. I—"

His voice breaks off as a buzzer sounds. I follow his gaze and see a pair of guards walking down the narrow corridor between the metal staircases and the brick wall. They pause at the foot of the staircase leading to my cell and begin to climb.

I stand and back away from the door until I hit the curved drinking dish.

Pass me by. Pass me by.

They stop in front of my cage. One of the guards presses his hand to the access pad and the door swishes open. I don't even have time to slip on my sandals before they grab me under the arms and drag me from the cell. As I stumble down the stairs, I glance back up at Mitch, who mouths something.

I can't hear his words, but I think he was saying "good luck".

2

Trey

The smell of strong coffee fills the room, but the cup in front of me remains untouched. I don't need caffeine or stimulants to keep me awake tonight. Thomas, Milicent's butler, had brought the coffee pot in when the hour hand on the antique grandfather clock in the corner had ticked past ten o'clock and it was clear we were in for a late night.

Milicent's butler. That makes him my butler now, I guess, though it's not something I've had much time to come to terms with. I have more pressing things to worry about.

"So no one has any idea where they've taken her?" Richard Masterton, the Chain's leader and Aleesha's father, slams his fist on the table and glares at me, as if holding me personally responsible for his daughter's disappearance. I sink further into my chair under the weight of his gaze.

Next to him, Bryn gives me a sympathetic look, though his eyes are tight with worry. They'd both arrived at Milicent's house while I was still slumped in the doorway, trying to come to terms with the fact that I'd been too late to prevent the Metz from taking Aleesha away.

"That would seem to be the case." At the other end of the table, Samson wraps his fingers around his cup of coffee. His huge hands could easily crush the delicate china. "Can I see the note?"

Richard turns his scowl on him. "What I don't understand is how you knew exactly where to find us if you weren't aware of the contents of this." He holds up the thin film between two fingers. It was the first thing he'd shown me when they'd arrived at the house, and the words are still branded in my mind.

Trey is in trouble. The Metz have come for him. Meet me at Milicent's house. Ella.

The note raises more questions than it answers.

"Rogue saw Aleesha running out of Phoenix headquarters," Samson says, nodding to the ex-Metz officer sitting next to him. "He questioned Abby after you left, and she said you'd be heading for Milicent's house."

"And you knew Milicent?" Richard's eyebrows knit together.

"I knew *of* Milicent." Samson smiles, a flash of white against his dark skin.

He also must have some way of getting through the Wall, because he turned up at the front door of the house rather than using the secret tunnel that connects it to a small shop in Area Six. His cane leans up against the wall behind him. He is still recovering from the injuries the President and his men inflicted, which makes me wonder why he's here. I'm not convinced it's solely out of concern for Aleesha.

"I still don't understand what happened." Rogue looks from Samson to Richard, before his eyes finally come to rest on me. "Who is this Milicent person, and what did she want with Aleesha?" Face flushed, his fingers tap an impatient rhythm on the arm of his straight-backed wooden chair. Unlike others around the table, his emotions are easy to read.

I glance at Bryn, but everyone's eyes are on me.

We've been through this already.

But to Rogue, this will all be new. And I wasn't exactly speaking coherently earlier, still too shocked by what had just happened.

"Milicent worked for the Chain. When I started working at Coleman's factory, she asked me to find out information about the factory and food distribution systems. She said she would pass it to Bryn and the Chain so it could feed into their plans. What she really wanted was for me to find out about the Coleman family so she could get revenge for her son's death. That's what all this was about."

"And this was her house?" Rogue looks around at the wood-panelled dining room, oil paintings hanging on the walls.

"Yes."

"So what's Aleesha got to do with it? Why did she run off again?" His rhythmic tapping stops as he curls his hands into fists.

I take a deep breath. "Milicent made a deal with the President that she would give him Aleesha if he told her where Elmo Coleman was hiding. She wanted to kill him in revenge for him ordering the execution of her son after the Rose Rebellion, but I reckon the President warned him in advance that she was coming because when she arrived, he was already dead. Killed himself. Anyway, the President wants to use Aleesha to get to Richard. Milicent admitted as much just before they put her to sleep. I ran as fast as I could to get here and warn Aleesha, but I was too late. The Metz had just left."

"He won't get away with this." Richard's voice is controlled, but a fire burns in his eyes. "I will personally hunt him down and kill him."

Bryn eyes him warily. "Shall we focus on trying to get Aleesha back first?" He turns to me. "Look, I know you don't want to involve

Ella, but she may know something about this. It was her name on the note."

"No." My fingers tighten on the arms of my chair. "We are *not* bringing her into this."

I'm as confused as Bryn about why Ella's name is at the bottom of the note. As far as I know, Aleesha's never met her.

"Ella?" Samson raises an eyebrow.

Richard slides the piece of film down the table. Rogue reads it, then passes it to Samson.

"Interesting," he mutters.

"What do you know about this?" Richard's voice is dangerously low.

"Only that Aleesha spoke to me about a woman named Ella who wanted to make a deal. Apparently, she's part of a group of Insiders who wants to help our cause."

"*Your* cause?"

I barely register Richard's words. My chest tightens. Ella had said if I didn't link her up with the Chain or Brotherhood, she would find some other way of doing it, but I hadn't thought she would go through with it. Not after my warnings. And I'd never even considered that Aleesha would help her.

How could she do that? After everything that's happened?

The room seems to close in around me as I struggle for breath. I was only just beginning to forgive Aleesha for her role in my father's death, and now she puts Ella at risk, too? Without even *telling* me?

"Trey?" Samson's voice breaks through my thoughts, and I look up to find everyone looking at me.

"What?"

"Do you know this Ella?" Samson's voice is oddly gentle.

I swallow. "She's my sister."

"Ah. That would explain things."

He doesn't say what it explains, and I don't really care. I squeeze my hands around the arms of the chair until my knuckles turn white. *I will not let Ella get involved in this.*

A hand covers mine. "We need to ask her about the note," Bryn says. "It's our only lead."

Conflicting emotions war within me. Bryn is right. None of us know where the Metz have taken Aleesha, and if we're to find her, every hour is vital. But if I bring Ella here, I know this won't be the end of her involvement. When my father died, I swore I'd take his place and look after my family. I can't let her get messed up in this.

"Just comm her and ask."

I look up into Bryn's eyes, the same blue as mine.

"Go into another room and speak to her alone." He gives me a small smile. "You'll feel better for doing something. It's not your fault Aleesha was captured, you know."

I stare down at the table. *It is my fault. If I hadn't trusted Milicent ...*

Bryn's hand tightens on mine. "It's *not* your fault, Trey. But you must trust me. If we just sit here doing nothing, there's no way we can find and rescue Aleesha."

If I can trust anyone, it should be Bryn. But if he were forced to choose between supporting me and the organization he believes so deeply in, I'm not sure which he'd prioritize.

I shove my chair back and stand. "I'll talk to her."

Their gazes follow me as I cross the room and yank open the door. Thomas jumps back, shoulders stiffening. From the guilty flush of his cheeks, he's been listening at the door.

"Would you like me to bring more coffee, Master Trey? Or some food?"

"No. Just leave us alone. And don't call me 'master'. It's just Trey."

He stares straight ahead, his top lip quivering. A bruise darkens his jaw where Richard had punched him after learning he had let the Metz take Aleesha away without protest. The butler had said he'd just been following his mistress's orders.

Because he obviously can't think for himself.

I turn away from him in disgust and pull open the nearest door. Shelves piled high with laundry stare back at me.

"The drawing room is in here, Ma— Trey." Thomas springs into action, opening another door to reveal a large sitting room. I walk past him into the room.

The door clicks shut behind me. I run my finger over the comm band on my wrist to call Ella. No one answers, but when I try again, a holo flashes in the air above my wrist, an image of my sister blinking sleepily.

"Trey? Where are you? Are you okay?"

"No." A flood of emotion washes over me, but I can't break down. Not yet. "What have you and Aleesha been doing?"

Ella's brown eyes widen, and she suddenly looks more alert. "She told you? I'm sorry, Trey, but you wouldn't help me, and you said she had links to the Brotherhood. I was the one who persuaded her to help me. She didn't want to. Is she with you? Can I speak to her?"

"Of course she isn't here!" I take a deep breath, trying to calm myself. "Did you have anything to do with the note that told Aleesha to come here, to Milicent's house?"

Ella looks confused. "What note? What are you talking about?"

"Aleesha received a note telling her that I was in trouble and that the Metz were coming for me. It was signed by you."

There's a pause, then the holo shifts as Ella sits up and brushes back her hair. "Trey, I never wrote a note for Aleesha. Has something happened to her?" Her voice is laced with concern. It sounds genuine, but then again, until today, I'd never had any reason to doubt anything Ella said. She's my big sister.

But even she lied to me.

"The Metz were waiting for her." My voice is flat. "We don't know where they've taken her."

Ella sucks in a breath. "Okay. You're at Milicent's house? I'm coming over. We'll work out a plan. We will find her, Trey. I—"

"*No!* You're not coming over. Just stay home."

She blinks. "But I can help. I've got friends who work in the government. They may be able to find out where she's been taken."

I hesitate for a moment, torn. I want to believe there's some way of finding Aleesha without involving Ella. But right now, I can't think of one.

"Fine. You can make some *discreet* enquiries. But you're not coming over here. I think we're about to stop for the night anyway. We're not getting anywhere." I stifle a yawn, my brain fogged with the exhaustion that follows adrenaline and shock.

"We? Who's there with you?"

"No one, Ella. It doesn't matter. Go back to sleep. I'll talk to you in the morning." I cut the connection before she can reply and walk back into the dining room.

Thomas had obviously ignored my instructions, because there's a half-empty tray of sandwiches on the mahogany table. The stack of plates beside it lie untouched. Rogue stuffs sandwiches into his mouth as if he hasn't eaten a proper meal in weeks.

"Well?" Bryn asks around a mouthful.

"She's going to talk to her friends to see if they know anything. But they won't be able to get any information until tomorrow." I turn my gaze to Richard. "You'll rescue her, won't you?"

"Of course."

But he doesn't meet my eyes.

"What about the mole?" Bryn asks in a low voice.

Richard gives a tight shake of his head. "Not now," he murmurs. "It's not the right time."

Not the right time for what?

"Well, I think we've done as much as we can do tonight," Richard says in a louder voice. "Let's see what tomorrow brings. We'll meet back here at seven in the evening. Perhaps you can arrange some food for us, Trey?"

He doesn't wait for my reply before he pushes back his chair and stands. "We need to make sure we don't draw attention to ourselves leaving this house. Samson, Rogue, you should come back with us through the tunnel."

Bryn hangs back as they leave the room. "Do you want me to stay?"

"No. It's okay. I need to go to work tomorrow anyway. If I take another day off, they'll be suspicious."

The thought of going into the factory and acting normal seems impossible. But I skipped work on Monday to watch Aleesha's leadership fight. If I miss another day, someone will notice and start asking questions.

"You know, you don't have to work there anymore. If Milicent left you everything, that'll be more than enough money to pay your mother's medical bills. I ... I don't want you putting yourself in danger."

I turn away. "And what would I do if I didn't work? Help you?"

Bryn is silent. He doesn't want me getting any more involved in the Chain's work than I already am.

"Besides, I'm pretty sure the government will start paying closer attention to what I'm doing if I don't go to work every day. And there's still that additive in the Outsiders' food I want to get to the bottom of." I hesitate for a moment. "The information I gave Milicent, about the distribution centres ... Is that helpful to you? Or was she just making that up so I'd think I was doing some good?"

Bryn sighs. "It could be very useful. And you may be right about the government. Just keep your head down for a few days and don't do anything to attract attention. Let's focus on getting Aleesha back, then we'll have a chat about what you found out."

"Okay."

It's a relief to have someone else tell me what to do, to reassure me things are going to be okay, even though I know in my heart that it's just words.

"Bryn, who's the mole you asked Richard about?"

"I'm sorry, Trey." He shakes his head. "I can't tell you."

Right. More secrets.

He blows out a breath, seeing the hurt expression on my face. "It's someone working for us inside the government. Quite high up, actually."

"High up enough to find out where Aleesha is being held captive?"

"Possibly. But it would be a huge risk for them to try and find out. It could completely blow their cover."

"And that's why Richard's refusing to speak to them? Because this person is more important to him than his own *daughter*?"

"I know that's how it seems, but you don't understand everything that's going on." He places his hand on my shoulder. "The situation is complex. We don't even know for sure that it *was* the President who ordered Aleesha's capture. We only have Milicent's word for that. Power is a complex thing. You don't always know who or what is behind something. Richard is right not to rush into things."

He lets his hand fall from my shoulder and tries to catch my eye. "He knows what he's doing, Trey."

I try to find reassurance in his words, but I can't.

"I'll see you tomorrow, okay?"

"Tomorrow," I echo.

I follow Bryn out of the room and watch him disappear into the cellar under the kitchen, then I scrub at my eyes and head toward the front door.

"I've made up a bed for you here, sir."

I halt, momentarily confused. Then I remember that this is my home now, or it could be, if I wanted.

Another thing to deal with.

"I ... I can't think about that tonight. All my stuff's at home ... at my apartment. I'll come back tomorrow night." I hesitate. "Just, um, keep things running as normal, please?"

Thomas smiles stiffly. "Of course, sir." He opens the door for me. "Good night, sir."

"Not 'sir'. Just Trey."

The night air feels thick and muggy, the streets empty as I make my way back to the apartment. I wonder where Aleesha is tonight. If she's hurt, alone, afraid.

I don't want to have to send the boys out to rescue you.

Those were the last words she'd said to me. But she hadn't sent anyone. She'd come herself, like always.

I reach the apartment block and lean my forehead against the cool, Plexiglas door.

I'll find you, Aleesha. I promise.

3

Aleesha

"So, what have they been doing to you?" Mitch's voice filters into my cube through the tube above my head.

I lie in my coffin-like bed, staring up at the base of the bed in the cube above me. It's the only place in this prison where I don't have to look at anyone else. The only vestige of privacy they give us.

"Come on, Aleesha. I know you're not asleep. Tell me something interesting. I'm dying of boredom here."

Dying of boredom. That's about right. After only one day here, I can't understand how people survive weeks in this place. No wonder Mitch talks so much. There's nothing else to distract you from the nothingness you're surrounded by.

With a sigh, I sit up and look at him. "Not much so far. They took some blood from me, gave me some weird drink, then took more blood. That's it."

"What kind of drink?"

"Dunno. But it was green and tasted awful." I scrunch up my face. "Have you had it?"

"Nah. I've not heard of that one." Mitch looks thoughtful. "Usually they inject stuff into you or force pills down your throat. If you're really unlucky, you get taken in for surgery."

"Surgery?"

"Yeah. Skin transplants, limb replacements. I'm surprised they haven't tried it with that bone healer on yer arm. You're a natural candidate. Whip it off and give you a new arm. Prototype, to see if yer body takes to it." He makes a slicing motion with his hand and grins.

My eyes widen. "They'd chop off my *arm*?"

Mitch shrugs. "Better than what some folks have had to deal with. The woman in that cell before you had her head cut open. I reckon they were testing some new implant or something. Anyway, it didn't seem to work, because they carried her out drooling."

I look down at the white, spongy fabric of the bed, suddenly feeling sick.

How can they get away with this?

But I know the answer to that. They get away with it because we're Outsiders. We don't matter.

Mitch's gaze flicks to the cube behind mine. "Ah, looks like Sleeping Beauty has finally woken up. Say hello. A pretty face like yours might cheer him up, poor bastard. They've really messed him up this time."

I look over to see a skeletal man hunched over his knees, head in his hands. He pulls at his dark hair, sending dull, matted strands floating to the floor. Dried blood stains his tunic, and to my horror, I see he's missing two fingers, the stumps covered by white gauze.

"Hello?" I swing my feet over the side of the bed and stand, then walk the three paces across the cube. "I'm ..."

The words die on my lips as the man turns to face me. Angry, red lines crisscross his face where someone's taken a blade to his skin. He squints at me, as if he can sense someone there but can't make

23

out who, then rubs a finger across the bridge of his nose.

"Jameson?" I reach out, forgetting the double Plexiglas wall separating us. My fingers spread across the unbreakable surface, then clench into a fist. "Jameson," I whisper again.

The Chain's technical expert is almost unrecognisable.

"Who ... Who's there?" the man rasps out.

"It's me. Aleesha."

Jameson tilts his head, his face screwed up in concentration. He raises a bloody finger to his lips, his hand shaking uncontrollably. "Aleesha ... The name is ... f-familiar."

"You know 'im then?" Mitch's voice comes from the other side of the cube. I wave a hand to shut him up, my eyes never leaving Jameson's face.

"What have they done to you?"

His lips part, revealing swollen gums, several teeth missing. He seems to be trying very hard to think of something, the strain and frustration showing in the tension of his body. Finally, he lets out a wheeze.

"Aleesha ... You're friends with Trey."

"Yes. Have they ... been torturing you?"

"Stupid question. What you think they've been doing?" Mitch says.

I turn and glower at him. Mitch shrugs, unrepentant.

When I turn back to Jameson, he's hunched over again, his shoulders trembling as he wraps his hands over his head.

Is he crying?

"I'm sorry. I shouldn't have asked." I trail my fingers over the wall, wishing there was some way I could get into his cube. Trey told me the Metz had taken Jameson after killing Matthews during the fighting in Area Four, but I'd assumed he was dead. I think we all did; otherwise, the Chain would have tried to rescue him.

Wouldn't they?

"I tried not to say anything." Tears leak from Jameson's eyes and roll down his thin face. "But it hurt so much. Then they put me into this machine, and the truth just came out. Like I couldn't control what I was saying."

He rubs the bridge of his nose again, and I remember that he'd worn glasses whenever I'd seen him at the Chain headquarters. Guess that would have been the first thing they took away from him – his sight.

"It was like … like a machine that could read minds."

A shiver runs through me. I wasn't sure how involved Jameson had been in the Chain's work or strategy, but at the very least, he knows where their headquarters is in Area Six.

Which means all of them are in danger.

The sound of the buzzer cuts through my thoughts. It goes off every time the guards enter, but there's no indication as to who they've come for until they arrive at your door.

Jameson cowers at the noise, his gaze flicking to the door as he rocks back and forth.

"I'll find a way to get you out. I promise."

Getting no answer, I retreat to sit on my bed.

"You shouldn't say stuff like that, you know."

"Like what?"

"Makin' stupid promises. Talkin' of escape. Once you've been in here a while, you'll realize that it just makes things worse." Mitch gives me a dark look and turns his back.

I pull my legs up to my chest and rest my head on my knees. Mitch is right. It's like talking about fresh bread and meat when you haven't eaten in days, or trying to tell a street hobie that he'll find a home soon. But Jameson looks so broken, so defeated, that I needed to give him *some* hope.

Or perhaps my words weren't for Jameson at all, but for me.

The door to my cube hisses open and strong hands grab my arms, pulling me roughly off the bed.

"Time to go, pretty girl. There's someone who wants to see you."

They march me down a long, sterile corridor that leads to a collection of small rooms. I'd been taken to one of them yesterday, where they drew my blood and gave me that strange liquid to drink. Today, we walk past them and into a huge metal box at the end of the corridor, the doors sliding shut.

One of the guards presses a button on the wall and the elevator shakes slightly, then begins to rise. I open my mouth to ask where we're going, but one look at the guards' faces makes me snap it shut again. My toes curl on the cold metal of the elevator floor, and the hairs on my arms rise under the rough tunic. It's several degrees colder here than in my cube, and I eye the guards' heat-regulating suits with envy.

The elevator shudders to a halt and the doors open. At a prod from behind, I step out into another corridor. Unlike the bare concrete of the tunnel below, this corridor has a carpeted floor and soft, yellow lighting.

But are we above or below ground?

Mitch wasn't able to tell me much about where we were, only that he thought the main chamber was underground. I've no idea how long I was sedated before waking up here. The journey could have taken minutes or hours.

My fingers curl into fists.

How far am I from London? From home?

Halfway down the corridor, a hand on my shoulder halts me. One of the guards raps on a plain wooden door and ducks his head inside. There's a muted conversation, then the guard pulls back and pushes me into the room. I reach out to stop myself falling, grasping the back of a tall chair. It's covered in a soft, luxurious material as fine as the brightly coloured scarves Insiders wear. The rough pile of the carpet tickles the underside of my feet.

The door slams behind me.

"Hello, Aleesha."

His voice sends a chill racing down my spine. I hadn't imagined I would find *him* here.

I lift my eyes and look across the room.

It's small, furnished with two chairs separated by a low table of polished wood. There are no windows, but a large holo screen on one wall gives the illusion of a countryside landscape. Sitting in the other chair, legs crossed and fingers steepled in front of him, is a man I never expected to see again.

The President.

His slicked-back hair is dark against his warm, brown skin, frown lines scar his forehead and light stubble, flecked with grey, traces his jaw. I dig my fingers into the back of the chair and stare at him, unable to speak.

Then my brain kicks in. "You brought me here?" I whisper.

"You really need to stop trying to rescue everyone, Aleesha. It always seems to land you in trouble." A cold smile turns up the corners of his lips. "Milicent made a deal with me. I had some information she wanted, and she was able to get me something *I* wanted."

"Me."

He gives a slight nod.

"What do you want with me?"

The President gestures to the chair I'm leaning on. "Why don't you sit down?"

I shake my head. As tempting as it is to sink into that soft surface, I need to be ready in case there's any chance of escape. I look around the room again, a door at the far end catching my eye.

"It leads to a store cupboard," he says with a low chuckle. "And the two guards who brought you here are waiting in the corridor outside. There's no way out."

He sighs when I don't answer. "Have it your way."

"What do you want with me?" I repeat.

"A couple of things. I wanted to know how you're able to get through the Wall. It's bothered me since you broke into the government headquarters, but it turns out the answer is much simpler than I'd thought." His fingers tap a light rhythm on the arm of his chair. "But my main reason should be obvious."

I stare at him blankly, still trying to process his words.

He knows how I can pass through the Wall?

My heartbeat quickens. He has the answer to the question that's haunted me ever since Jay pushed me off the roof. I should have died that day, but somehow, I passed through the Wall unharmed.

What is different about me?

"Come on, Aleesha. You're not stupid. I made you a deal last time we spoke. Surely you haven't forgotten."

His words drag me back to the present. "You wanted to use me to find my father," I say flatly.

And now my father's in London. And the President knows that. Milicent must've told him.

"So you've met him. What's he got to say for himself? Has he told you why he abandoned you? How he was responsible for your mother's death?"

My chest tightens. "He didn't have anything to do with her death. I saw the records. I was there, inside—" My voice breaks as I recall the holo footage of the Metz operation that had led to my mother's death. It had felt like I was there, in Rose Square with her. I'd felt her pain, saw the bullet end her life.

28

I fight for breath. My ribs feel like an iron cage constricting my lungs. "Primo killed her."

"Primo?" The President raises an eyebrow, then frowns. "Oh, that's what the Metz captain called himself. The one who set himself up as the leader of some Outsider gang. His chip went dead three days ago, so I presume he's no longer alive?"

I shake my head and glance down at my hands. I can still feel the heat of Primo's blood on my skin.

"I knew Ricus would come back eventually."

The President's use of my father's birth name jolts me for a second.

"He always wanted what he couldn't have." His fingers curl over the rounded wooden arms of the chair, his knuckles paling as the tendons on the back of his hand bulge. "It wasn't enough for him to take over half of Europa's cities. No. He would always come back to London. Always come back for me."

I stare at him, surprised by his words and the intensity in his voice. "You knew my father?"

Against my better judgment, I step around the back of the chair and sink into it, pulling my legs up to my chest. I'm close enough to see the flecks of amber in the President's brown eyes, as well as the anger and pain filling them.

"Yes, I knew him. Perhaps better than anyone, apart from Maria." His eyes tighten at my mother's name. "Ricus didn't really let anyone close enough to be a best friend, but if he had, I would have been it. We went to school together."

He falls silent. I hug my knees a little tighter, waiting for him to continue.

"You may blame Andrew Goldsmith or the Metz for her death, but if it were not for your father, her life would never have been at risk in the first place."

I glare at him, feeling anger coil in my belly. "You seem very keen to blame others for her death. How do I know *you* weren't involved, too?"

A spasm of pain crosses the President's face. "I was not involved in the Metz operation. I had no idea it was happening until it was too late." He looks away. "I did not cause Maria's death, but I have lived with the guilt of it for the past twelve years. Wondered what might have happened if—" He breaks off, as if remembering who he's talking to. He waves his hand through the air. "But that is all in the past. Ricus is not the man he once was."

"He's a better person than you. At least he wants to do the right thing."

The President arches an eyebrow. "Wanting something and achieving it are two very different things. One person's view of what is right may be very different from another person's. And, of course, there is the *cost* of achieving what one believes to be right. That must be taken into account, don't you agree?"

I open my mouth, then close it again. I'm not going to play his game. "You said you know why I can get through the Wall. What's different about me?"

The President chuckles. "Well, I suppose there's no harm in telling you. You know, when the three of you broke into the headquarters, I was actually worried that perhaps someone had discovered how the Wall *worked*. The foreigner was easy to explain, as was Andrew's son, once I realized it was him. But you ..." He shakes his head. "You were more difficult. Your blood tests revealed a natural immunity. It was a one in ten thousand probability. Do you know what that means?"

I shake my head, wondering what an immunity is.

"It means that for every ten thousand people, only one would be able to pass through the Wall unharmed. In a city this size, there's bound to be a handful of Outsiders who are able to do so." He shrugs.

30

"We always knew that. It's just bad luck that it happened to be you."

Bad luck? Or good luck?

From what he says, if I didn't have this immunity – whatever that is – I would have died the day Jay pushed me into the Wall.

"This immunity ... Is it reversible?"

"I don't think so. We tested that."

I think back to the green juice. What was in it?

"But it doesn't matter."

I lift my eyes to his. "Why? Because you're going to keep me here, use me as one of your test subjects?"

The President flicks his fingers impatiently. "We have plenty of test subjects. You're far too valuable for that."

The coldness in his eyes returns, and I place my feet back onto the floor, suddenly afraid of what he's going to say.

"You didn't think I would let Andrew Goldsmith's death go without reprisal, did you? Or the Metz Commander's? Your father needs to be taught that actions have consequences, and *this* government will not lie down and let terrorists destroy our city."

"What do you mean?" I whisper.

He holds up his hand, ticking off my crimes on his fingers. "Breaking into the government headquarters, stealing secret documents, breaking into the Metz compound, holding Metz officers hostage." He shakes his head. "All these are crimes of treason, and you know what the law says about that."

My blood turns to ice.

His eyes are unforgiving. "The penalty for treason is execution. Friday afternoon, you will be taken to Lincoln Square. There, in front of the cameras and the biggest crowd I can muster, you will be shot dead by a firing squad."

My jaw drops. I try to form words, but my mouth is too dry, my tongue thick. All my thoughts are consumed by that one word.

31

Execution.

"You … Why …" I close my eyes and try to form a coherent sentence. "If you cared for my mother, why are you doing this? She wouldn't have wanted you to kill me."

When I open my eyes, he's turned away and stares into the distance, as if focused on another time and place. "Maria made her own choices. She knew what the consequences would be. Your mother can't save you now, Aleesha. No one can."

4

Trey

"Earth to Trey!" A hand waves in front of my face, jerking me out of my daze.

"Sorry. What?"

Tiny frown lines gather between Emilie's perfectly shaped eyebrows. Her corkscrew hair is even more wild than normal, seeming to defy gravity. "I was just asking what's wrong? You've been in a daze all day. Are you still sick?"

"What? Oh, no." I rub my eyes against the exhaustion clouding my brain. "Sorry, Emilie. It's been a rough week. A friend of the family passed away last night."

Her hand flies to her mouth. "Oh, I'm sorry." She takes a step closer and places a comforting hand on my shoulder. "Were you close?"

I think of Milicent's betrayal and how little I really knew of the woman. "No, but it was still a shock. I'm just tired. Need a good night's sleep." I attempt a smile. I don't tell her about the nightmares that haunt my sleep. The way my mind replays the Battle of Rose Square and my father's execution until I wake up screaming. Some nights, I'm so afraid of the dreams, I fight to stay awake, despite the

33

weariness dragging my eyelids down. In a way, it's a relief to come to work and push all that to the back of my mind for a few hours.

"Well, I don't want to add to your problems, but I've been sorting through your holo messages. There's one from Louis that I can't work out."

I frown. "You were going through my messages?"

Emilie's hand falls from my shoulder, a hurt expression crossing her face. "I'm your assistant. That's my job."

I rub my eyes again and take a large gulp of the coffee on my desk, grimacing at the coldness. "Sorry. I didn't mean it like that. What's the message?"

She holds out a data pad. "I presumed it was work-related; otherwise, he'd have sent it to your comm band."

I squint at the text in front of me.

Darwin! Where were you Friday? How long am I holding this shipment? Need the space back next week.

I sigh. "I was supposed to meet him on Friday for a drink, but something came up. Please reply and tell him I was ill. I'll apologise later."

"What's this shipment he's talking about?"

Just piles of food I was supposed to have destroyed.

"Oh, nothing. Tell him I'll have it cleared next week."

In the chaos of the past few days, I'd barely thought about the visit from quality control and the mysterious ingredient that had been missing from the food production lines. I need to speak to Barnes about that.

"Okay. I'll send that now." Emilie walks over to her desk.

"See if he's free on Friday for a drink after work," I call over.

I can't deal with Louis' exuberance right now, but I need to stay on his good side. As Coleman's son, he has access to information that nobody else can get, and as I've already found out, he's pretty relaxed when it comes to security.

I finish the cold coffee and stand to look out of the window that forms one wall of my office. It overlooks the factory floor and the food production lines. I press my head to the cool Plexiglas, feeling slightly nauseous as the coffee twists my gut.

Below me, white-suited technicians scurry between the huge vats, in which the artificial meat is grown, and the rows of robotic arms that process and package it. Behind the production lines sit the humming dehydrators – giant metal boxes that suck the moisture from the meat so it can be stored for months, even years, until some poor Outsider can save up enough money to buy it.

At school, we'd joked about the meals, complaining about the tasteless food. But we'd had meat, fresh bread and vegetables every day. What I'd eaten in a week was more than most Outsiders had in two. More than the hobies lining the streets of Area Four would have in a month.

Guilt sours my mouth.

That was why I'd asked Louis to hide away the food that quality control had deemed unfit. I'd hoped Milicent would find some way of smuggling it out to give to people who didn't have food. It wasn't as if there was anything wrong with it. It just had one ingredient missing that the powers above seemed to think important.

Androcibus nanite. Whatever that is.

As if reading my mind, Barnes glances up from the factory floor. Her green eyes narrow as she catches me watching. I wonder if she knows Aleesha is missing. I guess Samson might have told her.

There are many things I need to ask Barnes, but they can wait. Until Aleesha is safe, I can't focus on anything else.

She drags her gaze away as a white-clad man approaches. As foreman, she keeps these production lines running better than anyone else in the factory. It makes my job as production manager easy, most of the time.

When five o'clock finally rolls around, I practically bolt out of the door, surprising Emilie, who's not used to me leaving so promptly. I rush out of the building and hurry to Milicent's house, run up the steps to the front door and press the discrete buzzer embedded in the decorative stonework.

The door opens almost immediately. Thomas steps to one side to let me enter. "Did you have a good day at work, Master Trey?"

I scowl at him and stalk down the marble corridor. "Can't I get into this place myself now?"

"Of course, Master Trey. The security system has been configured to your fingerprint and facial recognition. If you'll just let me show you how it works—"

"Perhaps later." I toe off my shoes and toss them into a corner. The cool marble soothes my hot, aching feet.

I know I'm being insufferably rude, but something about Thomas grates on my nerves. It's partly the role he played in Milicent's plan to hand Aleesha over to the Metz, as well as the fact he insists on calling me "Master Trey". But mainly, he just makes me uncomfortable. This whole house makes me uncomfortable.

Having servants waiting on me is just ... wrong.

I guess that's not Thomas's fault, though.

"Has anyone arrived yet?"

"None of the guests who were here last night have arrived, sir. But there's a gentleman waiting for you in the drawing room. Mr Devizes. He is ... was the mistress's lawyer."

I groan inwardly. That's the last thing I need.

"Would you like me to bring you some coffee, sir?"

"No, thank you," I say, a little too sharply.

Thomas's mouth tightens.

I sigh. "I'm sorry, Thomas. Some mint tea would be nice. And, please, call me Trey. I'm not your master."

Dismay flashes in the butler's eyes, but he quickly hides it and smiles stiffly. "Of course, Master Trey." His heels click on the marble floor as he walks toward the kitchen.

I let it go, wondering what he's so worried about. A pair of men's slippers has been placed on the shoe rack. They look to be my size. I slip them on and walk over to the drawing room door, pausing with my hand on the door handle, steeling myself for the upcoming conversation.

Plastering a smile onto my face, I push the door open and step into the room. A short, sprightly man wearing a burgundy suit springs to his feet. He smooths his greying hair nervously before holding out a hand and walking toward me.

"Darwin Goldsmith?" His voice is high-pitched. "My name is Henry Devizes. I am Mrs de Montfort's lawyer."

I take the proffered hand, his fingers cold and limp. "Do we need to talk now? Can it not wait until next week?"

The man gives a nervous laugh. "I'm afraid not, Mr Goldsmith. Please, shall we sit down?"

I sink into a chair. Mr Devizes takes the sofa opposite.

"Firstly, may I offer my humblest condolences for your loss. I have been Milicent's lawyer and friend for many years. I always thought she would outlive me, but, well ... I suppose the weariness of age eventually catches up with us all."

He pauses, obviously expecting a response.

"Thank you," I manage.

"This situation we find ourselves in is rather unprecedented," he continues. "If I hadn't known Milicent so well, I might have suspected ... Well, never mind. When she came to speak to me about changing her will last week, she seemed in perfectly sound mind, so I am required to act upon her latest wishes."

A spark of annoyance tickles my stomach. I gesture around the room. "I didn't ask to be left this, if that's what you mean."

Pink tinges the man's cheeks. "I wasn't implying anything of the sort, Mr Goldsmith. As it happens, my client left you rather more than just this house."

"More?"

Mr Devizes nods. "Yes. Milicent was a very wealthy woman. She had a wide investment portfolio, including fine art, gold, considerable reserves of digital currencies. There are several bequeaths to charities and gifts to the servants, but she left everything else to you."

"How much?"

He names a sum that makes my head spin.

I blink at him, sure I misunderstood. *She left all that to me?*

"She also left you a private message." He holds a data pad out to me. "Press your finger here to access it."

I press my index finger to the screen. It flashes and a message opens. It is short but to the point.

Use the money as you see fit. I have gifted each of the servants enough to retire, but some of them may wish to stay on. If they do, I beg you to respect their wishes. They are good people, and this has been their home for many years.

I remember Thomas's red-rimmed eyes and the worried gazes of the middle-aged couple who prepared such delicious food. I sigh inwardly. This is more their home than it is mine. I can't take that away from them.

Mr Devizes eyes me expectantly. "Is everything all right, Mr Goldsmith?"

"Yes. What do I need to do?"

"We can go through a few security procedures now, and I will give you a list of your assets." He pauses and eyes me uncertainly.

"I would suggest you talk to a financial advisor who can offer you further guidance on how to make the most of your investments. Unless your mother or father could assist?"

Heat rises to my cheeks. "My father is dead, and my mother is … not well."

Mr Devizes flashes glistening teeth. "Well, if you would like me to recommend someone, let me know. Once we get the security done, I will leave you in peace."

Ten minutes later, he departs in a flurry of handshakes, fake smiles and assurances of his support. When the door closes behind him, I lean back against the wall and close my eyes. Everything feels so overwhelming.

"Are you all right, sir?"

I open my eyes to see Thomas eying me with a concerned look. "Yes, thanks. How many people work here, Thomas?"

"Myself, Derek and Lydia, who do the cooking and gardening, and Dana, the housemaid."

"And you all live here?"

"Yes. Dana and I have rooms on the top floor, Derek and Lydia on the floor below, above the family's bedrooms." He swallows. "Will you continue to require our services, sir?"

"Yes," I reply, though the word hangs heavy in my throat. "If you wish to stay. Milicent left you each some money in her will, but if you would like to continue living here and keep the house running, that would be helpful. My …" I swallow hard. "A friend of mine is in trouble. I can't really deal with anything else right now."

Thomas's face softens. "Understood, sir."

I give him a look.

"Sorry … Trey." The corners of his mouth twitch.

"Thanks, Thomas." I flash him a wan smile.

While I wait for the others to arrive, I wander around the empty house. The bedrooms on the first floor are each larger than the living room in my family's apartment. In three of them, the furniture is hidden under dust covers. The fourth must have been Milicent's bedroom.

It looks untouched by her death. A dress hangs on the wardrobe door, ready to wear, a glass of water on the antique dressing table. A framed photograph, yellowed with age, sits on the low table beside Milicent's bed. In it, Milicent sits in front of a tall man, holding a toddler on her knee. The family she lost so many decades ago. Perhaps it's no wonder she became so bitter and disillusioned with the system.

The sound of voices from downstairs makes me think about Aleesha. I run down the wide, curved staircase to find Samson and Rogue talking to Thomas in the hall. They cut off their conversation as I approach.

"Is there ... Have you heard anything?" My tongue ties itself in knots under Samson's penetrating gaze.

"No." His deep voice reverberates around the high-ceilinged hall.

Thomas ushers us into the dining room and closes the door behind us. Samson limps over to the table and sits down heavily in a chair. I notice he's left his cane behind today.

"How are your injuries?" I ask.

"They'll heal."

My face flushes at the annoyance in his voice. "You've worked with the President, haven't you? What do you think he'll do with her?"

Samson rests one hand on the table, his thick fingers splayed. "I think the assumption he will use Aleesha to get to Richard is valid."

Samson's accent is a strange mix of Insider and Outsider. His language and manner of speaking suggest a wealthy background, but his accent is rough, as if he's spent a lot of time Outside the Wall.

"So he won't kill her?" Rogue leans forward, concern etched into his features.

"Not immediately." Samson shrugs. "But I wouldn't second-guess the man. I've made that mistake already."

We fall into silence. There's so much I want to ask this man – who he is, what he's trying to do, his relationship with Barnes – but I'm too scared.

"How is the gang?" I ask Rogue instead.

He scowls. "People wonder where she is. She got everyone riled up with that big speech of hers, but now they're questioning if she meant any of it. Anders is doing a pretty good job of keeping them calm, but after Primo, no one wants one of *us* in charge. If she doesn't come back soon, someone else will make a play for leadership."

Aleesha had created a new gang from the remnants of the Snakes and the Metz officers who'd chosen to remain Outside after being deactivated. But the alliance between the Outsiders and the men and women who had been their enemy was tenuous, at best. Without Aleesha there to bind them together, it could easily fall apart.

Footsteps and echoes of conversation filter through the door. A moment later, it opens and Bryn walks in, followed by Richard. Thomas enters behind them, carrying steaming platters of meat and vegetables. He's just about to leave when the dining room door flies open and Ella rushes into the room, breathing heavily, her translucent skin flushed pink.

"Sorry. Am I late?" Her gaze flits nervously around the room, finally coming to rest on me. She gives a small smile and tucks a loose strand of dark hair behind an ear.

"No. We were just about to start," Richard replies. "I assume you are Trey's sister?"

Ella nods and takes a seat beside me. I make quick introductions, noticing her eyes lingering on Samson. I wonder if this is the first time they've met.

"Did you ask your friends about Aleesha?" I ask anxiously.

She nods again, her nostrils flaring as the scent of spicy beef wafts toward us. No one has started eating, though I can see Rogue resisting the urge to be the first to tuck in.

"I put out a secure message to everyone in our group," Ella says. "She's being held at one of the Labs."

Relief rushes through me. *She's alive.* Then I frown. *But being held at one of the government laboratories.*

Icy fingers trail down my spine as I think about what that might mean. The Labs develop all our medical technologies, but their work is shrouded in secrecy. Like the Farms, Outsiders speak of them with fear.

"Which one? Where?"

Ella cowers under Richard's gaze. Between him and Samson, the room feels awash with testosterone. I shift uncomfortably in my chair.

"Frankie wouldn't tell me. Apparently, the location is top secret. But she did say she wouldn't be there much longer." She bites her lip and glances down at the table.

I recognize that look. There's something she's not telling us.

"What is it?" I ask sharply.

"The Labs have a small number of criminals they use as test subjects for medical treatments."

"Aleesha is not a criminal!"

Ella winces. "I know, Trey, but that's what they're treating her as. Anyway, that doesn't matter. Her file is protected. Frankie couldn't read the details, but there's a note attached that says she's not to be included in the testing programme."

"So they're *not* testing on her? That's good, isn't it?"

My sister swallows. Underneath the table, her fingers pick at the hem of her long top. "N-not exactly. I …" Her eyes finally meet mine. "They're going to execute her on Friday. In public. It's the President's orders."

Execute her?

It takes a minute for my brain to process the words. When they do, the icy fingers that had chilled my spine radiate through my body until I'm frozen in place, unable to move or utter a word.

Silence thickens the air.

"Damn that man!" Richard slams his fist down on the mahogany table and curses. "I should have known he'd do something like this."

"You think it's a trap?" Bryn asks.

"Of course it's a trap." His jaw clenches. "He's using her to draw me out."

"And why would the President be interested in drawing you out?" Samson's tone is casual, but his muscles tense. "I can see why he might want to get rid of the Chain, but this sounds very … personal."

The two men stare at each other like two cats facing off in an alley.

"I knew the President when I lived in London many years ago. We didn't part on good terms."

Samson raises an eyebrow. "Seems like you must have done something pretty bad for him to hold a grudge for so long."

"Whose side are you on, Samson?" Richard's voice is dangerously low. "As far as I understand it, you were working with the President up until a few days ago. How do I know you're not reporting all this back to him?"

The tension in the room rises a notch.

"Well, I guess you'll just have to trust me," Samson drawls. "Can you do that, Mr Masterton?"

Bryn places a hand on his leader's arm, but Richard shrugs it off. He's like a coiled spring waiting to explode. "People must *earn* my trust. And I've yet to see anything from you or your organization that proves you are worth trusting."

Samson stands quickly, his chair flying back so hard it topples to the floor with a crash. He doesn't bother to pick it up. "If that's the case, it seems unlikely we can work together." He heads for the door.

"Wait!" My voice comes out as a squeak.

Samson flashes me an inquiring glance over his shoulder.

I take a deep breath. "Can we just agree we're working toward a common goal? We need to prioritize rescuing Aleesha, and we must have everybody we can get for that."

Their silence doesn't reassure me.

"There is more at stake here than one person, Trey. But I'm sure Richard has a plan to rescue his daughter." Samson's voice is laced with sarcasm.

The door bangs shut behind him.

Rogue glances at the door, then Richard, obviously torn as to whether to stay or go. His eyes fall on the untouched food in the middle of the table, making up his mind. He settles back in his chair, eying me uncertainly.

"Was that necessary?" Bryn asks quietly.

The comment earns him a glare from his boss, but Bryn brushes it off.

"Samson has a lot of connections out here and knows the city better than we do."

Richard blows out a breath and his shoulders relax slightly. "Perhaps, but I don't trust him." He looks at Ella. "Is there any other way of finding out the location of the Lab?"

"I don't know. I'm not sure Frankie will risk asking questions." She chews her bottom lip. "If she got discovered, it's not just her job she'd lose. It would be classed as a criminal offence."

And she would end up as one of the Lab's test subjects.

"If he plans on executing her in public, perhaps we can intercept them before they can carry it out," Bryn suggests.

"That's what he'll expect," Richard replies. He traces a finger along the wood grain in the tabletop.

I open my mouth, closing it again when Bryn gives me a sharp look.

Richard pushes his chair back. "I need to think this through. I can't allow his games to disrupt our plans. There is too much at stake." He strides over to the door and walks out.

I stare after him, gobsmacked. "His daughter is about to be executed and he's worried about it disrupting his *plans*?"

Bryn sighs. "I know it sounds like that, Trey, but that's just how Richard is. It doesn't mean he doesn't care about Aleesha. I've known him a long time and have never seen him this conflicted. You have to understand. He's been planning on how to free London for more than a decade. It's like all the other cities and people we've helped have just been trial runs."

"So a city is more important to him than his own daughter?" I don't understand. How can he even be debating this?

"I don't know. If it was anyone else, well ... Richard's always said saving millions of people is worth the loss of one life. But perhaps meeting Aleesha has changed him." He casts me a sideways look. "Meeting you certainly changed me."

There's an awkward silence. I feel Ella shift uneasily beside me.

"Um, is anyone going to eat?" Rogue asks, looking longingly at the food on the table.

"Go ahead." My stomach feels the size of a marble.

"Richard will come up with a plan, Trey. He always does."

Ella's hand covers mine and squeezes gently. But neither Bryn's words nor my sister's touch reassure me.

I must be able to do something.

But I can't think what.

5

Aleesha

I spend the final hours before my execution lying on my bed,
staring up at the cube above me. There are a hundred things
I'd rather be doing to make the most of my remaining time on
this planet, but none of those options are open to me. It's been two
days since the President told me what was going to happen. Every
time I hear the buzzer, I expect the guards to stop outside my door,
but they always pass me by.

I've been counting the minutes and hours as best I can, based on
the regular timing of our meals. It can't be long now.

At least lying down means I don't have to talk to Mitch or Jameson.
Not that it's stopped Mitch from trying. I wonder if I could ask the
guards to plug the tube between our cubes so I don't have to listen
to him. The last thing I need right now is pity.

Tears prick my eyes.

Eighteen years ... It doesn't seem very long at all. Not long enough
to really live or make a difference in this world.

I never thought about what I wanted to do with my life. For the
past twelve years, my sole focus has been surviving. But now that
my time draws near, my mind explodes with possibilities. There are

so many things I want to do. So many places I want to see.

The little I know of the world outside Britannia comes from what Bryn and my father have told me. They described bustling cities, high mountains, jungles, deserts. My father even said there were people living on the moon, though I don't see how that is even possible. The moon is just a glowing orb in the sky, the night-time reflection of the sun. It looks so impossibly far away.

Yet my father said he would take me there someday.

If I had accepted his offer that day, everything would be different today. Instead of waiting for my death, I'd be starting a new life in a new country. Him and me. A family.

But if I *had* accepted his offer, Primo would still be terrorizing Area Four.

My thoughts stray to the one person I have refused to think about. Trey. I wonder if he knows where I am, that I'm about to be executed. There are so many things I wish I'd had a chance to say. I want to tell him he's the best person I've ever known. That he makes me want to become a better person.

I want to tell him how much he means to me.

An ache starts in my chest and blossoms outward, driving more tears to my eyes. I clench my fists and dig my nails into my skin to stop them from falling. I turn on my side to curl into a ball, but the bed is too thin and narrow to allow even that comfort.

I will not cry.

They may take away my life, but I can still choose how I die. I will not beg for mercy. I will not let them see my fear.

I will not cry.

I push away thoughts of Trey, my father, Rogue and Megan, Danny and Anders, Abby, Bryn and little Tommy. The idea that I will never see my friends again is just too painful. So I just focus on what is to come. Slowly, the pain in my chest fades and I stretch out on my back again.

The President had said it was going to be done by firing squad. At least that means it will be quick. Perhaps I won't have time to feel any pain. It would be a better death than my mother had.

I wonder what the Insiders in the crowd will think of me. Will they form a baying mob like the Outsiders who crowded up against the steps of the monument, screaming for Andrew Goldsmith's death? Or will they stand there calmly and watch as the bullets rip through my flesh?

I wonder if they will see me as a young girl or just a criminal.

The buzzer sounds. My heart speeds up. The guards are coming.

I strain to hear their footsteps. Faint at first, then louder and louder until the metal staircase outside my cell rattles under their weight.

It is time.

I sit up and swing my legs over the side of the bed. My left arm itches under the bone healer. Not for the first time, I wish I could get rid of the damn thing and give my arm a good scratch.

"Aleesha?"

Mitch sounds genuinely concerned, but that doesn't mean I want to talk to him. Still, he may be the last person, other than a guard or Metz officer, I'll be allowed to speak to.

"I'm fine," I say and feel a flush of pride at the confidence in my voice. I sound as if I've just woken from a nap and am wondering what to do with the rest of the day.

"You might get rescued, you know."

I snort. "What was that you said the other day about false hope?"

Mitch gives an apologetic shrug. "It's possible, right?"

Possible, but unlikely.

What is one life compared to the lives of many?

It is a difficult question to answer when the life being sacrificed is your own.

The only hope I have left is that my father will think my life is worth enough to risk the President's trap. Although my head tells me it would be better if he stayed away, that I don't want people to die trying to rescue me, that the world needs him far more than it needs me, my heart wants to live.

The guards, a man and a woman, stop outside the door to my cube. The woman presses her hand to the access panel, and the door opens with a faint hiss.

"Aleesha?"

I turn to look at Mitch.

"Good luck."

I can't bring myself to smile as the woman grabs my arm and pulls me toward the door.

They lead me out of the cavern, down the rough, concrete tunnel and into one of the small, clinical rooms where scientists run their tests on the prisoners. A woman dressed in a white tunic and trousers waits. The guards stay in the room as she cuts the bone healer from my arm, then hands me a pair of black trousers and a vest. I even get a pair of boots, but they're not half as good as my old ones, which I suspect ended up incinerated with the rest of my clothes.

Still, I guess there's not much point in wasting good boots on someone who's going to be dead in a few hours.

At least it's a relief to have the bone healer off. My fingernails leave red lines on my pale skin as I vigorously scratch the dead skin that's accumulated over the past few days. The woman gives me a disapproving look and rubs some lotion onto my arm. It smells funny, but it stops the itching. I flex my fingers and twist my arm. Apart from a slight twinge at the elbow, it feels fine.

That in itself is a miracle.

My joy is short-lived as one of the guards pulls my hands behind my back and fastens a pair of metal cuffs around my wrists. Then I'm led out of the room, up in the giant elevator and along the same carpeted corridor as when I'd been taken to meet the President.

I pause at the door to the room where I'd last seen him, expecting to be ushered inside again, but one of the guards grabs my arm and pulls me forward. We turn a corner and come to a halt in front of a different door. The guard knocks, then twists the handle and pushes me inside.

He is waiting.

He stands with his back to the door, dressed in the suit he wears when he knows he's going to be in front of the cameras. It's a rich blue, a shade or two lighter than the regulation government suits his officials wear.

"Do you know what time it is, Aleesha?"

When I don't answer, he turns to look at me.

"Two in the afternoon. Your execution is due to take place in one hour. I have to say, I'm disappointed I have heard nothing from Ricus. Perhaps he is planning to disrupt the event. It would be like him to cause a scene. Or perhaps he just doesn't care."

He holds something in his right hand, twirling it between his fingers. "Maybe this will convince him."

He holds out his hand, palm open. The green glass, nestled between the three points of the triquetra, flashes in the light.

My breath hitches.

"Ricus never went anywhere without this. Did he give it to you?"

"He gave it to my mother."

A scowl flits across the President's face before his usual blank expression returns. "She was too good for him," he mutters.

I lick my dry lips, the saliva feeling like a thousand tiny needles pricking my skin. How can this man know more about my own father than me?

"Do you know where he got it?"

I shake my head slowly.

"It was his mother's. She was a religious woman and brought Ricus up to believe the teachings of the church. Though when God failed to save his parents, he left that path behind."

"His parents died?"

"They were murdered." The President closes the distance between us until he's just two paces away. My fingers twitch behind my back, aching to reach out for the amulet. "That's why Ricus was sent to London. His father's sister, his last surviving relative, lived here."

So he lost his parents, too.

I feel a pang of sympathy for my father. Why didn't he tell me about them?

"What happened to his aunt?"

"She stayed in London after he left. Passed away peacefully a few years ago. Ricus didn't attend the funeral."

The President steps forward and holds up the amulet. The short piece of cord I used to tie it around my ankle has been replaced by a long, leather thong. He loops it over my head. The cold metal rests on my skin just below my throat.

"Any final requests?"

"Let me go?"

He chuckles. "You're brave. I'll give you that." He studies me for a moment. "I'm sorry I have to do this, Aleesha. Really. I know you think of me as a cruel man, but I'm not. I know your father well, and I believe that if he has his way, many people in this city will suffer. My duty is to protect them. Do you understand that?"

"You call starving people and dragging them off to be tortured *protecting* them?" I strain against the cuffs, but they don't give, so I settle for forming a globule of spit in my mouth and firing it from my lips. It lands squarely on his cheek, and I smile as he lifts an arm to wipe it away. "You don't know my father at all."

"I can see there's no reasoning with you," he says stiffly. "But I did bring you something to help you deal with your ordeal." He pulls something from his pocket and holds it up.

Tronk.

I clench my jaw. "I don't take that stuff."

He raises one eyebrow. "Really? My spies tell me you're an addict."

I try to swallow, but my mouth is dry. I can't tear my eyes away from the packet of white powder. "I quit."

"Is that even possible?" He steps closer and dips a finger into the packet, then reaches forward.

I rear back, but I'm not quick enough to escape him running his finger over my lips.

My tongue flicks out instinctively. Once, twice.

A bitter tang. My mouth waters, wanting more. I close my eyes and swallow.

No more.

When I open them, I see a satisfied gleam in his eyes.

"It's here if you want it." He waggles the packet.

I shake my head, but my tongue flicks out again of its own accord.

What harm can it do?

At least I'd go to my death happy. And maybe ... Maybe I'll get to see *her* again before I die.

Mama ...

My limbs feel weak and heavy as he opens the packet. For once, I'm glad of the cuffs binding my hands. They stop me lunging forward to snatch the packet and pour the contents down my throat.

The President pulls a small spoon from his pocket and dips it into the powder before holding it out to me. My mouth parts, and I find myself leaning forward. Every fibre in my body strains toward the white powder. I want it. I need it.

Deep inside, a voice niggles. It reminds me of a girl named Lily and a promise I made. But what do promises matter now, in the final moments of my life?

The President tips the spoonful of powder into my waiting mouth.

The taste explodes on my tongue. Salty and sour. Before the tronk has even had time to work its way through my bloodstream, a wave of contentment washes over me, soothing me. Tension drains from my muscles like a coiled spring slowly unwinding. The corners of my lips lift as I close my eyes and slowly blow out a breath.

Peace. Happiness.

But still, that persistent voice won't go away. Now it's talking about a boy named Trey. No. Not a boy. A man. A man who made me feel … What?

Loved?

My brain sparks into action, trying to fight against the tronk-induced lethargy.

Trey wouldn't want you to give in. He would want you to fight to the end.

And my father … How ashamed would he be if they were to drag me out to my execution drugged up to my eyeballs?

My fingernails dig into my palms, and the pain momentarily cuts through the fog in my mind. But not for long. The smile on my lips broadens. Why should I fight it? It makes me happy. Tronk makes everyone happy.

The room around me spins. As if from a distance, I hear the President calling for the guards to catch me as my legs give way and I fall down into darkness.

6

Trey

"You need to keep your emotions in check," Barnes hisses. Her words are drowned out by the clatter of robotic arms above us. The production lines are about the only place in the factory we can have a conversation without the risk of a hidden microphone picking up our voices. I lean a little closer, seemingly to study the production figures on her data pad.

"Yeah, well, that's a little difficult when my girlfriend is due to be executed. Are you sure Samson's not doing anything to save her?"

"I told you. I don't know. I haven't seen him since last weekend." She jabs the screen of the data pad with unnecessary force. *"They're* keeping a closer eye on me since that bitch made a fuss over the androcibus nanite. Speaking of which, we need to do something about getting it out of the production lines. Every day you stall, more people are poisoned."

"We don't know what the androcibus nanite is yet. It might be a perfectly innocent ingredient."

Barnes snorts and opens her mouth to retort, but I get in first.

"I'll look into it next week. Are they following you?"

"Not sure. But they've definitely tapped my comm band. Normally,

I'd meet Samson at one of the gyms he owns, I go there often enough, but with his injuries and trying to sort out this mess with Aleesha, he hasn't been able to make it. He shouldn't even be out of bed yet – not that that's ever stopped him before." Her face softens momentarily.

A bell rings out, indicating the start of the lunch break. Barnes cuts the power to the data pad.

"I have to go." She flashes me a rare, sympathetic smile. "I know it's hard, but try to act normally. Or, rather, act like an Insider. After all, you're one of *them*."

I rear back as her ponytail whips around and watch her stalk up the aisle.

One of them …

Her words bite, but she's right. She's also right about the androcibus nanite. There's something odd about the secrecy surrounding it. If it were just an innocent ingredient, why did quality control refuse to tell us what it was? If Barnes is right and it is a substitute for tronk, we need to figure out a way to get it out of the food supply.

Is it worth risking your job over?

Ah, that voice in my head again. The voice that reminds me of the promises I made to my mother and sister. The promise I made to my father, after his death, that I would finally step up and be the son he wanted me to be. The man who would provide for his family and keep them safe.

My mother had little left after he was murdered. Forced to leave her home and sell her possessions, all she had left was her pride. And she sacrificed that when she begged Coleman to give me this job.

I can't risk getting caught. It's not just about the money – I guess with Milicent's legacy, I don't need to worry about that now – but the shame it would cause my mother if I lost my job or got arrested.

"Are you all right, sir?"

55

The hesitant voice of a middle-aged technician snaps me out of my reverie. I school my features into a neutral expression. "Y-yes. Thank you."

He slips past me with a nervous glance. I turn and force myself to stroll back to the elevator. As I cross the open space in front of the production lines, I sense someone watching me and glance up. A sculpted face shadowed by a flop of blond hair stares down from my office window. My heart sinks.

Louis Coleman.

Possibly the last person I want to see right now.

I slowly walk through the decontamination chamber, letting the rush of air suck at my clothing and skin, then smooth my hair down and step into the elevator. Outside my office door, I pause, take a deep breath and plaster a smile onto my face before stepping into the room.

"Louis! What can I do for you?"

He turns as I enter, a broad grin spreading across his face. With his straight nose, chiselled jaw and muscular build, he looks like a Greek god. Of course, he was designed that way. As the youngest son of the Coleman dynasty, he would have had the best genetics money could buy.

"Darwin!" He claps me on the shoulder, his face clouding momentarily. "How are you doing? Emilie told me a friend of yours passed away this week. I'm so sorry."

"Thanks." Then I remember something. "I'm sorry for your loss, too."

A flash of surprise crosses his face. "You know about Great-Uncle Elmo? I didn't think they'd made that public." He frowns. "Who told you?"

I curse my stupidity. *Think before you speak, idiot.* "I don't remember. I'm sorry."

"It's okay. I don't know why it's being kept such a big secret anyway. They don't have to say he—" Louis snaps his mouth shut and smiles, though it seems forced. "Anyway, you still on for drinks this evening?"

I wonder again why Elmo Coleman had taken his own life. If he knew Milicent was coming for him, why didn't he run? Perhaps he was just sick of hiding from her and tired of life. Or maybe he just didn't want to give her the satisfaction of being the one to end his life. Either way, I guess suicide isn't something the Coleman family would be proud of.

I open my mouth, then hesitate. How can I agree to go out drinking when Aleesha could be dead by then?

The thought sends a spasm through my gut.

Louis' face creases in concern. "Are you sure you're all right, Darwin?"

"Fine," I say through gritted teeth. "It's just been a tough week."

"Well, I always find a few beers help me forget life's problems," he replies cheerfully.

His answer is typical Louis, though what problems he could possibly have to deal with, I don't know. It must be hard having to decide which girl to date next, or which extortionately expensive suit to buy.

I realize I'm clenching my jaw and force myself to relax. "Let me see how this afternoon goes," I say, putting off the decision a bit longer.

"Are you two going to the execution then?" Louis looks from Emilie to me.

My heart skips a beat. "What?"

"The execution. Did you not see the memo? Father's giving anyone who wants to go the afternoon off."

"But what about the production lines? If we stop them, it'll take weeks to get them back online."

"Who said anything about stopping the lines? The memo doesn't apply to the factory workers. They won't be allowed Inside anyway." Louis shrugs, then looks from Emilie to me. "You two can go, though."

I had thought about making some excuse to get out of work early to go to the execution, but Bryn's words still blaze in my mind.

Richard will come up with a plan, Trey. He always does.

Bryn may trust his boss, but I'm not sure I can. Not with Aleesha's life. But what can I do? Even if I were to disrupt the execution, run to stand in front of her, all they would do is shoot me, too. I'm of no importance to the President. No, I must trust Richard. There is no other option.

But there is one thing I can do for Aleesha. I can be there. A friend in the sea of hatred. Bryn wanted me to stay away, *ordered* me not to go. But if she ends up dying today, I will not let her die alone.

"I'll go." I check my comm band and make a move toward the door. "You coming, Louis?"

"You're going to watch the execution?" Emilie purses her lips.

"What's wrong with that?"

She turns back to her holo screen, her shoulders stiff. "Didn't think it was your kind of thing. Disgusting, making a public spectacle of a woman's death."

"She's a criminal, Emilie," Louis says, though the smile has fallen from his face.

"That doesn't make it right," she snaps. "I thought better of you, Trey."

Heat rushes to my cheeks. I don't want Emilie to think badly of me, but I can't tell her the truth. It would be too dangerous for both of us.

"Well, I don't think I'll get anything productive done this afternoon anyway." I hesitate, seeing Emilie's lips tighten. "If you want to leave early ..."

"No chance of that. You have a message from Phillips. Two of the food lines at the government factory went down yesterday, so they've asked us to increase production while they get them fixed. *And* he's said we might have to work the weekend. If you're not going to be around this afternoon, I guess it'll be up to me and Barnes to sort out the logistics."

I flash Louis an apologetic smile and cross the room to perch on Emilie's desk. "I'm sorry. Honestly, I don't want to run out on you, but this execution ..." I hesitate, wondering how much I can trust her, and lower my voice so Louis can't hear. "It's not what you think, okay? I just need to be there for someone."

Her eyebrows knit together. "You're not going to do anything stupid, are you?"

The unspoken "again" hangs in the air.

I can't say it. Can't make her a promise I know I could very well end up breaking. "I'm just going to sit in the crowd and watch. If you need my help with anything, comm me. And I'll come in tomorrow to make sure everything's running smoothly. You take the weekend off, okay?"

"Fine." I'm treated to a small smile. "I promised to help my sister with her exam revision tomorrow, so I'd rather not have to cancel on her."

"We'll manage without you." I stand and rest a hand on her shoulder. "Thanks. I really appreciate this."

Out in the corridor, Louis makes a face. "What's up with her?"

"I don't know. I guess I haven't been a very good boss this week." Guilt seeps through my veins as I remember the look of disgust on her face.

She seriously believes I want to watch a woman get executed, like it's some kind of spectacle?

No wonder she's disappointed in me.

"I reckon she thinks I'm a bad influence on you." Louis grins at me. "She never has much time for me. Shame. If she let her hair down, she could be a lot of fun."

It takes us half an hour to catch a pod from the factory roof, then walk the short distance from the pod point to Lincoln Square. The queue to file in through the cordoned-off entrance stretches back along the street. A pair of Metz officers guard the entrance and check the chips of everyone passing through. My pulse quickens as I draw closer, wondering if they'll stop me, but when one presses the chip scanner to my arm, it beeps and I'm waved through.

Tall screens funnel us through a narrow opening and into the main part of the square. The crowd disperses in front of me, and as I step out of the shadows, I stifle a gasp.

The tall buildings lining the square are barely visible behind the rows of stadium seating that stretch up and back on three sides of the square. Two-thirds of the seats are already filled, and more people stream in behind me. It feels as if you could seat half the city in here.

A low platform backed by a tall screen stands on the fourth side of the square. A solitary metal pole rises from the centre of it.

That's where they'll do it.

My gaze locks on the pole, my feet frozen to the ground. I'm dimly aware of someone tugging on my arm, but all I can think about is how impossible it would be to rescue anyone from that platform in front of all these people.

I was a fool to believe Bryn. A fool to believe Aleesha's father could do anything to save her.

"Come on, Darwin. Don't just stand there."

I turn to see Louis frowning at me. Numbly, I let him lead me up the stairs of one of the stands. He stops at two vacant seats at the end of a row, near the top.

"Here okay?"

I nod and slump into the seat next to him. My gaze is drawn to the platform again. I wonder where Aleesha is, how she's feeling, if she still hopes for a reprieve or has already resigned herself to her fate.

Sweat moistens my shirt under my arms. I shouldn't have come. Why did I think being here could help?

"Are you all right?"

Louis' voice breaks through my thoughts. I follow his gaze to where my hands grip the arms of my chair, my muscles tense, as if I'm about to push myself up.

"Y-yes. I mean, I am feeling a little unwell. Perhaps I should go."

But as I begin to stand, I catch sight of the last few people trickling into the square and the bulky Metz officers closing the entrance tunnel. I sink back into my seat.

We're trapped. The execution is about to begin.

7

Aleesha

A blow to my cheek wakes me. My eyes blink open, but I'm too dazed to avoid the second slap, which whips my head back the other way.

"Time to wake up, pretty girl."

The guard's face comes into focus. A deep scowl furrows his thick eyebrows. They look like a caterpillar, wiggling its way across his sullen face. A giggle bubbles up inside me. I manage to clamp my mouth shut just in time to stop it from escaping.

Thoughts trudge through the treacle of my mind. Ever so slowly, memories return.

Rough hands pull me to my feet. I stumble but manage to stay upright.

"That'll do. Let's get this over with."

I blink woozily as I'm pushed forward. It takes all my effort to put one foot in front of the other, but I'm so happy I don't care.

As they push open the door, a blinding light hits me. I close my eyes and breathe in the fresh air. Not the stinking air of Area Four, which smells of trash and too many people, but the fresh, clean air Insiders breathe. It rushes through me, pushing away the haze of the tronk, taking with it the sense of happiness that had tickled at my belly and made me forget what was about to happen.

A hollow emptiness replaces it.

Steps appear in front of me, and I'm led up onto a raised platform. With every step, the drug's grip on me lessons. The stuff the President gave me must have been weaker than the tronk sold on the street. My body is used to stronger stuff. Just thinking of it makes me lick my lips, as if some trace of the powder may linger, but my saliva just stings the cracked skin, the twinge of pain making me more alert.

One of the guards tugs at the cuffs binding my hands. I feel them release, and for a moment, I'm free. But my relief is short-lived as I'm pushed back into a metal pole, my wrists cuffed behind it.

The guards' footsteps tremble through the wooden planks of the platform as they walk down the steps, leaving me alone.

Finally, I look up, squinting against the sun shining into my eyes, and gasp.

The platform stands at one end of a huge square. In front of it is a large, open space surrounded on three sides by tiers of seating rising up to almost the height of the old, stone buildings behind. Every seat is full.

There are hundreds, perhaps thousands of Insiders.

Their bright clothing sparkles in the sunlight. I've never seen so many different colours in one place, nor such intricate detailing. A young woman in front wears a fitted jacket that must be worth more than everything I possess lumped together.

All of their eyes are on me.

I scan their faces, searching for pity. After all, I'm just a girl. Surely I don't look like a dangerous criminal. But their expressions are carved from stone, and I find little sympathy. Some meet my gaze with cold, hard eyes. Others turn away, as if embarrassed they have to be here to witness this.

The metallic taste of blood fills my mouth, and I realize I'm chewing my lip.

My stomach clenches, my bladder beginning to loosen. Leaning my head back against the pole, I close my eyes and draw in a long breath. I will *not* piss myself. Not here in front of everyone.

You are fearless. You are strong.

The sun blazes down, heating the amulet around my neck, which sits in plain sight on my chest. I long to wrap my hand around it and feel it dig into my palm. Anything to distract me from what is to come.

"Welcome, everyone."

My eyes snap open as the President's voice booms out. He stands to one side of the platform, his voice amplified by some hidden microphone. His dark hair is slicked back, his light blue suit clean and fresh, his calm composure broken only by the slight twitch of his hands.

Is he worried my father will try to rescue me? Or worried that he won't?

This is a carefully laid trap. I am the bait, and my father is the prize.

But will he bite?

"Before you stands a criminal." The President waves a hand in my direction. "Most criminals are dealt with by our trusted law enforcement officers, but the crimes this woman has committed are far too serious for our usual system of justice."

He turns to me. "Aleesha Ramos, you have been found guilty of evading the law, stealing food, weapons and other supplies, illegally roaming the city, breaking and entering the government headquarters and the Metz compound, attacking members of our law enforcement and ..." He pauses for emphasis. "Conspiring to capture our loyal Metz officers and forcing them into servitude."

A hushed silence follows his words. Then a murmur ripples through the crowd. The faces looking at me are both angry and fearful.

Do they believe him? Believe that this girl, barely taller than a child, could commit such crimes?

Judging from their expressions, they do. And why wouldn't they? He is their trusted leader who keeps them safe from dangerous Outsiders. I am a threat to their world, their way of life.

Heat burns inside me, fire filling the emptiness in my stomach. The last remnants of my drug-induced haze disappear. I understand now why he gave me the tronk. It wasn't out of pity but out of fear.

Fear of what I will say.

"As a result of this long list of crimes, and to set an example for anyone else who may feel that breaking our laws and conspiring against the government is worth the risk, you have been sentenced to death for treason."

His words wash over me as the heavy footsteps sounding behind me pound terror into my heart.

I whip my head around. A tall screen separates the platform from the building behind. I can't see through it, but I can hear them approaching.

My executioners emerge, three from either side of the screen.

The crowd falls silent.

The fire burning inside me dims. Against my will, my body begins to tremble.

The Metz officers form a line ten paces in front of me. There are six of them. Six trained killers to murder one girl.

The President isn't leaving anything to chance.

A tall woman dressed in the grey uniform of the palace guard moves out of the shadow of the building and touches the President's arm. Her shoulders tense, she constantly scans the crowd and the rooftops lining the square.

She murmurs something into the President's ear. He nods in reply. The woman steals a glance at me before backing away. She looks oddly familiar, though I can't figure out where I've seen her.

"Without law and order, our society would fall. You have elected me to protect you and uphold our laws. On this sad occasion, you are all witnesses to the power of the law."

A woman cheers. It spreads like a wave, and the shouts grow louder until it is like a crowd of Outsiders at a leadership contest, everyone jostling for their voice to be heard.

The President lets the cheering go on for a minute before holding up his hand for silence. As the din fades, the Metz officers in front of me lift their weapons.

"Wait!"

It takes me a second to realize that the dry, cracked voice was mine. When I do, I shout again, louder.

"Wait!"

The President turns toward me, a smile playing at the corners of his mouth. "You wish to say something, Miss Ramos?"

I swallow, trying to force some moisture into my mouth. My heart pounds against my ribcage. "Yes."

Everyone stares at me. Cold, hard, Insider faces. They don't care about me, a girl who shouldn't even be here today. A girl who was never even registered as being born. All they see is a criminal. What can I say that will change their minds? To make them open their eyes and see that their wonderful, perfect lives come at a price?

Then I see him out the corner of my eye, and some small part of the fear inside me melts away.

The sunlight sparkles off his blond hair, making it shimmer like a halo around his head. It takes me back to the first time we met. When the sun had shone in through the window of the small, white house the Chain had used as a meeting point and made his pale skin glow. He had looked like an angel.

I remember thinking that he was the light to my darkness. How right I was. All he tries to do is good. All I seem to do is hurt.

His eyes meet mine. The fear etched into his face almost paralyzes me. My chest aches, and I want to cry out at the injustice of it all. That having finally found someone who's worth living for, my life will be taken away.

I blink back my tears and force my knees to lock, my shoulders to straighten against the metal rod at my back.

I'm not sure if I can be brave for me, but I can be brave for him. He gives me the strength to speak. If it is my fate to die today, I'll go out fighting, even if the only weapon I have is words.

"You call me a criminal." My voice is weak. Too weak to carry to those at the back of the crowd. I try again, this time with more force to my words. "You say I am a criminal, yet you know nothing about me. Imagine that I am your daughter or your son. Because that is my only real crime. Being born."

I pause for breath, my throat already hoarse from the dry air. The sun feels like a furnace and sweat trickles down the back of my neck.

"My mother was an Insider, like you." Murmurs of consternation ripple through the crowd. "Because of who my father was, she knew if she registered my birth to make me a legal citizen, we would be hunted down and I would be taken by the Metz." I glare at the President. "On *his* orders. To save me, she fled Outside the Wall."

A frown creases the President's forehead. He opens his mouth to speak, but I get there first.

"All my mother wanted was to save her baby. Wouldn't any of you do the same? Or would you willingly give up the child you had birthed knowing she would be taken away and murdered?" I glare around the square, feeling a glint of satisfaction as people who had looked at me with hatred before now refuse to meet my gaze. There are children in the crowd, their parents bringing them along to see justice done. It makes me sick.

"Look at your child." I speak directly to a woman in the front row, who has a toddler on her lap. She gives me a malevolent look and turns his face away, holding him protectively, as if my words have the ability to kill. "What would you do to save him? Would you give up your money? Your pretty things? Your *life?*"

"Silence!" The President's voice rings out above mine, but I don't stop. They can shoot me mid-sentence if they want, but I *will* say what I need to.

"I was six years old when my mother was murdered. I had no one. Yes, I stole food. To stay alive! I lived off crusts of hard bread that even the street hobies discarded. I wasn't able to go to school. My only education was on the street. And for those of you who've never been to Area Four, who choose not to look at what it's like on the other side of the Wall, I'll tell you this. Survival is tough."

Out of the corner of my eye, I see the President motion to someone. A man in a grey uniform pulls a piece of cloth from his pocket and begins to walk toward me.

"If I had been your child, I would have been in school, learning history, technology, science. Instead, I learned to run from men who wanted to rape me. I learned to fight those I couldn't run from. I had no future, except surviving each day. And I am not the only one. You are afraid of us Outsiders. You think we're all addicts and hobies. But it's you who have made us that way. And *you* can change things."

The guard is just a few steps away. He pulls the cloth tight between his hands. A gag. I rush to get out the rest.

"For once in your life, think of us as people. People who have little food, no money and no chance of a job. And think what you would do in our position. Could you survive? Or w—"

The gag is pulled tight on my mouth. I twist my head, trying to break free, but the guard is fast, and the knot digs into the back of my head, pulling at the corners of my mouth.

Something catches in my throat and I cough, doubling over as I fight for breath through the thick cloth. Black spots dance across my vision, and for a moment, I think I'm going to pass out.

"This has gone on long enough." The President's words seem strangely distant.

I stare at the patterned wood of the platform in front of me until my lungs stop spasming and I can draw in air through my nose.

"Metz, prepare to fire."

I look up into the barrels of six guns. It's hard to look away, but I manage it. The faces of the Insiders in the stands look down on me, cold and unyielding. I have failed to change their views, to make them rethink how their society should work. It is too late now.

My eyes find Trey's in the crowd. I try to tell him so much in that final gaze. That he is too good for me. That he'll now be free to live a better life. That I'm sorry things had to end this way.

"Take aim."

My shoulders straighten. I feel strangely at peace. There is no longer any fear or anger.

"Ready."

I close my eyes and picture my mother. She stands in front of me with her hand outstretched, waiting for me to join her.

"Fire."

8

Trey

Around me, the murmur of the crowd dies down as everyone's gaze turns to the platform. More Metz officers filter into the square, forming a line in front of the stands. Their guns are held steady, their masked faces turned up to us as if we are the threat, not the people they are protecting.

The President emerges from the screen behind the platform, followed by the grey-clad palace guard. I spot my sister, Anabel, her uniform identical save for the two, bright flashes on each arm that mark her position as Head of the Palace Guard. Her hair is pulled back into its customary bun, and her gaze flicks around the crowd, one hand resting on the gun at her belt.

The President climbs the three steps up onto the platform. He doesn't need to ask for silence. You could hear a pin drop in the square.

I wonder what Anabel thinks of all this. She hasn't visited Mother, Ella or me this week. Would she intervene to stop this – for me?

But in my heart, I know she won't. She can't. Her job is to protect the President and carry out his wishes. If she tries to intervene, she'll lose her job, maybe even be imprisoned herself. Besides, I'm not sure she wants to stop this. She still blames Aleesha for Father's death.

The President begins to speak, his words flowing through my mind like a gentle rain. It's only when more guards emerge, dragging a small, dark-haired figure, that I begin to pay attention.

Aleesha.

I lean forward in my chair. She looks so fragile next to the stocky guards. They roughly cuff her to the metal pole in the centre of the platform, and she stands there, blinking in the sunlight.

I frantically scan the square, looking for any sign of rescue.

This can't happen. I can't let her die.

But I am powerless to stop it. Even if I made it past the guards at the foot of the stands and across the empty square to the platform, then somehow figure out how to undo her handcuffs, we'd be gunned down before we'd taken two steps toward freedom. I have to trust that the Chain has come up with a plan to free her.

I rub my palms on my thighs. They've left beads of sweat on the plastic arms of the chair.

"She's a pretty little thing," Louis murmurs.

My hands clench, and I fight the urge to punch him.

"You know her, don't you?"

His comment catches me off guard. I force my hands to relax, grateful that everyone else seems to be fixated on the scene below us. I'm not quite sure how to reply. I could deny it, but even Louis would see through that lie and I'd lose any trust I'd built with him. But admitting I know a criminal could get me arrested. However, to deny knowing her, deny my feelings, would feel like the ultimate betrayal.

"Yes," I say finally. "I know her."

"I'm sorry."

I tear my eyes from Aleesha to glance at him. His look of concern seems genuine.

When I look back at the platform, Aleesha is staring straight at me. I try to smile, but the muscles in my face are frozen.

Then she begins to speak.

Her accent stands out amongst the cut-glass elocution of the people around me. This is no prepared speech. She stumbles over words, her voice cracking as she raises it, shouting her message. But there's an underlying power, a raw emotion that no speechwriter could create. She speaks from the heart. And her words, her desperate plea for people to listen, cause my own heart to splinter, and at the same time swell until my chest threatens to rip apart.

I'm so damn proud of her.

And so ashamed that no one listens.

The President doesn't let her talk for long. Perhaps he's afraid her words really will have an effect on the crowd. A guard gags her and steps back. My heart lurches, my breath faltering.

Where are you, Richard Masterton? Where are you, Bryn?

I scan the crowd, hoping against hope to see someone I recognize. But if the Chain has people planted here, they're well disguised. The anticipation on some of the faces makes my gut twist. Three rows in front of me, a child begins to cry and is quickly hushed, her face pressed into her mother's shoulder.

A flicker of movement on the roof of the building opposite catches my eye. But when I turn to look, there's no one there.

"Metz, prepare to fire."

On the platform, Aleesha stares out defiantly. She meets my gaze and holds it for a second. I open my mouth. I want to scream for them to stop. Want to tell her I love her. That I'm sorry for not saving her, for not being the man she needed me to be.

"Take aim."

The President's order rings in my ears. I close my mouth, knowing it is too late, but hating myself for not doing this one thing for her.

For not being quick enough and smart enough to speak.

Moving as one, six Metz officers raise their guns.

"Ready."

Whatever Aleesha's father had planned – if he had anything planned – is too late.

She is going to die.

I close my eyes, then force them open again. I won't turn away from this.

"Fire."

Gunshots rip through the square.

But they don't come from the execution squad.

"What the ..." Louis breathes.

I stare at the platform where Aleesha stands, her body rigid as grey-uniformed guards fall to the ground around her.

My brain tries to process the scene in front of me. It's all happening so fast. Shots rain down from hidden snipers on the rooftops surrounding the square. Those that miss their target send fragments of stone ricocheting into the air. The Metz firing squad has fallen apart. One of the officers lies motionless. Two more wrestle each other on the ground, the other three firing on the palace guards rushing toward them.

Anabel hustles the President off the platform, but just before he disappears, he twists his head to survey the square. He doesn't look shocked. Quite the opposite.

A sick feeling fills my stomach. *What has he got up his sleeve?*

Around me, people scream and shout as they begin to move, rushing from their chairs, only to clog the stairways as there's nowhere for them to go.

"Stay in your seats!" booms a Metz officer standing at the entrance to the closed-off tunnel.

No one listens.

I stand and look around. The remaining palace guards have taken refuge behind the platform, firing out at the remainder of the execution squad, who I presume must be under Richard's control. Aleesha is horribly exposed between the two sides, trapped by the cuffs securing her to the metal pole.

I have to get to her.

The Metz officer shouts again for people to sit, but its gravelly voice is barely audible over the screams of the crowd. A man climbs over the barrier into the square and runs toward the tunnel entrance. Others begin to follow.

I'm yanked down seconds before a bullet whistles through the air above me. There's a grunt. Two rows back, a woman topples forward, sprawling across the empty chairs behind me. She doesn't move.

"Stay down. They're on the rooftops," Louis shouts into my ear.

There are more shots, more screams.

"No one move!"

On the rooftop opposite, masked figures appear, firing wildly into the crowd. I recognize the combat uniforms of the Chain – the people Richard brought here from overseas.

Why are they shooting at us?

"Stop!" I jump to my feet and wave my arms in the air before realizing that might not be the best idea. They probably don't know who I am. Besides, I'm not supposed to be here.

Was this why Bryn told me to stay away? Surely killing innocent people wasn't part of their plan.

It dawns on me that perhaps the Chain's leader doesn't see Insiders as innocent bystanders.

A figure on the roof sweeps his gun in my direction.

I drop behind the chairs just in time.

"What the hell do you think you're doing?" Louis' face is pale, his eyes wild. "The idiots are trying to shoot us."

Hunched awkwardly behind the dubious shelter of the chair backs in front of us, he fumbles with his comm band. "Dammit. I have no signal. It must be jammed."

If the shots were intended to frighten the crowd into subsiding, the Chain's plan hasn't worked. The trickle of people running to the tunnel entrance has turned into a stampede.

"They'll trample each other. There has to be another way out," I mutter under my breath.

On the platform, Aleesha struggles to get free, bullets peppering the wood around her.

I glance behind us. A walkway runs behind the rows of seats at the top of the stand. At the far end, there seems to be an exit, a barrier at waist height.

"Where are you going?" Louis tugs at my trousers as I crawl out into the stairway. "You can't get out that way."

"Going to see if there's a way down to that end of the square." I nod toward the platform. "Anything's better than sitting here waiting to be shot."

I jostle through the people fighting to get down the stairs and make it to the walkway, grateful that the shooting seems to have abated. Halfway along, I sense I'm being followed.

"Wait up," Louis pants. His face is flushed, hair ruffled.

Our feet pound on the metal grating. I skid to a halt at the barrier and duck under it, then rush down the winding staircase, Louis a few paces behind. At the bottom, instead of turning right to run behind the stands toward the entrance to the square, I turn left, ignoring Louis' shouts.

As I reach the corner of the stand, a figure looms up out of nowhere. I slide to a halt.

"What are you doing here? You need to go that way." The guard jerks a pistol in the direction over my shoulder. Beads of perspiration run down his forehead as his eyes flick anxiously to the square behind him. "Damn Metz officers have turned rogue."

Over his shoulder, I catch sight of Aleesha on the platform. I blow out a breath in relief at the sight of Bryn crouched behind her, seemingly trying to cut her cuffs.

I hold up my hands and take a step back. "Right. Sorry."

The guard reaches up and touches his earbud. "Reinforcements? About time."

At that moment, a dull pounding begins, the ground vibrating under my feet.

Louis' breath is hot on my neck. "At last."

Metz officers spill from either side of the screen behind the platform, moving out and around to form a semi-circle in front of it. They begin to fire out into the square and up at the figures on the roofs of the buildings. Bryn and Aleesha drop to the platform as the air above them explodes with the hiss of tasers and the crackle of gunfire.

A noise from behind makes me turn. More officers march from the far end of the stands toward us.

A sour taste fills my mouth. *So this was the President's plan.*

Aleesha lifts her head to look around. For a second, our eyes meet, and she mouths a single word.

Run.

9

Aleesha

Splinters dig into my cheek as I lie awkwardly on the platform, face down, my hands still cuffed behind my back. I can feel Bryn working to free me as gunfire rages through the air above us.

"Nearly there," he grunts.

A moment later, I hear a snap, and my hands fall free of the pole. I bring them around in front of me. The cuffs are heavy on my thin wrists, but at least I can move my arms.

"Shuffle back," Bryn says in a low voice. "If we can drop off the platform, we may have a chance of getting away before they realize we're gone."

"What about them?" I gesture toward the Metz officers who had been about to execute me before they'd turned their guns on the guards.

"They'll have to get themselves out of here," Bryn says grimly. He begins to push backward on his belly.

The officers have bunched together into a tight group. Bullets slam into them, and I wonder how long their armour will hold up to this kind of assault.

"Come on, Aleesha!"

I begin to wiggle backward, then stop upon hearing a sharp intake of breath. I glance over my shoulder and freeze.

Two Metz officers haul Bryn up and hold a gun to his head. Cold hands grab me and yank me up beside him.

"Drop your weapons!" The guttural voice of the officer holding me rings in my ear.

Bryn curses.

My execution squad slowly place their guns on the ground and raise their hands in the air. I wish I could see through their masks to the faces underneath and know who chose to risk themselves to save me.

We're surrounded. The rescue attempt is over.

I should have known it was too good to be true.

But at least I know my father cared enough to try.

Silence hangs in the air. Even the crowd standing at the closed entrance is quiet, staring at the scene in front of them. For once, they look at the Metz in relief, not fear.

There's a low chuckle and the sound of footsteps, then the President emerges from behind the screen and walks out onto the platform. He raises his arms, as if welcoming a long-lost friend.

"Come out, Ricus! I know you're here."

Silence follows. I glance at Bryn, who tilts his head a fraction. So he *is* here.

My pulse quickens and the hollowness in my belly opens again. I'd made peace with the fact I was going to die, but given the small glimpse of a reprieve, the dread that had run through my veins returns with a vengeance.

I try to catch Trey's eye, but he's focused on the rooftops around the square. A tall, blond Insider stands next to him, his expression more affronted than afraid.

The President's arms fall to his sides. "Ricus? Are you going to run away again? This is becoming something of a habit of yours." He jerks his head at the officer holding me. "Bring her forward."

I plant my feet and throw my weight backward as the Metz officer grips my arms, but it's a token resistance. It could probably pick me up with one arm. It yanks me forward until I'm standing next to the President. Our eyes meet, and I think I see a spark of pity behind his cold exterior before it's quickly gone again.

Perhaps I imagined it.

"Hold the gun to her head," he says quietly.

The Metz officer obeys. Cold metal presses into my hair, just above my left ear. It trembles slightly, and I wonder what has the officer so scared. Then I realize it's not the gun that's trembling. It's me.

"This is your daughter, Ricus! Are you prepared to watch her die?"

Still, there is no response.

There's the sound of raised voices from behind the screen, then the female, dark-haired guard I'd thought looked vaguely familiar rushes over to the President. Her cheeks are flushed and she's out of breath.

"Sorry to interrupt, sir," she says in a low voice. "We need to get you out of here. We think they may have reinforcements."

Her gaze flits around the square. When her eyes find Trey, they widen momentarily.

The President looks annoyed. He puts a hand to his chest to muffle his microphone, but I'm close enough to hear. "I told your team no interruptions, Anabel. We need to draw him out."

Anabel ...

Things suddenly click into place. This must be Trey's older sister, the one who leads the palace guard. The President's primary bodyguard.

So where has she been that she's out of breath?

"It's too dangerous, sir. I can't protect you properly here. Let's take the hostages away." She scans the rooftops, her body tense, ready to defend her boss at the first sign of a threat.

The President shrugs her off and steps forward. "You have five seconds, Ricus!"

He begins to count down. The barrel of the gun presses into my skull. I try to swallow, but saliva catches in my throat. Beside me, Bryn shifts uneasily. He knows my father better than I do. Does he expect him to save us or call the President's bluff?

When the President gets to "two", a voice rings out.

"Stop!"

I swing my head to the right, seeing a figure on the roof of a tall apartment building. Even from this distance, I recognize my father. He stands tall, his shoulders back. A bandage has been hurriedly tied around his collarbone, blood seeping through.

The two men stare at each other.

My father is the first to speak. "Let them go. Then I'll come down."

The President gives a hoarse laugh. "Do you think I'm stupid? You come down here first. Once you're in custody, I'll let your daughter go." He jerks his head at Bryn. "This man is a terrorist and will pay for his crimes."

My father doesn't reply.

"Come on, Ricus. You're in no position to negotiate. Whose life do you value more – yours or hers?"

I wonder what my father's thinking. Part of me doesn't want him to turn himself in, to give up and admit defeat. I don't want to lose the only family I have. But a selfish part wants him to prove he cares about me. That I *mean* something to him.

Still, he doesn't speak.

Then something odd happens.

The cold metal pressing against my head disappears. The officer's grip on my arm slackens, then falls away, as its other arm raises and points the gun straight at the President.

At first, the President doesn't notice, too busy staring up at my father. Cautiously, I take a step back, then another.

No one stops me.

I turn to see Bryn stepping away from his captors. He looks as confused as I feel.

Then, as one, the Metz officers surrounding us, save the one in front of me, place their weapons on the ground and stand at attention, as if ...

As if they've been given an order.

Only then does the President look around. His face blanches. "What the ..."

Anabel shakes herself and grabs his arm, dragging him away. This time, the President doesn't resist. His face twists into a snarl as he shoots one final look up at the man standing impassively on the roof, staring down at us.

Then he's gone.

Murmurs of concern ripple through the crowd. They don't know how to react to this sudden shift in power. Is this a new threat or not?

Bryn moves forward to grasp my arm. "Let's get out of here."

"What's happening?" I whisper.

"I don't know," he says darkly. "This wasn't part of the plan."

We hurry from the platform and make our way over to where Trey pushes through the Metz officers surrounding him. He throws his arms around me, and I cling to him as a wave of dizziness washes over me. He smells of pine needles and water – the calm after the storm.

"You're safe," he mumbles into my hair. "You're safe now."

A touch on my shoulder pulls me back to the present.

"We need to go," Bryn says.

I draw back and look around. The blond man who'd been with Trey stands a few paces behind us. He looks at me curiously, as if I'm a creature he's never seen before. Bryn eyes him warily.

Trey twists his head to look over his shoulder. "Oh, this is Louis. I work with him."

"I think you'd best be going ... Louis." Bryn's voice is hard. "Now."

The blond man narrows his eyes and opens his mouth to protest. Then seems to think better of it and shuts it again. He gives Trey an odd look, before turning and shoving his way through the officers to disappear behind the stands.

"What the hell were you thinking bringing him here?" Bryn mutters.

Trey makes an apologetic face. "He followed me."

"I told you not to come." Bryn sounds angry, but his voice is laced with worry.

Trey's about to reply when the tall, black figures around us begin to move. Bryn pushes us both behind him and pulls a knife from his boot. Trey crushes me to him, his heartbeat pounding rapidly against my chest. The Metz officers march to the centre of the square and line up in neat rows, like soldiers awaiting their orders.

Three members of my execution squad hurry over to us, carrying the unmoving form of a fourth between them. Two limp severely, their dull grey armour riddled with pockmarks. A thread of smoke rises from the back of one of the helmets. They lay the body of their companion in front of us, then one of them turns toward me. Instinctively, I take a step back.

"Can you get this helmet off?"

The voice is toneless and guttural, but the officer crashes to his knees and bends his helmeted head toward me.

Silently, Bryn hands me his knife. I slip the tip into the tiny catch where the helmet meets the neck of the suit. There's a click.

The officer reaches up with its gloved hands, twists the helmet, then pulls it off its head.

Anders' freckled face is weary. The helmet has flattened his sandy-blond hair, making him look even more boyish than normal, and the broad smile that usually brightens his face is absent. His expression is that of an old man – one who has seen too much of life. He takes the knife from my hand and unlocks the helmets of the others, revealing Rogue and Leon, another of the ex-Metz officers who'd chosen to join my gang, before kneeling beside the figure on the ground.

He carefully removes the helmet to reveal a woman's face, pale and still, then bends over her, holding his ear just above her mouth. When he rises, his face is grim.

"She's gone."

I fall to my knees beside the woman, reaching out to her neck to feel for a pulse. Her skin still carries a trace of warmth. "Are you sure? I thought the armour was impenetrable." I take in the battered armour covering her body. Part of the chest area has crumpled, and my stomach plummets when I see blood glistening through it.

"Not quite," Rogue says. "They focused all their firepower on her. The suits can only take so much."

Guilt dulls the eyes of all three men.

I search my mind for the woman's name. *Radha*. I'd barely spoken to her, yet she had given her life to save me.

There's the sound of running footsteps, then Danny skids to a halt next to Anders, breathing heavily. Sweat beads on the snake tattoo covering his shaved head. Two men dressed in the combat uniforms of my father's team follow him more slowly.

Danny pokes at the dents in Anders' suit. "You all right, big man? I managed to get a couple of the ones firing at you, but then they noticed we were up there." He holds up the gun slung over his shoulder. "These are great! First thing I've seen that goes through those suits. Good thing for you that lot didn't have them; otherwise, you'd be even more holey." He seems to catch sight of the woman on the ground for the first time, his face falling. "Oh."

I gawp at him. "What are you doing here?"

"Came to rescue you, of course. I was up on the roof with a couple of your da's lot until the plan went to shit. Who's our knight in shinin' armour?"

The question's directed at Anders, who shrugs and looks to Bryn.

"I don't know," Bryn says tightly. "It's not one of our team."

"Isn't that one of Samson's men?" Trey asks, looking over my shoulder.

I turn to see a slim man with a half-shaved head and long, thin braid dart across the square toward a figure wearing a dark, hooded cape. "Yes. That's Petal."

But how did Samson get hold of a device to deactivate the Metz?

I look more closely at the figure Petal's talking to. He's completely covered by the cape, but I can tell he's slightly built. I have a sudden feeling I know who is beneath it.

"Giles ..." I breathe, starting forward.

Petal reaches out to grab the figure's arm, but the person jerks back, the hood falling away. Sunlight glistens off Giles's pale head. He shrinks in on himself and claws at the hood to pull it back up. My gaze falls to the black box around his neck.

"It's the ghost! What's he doin' here?" Danny asks loudly.

"Shut up." Anders' voice is a growl, but it carries across the silent square.

Giles's hand freezes on his hood. He turns to stare at us, his gaze stopping on Anders.

Danny looks at his friend in surprise. "What?"

84

Anders' jaw is clenched. Conflicting emotions play over his face – joy, relief, trepidation.

I look back to Giles. His face is filled with one emotion – adoration.

Suddenly, Giles's cryptic comments make sense. His fierce protection of the Metz officers, his initial reluctance to hand over his precious device.

You won't hurt them, will you? You were supposed to protect them.

Was he concerned about all the officers or just one?

"You … You're here." There's a tremor in Giles's voice.

Anders' mouth works silently. I've never seen the thoughtful, confident man look so speechless.

Giles stumbles toward us, the black box in his hands seemingly forgotten.

Danny turns to Anders, searching his face. "You know him?"

"Yes," Anders chokes out, then clears his throat. "Yes. He was … is a friend."

A friend to Anders perhaps, but as Giles comes to a halt in front of him, his pale eyes shining, I realize Anders is much more than a friend to Giles. He is his whole world.

For a long moment, the two men stare at each other, locked in a bubble of time and space where the rest of us don't exist.

Giles reaches out, then draws his hand back. Finally, Anders takes a step forward and pulls him into an awkward hug. In his arms, Giles seems to stretch and grow, his spine uncurling and straightening, as if after years of being bowed over, he can finally stand tall again.

Anders pulls back. His arms fall to his sides as his face flushes. "I …" He clears his throat. "I'm so glad you're alive."

"Do you remember?" Giles whispers.

"I think so. At least most of it." Anders ducks his head. "I'm so sorry, Giles. They sent me after you, didn't they? To bring you back?"

Giles bobs his head. "I knew it wasn't really you. They must have found out that you helped me escape and reset your chip."

Danny coughs loudly, his expression clouded. "Don't we have stuff to do?"

Anders starts and looks around awkwardly, as if just remembering that we're here.

Rogue steps in. "Is that the device Aleesha used to deactivate us?"

Giles nods. His pale eyes flash with alarm as he notices everyone staring at him, his bony fingers fumbling with his hood. I step forward and place a hand on his arm. Giles practically jumps backward and cowers, his eyes darting around.

"Hey. It's okay." I try to sound soothing. "What are you doing here? Who brought you here?"

"I did."

I jump at the deep voice booming in my ear and spin around, seeing Samson standing just behind me. *Why does he always have to sneak up on me?*

"How did you know about Giles?"

Samson flashes a smile. "You always ask me how I know things, Aleesha."

"And you never tell me."

"You don't tell me your secrets. Why should I tell you mine?"

I glare at him.

Samson raises his hands in mock defence. "Is that the thanks I get for saving your life?"

I notice he doesn't have his cane with him. Either his leg is recovered or he doesn't want to show any weakness. I suspect the latter. "I think *Giles* is the one we should be thanking."

"You think he'd have made it here without me?"

I turn back to Giles. He seems calmer, but probably only because his hood is back up over his head and Anders' hand rests on his shoulder. Being out here, surrounded by all these people, must be his worst nightmare.

"You came out here to save me?"

Giles looks up at me, his eyes luminescent under the shadow of the hood. He twists the box over and over in his hands. "He said you needed help."

My heart goes out to the recluse. Shunned by Insider and Outsider alike because of his odd looks and manner, no one sees the genius underneath. He is a true friend.

I smile at him, tears unexpectedly springing to my eyes. "Thank you, Giles. You saved us all."

He ducks his head, embarrassed.

"So, what happens now?" Danny jerks his head toward the Metz officers lined up in the square.

"First, I want to have a word with Richard." Samson's voice sounds grim, and I wonder just what he wants to say to my father.

"And then?"

Before Samson can reply, Giles lifts his head and looks directly into Danny's eyes. "Then we will take the Metz compound."

10

Trey

We all stare at the hunched figure. The last time I'd seen Giles, he had shown us the entrance to the old underground station we'd used to access the tunnels that run under London. It feels like a lifetime ago that Aleesha and I broke into the government headquarters to access the information bank. The horrors of Sanders' and Mikheil's deaths have been buried by my memory to make space for more recent tragedies.

"You want to break into the Metz compound?" Danny stares at Giles in disbelief.

"But it's a fortress," Rogue says. "Impenetrable."

Aleesha's face is creased into a frown. Anders opens his mouth to speak, then closes it again. Only Samson doesn't look surprised.

"We don't need to break in. We can use them to enter." Giles's eyes dart to Anders. "The Metz will return to their base, and when the compound opens, we follow them in and shut them all down."

Anders nods slowly. "It could work. The compound must be almost empty of officers, though there will be plenty of people in there we can't control. We would need to get to the control centre before they can initiate lockdown procedures."

"I have some people who can help," Samson says. "Though I suspect not the numbers we'll need. We must act immediately if we're to have any chance of surprising them."

Bryn glances around the square. "Agreed. This is an opportunity we can't pass up. When Richard gets here …"

I follow his gaze, wondering where the leader of the Chain has got to.

Aleesha steps away and bends over to talk to a man who's hunched over the body of a woman in a Metz uniform. As she straightens, I spot a flash of movement on the roof opposite.

A woman in a grey uniform peers furtively down into the square. Sunlight glints off metal. My legs spring into action before my mouth has time to form words of warning. I barrel into Aleesha, knocking her to the ground as a loud *crack* shatters the silence. Dust fills my mouth as the bullet ricochets off the ground to our right. My heart races as I lie there, panting, muscles on fire from the sudden surge of adrenaline.

There's a shout, followed by a rattle of gunfire.

Aleesha groans and blinks up at me. "What …"

I realize I'm lying on top of her and push myself up. "Are you okay?"

Gingerly, she pushes herself up to a seated position and clutches her head. "I think so." She looks around. "Who was that?"

"One of the palace guards got onto the roof," Bryn says, rushing over to us. He reaches out a hand to help Aleesha up. "We need to get out of here. We're too exposed."

"Nice moves, Insider." Danny swaggers over, his gun hanging from one hand. "Is that how you get women into bed? Never pictured you as the rough type."

Aleesha scowls at him. "Shut it, Danny."

"And we didn't give you a gun just so you could waste all the ammo,"

Bryn adds. "We don't have a never-ending supply, you know."

Danny mutters something unintelligible and slings his gun over his shoulder.

"Let's get inside," Samson says. His gaze moves around the square. "We're sitting ducks out here."

We take shelter in one of the apartment blocks lining the square. Rogue is the last to arrive, accompanied by the other man disguised as a Metz officer, who carries the body of the woman, now free of her heavy armour.

Samson and Bryn stand in the corner, conferring in low voices.

"Are you sure you're all right?" I ask Aleesha.

She nods, then winces. "Yeah. Just banged my head." She gives me a small smile that makes my heart flip. "Thank you. If you hadn't spotted her, I—"

"It's fine. Honestly, the number of times you've saved me …" I shrug awkwardly.

"Aw. You two lovebirds are so sweet," Danny croons. "You saved me. No, you saved me."

"Cut it out, Danny," Aleesha snaps. "What's got into you?"

"Nothin'," he mutters darkly, his eyes flitting to Anders, who talks to Giles in a low voice.

"Everyone okay?"

Richard strides into the room, followed by a man dressed in the bright clothes of an Insider. "Bryn, what's going on?"

Bryn quickly fills him in. Richard's eyes linger on Aleesha for a moment, as if reassuring himself that she's okay, then fall on Giles, who cowers under his gaze.

"So, you're the man with the ability to control the Metz. Perhaps you could give me the device? Then you can go back home and leave us to clear up this mess." Richard holds out his hand expectantly.

"No." Giles clutches the device to his chest and looks up at Anders, then over at Aleesha, who gives him an encouraging nod. He straightens, though he still can't meet Richard's gaze. "No. It's mine."

A flash of annoyance crosses the taller man's face, but when Samson walks over to stand next to Giles, Richard drops his hand. "Fine," he says tightly. "We'd better get moving. I'm sure the President has something else up his sleeve." He turns to the man who'd followed him in. "Do you know the quickest route to the Metz compound?"

Bryn sidles over to me as the others talk. "You need to get home, Trey," he says in a low voice.

I'm about to protest, but he cuts me off. "No, I'm not just being overprotective. You're chipped, remember? And the government knows you're connected to us. They could track you."

I groan inwardly. I have a chip blocker – a plastic sheath Louis gave me that blocks the location signal given off by the chip embedded in my arm – but it's in the pocket of my coat in the apartment.

Bryn squeezes my shoulder. "The best way you can help us is to go home, Trey."

His words crush me. I may have just saved Aleesha's life, but to the Chain, I'm still a liability. Someone who gets in the way. Someone they have to protect.

Bryn catches the look on my face and grimaces. "I didn't mean it like that, Trey. Just—"

"It's fine. You're right. I should leave." I reach out and touch Aleesha's arm. "Be careful, okay?"

"You, too." She seems about to say something more, then stops herself.

"Well, I'll see you later. Um … Good luck." The words sound as weak as I feel.

Only Aleesha watches me as I walk across the lobby, but when I open the door and glance back one final time, even she has turned away. A rush of loneliness washes over me. I'm only a pretender in these people's eyes. I don't have the skills required for them to welcome me into their world. Yet the one I step out into, the world I was brought up in, doesn't feel like home anymore.

I wonder if anywhere ever will again.

The streets immediately around the square are quiet as I make my way back to my family's apartment. I've just reached the entrance when my comm band beeps.

I check the message. It's from Louis.

We need to talk. 8 pm at Macie's in Soho.

Apprehension seizes my stomach. But it doesn't sound like he's turned me in as a traitor just yet. Perhaps there is time for me to change his mind.

I send him a quick message to confirm, then push open the door of the apartment block and walk up the stairs.

When I let myself into the apartment, I find my mother lying on the sofa, staring up at the ceiling. She twists her head as I walk in, and I'm struck by how haggard she looks.

"Trey." A smile cracks her paper-thin skin. "How was your day?"

Her question confuses me, until I catch sight of the old grandfather clock in the corner and realize it's just after five.

"Fine, thanks." I perch on the chair opposite her. "Can I get you anything? Coffee? Something to eat?"

She shakes her head and, with some effort, pushes herself up into a sitting position. "I'm fine, thank you."

You're far from fine.

Her muscles are wasting away. She's always been a slim woman, but now she looks as fragile as a bird after winter.

"I should probably sell some of this stuff." She waves a hand around the small room, which is packed with over-sized furniture. "I doubt you or Ella will want it when I'm gone, and I don't think Anabel can fit anything into that tiny place they've given her."

Mother hates this apartment. Home for her was the large apartment near the centre of town. The one they had to give up when Father lost his ministerial job. I wonder how much being in this dreary room day after day has contributed to her rapid decline in health.

"Milicent left me her house, you know. You could move in if you'd like. There's plenty of room, and it's much nicer than this place."

I curse myself for not suggesting this before. I'd mentioned Milicent's death to my family but not the details of her will.

Her eyes shine with hope as a spot of colour blooms on her cheeks. "Really? I don't want to step on your toes. This apartment is …" She seems to search for a word. "Adequate."

My stomach tightens. *I should have done this days ago.* "Of course. You and Ella should both move in. There's no point renting this place when there's an entire house available." Another thought hits me. "Milicent left me money, too. More than enough to pay for whatever treatment you need. When's your next appointment with the doctor?"

"Monday evening."

"I'll come with you."

"You will?"

The joy on her face causes another pang of guilt to rush through me. For all her faults, she is still my mother, and I haven't been the son she deserves.

"Of course." I stand and gently pull her up and into a hug. I'm careful not to squeeze her too tightly.

Mother lets out a contented sigh. "I don't know why Milicent took such a liking to you, but it was so generous of her to leave you so much."

For a moment, I debate telling her everything. That while my duty lies here, my heart longs to be doing something more. Something that will help change our country for the better.

But I can't burden her with more worries. Let her believe what she wants to believe – that this was just the gesture of a kind old lady.

Perhaps there's another reason I don't tell her. Perhaps I finally feel like the son she wanted me to be. No longer a burden, but a man who can provide for his family.

* * * *

When I walk through the door of Macie's, I see Louis chatting with the barman.

"Hey," I say.

Louis turns and pushes a tumbler of whisky toward me. "Here."

I toy with the glass as he finishes his conversation. Louis is a heavy drinker, but even so, I'm not sure starting on whisky this early in the evening bodes well.

Finally, Louis grabs his drink and hops off his stool. "Come on. Let's go up to the roof."

He doesn't wait for me to reply as he weaves through the people crowding the main room and up the narrow staircase. I follow him to the rooftop terrace. It's a peaceful oasis amid the hubbub of the city, but rather than calm me, the tranquillity heightens my sense of trepidation. I join Louis at a low table next to a babbling water feature.

He takes a swig of his whisky, then stares into his glass, as if the amber liquid holds the answers to all his questions.

"You haven't stopped working with the Outsiders, have you?" he eventually asks, not looking up.

I could lie to him, make up some excuse for my behaviour in the square, but I know he wouldn't believe me. If he wanted to, he could call his father, and I'd be arrested before I had time to leave the building. Perhaps he's already done that and this was just a ploy to draw me here.

My best chance is to be honest with him and hope there's more to him than the womanizing socialite he comes across as.

"No."

Louis twirls his glass idly. "Is that why you got the job in the factory? To spy on us?" His tone is more curious than accusatory.

"No. I took the job because my family needed the money." I hesitate, wondering how much to confide in him. "My father lost his job in the government because of me. He was murdered a few weeks ago. My mother's sick and has medical bills."

"I remember seeing something about your father's death on the news." He glances up at me. "I'm sorry."

Emotion thickens the lump in my throat. I wonder if I'll ever be able to think about my father without an overwhelming sense of guilt and loss. "Thanks."

"Is that why the President wanted to execute that girl? Because she was involved in your father's death?"

"Maybe. There are other reasons, though." I shake my head. "It's complicated."

I force myself to take a sip of the whisky. It burns my throat, making my eyes water.

"And she's your girlfriend? The girl who was being executed?"

"Kind of."

Louis gives a low whistle. "That must be rough. Having the hots for the girl who killed your dad."

My fingers tighten on the glass. His words hit too close to home. "She didn't kill him."

"Oh, right. Sorry." He pauses. "She's hot, for an Outsider. Kind of scrawny, but a pretty face."

95

A stab of jealousy hits me. An image of Aleesha appears in my mind, but instead of being in my arms, she's in Louis'. He strokes her hair, whispers into her ear ... As much as I know it's irrational and Aleesha would never choose someone like Louis, it's hard to shake the thought from my mind.

Louis downs the rest of his whisky and stands. "Want another?"

"No. I'm good."

I stare at his retreating back, wondering if I should use the opportunity to escape. But where would I go? They know where I live, where I work. Not to mention the fact they're tracking my every move. The only escape would be to remove my chip again and try to disappear Outside the Wall, but that would mean leaving my family, my job, my chance of making a difference.

When Louis returns, he places his glass on the table and sits down, leaning forward to rest his arms on his legs. "What did your father want you to do with your life? Before all this happened?"

Taken aback by the question, I sit silently for a moment before I answer. "He wanted me to do well at school. I think he hoped I'd follow him into government work." I pause, trying to remember the conversations we'd had about my future. "Though I'm not sure if he ever said that specifically."

"I'm guessing being a production manager at Coleman's probably wasn't your dream job." He flashes me a wry smile. "What did you want to do?"

"I'm not sure," I say honestly. "I mostly tried to avoid thinking about it."

"Me, too." Louis sighs heavily. "Except I never had a choice. My life's been mapped out from the beginning. University, take over the family business ... And Mother's already trying to set me up with an *appropriate* woman to marry."

I glance at him, surprised by the bitterness in his words. "But you have everything you could want. What's not to like?"

He chuckles, no humour in the sound, and takes a sip from his glass. "I guess it must seem that way. Everything except the freedom to choose."

"Why don't you just tell them you want to make your own decisions?" As the words leave my lips, I realize how hypocritical they are.

Louis grimaces. "I guess I should. But you're right. I've been given everything on a silver platter my whole life. I feel like I owe them." He knocks back his whisky.

"Anyway, you must be wondering if I'm going to tell my father about your exploits. Well, I'm not. At least not yet."

Relief rushes through me. My hand trembles as I lift the glass to my lips.

"I'm not sure what I expected to see today, but the execution…" He shakes his head, running a hand through his hair. "It wasn't anything like I thought it would be."

"Well, I don't think it went as the President planned, either."

Louis is silent for a moment. "When I asked you what it was like Outside … I guess I thought it would be pretty exciting, being part of a secret organization. But being shot at isn't much fun." He sighs. "I won't turn you in on one condition, Trey."

"What's that?"

"Don't do anything that will harm the factory. Whatever your gang wants, leave us out of it. My family has worked too hard to build the business. I couldn't face my father if got destroyed because of something I failed to do." Louis looks me in the eye. "Deal?"

"Deal," I reply. It's not like I have a choice.

He holds out his hand. We shake, but it feels like another knot tied in the web of lies and deceit that has me trapped. Because, despite my promise to Louis, I know there are secrets in that factory that I have to unravel.

11

Aleesha

You'd have thought breaking into the most fortified building in the city would be difficult, but as it turns out, getting in is the easy part. Either the compound hasn't been notified of what happened in the square or the behaviour of the officers with us is convincing enough for them to open the hangar-like entrance to let them in.

One of my father's men operates a device that cloaks us from the cameras, and there's no sign we've been noticed as we follow them down a wide, sloping tunnel that leads to a vast room underground. The Metz officers stand like soldiers between rows of round pillars, each with a low, circular platform at its base. Some of the platforms – those with armoured, exoskeleton suits awaiting occupants – glow blue, but most are empty and cast a red light across the space between them.

In addition to Rogue, Anders, Leon and Radha, who had infiltrated the President's firing squad, Danny and three other members of my gang had joined the Chain to help rescue me. Danny is the only Outsider. When I mention this to him, he says he wasn't picked for the mission but insisted on coming anyway. I file this away for future reference, wondering what the rest of my gang made of my father selecting only the ex-Metz officers for the mission.

Leon still carries Radha's body, his dark face pinched with the strain of her weight. There was nowhere safe to leave her, and he said he wanted to cremate her here, in the place that had been her home for so many years. He sets her down gently, away from the silent Metz officers, and returns to join us.

Despite her death, which I know will come back to haunt me, I feel as light as air. My father came to rescue me. The President's plan had failed, and he is about to lose his biggest asset – the Metz compound. But it is more than that. I had accepted death, but I am still alive.

The air tastes sweet. The white buildings we passed on our way to the compound seemed brighter than before, the greens and blues more vibrant. I relish the ache from the bruises on my jaw and the cramping of my toes in the too-tight boots, because they are reminders than I can still experience pain.

It took being a second from death to remind me how much I wanted to live.

My father strides over to us. If his wounded shoulder is bothering him, he doesn't show it. He hasn't spoken a word to me since my rescue. There's been no hug, no touch. But I guess he has to stay focused on the operation.

"We can't get the doors open. Any ideas?" His words are directed at Rogue.

Rogue glances at me before answering. "The doors in the compound only respond to the chip inserted in your hand when you become an officer. Our chips were removed so they couldn't track us Outside, and Giles can only control the implants in the officers' brains."

My father scowls. "What are you saying? We're trapped in here?"

Rogue looks uncomfortable. "We could use the officers to get us through, but you'd need to deactivate them first. I don't think the chips will work through the suits."

"Fine. We only need to get to the control room. Once we have, we should be able to unlock all the doors remotely."

My father quickly confers with Bryn and Samson, ordering them to split their forces into two teams. Anders goes with one, Rogue with the other, both knowing the location of the control centre. Giles deactivates three of the officers and a captain to go with the groups, though I can see he's not happy about it.

The officers don't put up much of a fight, but the captain is another matter. He knocks two people to the floor before Samson manages to twist an arm behind his back and presses the barrel of a gun to his head. The man looks around with wild eyes.

"Let's go," Samson says tightly.

I step forward to follow, but a hand on my shoulder pulls me back. "You're staying here."

I twist out of my father's grasp and turn to face him, opening my mouth to protest.

"Someone needs to stay here with Giles. There's going to be shooting out there. We can't afford for him to get killed. He's the only one who can use that device."

He beckons Danny over. "I want you two to stay here in case anyone tries to escape this way. If you need to, use them to fight back." He jerks his head toward the silent officers scattered around the room.

Danny scowls, but he's too intimated by my father to say anything.

Warm fingers tilt my chin upward, forcing me to meet his gaze. "Don't do anything stupid. I've rescued you once today. I don't want to have to do it again."

I gulp and nod.

He turns and stalks off to take command.

"Scary as hell, your da," Danny mutters as the armed fighters file out of the room.

I don't reply as I brush my fingers against my chin, trying to pretend they're his. Danny's right. He's not a giant, like Samson, and he doesn't have the scars and muscle from years of fighting, like Bryn and Murdoch, but my father exudes power. He acts as if he can't be beaten, and that is far more intimidating than physical strength. Sometimes he seems more inhuman than the Metz officers surrounding us.

I just need to get to know him better, that's all.

With Anders' departure, Giles retreats back into himself and moves to a corner of the room, leaning against the wall and sinking down to sit, cradling his black box. Danny's dark eyes rest on the hunched figure.

"Who'd have thought the freak would save the day."

I sense the undercurrent in his words and shoot him a warning look. "You know, just because Anders and Giles are friends doesn't mean Anders can't be your friend, too."

"Did I say he couldn't?" There's a pause before he mumbles, "None of my business if the freak goes all gooey-eyed around 'im."

"Don't call him that."

Danny snorts. "Well, he is, ain't he? Looks like a bleedin' skeleton."

I glance over at Giles, hoping he can't hear us. "He was *born* like that, Danny. It's not his fault. His device saved us in the Battle of Rose Square, and if he hadn't turned up today, both of us would be dead."

Danny huffs. "Well, I don't see why I have to stay here playin' babysitter to you both. Missing out on all the fun."

Anger flares inside me. I shoot my hand out and grasp his wrist, twisting it sharply so he's forced to release his gun. I yank down on the weapon's strap, pulling it tight around Danny's neck. Caught off guard, his eyes bulge.

"Who are you babysitting?" I ask through gritted teeth.

His hands claw at the strap as he fights for breath.

I release my grip, and he staggers forward. Gasping for breath, he shoots me a malevolent glare. I give him a cold look in return.

"Are we good?"

For a long moment, we stare at each other. Danny is the first to look away. "Yes, boss."

He wanders around the Metz officers, occasionally prodding one and muttering something under his breath. I walk over and crouch down by Giles.

"Thanks again for coming to rescue me. It must have been tough for you, being around all those people."

He doesn't answer. Under the fold of his cloak, I catch sight of his long fingers clutching the box, as if his life depends on it.

"Anything I can do to help?" I ask quietly.

The hood moves from side to side.

"Once they've got control of the compound, we'll be able to free the other officers. That's what you wanted, wasn't it? Or was it just Anders you wanted to free?"

Giles starts at the name.

Silence stretches between us.

"They used to tease me, the other kids in the compound," Giles whispers. "My parents sent me here when I was young, once they'd given up on any hope of finding a cure for my … condition. The compound accepted me because my IQ levels were off the charts. I think they thought I'd eventually put on weight and muscle. But despite the steroids, I was always a skinny runt."

He falls quiet for a moment, then continues.

"It's hard being different. But then Anders arrived." His voice

103

blossoms with warmth. "He didn't seem to care that I looked different, that I didn't want to play games or fight like the other kids. Everyone wanted to be friends with Anders. Yet he chose to be friends with me."

"He helped you escape?"

Giles nods. "When he first became an officer, he was just like the others. The implant changed him. I felt as if I'd lost him. But slowly, the old Anders returned. He remembered things that happened when he was outside the compound. I ... I wanted him to come with me, but he refused. Said he could do more good on the inside. But they must have found him out and reset his chip. When they sent him Outside to bring me back, he didn't remember me at all."

He falls silent. After a few minutes, I stand and leave him to his thoughts.

Time stretches. The longer we wait, the more I worry that something has gone wrong. Visions of my friends being shot, an army of Metz officers exploding out of the walls and chasing them down, run through my mind. My gaze flits constantly toward the door, waiting for someone to come through it.

Danny seems as nervous as me. Bored of playing with the officers, who are unresponsive to his prods and jeers, he stands facing the door into the compound, his fingertips beating an irregular rhythm on his gun.

When the door finally slides open, Danny's so jittery, he lets off a burst of gunfire that sends sparks raining down around the entrance.

"Stop, you idiot!"

I see Bryn crouched by the door, his hands over his head. I rush over to help him as he limps forward.

"Bloody trigger-happy Outsiders. Knew Richard shouldn't have given him that gun," he mutters.

"Are you okay? What's happened? You've been gone forever."

Bryn rolls his eyes. "Hardly. It couldn't have been more than an hour. The control centre's secure." He rotates his neck and winces. "Those Metz officers are good fighters, though."

"Did anyone … Is anyone badly hurt?" I dread his answer, but I must know.

"Few broken bones. Zane got knocked out for a bit. That's about the worst of it. Anders asked me to fetch you and Giles. There's some mad scientist he wants Giles to talk to."

"The Professor," I murmur.

I walk over to Giles and tell him what's happened. He shrinks back when I mention the Professor, but when I tell him Anders asked for him, he scrambles to his feet and shuffles forward.

Bryn leads us through a maze of corridors. Some are empty, but in others, we walk past bodies of Metz officers, dressed in the thin, black undersuits they wear around the compound.

This was their home.

I try not to look at them.

We walk into a wide corridor that I recognize from my previous visit to the compound. Circular cutouts in the ceiling let in an odd, green light. At the far end, a huge set of doors separates this part of the compound from the recruits' quarters.

Bryn pushes open a door and we enter a second, smaller corridor. The air in here tastes almost antiseptic, like a medic unit. I sense Giles close behind me, his breathing shallow and fast. Rogue waits by another set of doors that leads to the Professor's laboratory. His eyes meet mine as we approach, and I wonder if he's remembering the last time we were here.

Inside the laboratory, Anders stands beside my father. In front of them, next to a workbench, stands an elderly man with frazzled grey hair who wears a lab coat.

His eyes narrow at me. "You!"

Then Giles steps out from behind me and raises his head. When his hood falls back, he blinks owlishly in the bright light.

The Professor stares at him. "They said you were dead," he whispers. His eyes fall to the box in Giles's hands and his face flushes. "You did this?" He steps forward, but my father's arm whips out, grasping the man's shoulder and yanking him back. The Professor lets out a yelp of pain.

"Don't hurt him." Giles steps forward. "He can help us."

Behind me, Bryn snorts.

Giles shrinks back. I place a comforting hand on his arm while flashing Bryn a warning look.

"Please, Professor," Giles whispers. "These people want to do the right thing."

The Professor's eyes flit to the guards surrounding him, then his shoulders sag and he sinks down onto a high stool. "You didn't even leave a note," he says hoarsely, closing his eyes and pinching the bridge of his nose. "I thought you were happy here. I treated you … You were like my son, Giles. Then you disappeared. They told me you'd run off and they'd found your body in Area Four. When I asked to see it, they said it wasn't in a suitable condition." He looks up, his eyes bloodshot. "Why did you leave?"

Giles looks down at the floor. "I'm sorry, Professor. I never wanted to go. This was my home. But when I tried to explain to you that the device we were creating wouldn't be used to help the Metz keep the streets safe, as they told us, that they wanted to create an army to kill people, you refused to listen."

He takes a tentative step toward his mentor, and my father's grip on the Professor tightens. The scientist winces and tries to shake off his hand. "You don't have to be so brutal, you know. I'm a scientist, an old one at that, not a fighter."

"We have freed many of the officers," Giles continues. "If you'd speak with them and listen to what they were made to do ..."

The Professor's eyebrows shoot up. "You managed to free them? How?"

"By deactivating the control chips." Giles lifts the black box from around his neck, his voice rising in excitement. "I can show you."

Anders steps in front of Giles. "Wait. Let me show him."

"It's okay, Anders. He won't hurt me."

Someone coughs behind me. "Richard? There's a door at the far end signposted to subjects' quarters. Permission to check it out?" a woman asks.

My father lets his hand drop from the Professor's shoulder and turns to the man next to him. "Cuff him and keep an eye on him."

He strides over to the woman, giving her instructions in a low voice. She nods and moves off with three of the fighters.

The Professor stands slowly, as if the movement pains him. He looks past Anders to the black box in Giles's hands. "Can I see it?"

Giles smiles softly at Anders, who looks torn. Slowly, he steps aside.

"You can see it with the cuffs *on*." My father's voice is sharp. The man guarding the Professor lets go of the gun slung around his body and reaches for a pair of restraining bands from his belt.

Giles places the box on the bench in front of the Professor. The man reaches for it greedily and turns it over in his hands. I glance over my shoulder at my father, who has turned away and is muttering something into his comm.

"I—" Giles begins.

Crack.

I whirl around. Giles stands with his hand outstretched, his mouth hanging open in disbelief. The Professor brings the box down again on the edge of the bench, sending fragments of plastic and metal skittering across the floor.

Giles lets out an odd, keening wail and lunges forward.

I don't quite catch what happens next. Everything's a blur of movement and limbs. One moment, the guard reaches for the Professor, the next, he's clutching his leg, blood spilling between his fingers, and the Professor has his arm around Giles's neck, pulling him backward with surprising strength.

The bright lights of the laboratory glint off the metal scalpel at Giles's throat.

Anders makes a move toward them, his hand outstretched, but he stops in his tracks as he sees the steely determination in the Professor's eyes. Beside me, Bryn raises his gun, aiming it at the Professor.

My mouth goes dry.

My father pushes past me, his face dark with anger. "Let him go."

The Professor's eyes are steady. "No."

Giles clutches at the man's arm. Despite his slight build, I'd have thought he would have an advantage over the elderly man, but years of subservience have taken their toll and he cowers into his former master.

"You brought them in here. Betrayed the *family*," the Professor whispers into Giles's ear.

Giles trembles, his eyes almost popping out of their sockets. He looks to Anders, and perhaps Anders sees a warning in his friend's eyes because he springs forward. But he's too late.

The Professor slices the scalpel across Giles's throat and pushes him away.

A slash of crimson appears on Giles's white skin. He sways, one hand covering his throat, then his legs give way. Anders catches him and lowers him gently to the floor.

My feet are frozen in place as I watch as my father and Bryn wrestle the blade from the Professor's hand and secure his arms behind his back. The man doesn't put up much of a fight as he glares malevolently at his former assistant.

Blood pulses from Giles's neck, soaking his cloak.

Anders stares down at his friend, as if he can't believe what he's seeing. He presses one of his large hands to Giles's throat, as if that can stop the blood from pouring out. Giles lets out a gurgle and his eyes roll back into his head.

"Medic to the laboratory. Now!" my father says into his comm. He glances down at Giles. "Dammit. We need him."

I stumble forward, dropping to my knees beside the man who, hours earlier, had saved my life. I lift my gaze to Anders', seeing the despair and anguish in my friend's eyes.

We both know the medic will be too late.

Bryn dumps the contents of a medic box on the floor beside us. He rips open a dressing and shoves it into my hands. "Here. See if you can stem the bleeding."

Anders removes his hand to let me press the dressing to Giles's wound. The white gauze turns red in seconds.

"Add another." Bryn's voice is taut.

The second dressing soaks through.

"It's not working." My voice trembles.

Don't die, Giles. Please, don't die.

Anders cradles Giles's head in his lap as his friend's life leaks out onto the laboratory floor.

The movement of Giles's chest slows. His eyelids flutter, then open, his eyes finding Anders. He opens his mouth to say something, but his body spasms, a gurgle of blood and saliva trickling out between his lips.

"It's okay." Anders strokes the man's face, his voice choked. "It's okay. I know."

Giles's face relaxes and his eyes close again. He sags in Anders' arms as his chest falls, then remains still.

The pool of blood on the floor expands, soaking my legs.

My father's curses ring in my ears, but they seem so far away.

I lift Giles's hand from the floor and place it onto his stomach. Delicate hands with long, thin fingers perfectly designed for the intricate work he loved.

He came Inside for me, saving my life. But I couldn't save him.

My father didn't save him.

None of us saved him.

All he wanted was for the Professor to see what he saw. That what had been done to the Metz officers was wrong. He trusted his mentor, had forgiven him. And the price of that forgiveness was death.

Numbly, I stand and look down at my hands. They're stained with blood.

Will it ever go away?

My stomach roils, sending acid shooting up my throat. I stumble away, trying to control the rising nausea. A hand on my back guides me to a sink just in time. Someone turns on the tap, and the flow of water removes the acrid stench of sickness from the air. I stick my hands underneath it, the water turning red, then pink, then finally clear.

Even so, I keep scrubbing until Bryn turns off the water and gently pulls me away. He holds me as my body shakes, making soothing noises that are quite unlike the rough, surly man I know.

After several moments, he pulls back, holding me at arm's length. "Okay?"

I nod and suck in a deep breath.

My father stalks over, muttering something into his comm. His gaze softens momentarily. "I'm sorry."

I don't trust myself to answer.

He raises a hand to his ear and frowns, turning back to me. "I think there's something you need to see."

"Richard—"

I step forward, cutting Bryn off. "It's fine. I'm fine."

Whatever he wants me to see, it has to be better than facing Giles's body.

I follow my father across the lab and through a pair of double doors. There's a short corridor and another pair of doors that open into a long, carpeted corridor with soft, yellow lighting. My boots sink into the carpet, and a jolt of recognition hits me.

A series of doors lead off the corridor, and there's a large, metal elevator at the end that I know leads down, deeper underground.

12

Trey

The bleeping of my comm band wakes me. Groggily, I reach for it. Three new messages. I bring up the time display.

What could be so urgent at seven on a Saturday morning?

The first message is from Phillips, my manager. The holo image darkens the shadows under his eyes and he seems even more grumpy than usual. "Need you in here now, Goldsmith. The line's stopped and the boss is breathing down my neck."

The next two messages are also from Phillips, demanding to know where I am and why I'm ignoring him.

I type a quick response, telling him I'm on my way, and drag myself out of bed. I can't remember unpacking my clothes, but when I open the large antique wardrobe, my suits and shirts are neatly hung up. Thomas, I suspect.

I run down the main staircase, the plush carpet deadening my steps. At the bottom, a noise from the kitchen catches my attention. Rather than hurrying to the front door, I tiptoe over and peer through the crack in the door.

The kitchen is busy, despite the early hour. Lydia hums a tune as she pounds dough, flour rising around her. Derek, Thomas and

Dana sit around a small table, empty bowls in front of them. A small screen hangs from one corner of the ceiling, the news on, headlines scrolling along the bottom.

"The rebels are now surrounded," the newsreader says. "All entrances and exits to the Metz compound are heavily guarded, and the President has issued a personal assurance that there is no further danger to the public. However, some commentators have speculated that the rebels could survive the siege for weeks, living off the food stockpiled in the compound."

My breath hitches. I glance down at my comm band again, though I know there's little point. With the government monitoring all communications, Milicent was the only member of the Chain I was able to communicate with. Now I have no way of speaking to them, no way to find out if Aleesha is safe.

Richard's face appears on the screen in the kitchen, though they refer to him by his birth name – Ricus Meyer. The newsreader solemnly talks about the failed execution and the innocent by-standers murdered by the terrorists.

They show a short video of a young girl playing in a park with her mother. Two of the victims of the stampede trying to exit the square.

Ten people who turned up to watch the execution never made it home.

Had that been part of Richard's plan? I don't want to believe it. He's Aleesha's father and the leader of the organization I have sworn to help, but doubt clings to me. Richard had said he would stop at nothing to free London. I can't help but wonder how many lives he's prepared to sacrifice to achieve his goal.

I turn to leave, but Derek's muffled voice stops me. "You don't think we should report him? If the Metz find out they were here ..."

A chair scrapes across the floor. "He's the master now. And the mistress was involved, too, you know."

I peer through the crack in the door, then jerk back as a figure passes right in front of it. My heart skips a beat, but it's only Thomas stacking the dishes in the cleaner.

"But if they find out we knew and didn't report it, they'll arrest us." Dana's voice is thin and high-pitched.

Air hisses through my teeth. I hadn't thought about the risk to the staff from having the Chain meet here. The house is in an upper-class neighbourhood, and despite the secret tunnel, there have been enough oddities recently that the neighbours are probably keeping a close eye on us.

"I'll speak to Master Trey about it," Thomas says after a pause.

I pad back up the corridor to the front door, my mind whirring. Even in my own home, it appears I'm not safe.

* * * *

"What took you so long?" Phillips asks as I walk into his office. The air smells stale, and the faint hum of the air filtration system is absent.

"Sorry, sir. I got here as quickly as I could. What's the problem?"

"That's for you to find out." Phillips tugs at his collar. Rolls of fat threaten to spill out from it. "The report should have gone to you, but the night foreman didn't have your contact details. Which is why *I* ended up having to come in at five this morning to calm him down."

A lump forms in my throat. I hadn't even thought about giving the foreman my comm number. I'd assumed that if there were any issues at night or over the weekend, he would deal with it.

"Sorry, sir. If it's an issue with the machines, though, I'm not sure what I can do to help."

Phillips looks exasperated. "I know you can't fix them. Just find Barnes and get her here as quickly as possible. This is the worst possible time for something to go wrong. If it's not back up and running in the next two hours, I'm going to have to report it to Coleman. I'm sure you don't want him coming down to ask questions."

"Y-yes, sir." I wait to see if there's anything else, but Phillips just sighs and turns back to his holo screen. I take that as a dismissal.

The factory is eerily empty as I make my way down to the factory floor. The production lines run twenty-four hours a day, staffed by low-paid Outsiders who come and go through a different wing of the building. This side of the factory houses the management and administrative functions.

I find Taylor, the haggard night foreman, halfway down one of the lines where the artificial meat is shaped into burgers, sausages or whatever else it's pretending to be. A couple of workers lie underneath the conveyor belt, tools scattered on the floor. The machinery is silent, though some of the other lines are still running and there's the background hum of the dehydrators.

"I've been trying Barnes every ten minutes but can't get through," he snaps as I approach. "We've had a look but can't figure out what the problem is."

I spend five minutes trying to calm him down, then leave with a promise that Barnes will be here within the hour.

Thirty minutes later, I'm regretting that promise.

When Barnes doesn't answer her comm, I dig her home address out of the employee records, then spend five minutes repeatedly pressing the buzzer for her apartment before an angry neighbour on the fourth floor shouts down at me that she's not home. I even try going to the underground bar where we'd met before, but seeing as it's eight-thirty in the morning, the door is locked and barred.

Leaning against the graffitied wall in the stinking alley, I mull over my options. Going back to the factory without Barnes will only get me into more trouble. Ignoring the problem will probably get me sacked. Searching for her in a city this size could take weeks.

In the end, I return to her apartment block and sit on the steps outside, asking every person who comes in and out if they know Rae Barnes. Most of them don't. It's a big block, and Barnes doesn't strike me as the chatty, neighbourly type.

Eventually, after my backside's gone numb from sitting on the stone step for an hour, I spot her walking down the street.

She raises an eyebrow when she sees me. "That doesn't look comfortable."

"It's not." I wince as I get to my feet. "Where have you been?"

Barnes pushes past me. Her hair is pulled back into a knot and she's dressed in workout gear. "Last I heard, my weekends were my own. I only report to you at work."

I try to temper my irritation. "There's a problem at the factory. I need you to come in. Please," I add as an afterthought.

Barnes presses her thumb to the security pad and yanks open the door to the apartment block. "I'm back in on Monday. I'll deal with it then."

I catch the door just before it closes and follow her inside. Rather than taking the elevator, she heads toward the stairs.

"The production line's broken and Taylor can't fix it. Phillips wants it back up and running as quickly as possible." I glance at my wrist, my heart sinking. "He'll have reported it to Coleman by now, and if we don't get it fixed asap, we'll all be in trouble."

"Will we?" Barnes doesn't slow her pace.

"I've checked your contract," I pant, my lungs burning as I try to keep up. "There's a call-out requirement ... You have to come in ... within two hours."

"Well, in that case, I'll see you at the factory in precisely two hours."

I run up the last few steps to the landing and grab her arm. "Rae, please—"

"It's Barnes to you." She tries to yank her arm away, but I keep hold, forcing her to turn to face me. Dark circles rim her swollen eyes.

I frown. "Are you okay?"

"I'm fine. Or I will be when you let go of me."

"Will you please just listen to me for five minutes?"

We stare at each other for a long moment. Finally, she sighs. "You'd better come in."

Her apartment is small, plain and sparsely furnished. The only thing that stands out is an expensive coffee machine on the tiny kitchenette counter. Barnes pushes a button, and the smell of coffee soon fills the room.

"What's gone wrong then?" She dumps the bag she was carrying on a battered chair and turns to look at me.

I explain what the foreman had told me. "We're having to up production as the government lines are still down."

Barnes quickly downs her coffee and sets a second cup under the machine. "I'll get changed. Help yourself to coffee."

She disappears into what must be the bedroom. I wait for the machine to finish, then take the coffee and grab Barnes's gym bag to set it on the floor so I can sit. It's heavy and makes a clinking sound when I set it down. Frowning, I glance at the closed bedroom door, hearing the faint hiss of a cleaning unit. Setting my cup on the small table, I lean forward and open the bag.

A folded towel lies on top of a pair of overalls. I push them aside, frowning. Underneath, the bag is filled with tools. Spanners, wrenches, digital boxes. A half-cracked data pad and a small box with a symbol indicating it's explosive.

Everything a mechanic would need to fix a machine ... or break it.

"What are you doing?"

I jump and straighten, heat rushing to my cheeks. "I ..." My voice trails off. "You weren't at the gym," I say lamely.

"Did I say I was?" Barnes pushes past me and closes the bag. Her hair's damp – she couldn't have gone through the full drying cycle – and a lingering smell of oil cuts through the scent of soap. "Shall we go?"

I glance around the room and lower my voice. "Is it safe to talk in here?"

Barnes shrugs. "As safe as anywhere."

"Have you heard from Samson since the execution yesterday?"

Her shoulders stiffen. "No," she admits. "I got a message from one of his runners that they'd managed to stop the execution and were going to take the Metz compound. Since then, nothing." She turns to face the window, but not before I see the worry lines creasing her forehead.

"According to the news reports, they're trapped in the compound."

"That's what the media *would* say." A ghost of a smile crosses her face. "Samson and Petal are pretty good at finding their way out of places, though. If they wanted to leave, they'd be out by now."

"And the government production lines ... Did you have anything to do with them breaking down?"

Barnes lets out a snort. "Unless they've had a significant upgrade since I worked there, which I doubt, they're probably crumbling from old age and poor repairs. The government doesn't believe in investing in quality machinery."

She pulls on a pair of scuffed, black boots. "Shouldn't we be going? I thought you said it was urgent."

I trail her to the door, feeling ill at ease. Outside, I order a taxi pod, figuring Phillips won't mind the cost if it gets us there quicker.

Once we land on the factory roof, we take the elevator down. Barnes peers through the glass walls, unable to hide her curiosity.

"Pretty nice, this side of the building," she comments as we exit into a carpeted hallway.

I don't reply, thinking about the rough, concrete walls and cramped dining area in the East Wing. There may not be a wall dividing the building, but there are definitely two sides to Coleman's factory.

Just like the city.

I send Barnes straight down to the factory floor, then go to Phillips's office. After being interrogated as to why it's taken me so long to return, I get dismissed with an order to not leave the factory and a warning that Coleman's on the prowl.

Returning to the factory floor, I spot Barnes's legs poking out from under the production line.

"How's it going?"

"It'd go better if I didn't get interrupted," comes the muffled reply. A few minutes later, she sticks her head out from underneath. "Seriously. There's no point in you standing there. I'm still trying to work out what the problem is. Those idiots haven't helped by taking everything apart. You have your comm, right?"

I nod.

"I'll let you know as soon as I've figured it out. The best thing you can do is start processing my overtime claim." She flashes me a grin and disappears back under the machine.

I wander up to my office and collapse into my chair, wondering just how much I can trust Barnes. She's already tried to remove the androcibus nanite from the production line once, and I wouldn't put it past her to sabotage it again.

I drum my fingers on the desk. Quality control said the androcibus nanite was a preserving agent, but Barnes had a different theory. She remembered seeing the additive in the ingredient list for the government rations when she worked at the factory and thinks it's some kind of poison that works with co-tronkpretine to dull the brains of Outsiders and make them more compliant. It seems a wild leap to me, but it did strike me as a bit too coincidental that androcibus nanite was introduced into the lower-grade meat production line around the same time Outsiders started rejecting the government rations.

I'd searched the files I was able to access on the factory database but had so far failed to find any clue as to why it had been added to the production line in the first place.

My fingers slow their rhythm. I'm alone in the factory, with a perfectly good reason for being here. What better opportunity will I have to poke around?

Half an hour later, all I've discovered is that security at the factory is better than I thought. My employee chip gives me access to all the communal areas and most corridors, but the offices and restricted areas are all closed to me. Frustrated, I head up to see Phillips, wondering if I can persuade him to give me the contact details for the Lab that sent us the nanite.

His office is empty, the chair pushed back from the desk, his holo screen still on. My eyes fall to a half-open drawer filled with packs of faglights. If he's gone for a smoke, I'll have at least ten minutes.

Quickly, I bring up his filing system before the holo screen locks. It's neatly organized, so it doesn't take me long to find the ingredient lists for all the production lines he's responsible for. I scan through the most recent updates. It's not just my production line that had the androcibus nanite added. The files for lower-grade products across all lines had recently been updated for the new additive.

My pulse quickens as I bring up his email and type the additive into the search bar. The search returns five results, all labelled confidential. In the fourth message, I find what I'm looking for.

An email from Coleman that consists of one sentence.

To be introduced across all lower-grade product lines as discussed.

Below that is a forwarded email from Laboratory Five with an attachment. I scan the email, memorize the name at the bottom, then open the attachment. It's an official government communication requiring androcibus nanite to be added to any food lines sold to Outsiders to ensure "continuity of supply at this difficult time".

What does that mean?

A faint tap on the door catches my attention. The hairs on the back of my neck rise. Frantically, I close down the files I've opened, but I'm not quick enough.

The door swishes open to reveal a tall, imposing figure with a streak of silver through his dark hair.

My heart drops into my stomach.

Brad Coleman steps into the room, his gaze falling to the holo screen in front of me. "What the hell do you think you're doing?"

13

Aleesha

I find my father breakfasting alone in what had been the Commander's sitting room. Someone has brought him food on a silver tray, and he sits like a king, staring out of the window. "Morning."

He glances over at me and waves a hand toward a chair. "Sit down. Food?" He pushes a plate of pastries toward me. "We found some of the catering staff and a couple of scientists who didn't make it out. They're only too keen to assist us."

"It's amazing how a gun to the head inspires loyalty," I reply, grabbing one of the pastries.

The buttery pastry barely has time to melt in my mouth as I stuff the treat in. I should savour it, I guess. It's the first time I've ever had a pastry. I reach out for a second and chew it more slowly, ripping off small pieces at a time. This one has chocolate inside. *Real* chocolate, not chocco. It's the most delicious thing I've ever tasted.

I walk over to the window and look down at the street below. The government has set up barricades in the surrounding streets. So far, every exit we've found from the compound has been heavily guarded. We're trapped, and by the looks of things, it appears they're willing to wait. There's a constant supply of water and a pile of food bigger than any I've seen outside the Area Four food depot, but with the number of mouths we have to feed, it won't last more than a week.

I pop the last of the pastry into my mouth and turn back to my father. "So, what's your plan?"

He sighs and sets down his cup of coffee. "Ration our food and sit tight. If we can't find a way out, we don't really have another option. I hadn't planned to take the compound yet, but now we have it, it's too valuable to surrender, and there are too few of us to take on the government's army."

"What about the Metz officers we brought back? Surely they can be controlled from here?"

"Just before we broke in, the staff in the control centre released some sort of virus into the computer network. I've got people working to see if there's anything left, but at the moment, we have no way of controlling them." He sighs. "Giles's box is beyond repair, and the Professor had a poison capsule tucked inside his mouth." My father snorts in disgust. "Dead before we could question him. So, for now, we just have to keep the officers locked up."

Guilt sours my mouth at the mention of Giles. The compound has its own crematorium, so we'd held a small service for him and Radha the night before. Bryn was the only member of the Chain who'd attended, but Samson and Petal were there. Anders had said a few words. He'd asked if I wanted to say something, but I wasn't sure what you were supposed to say at funerals, so I'd declined.

I guess I should feel satisfaction that the Professor is dead, but I don't. Just anger that he won't face the justice he deserves. But I know that only part of the anger I feel is directed at him. Most of it is for me.

I should have been able to stop him.

"Rogue's asked to speak to the officers. He thinks he may be able to explain what's happened and persuade them to join our side."

"And they might just say whatever he wants to hear if it'll get them out of the cell." My father shakes his head. "We can't trust them."

Perhaps he's right. Trust got Giles killed.

"Jameson was working on a similar device to control the Metz. Can he help?"

My father sighs heavily. "Jameson can't even help himself at the moment. And that's another issue. If we can't find a way out of here soon, I'm going to have to risk sending a message to Murdoch. He needs to clear out of the headquarters and find a new building before the government moves in."

Turns out that Laboratory Two was directly connected to the Metz compound. It was a relief to be able to free Mitch, Jameson and the other prisoners, though freedom was a relative term. They have better accommodation and food, but until we can find a way out of the compound, they're trapped here, too.

When I'd released the lock on his door, Mitch had pushed past me and stretched his arms over his head, his grey tunic hanging loose on his thin frame. "Well, I guess your rescue party did turn up, after all. Remind me to stick near you in the future."

I figured that was the closest to a thank you I would get.

Jameson hadn't been able to walk, so Bryn had carried him to a small bedroom that had belonged to one of the Metz captains. He'd lost so much weight that Bryn had barely been out of breath when he gently laid him on the thin bed. Jameson babbled incoherent apologies, while Bryn tried in vain to soothe him. Part of me wondered if the man was so broken as to be beyond recovery.

I slump down into the chair opposite my father and scratch the back of my hand. One of the remaining scientists had removed the monitoring chip they'd put in me when I'd arrived. They'd smeared some healing gel on the cut, but it itches worse than a double mosquito bite.

When I look up, the corner of my father's mouth is twitching as if he's trying to hold in a smile.

"You have a bit of pastry just here." He points delicately to the corner of his mouth.

"I was saving it for later," I mutter, swiping the back of my hand across my mouth. I suck in a lungful of air and hold it for a moment before releasing it.

"Was there a reason you came to see me, Aleesha? Other than to steal my breakfast?"

"I wanted to say thank you. For coming to rescue me." My hand strays to the amulet around my neck, hidden under my vest.

"You thought I wouldn't?" My father's voice is surprisingly gentle.

I shrug, embarrassed. "It was a trap."

"I know." He pauses. "But I couldn't take the risk that he would go through with it."

I pull the amulet over my head and hold it out to him. "This is yours."

He studies me for a moment, and I feel his blue eyes burning deep inside my soul. Then he reaches out and wraps my fingers around the charm. "Keep it. I gave it to your mother, and she chose to give it to you. It's yours now."

The only thing I have left of her. I swallow down the emotion rising in my throat and hang the amulet around my neck again.

"She would have been very proud of you, you know," my father says quietly.

My chest tightens. "I ... I miss her."

It's been twelve years, but I miss her more than ever. I cling to the few glimpses of her I remember, but every year, she seems to fade from my memory. I'm not sure I can even remember her voice.

But I remember her death. It has haunted my dreams ever since I saw the footage in the Metz compound. Over and over again, I have watched her die, powerless to stop it. Sometimes her death merges with Andrew Goldsmith's, their faces mirroring and dividing until they surround me on all sides and their blood soaks my feet, rising up my body until I think I might drown in it.

My father squeezes my arm. "I miss her, too."

"What was she like?"

His gaze turns distant and the corners of his mouth lift into a warm, unconscious smile that transforms his face. For a moment, I see not the man who has ruthlessly torn down governments and taken control of cities, but the man my mother saw all those years ago – a man in love.

"She was the most wonderful person I have ever met. I was captivated by her beauty, but it was her heart that won me over. Maria had a smile for everyone and always saw the best in people." He glances over at me. "When I arrived in London, I was in a bad place. I was angry. Angry at the people who'd murdered my parents, angry at myself for being the cause of their deaths, angry at the world in general. Maria pulled me out of that. She was the angel who tamed the devil inside of me. The light to my dark. Without her …" He shakes his head. "Anyway, I'm sorry I wasn't there – for you both."

His words about his past intrigue me and remind me of what the President had said. "What happened to your parents?"

He blows out a breath. "It's a long story. The short of it is there was a mix-up at the hospital after my mother gave birth to me. South Africa was pretty chaotic at that time. I think the hospital was attacked by some rebels and they had to evacuate. In the confusion, I was mixed up with another baby, the child of one of the richest families in the region. It went unnoticed for years. I was not that dissimilar in looks to my father, but when I started school, they began to wonder if something was wrong.

"South Africa was the same as London and most other countries. The more money you had, the more genetic enhancements you could bequeath on your unborn child. My parents were loving and kind, but they weren't well-off. At first, they just thought they had been blessed with a naturally intelligent child, but as I got older and surpassed my classmates in everything, they suspected I'd been given additional enhancements." He pauses. "For a while, I think they didn't want to believe that I was not biologically theirs. But my real parents, the ones who had paid for a perfect son, were not forgiving."

"They wanted you back?"

My father nods. "One letter was all the warning my parents had. We fled our home, leaving everything behind. I was fifteen at the time. But of course, *they* could hire the best people to track us down. My father bought us extra time to escape with his life. It was only when I was getting on the plane that I realized my mother wasn't coming with me. They only had enough money for one ticket.

"I flew to Paris, then London with just the clothes on my back and a hastily written note to an aunt I had never met. And that amulet." His expression becomes pinched and he turns away. "It was my mother's."

I don't know what to say. Should I offer him comfort? Although he's my father, he is still a stranger to me in so many ways.

"The President said you were friends," I say cautiously.

He flashes me a sharp look. "I would treat anything *he* tells you with caution. He can be very manipulative. But yes, we were friends at school for a time. He was sensible and smart – the model pupil. I was a natural rebel. I think that was what intrigued him most about me. He attached himself to me and we became friends, of sorts. But when I started dating Maria, he became jealous."

His face darkens. He pushes his chair back and walks over to the window. "I wasn't sure whether it was because he wanted Maria for himself or didn't like me spending time with her over him, but he started to change. We had all these plans about what we'd do after university. I believed the government and system of society was corrupt, and I always thought he agreed. But his views changed. Maria had always treated him kindly, but he began to scare her. Tried to turn her against me. Anyway, we fell out completely just before I left London. He seems to have born a grudge ever since."

He turns back to me and smiles sadly, holding out his hands, palms upward. "Now you know all my secrets."

I suspect that's not quite the truth. Ricus Meyer, Richard Masterton, whatever he calls himself, is a man with many secrets. But I'm grateful he has shared some of them with me. It makes me feel closer to him. He still intimidates me, but I think, in time, perhaps I could love him.

The thought sends warmth flooding through my chest. A family of two is better than no family at all.

There's a knock on the door and Katya, my father's second-in-command and lover, walks in. The spell is broken, the warmth in my chest disappearing. Perhaps we will be a family of three, but she is not the stepmother I would have chosen.

"Can I speak to you for a moment, Richard?"

My father raises an eyebrow and gives me a rueful smile. "Duty calls. I'm glad we had this chat, though."

I turn to leave, but stop, remembering the other reason I'd come to see him. "I forgot. When I saw the President before my execution, he told me why I was able to pass through the Wall unharmed."

I think it's the first time I've seen my father surprised. "What did he say?"

I frown, trying to remember his exact words. "He said I had a natural immunity … Whatever that is."

My father's face falls. "It's usually used in the context of an illness. If you are immune to a virus, for example, it means you won't get sick from it like other people."

"So there's a sickness in the Wall that kills people?"

"I don't know." His eyes bore into me, and I shift uneasily. "Did he say anything else?"

"He said the foreigner was easy to explain, as was Andrew's son, Trey." I chew my lip. "Does he mean that Insiders and foreigners *can* pass through the Wall?"

My father's brow furrows. "He said that? Interesting. I thought we had tested those options previously, but I'll have to check with Murdoch."

"Trey said now that he'd been chipped again, he didn't think he could get through the Wall anymore, but I'm sure Bryn said it had nothing to do with a person's chip." I feel more confused than ever.

He sighs. "Perhaps one of the scientists downstairs knows more. Thanks for telling me."

That's a dismissal if I've ever heard one. I eye the remaining pastry, then decide I've probably had enough for one morning and head to the door. It opens in front of me, and I take an inadvertent step back as Samson looms in the doorway.

He nods to me and walks in, not waiting for an invitation. Petal follows, a smug grin on his face. My nose wrinkles as an unpleasant odour trails him.

My father opens his mouth to protest, but Samson gets in first. "Petal's found a way out."

Petal swipes the last pastry from the table and retreats to lean against the wall. He begins to chew noisily.

"Where?" My father shoots Petal a dark look.

"Through the old sewers," he mumbles around a mouthful. "It's a bit of a climb down and a cramped walk, but it's doable. I came up about half a mile away, but you may be able to follow it all the way Outside."

"That would explain the smell," my father says acidly.

Petal grins and waggles his eyebrows. "Sometimes you gotta look in unusual places."

"Now that we have a route out, we need to decide on our next step." Samson sits in the chair I vacated. "You said we both have the same goal – to create a more democratic system of government in Britannia. How exactly do you propose to go about doing that?"

There's a pause while my father studies Samson. I sense him assessing the big man, weighing up the people and connections he can offer against the risk of trusting him with the Chain's secrets.

"We capture the President and key government ministers loyal to him. They're having a private dinner on Thursday night. We won't get a better opportunity. Once they're captured, we'll use them to access the government building and take control of their secure systems. Then we broadcast evidence of what the government has done to their people, including footage of the prisoners here. We announce a new democracy and execute the President and his allies. We've carried out the same process in many other cities."

"Has it worked?"

My father's gaze remains steady. "Yes."

"Well, you may find things a bit different here," Samson drawls. "For one thing, I know there are procedures in place to lock down the government headquarters if the President is compromised. And I don't fancy your chances of breaking in. Not unless you can take down the barrier around it."

"We may not have to resort to that," Katya says. "Not if we have the codes to get in."

Samson darts her a look. "You have someone on the inside?"

"Perhaps."

He leans back in the chair. "Interesting. Who would that be?"

Katya crosses her arms. "None of your business."

Samson smiles coldly. "If you want my help, it *is* my business. You said you only trust people once they have proven their worth. I saved your daughter's life, Richard. I believe I have done that. But trust goes both ways. And I am not sure *you* are worth trusting."

My father catches my eye and tilts his head toward the door. I slip from the room and leave them to their games. My steps are lighter now that I know there is a way out of this place, a way for me to return to my gang. But anxiety still gnaws at my stomach.

I had a responsibility to them. I'd promised to look after them and keep them safe, then hours later, I'd disappeared.

I worry about what's happened in my absence and what I'll find when I return.

I worry they won't want me back.

14

Trey

I push myself to my feet and stare blankly at Coleman, trying to find my voice. I dare not look at the holo screen. My fingers slide toward the escape key on the luminescent keypad, itching to close down the final file.

"A-are you looking for Phillips, sir?"

"Of course I'm looking for Phillips." Coleman's voice is smooth and low. "But I wasn't expecting to find you here. Don't you have a production line to fix?"

"Y-yes, sir. I have Barnes working on it right now. She—"

My comm band bleeps. A message from Barnes. I tap the band, praying it's good news.

"She's found the source of the problem and is working to fix it now. It should be back up and running in a couple of hours." I can hear the relief in my voice.

Coleman's eyes bore into mine. "Good. Your line has been having more breakdowns than usual. I want a report on my desk by the end of the day telling me why that is and how you plan to fix it without shutting the line down. We cannot afford any more interruptions."

I nod. "Of course, sir. Phillips mentioned the extra orders we've had from the government. I—"

I break off at the sound of rapid footsteps outside. Coleman turns, and in the split second his attention is diverted, I close the file and step away from the desk.

"I'm sorry, sir," Phillips pants from outside the room. "I'd just nipped to the bathroom."

"It's no problem. Goldsmith here was just updating me on the progress with fixing the production line."

Coleman steps further into the room and Phillips appears in the doorway, his face flushed. "Good. Barnes got it running yet?"

"She's found the source of the problem and is working to fix it now," I say, moving in what I hope is a casual manner toward the door. "If you'll excuse me, I'll go and make sure she's got everything she needs to get it sorted."

Phillips steps aside to let me out. As I pass Coleman, he reaches out to stop me. I drag my eyes up to his.

"Be careful, Goldsmith. Remember what I said last time we spoke."

I swallow hard at the veiled threat, remembering the conversation all too clearly. Coleman had discovered I'd impersonated Louis to snoop around the East Wing of the building. He'd accepted my excuse on that occasion but had hinted that my job and even my life might be in danger if there were any future transgressions.

"Y-yes, sir. Of course."

His grip on my arm relaxes as he turns to Phillips. I use the opportunity to slip through the door and walk from the office as quickly as I can without running.

When I get back to my office, I'm surprised to see Emilie behind her desk. "I thought you were taking the weekend off?"

She looks faintly embarrassed. "I was, but Leona arranged to meet some of her school friends to study today, so she didn't need me around. And I … I wanted to apologize for my comments yesterday.

It's none of my business what you do, nor is it my place to comment on it." She stares intently at the holo screen in front of her, but her fingers are still.

"It's me who should apologize," I say, coming over to sit on her desk. "I shouldn't have run out on you, especially with the problems we've been having." I hesitate, wondering how much I can trust her. "When I was Outside the Wall, I met the girl who was due to be executed. I wanted to be there for her so she wasn't totally alone."

"I saw on the news she managed to escape. Did you have anything to do with that?"

I shake my head, even though she's still looking at her holo screen. "Louis and I got shot at like everyone else. We managed to escape down the back of the stands. It was chaos." I shudder at the memory, an image of the small girl and her mother flashing through my mind.

Emilie turns to look at me, her expression softening. "It must have been terrible. I bet the last thing you wanted to do after that was come into work today."

Talking about the execution causes my thoughts to stray to Aleesha and Bryn. Are they still trapped in the compound? Are they even alive?

I manage a weak smile. "It's a good distraction."

Emilie's hand covers mine. It's warm, comforting. "You know, if you ever want to talk about anything ..." Her voice is gentle, her eyes kind.

I squeeze her fingers, then pull away. "Thanks." As much as I long to confide in someone, to share my worries, I can't bring Emilie into this. What I know could get her arrested.

A fleeting look of disappointment crosses her face, but it's quickly replaced by another smile. "On a different note, the application window for interns is coming up. I wondered if you might be able to put Leona forward for a place? She's really smart, smarter than me, and it would be so helpful for her university application. The position's unpaid, but if you do a good job, they give you a bonus at the end of the four weeks."

"Sure. Just tell me what I need to do." I remember something else she had told me. "You're helping fund her studies, aren't you?"

Emilie nods. "That's why I'm still living at home. Well, that and the fact there are no apartments I could possibly afford." She scrunches her face. "But it means almost all my salary can go to Leona's university fund."

"She's lucky to have such a generous sister."

Emilie flushes. "I just want her to have what I couldn't. Our parents are supportive, but, well ..." She waves a hand through the air. "Anyway, once she gets through university, I'm sure she'll qualify for an amazing job. Perhaps one that comes with an apartment."

It had never really occurred to me that some Insiders struggled for money. Saving to pay for a university education is a far cry from not being able to pay for food, but still, it was something I had always taken for granted until recently.

I make a mental note to arrange for Emilie to get a decent bonus at the end of the year. If not from the factory, from the money Milicent left me.

* * * *

When I finally make it back to the house, I find the street outside crowded with taxi pods and hover floats. Mystified, I weave through them to the front door, which is propped open. Boxes litter the hallway.

It seems my mother took the invitation to move in as soon as possible quite literally.

I follow the sound of my mother's voice to the drawing room. She's sitting in Milicent's high-backed chair, giving orders to Thomas, who looks both uncomfortable and bemused.

"Hello, Mother."

She stops mid-sentence and turns to me. Her eyes are bright, and she looks almost like her old self. "Trey! I hope you don't mind, but I'm asking Thomas here to rearrange this room in order to fit our furniture." She casts a critical eye around the immaculate sitting room. "Of course, the whole place needs redecorating. It's so old-fashioned. My friend used this fantastic designer for her house. I—"

"Mum, stop!" I take a deep breath and walk over to her, feeling a pang of guilt at the wounded expression on her face. "Look, you need to rest. There will be plenty of time to sort out the house. Why don't you go up and make sure your bedroom is just how you want it. Tackle one room at a time. I'll get the furniture moved into the front room for now, then you can take your time working out what you want to do."

"Well, okay ..."

"It's nearly dinnertime. Let's go upstairs, and Dana can help you unpack." I gently pull her from the chair and steer her in the direction of the door. "Thomas and I will bring in the rest of the stuff from the hovers, and I'm sure the cook has something nice planned for dinner. You could dress up if you like."

"It doesn't seem worth it when we don't have visitors ..." Her face brightens again. "Once we've redecorated, we can throw the most fabulous party. There's so much space here. Even Mary and Gisella will be impressed."

Despite her enthusiasm, we make painfully slow progress up the stairs. By the time we arrive at Milicent's bedroom, which my mother seems to have claimed as her own, the colour has drained from her cheeks. Quick footsteps sound outside the room as I help her lie down on the bed. To my relief, it's Dana. I leave my mother to instruct the housemaid on how to unpack her clothes and make my way back downstairs.

Half an hour later, the pods and hovers have left, and I shut the door on the front room, which is packed to the brim with furniture from her apartment.

"Just don't let her in there," I tell Thomas. "She can't worry about what she doesn't know."

His lips twitch. "Yes, sir. Dinner is planned for seven if that is convenient?"

"Sure." I hesitate. "Has my sister been here?"

"She was here earlier this afternoon and said she would be bringing a friend to dinner."

"Friend?"

"Yes, sir."

I massage my temples. "Right."

"Why don't you go and get changed, sir," Thomas says kindly. "It looks like you've had a hard day."

I grunt a reply and am halfway up the stairs before I realize he's still calling me "sir". And this time, I hadn't even noticed.

My comm band bleeps while I'm changing. The number comes up as unknown and the message is just three words – *Everyone safe. B. Bryn.*

My breath comes out in a rush, a little of the tension in my shoulders and neck releasing with it. Aleesha is alive. Bryn is alive.

* * * *

I walk into the dining room at seven to find my mother chatting with a tall, lanky young man I vaguely recognize. She wears a long evening dress and sips from a narrow-stemmed cocktail glass.

"Trey!" she trills. "Have you met Ella's boyfriend, Dexter?"

Dexter steps forward and holds out his hand. I take it reluctantly, and he pumps my arm enthusiastically. "So good to meet you, Trey. Ella's told me about everything you've been doing. We're so excited to help you make a difference."

I frown and open my mouth, but Ella appears behind him. At her pleading look, I close it again. "Sure. Nice to meet you."

Ella hands me a glass containing a fluorescent pink liquid. I take a cautious sip and my eyes widen. "What's in this?"

"Oh, just a few things I found in Milicent's cabinet." My sister grins wickedly. "There's a lot of stuff that needs using up."

I'm saved from replying when Thomas enters the room and announces that dinner is served.

I don't know if it's the alcohol in the cocktail, the good food or the banter between my sister and Dexter, but I find myself enjoying dinner. For the first time in weeks, I feel like I can relax. Everyone I care about is safe, or at least as safe as they can be.

After dinner, my mother excuses herself to rest. I move to help her up, but Thomas beats me to it. Mother beams up at him. "It's so nice to have some help around the house," she murmurs as he leads her from the room.

The moment the door closes behind them, Dexter leans forward, bracing his elbows on the table. "Right. Let's get down to business."

My heart sinks. I glance at Ella, but she refuses to meet my gaze.

"I've studied the footage of what happened at the execution. We stopped broadcasting to the public as soon as the shooting started, but the cameras kept rolling. You were there, weren't you?"

I nod. It seems pointless to deny it. I remember Ella saying Dexter worked for one of the media outlets. "You probably have a better idea of what happened than me. It was chaos."

"The footage was pretty erratic. Some of the cameras got taken out in the crossfire. Anyway, I identified who I thought were the leaders of the Chain and the Brotherhood, and Ella confirmed it. They're working together, aren't they?"

"Honestly, I don't know." I take a sip of my drink. "I'm not sure they're on good terms. I wasn't even sure Samson would help with Aleesha's rescue."

"Have you managed to speak to them since they took the Metz compound?" Ella asks.

"No. As far as I know, they're trapped in there." I think of Bryn's message, wishing he'd told me where they were. But he probably didn't want to risk giving anything away if the message was intercepted.

"I know Ella's spoken with you about our group. There are about thirty of us ..."

I give Ella a pleading look, but she refuses to meet my eye.

"The Chain is bringing in fighters from overseas." Dexter draws a line on the table with his finger. "The Brotherhood is trusted by Outsiders." He draws a second line leading off from the first. "But there's still one element they haven't accounted for – Insiders. That's where we can help." He draws a third line at the bottom, linking up the first two lines. "We complete the triangle."

His eyes burn with an intensity I find uncomfortable.

"We want to help, Trey," Ella says.

"I don't know what Samson and the Chain have planned," I say, stalling for time. It would be rude to get up and walk away, but I don't want to have this conversation with them. Don't want to get them involved. I squeeze my eyes shut, and for a second, I'm back in the square, bullets flying around me.

"We're in a unique position," Dexter continues. "We have people working in the government, the media, the food companies, every big organization."

Including the Labs ...

"Which Lab does your friend, Frankie, work in?" I ask before I can stop myself.

If they have someone working in Laboratory Five, perhaps even someone working on the team that produces the androcibus nanite ...

I try to quash the thought, not wanting Ella involved. But my traitorous mind won't leave it alone. Besides, I'm running out of excuses to stop Barnes from doing something stupid. If it is just an innocent additive, Dexter's friend will be able to find out. And if it's something harmful ...

Well, I'll deal with that if and when it comes to it.

"Laboratory Five," Dexter answers. "Why?"

My pulse quickens. "There's an additive that's recently been added to the lower-grade food lines – androcibus nanite. It may be nothing, but I wondered if it might be some kind of tronk replacement now that a lot of the Outsiders aren't eating the government rations. There's very little information about it on our systems, but it came from Laboratory Five. Someone named Mai Tanaka is involved with it."

Dexter makes a note on his comm band. "Great. We'll get a message to Frankie and see what she can find out."

"Tell her to be careful. If it *is* something they don't want people knowing about, she could get into trouble, maybe even be in danger." I bite my lip.

"Of course." Dexter looks serious. "We'll take every precaution."

I make my excuses and push my chair back. At the door, I look back to where Dexter and Ella sit with their heads bent together, talking excitedly. I can see why she was attracted to him and how he has drawn people into his group. He's charismatic, but it's more than that. He believes every word he says and is so passionate you can't help but be drawn in.

But I fear for them. I fear for my sister.

They don't know what they're getting themselves into.

15

Aleesha

The guards at the main door to Phoenix headquarters let us in with a sullen nod. The huge mural of the snake that marked the old warehouse as the property of the Snakes flows along the boundary wall and up over the entrance. I'll have to get Jax to paint over it now the gang's been renamed. A phoenix signifying renewal, rebirth and a new start for Outsiders and Insiders alike.

Immediately upon stepping into the building, I sense that something is wrong. The place smells of stale urine and beer. Worse, it is quiet. Not even the sound of training breaks the heavy silence. My fingers curl into a fist, wishing I'd thought to steal a knife. Unarmed, I feel vulnerable.

Ahead, the dark corridor ends at a door leading to the main hall. I'm afraid to open it. Afraid to see what's inside.

But I don't have a choice.

Skylights run the length of the high ceiling in the main hall, letting in shafts of light that don't quite reach the edges of the room. The room looks much as it ever did – a padded floor in the centre for wrestling, punch bags hanging in an alcove off one corner, couches and chairs scattered around. At the far end is a platform, where I'd stood to make my speech just four days ago. On the wall behind it is Jax's masterpiece – a towering phoenix with its flaming wings spread wide, painted in reds, oranges and golds.

My eyes narrow. Someone has sprayed black paint across the bottom of the mural. One word in two-foot-high letters.

Paigon.

Rogue follows my gaze. "What does it mean?"

"Backstabber. Someone who lies and betrays their friends."

I get a sinking feeling as I look around the room, now seeing the hunched figures in the shadows. Some stare at us, their eyes cold. Others are sleeping, perhaps unconscious. Many of them wear rough bandages.

There is no welcome for their returning leader.

"Who did you leave in charge?" I ask under my breath.

"Megan and Jax," Anders answers. He shrugs. "There wasn't anyone else."

"What are you lot starin' at? Don't you have stuff to do? Lazin' around here like a bunch of street hobies." Danny's voice echoes around the hall. He has tight grip on the gun the Chain had given him. His finger twitches on the trigger.

"Danny," I say quietly. "Give your gun to Anders."

"But the Chain gave it to—"

"Do it," I snarl.

He casts me a disgusted look but unhooks the weapon from his shoulder and hands it over. I relax a fraction. Having a trigger-happy Danny in this kind of atmosphere will only make things worse.

"Where are Megan and Jax?" I call out.

Silence. Anger flares in my belly. I stalk over and grab one of the men by his jacket collar. He stares up at me with vacant eyes, and a twist of paper falls from his grip, releasing a trickle of white powder.

I give him a shake. "Is this what you've come to? Moping around here in the dark getting high on street tronk?" I shove him against the wall and release my grip. "You know what that crap does to you."

Shame taints my words.

The sight of the powder causes saliva to burst in my mouth. The taste of the tronk the President had given me still lingers, if only in my mind.

A spark flickers in the man's eyes. I search through my memory for his name. *Ishaan.* He'd been one of Vihaan's cronies, possibly a relative. He has the same black hair and sallow skin. Coughing, his chest rattling, he unfolds himself and slowly climbs to his feet.

"Yer back then."

I try not to recoil as his stench hits me. "Yes, I'm back. And by the look of it, just in time to stop this place from going to shit. What the hell's been going on?"

The man nearly overbalances, but thrusts a hand out to the wall to steady himself. He throws his head back and spits. *"Paigon."*

The sound of my palm connecting with his cheek rings loudly in the empty silence. I stare at him, then down at my hand, unable to believe what I've just done. I wipe the spit from my cheek with the back of my hand.

He deserved it.

I deserved it.

Rogue steps forward, but I hold out a hand to stop him, my eyes not leaving Ishaan's. "Megan?"

"In the office." Ishaan jerks his head toward the end of the hall.

I feel their eyes on me as I turn and walk away, my heart pounding in my chest. I knew getting myself captured was a mistake, that the fragile truce between the ex-Metz officers and the gang members needed constant nurturing, but I hadn't dreamed things could fall apart so quickly.

"I'm sure it's not as bad as it looks," Anders murmurs into my ear as we approach the door to the small room I'd been using as an office. "It wasn't like this when we left."

I kick the door and it slams open, bouncing off the wall. Jax looks up from the table. Megan doesn't.

Rogue, Danny and Anders file in behind me, and Anders quietly closes the door. Rogue walks over to Megan and places a hand on her shoulder, withdrawing it when she flinches. Hurt flashes across his face.

I break the silence. "What's been going on?"

Jax eyes Megan uncertainly. When she doesn't answer, he shifts uncomfortably in his seat. "Bigland Boys attacked yesterday. Dunno if they knew you was gone or what. It was a bit of a half-hearted effort, so we were able to fend 'em off."

I close my eyes and draw in a slow breath. I knew I'd have to deal with the Bigland Boys' leader at some point. After they'd helped rescue us from Primo's attack, he'd made it clear his help would have a price. I'd just hoped it wouldn't come to a head this quickly.

"Any casualties?"

Jax shrugs. "Couple of people got nasty wounds, need to make sure they don't get infected, but we got off fairly light."

"And the graffiti on your mural?"

The older man looks down at the table and runs a hand over his steel-grey hair. "People are pretty pissed."

"Can you blame them?" Megan finally looks up and fixes me with a hard look. "You promised us everything, and then, an hour later, you run off after your *boyfriend* and disappear. Next thing we hear, you've got yourself captured by the Metz. Is it any wonder people don't trust you?"

"Megan—"

She turns to Rogue. "Don't *Megan* me. You weren't the one who had to try to explain that we're all supposed to be friends now, even if we ain't got enough food to go around." She looks back to me. "It's only because of Jax that we're still here at all. He's had to fight off four wannabe leaders so far. For *you*. You know what people are sayin'? That things are worse now than they were with Primo. That the girl who promised us things would be different, that life would be *better*, has turned traitor and run off to become an Insider. *Paigon* ... That's what they're calling you. You goin' to deny it?"

She slumps back in her chair and turns her head away, but not before I see the glint of tears in her dark eyes. "I was such a fool to believe," she mutters, almost too low for me to catch.

It's those words more than her outburst that hit me like a punch to the chest.

D'ya think things'll ever be different, Aleesha?

We can change things ... Build a different type of gang.

How many promises have I broken?

I pull out the chair next to her and sit. "You're right. People are pissed. And they have every reason. I failed you." I take a deep breath. Anger still boils inside me, and part of me wants to storm out into the hall and settle this with fists and knives. I know I'm a better fighter than most of them. That's how this would have been dealt with in the past. But I promised them things would change. I promised them something better.

"I shouldn't have run off after Trey. It was stupid of me. I walked right into the trap the President had set."

"The President?" Jax's eyes flick to me. "What's he want you for?"

"It's a long story. I'll tell you once we've got this mess sorted out." I try to catch Megan's eye, but she's not having it. "Look, I made a mistake, but it won't happen again. And I'll do whatever it takes to put it right."

For a moment, there's silence. Then Megan draws herself up in

146

her chair and meets my gaze. I see the weight she and Jax have been carrying these past few days. She may blame me for running off, but she also blames herself for failing to control the gang in my absence.

"Well, you can start by findin' us some food. People have started raiding the shops again. I told 'em not to, but what can you do when everyone's hungry?"

Anders sits down opposite me, placing Danny's gun on the table. "Are we completely out? How about water? Medicine?"

Jax eyes the gun warily. "Out of food. We're all right for water, as long as we don't waste it."

"How have things been between the old gang and the ex-Metz officers?" I ask. "I didn't notice many of them in the hall."

Megan shrugs. "Not great, but if we can get everyone a decent meal, we might have a chance."

I lay a hand on her arm. She stiffens but doesn't pull away. "You've done more than I could have asked of you. Both of you. We'll make this right."

Food can make or break a gang. Normally, a gang survives on food donated by people in the surrounding area, in return for looking out for the Metz and protecting them from other gangs. But everything's changed in the past few weeks, what with all the fighting and Primo terrorizing everyone, not to mention everyone refusing to eat the government rations. Even if the people of Area Four trust us, which they have no reason to, there's not enough food to go around.

"What are we goin' to do about the Bigland Boys?" Danny asks. "We can't let 'em get away with this."

"Nothing. Our first priority is getting people fed and healed."

"But—"

"I mean it, Danny. The Bigland Boys can wait." The last thing my people need now is another fight.

He gives me a dark look. "They're not goin' to go away, you know.

Denzel ain't smart, but he ain't stupid, either. If you don't put him in his place, he'll think he can take what he wants."

I narrow my eyes, and he raises his hands in the air. "Just sayin'."

"Comment noted." I turn back to the table. "Now, does anyone know what food's available out there?"

"Not much," Megan says. "The government ration stores are full, but no one wants that stuff. Everything else has been cleared out."

An idea forms in my mind. It's not ideal, but right now, we don't have many options. I turn to Danny. "Have you got any of those chits left that you used to pay the monks for our food?"

He purses his lips. "Should be a few. I hid 'em away before we left." He shoves his chair back. "I'll go take a look."

I turn back to Megan. "We need everyone who can draw rations to go get as much food as they're allowed. If they've got stockpiles, they may even be persuaded to give us some extra."

"But isn't it bad?" Jax asks.

I shrug. "It's the same food we've been eating for years. Even if the government has messed with it, starvation's going to kill us faster than they ever could. And tell them not to get stuff like protein bars. We need the basics – flour, powdered milk, salt. Some of that fake meat crap if they've got it." I don't hold out much hope of that.

Megan wrinkles her nose. "Flour? What do we do with that?"

Before I can reply, the door bangs open and Danny walks back in. He drops a small, battered lockbox on the table. "This is all I've got. An' most of it's mine, not the gang's." He tips out a small pile of chits.

"You'll get it back, Danny. I promise."

He makes a huffing noise and slumps into a chair.

I sort the chits into two piles and push one to Jax. "You know the man who deals with the anti-infection pills, right?"

Jax nods.

"Get as many as you can. Don't let him rip you off." I push the rest of the metal scraps to Danny. "Go and see if the monks have any vegetables they'll sell you."

"Vegetables?" He frowns. "What are you suggestin'?"

I place my hands on the table and take a deep breath. "I'm suggesting we learn to cook."

My idea doesn't quite get the response I'd hoped for.

"Cook?" Megan looks at me as if I've just suggested she take on an army of Metz officers single-handedly.

"Like the monks did for us. We can make food go further that way and use what other people don't want."

There's another silence.

"But we don't know *how* to cook," Jax says, his blank expression mirrored on the faces of my friends.

"That's why we're going to recruit some help," I say, more confidently than I feel.

Once Jax, Danny and Anders have headed out and I've found Tommy and sent him on a mission of his own, I get Megan to help me round up what remains of my gang in the main hall.

I have to shout for silence. Once everyone quietens down, I clear my throat. "I owe you all an apology. I promised you a new start, then disappeared to let you fend for yourselves. For that, I am truly sorry. Unfortunately, the Metz got hold of me. But I escaped and am back."

I run my eyes over the people in front of me, meeting their hateful and resentful gazes. "What I did was inexcusable. But what I came back to was also inexcusable. In a few days, you've let this place become a hovel. You've been too busy fighting each other to listen to Megan and Jax. Too busy bitching to figure out where your next meal's coming from. I may be your leader, but that does not make me your mother. You're survivors, so *think* like survivors. Use whatever brains you've been given and work together."

I pause, wondering if I've gone too far. An uneasy murmur ripples through the crowd in front of me. But amongst the sullen looks are some faces downturned in shame.

"Starting now, we work together. Our first priority is to get everyone fed. Everyone who can draw government rations, speak to Megan." I hold up my hand at the muttered protest. "I know what people say about them, but any food is better than starving. Everyone else, including me, is going to help clean this place up. We're going to make it into a home, and once we've done that, we're going to start training. If the Bigland Boys come back, we'd damn well better be strong enough to show them exactly who rules this part of Area Four."

I get a mild cheer for that, though it's quickly quashed by the glares of those who aren't convinced by my words. But I know how they feel. We're Outsiders. We're used to being let down by others. Actions mean more than words out here.

"One last thing. If anyone has any tronk, hand it in to Rogue. That drug is *not allowed* in this building."

"Or what?" someone shouts.

"Or you'll be out of the gang," I reply. "Now, let's get going."

I jump down from the stage and start assigning tasks. By the time Tommy returns with Abby, someone's found a mop and is dragging it across the floor. It may be just moving the dirt around, but it's a start.

Abby pulls me into a hug. "I'm so relieved you're safe." She pulls back and looks around. "Sorry. I keep forgetting you're the boss now."

"What do I do with these?" Tommy sticks his tongue out in concentration as he juggles four plastic tubs containing plants.

At that moment, Anders walks into the room, a sack over his shoulder. He's followed by Danny, who carries a bunch of dead rats by their tails.

"Can you teach us how to cook?" I ask Abby anxiously. "We've got vegetables, rats, flour and stuff from the government rations. Can you do something with that?" I pull her over to the giant pot Leon had found in an old storeroom. It looks about a hundred years old but seems to be watertight.

"Of course." The corner of her mouth twitches. "You have changed, Aleesha. The girl who wandered into my kitchen a month ago would have *never* considered cooking."

I flush and turn away, shouting to Ishaan and the girl he's talking with to clean the pots.

Seeing everybody hustling around, some joking, a warmth grows in my chest that begins to replace the cold fear I'd felt upon walking into the building. Giving people something to do is already distracting them from their complaints. With Abby's help, perhaps I'll be able to get everyone fed, as well.

I look at Leon scrubbing the floor, then Jax painting over the graffiti on his masterpiece and smile. I've been given a second chance, and there's no way I'm going to blow it this time.

16

Trey

I'm juggling two coffees and a plate of cake in the elevator when my comm band rings. By the time I get back to my office and deposit the drinks and food on Emilie's desk, Ella has rung off. A few seconds later, a message comes through.

F couldn't find anything specific about AN, but she said MT's in charge of a top-secret section of the lab that has files she can't access. It has a code name. Project Griffin.

My heart drops into my stomach. Top secret. If androcibus nanite was just an innocent additive, it wouldn't be under the control of a top-secret department.

"Chocolate, lemon or ginger?" Emilie asks.

"Your choice," I say distractedly, sending Ella a quick reply, telling her to save anything else until we're back home, then deleting the messages. I hope the government is too busy fighting the Chain to worry about monitoring our comm bands.

So much for Dexter taking every precaution.

"Elaine called saying Louis wants to speak to you."

"Good," I reply, turning back to Emilie and grabbing the plate. "Tell her I'm on my way over."

She surveys the remaining pieces of cake and sighs theatrically. "And I thought the extra cake was for me."

I grin at her as I pick up my coffee and head for the door. "See you in a bit."

The door to Louis' office opens as I approach. I step into his waiting room, where Elaine sits behind a desk. She tosses her blonde curls over her shoulder and gives me a dazzling smile. "Go right in, Mr Goldsmith. He's waiting for you."

I offer her the plate of cake, but she declines, as I knew she would. Louis said she's on some detox diet. Three pills a day containing all the vitamins and calories you need without the inconvenience of consuming food.

Louis sits at his desk, his brow furrowed as he looks at something on the holo screen in front of him.

"I brought cake," I say, setting the plate next to him.

"Chocolate or ginger ... What a choice." He picks up the chocolate cake and takes a big bite, then waves at me to pull up a chair. "Good weekend?"

"It was all right. Barnes managed to get the line fixed, so at least I had yesterday off."

"Ah, yes. Father said there were a few issues. Glad it's sorted. Barnes knows her stuff, even if she is an ice queen."

Before he'd been promoted to Head of Distribution, Louis had my job. I remember Emilie telling me he'd hit on Barnes and been firmly rejected. Seems it was a rare enough occurrence for him to hold a grudge.

"So, what am I doing with this food you asked me to stockpile?" Louis asks, licking his fingers. "I need to get it out today; otherwise, I'm going to have to answer some difficult questions."

"Can you send it anywhere?"

"Pretty much."

"Great." I give him the address of Aleesha's headquarters.

His face darkens as he consults a map on his holo screen. "Isn't that a gang's building?"

"Maybe. But they'll see it's distributed throughout Area Four."

Louis leans back in his chair. "I can't send it there!"

"But you said you could send it anywhere?"

He rolls his eyes. "Yeah, but I didn't think you meant a gang headquarters in one of the roughest parts of the city. There's no way my people will agree to go there, and if I force them, they'll talk about it with others. Besides, the pod won't be able to land on that roof."

I chew my lip. There must be a decent amount of food stockpiled – everything that had gone through the production line after Barnes has removed the androcibus nanite from the system. Quality control had ordered me to destroy it, but I'd persuaded Louis to hang onto it until I could figure out what to do with it. Giving it to Aleesha seemed like the best option.

"Look. There's an old, disused warehouse not far away." Louis points to a rectangular building on the map. "It was the old distribution centre before we moved to the high-security one, so we can land the pod right inside. I'll give you the code to get in for you to pass to your friend."

I blow out a breath in relief. "Thanks, Louis. That'd be great."

"No problem. Just don't message them the code, okay? I don't want to risk any of this coming back to me." He types a quick email. "Done. It should be there by this evening. Anything else I can help you with?"

I hesitate, wondering whether to ask him about Project Griffin. The likelihood of me getting access to Phillips's computer anytime soon is minimal, and I bet Louis has clearance to access more of the factory's files than me. I'd promised him I wouldn't do anything to harm the factory, but this really wasn't *doing* anything. It was just gathering information.

"Can you see if you can find anything that mentions Project Griffin?"

Louis raises an eyebrow. "Project Griffin? And what would that be?" There's an edge to his words, and I wonder if I've made a mistake trusting him.

Too late to back out now.

"I don't know," I say honestly. "Remember I told you about that additive in the production line?"

He nods.

"Well, there's no information on it that I can find in our system, which is odd, don't you think?"

"Not necessarily. You don't need to know the details of the ingredients in order to run the production line."

"I guess, but it's been niggling at me. I heard mention it was part of something called Project Griffin." I look straight into Louis' golden eyes. "I'm not suggesting we do anything about it. I just want to know why it's been put into the food. Quality control was pretty secretive about it."

Louis snorts. "They're secretive about *everything*." He grins wickedly. "But I did manage to get access to their files."

He turns back to his screen and types in a command. "Hmm ... There are a bunch of files that mention Project Griffin. Some are in quality control, some in my father's private files."

"You have access to them?"

"Yes ... But I'm not supposed to look in them without Father's permission. It's just as a backup. In case he gets sick or something. Anyway, there's one here in the QC section that mentions both Project Griffin and the androcibus nanite. I'll forward it over to you."

Louis' eyes are fixed on the screen, so he doesn't see me nudge my half-full cup of coffee off the desk. I leap up, uttering a curse Aleesha would have been proud of. Louis' gaze follows mine to where the dark liquid soaks into his cream rug.

"Dammit, Goldsmith. That's real sheep's wool." He pushes past me and sweeps the rug into his arms, calling for Elaine as he carries it to the outer office.

I reckon I have about ten seconds. I scramble around the desk and highlight all the Project Griffin files in Coleman's private file system, then attach them to the email, praying Louis won't notice the file size.

When he walks back in, I'm kneeling, frantically dabbing at the carpet with my handkerchief, grateful Thomas thought it necessary to furnish me with such an old-fashioned item.

"Oh, leave it. I'll get Elaine to get the cleaners on it. It's not the first time it's happened."

I get to my feet. "I am so sorry, Louis. If it needs any specialist treatment or replacing ..."

He waves his hand. "Honestly, it's fine. Worst case, I beg Father to get me another one." He glances up at the clock on the wall. "I'm sorry to cut things short, but I've got a meeting to get to."

"Of course. Could you just send that message before you go?" I step aside to let him pass.

He barely glances at the message before hitting send. "There you go."

I resist the urge to run back to my office, desperately hoping Emilie's buried in some other task and won't open the message first. But she's not in the office when I return. I bring up the email, download the attachments to a microchip and delete the incriminating message before she gets back.

The chip burns a hole in my pocket for the rest of the day.

* * * *

When I finally leave the office, I pull the chip blocker Louis had given me over my forearm and walk down to Area Four. The guards outside Phoenix headquarters look at me suspiciously, but when I ask if Aleesha's inside, one of them slinks away. He returns a few minutes later and gestures for me to follow him.

The building is cleaner than I remember, and the smell coming from a giant pot at one end of the main hall makes my mouth water. I find Aleesha in a small room off to one side, sitting around a table with Rogue and a girl with long, dark hair. Blueish circles ring Aleesha's eyes and her forehead's creased in a frown.

"Hi, Trey," she says dully.

Rogue gets to his feet and offers me a smile. "We'll leave you two alone."

The girl scowls at me and only moves to follow him when Aleesha jerks her head toward the door. "Stay away from her," she mutters as she brushes past me.

I glance at her retreating back, then close the door and sit down next to Aleesha. She's slumped in her chair, her elbows resting on the table, head in her hands.

"Are you all right?" I place a hand on her shoulder. She doesn't push it away, but neither does she lean into me. "I got a message from Bryn that said you were safe, but nothing since. How did you get out of the compound?"

Aleesha sits up. My hand falls from her shoulder, but she doesn't seem to notice. "Petal found a route out through the sewers. I got back Saturday."

"And you didn't think to get in touch with me?" It's not my intention to make her feel guilty, but I can't hide the hurt in my voice.

"How, Trey? You think I've had time to wander over to your house and wait for you to show up?" Her mouth tightens. "I have more important things to worry about, like how to feed dozens of people out of thin air." She waves a hand in the direction of the hall.

I swallow back a retort. She's clearly stressed, and I didn't come here to argue. But this wasn't the reunion I had hoped for. "It smells pretty good out there. How did you find a hotplate big enough for that pot?"

"One of the ex-Metz officers managed to figure out how to fix a few of them together." She shrugs. "I've no idea what he did, but as long as it works, I don't care. Abby taught a couple of us to cook so we could stretch things further. But what's out there now is the last of what we managed to scrounge up, and it's barely enough to give everyone a cup full."

She sighs. "We're out of chits – and favours."

"Well, it's a good thing I dropped by then." I tell her about the food Louis has arranged to drop at the warehouse and the code to access it.

Her eyes widen. "Are you serious?"

I nod, surprised to see tears glistening in her eyes.

Aleesha lets her head fall into her hands and whispers something too quiet for me to catch. After a moment, she sucks in a deep breath and sits back, wiping her eyes with the back of her hand.

She offers me a soft smile. "Thank you."

"You're welcome."

I stand and hold out a hand to her. After a slight hesitation, she takes it and lets me pull her up and into my arms. I bury my face into her hair, breathing in her scent, then gently tilt her head up. A flicker of indecision races across her brown eyes, then she lets out a small sigh and lifts her lips to mine.

Heat pools in my stomach as her breath caresses my skin. She kisses me hungrily, reaching one hand up to grip my hair. A groan escapes my lips as the heat in my body moves lower. I cup her face, pulling back to stare at her for a moment before bending to kiss her again, my lips not wanting to leave hers for even a second.

This. This is what love feels like.

There's a loud banging on the door. Aleesha practically leaps from my arms, her face flushed. "C-come in."

Danny swaggers in and closes the door behind him. "Sorry to interrupt," he says with a leer, "but people was wonderin' if there's anythin' else for dinner. I know there ain't, but I can't tell 'em that."

"It's okay, Danny. I think Trey's brought us something pretty special for dinner." Her face glows. "Get Anders, Leon and Jax. We're going foraging."

She strides past me out of the room, avoiding my outstretched hand. Danny smirks, then turns to follow his leader. I touch my fingers to my lips, still warm from hers, and sigh.

I think I've just been dismissed.

* * * *

I've never been to a private hospital, but it's not what I imagined. From the outside, it looks like a smart, new office block, but inside feels more like a spa than a medical facility. There's no medicinal smell, no robotic staff, no white lab coats.

I have to support my mother as she gets out of the taxi pod and end up half carrying her to the waiting area. As always, she's immaculately dressed, but the clothes hang loose and her hip bones crunch ominously under my hand.

We're not kept waiting long. About five minutes after we arrive, a polite woman tells us the doctor is ready to see us. She offers a hover float, which Mother declines. I roll my eyes. Apparently, it's fine to lean on me for support, but sitting down would be a step too far.

The doctor, a man in his fifties, stands to welcome us into his office, gesturing to a comfortable looking sofa. "Welcome, Mrs Goldsmith. Is this your son?"

My mother gives him a tired smile as she sinks down. "Yes. This is Darwin."

I don't bother to correct her.

The doctor flashes me a smile. "Thank you for coming along, Mr Goldsmith." His expression turns serious. "How have you been feeling, Mrs Goldsmith?"

My mother twists her hands in her lap. "Oh, about the same."

"The pain is still worse at night?"

"Yes, though it's almost constant now. I'm not sure the painkillers are working anymore."

Worry flashes in the doctor's eyes, but he quickly composes himself. "I'm afraid we can't give you anything stronger."

My mother's shoulders sag.

"Why not?" I ask. "You can see how much she's suffering."

The man gives me a sympathetic look. "We don't *have* anything stronger, Mr Goldsmith." He picks up a folder from the table in front of him and opens it. "I got your latest test results back from the laboratory this morning." He closes the folder and places it back on the table, then leans forward and clasps his hands together.

I swallow hard. I know that gesture. The sympathetic, yet pitying look in his eyes. It's how the man at the crematorium had looked when I'd accompanied Milicent to her death. My mother reaches out, and I take her hand.

"I'm afraid your condition is progressing faster than we thought."

"So there's still no progress on a cure?" My mother's voice is barely a whisper.

"I'm afraid not, Mrs Goldsmith. The scans we did show that the disease has spread throughout your body. I'm afraid that's why the painkillers don't seem to be working anymore. There are too many inflammations for them to dull."

The room suddenly feels stifling. I clear my throat. "What are you saying?"

The doctor presses the tips of his fingers together. "I'm afraid we've done all we can, Mrs Goldsmith. I'm very sorry."

A small gasp escapes my mother's lips. She sways, and I grab her shoulder, afraid she's going to faint. My palms turn clammy.

"There must be some more tests you can run. Try something else." The anger in my voice doesn't sound like me. "I have money. Whatever it costs, I'll pay." I glare at the man, daring him to defy me.

The doctor holds up his hands. "Mr Goldsmith, I assure you, money is not the issue here. Your mother's condition is highly unusual. We have tried everything we can think of, had our best people working on her case, but you can see for yourself how quickly she has deteriorated." He pauses. "Whatever this is, it's eating her alive from inside. The longer she hangs on, the greater her pain and suffering."

His words ring in my ears, but I refuse to believe them.

I can't believe them.

I withdraw my arm from around my mother's shoulders and lean forward. "You're a doctor. Do your job!"

"My job is to relieve pain and suffering," he says quietly. "We have made incredible technological advances over the past hundred years, but occasionally, even we are beaten. I truly am sorry."

"It's okay, Trey." My mother looks up at me, tears shimmering in her eyes. "I've known for a while this was coming. I just hoped I would have more time."

Her previous words ring in my ears.

I should probably sell some of this stuff. I doubt you or Ella will want it when I'm gone.

She has known all this time and didn't say anything.

Her face relaxes into a smile. "Perhaps your father will be waiting for me on the other side."

My jaw clenches. Does she now suddenly believe there's an afterlife? Some happy place you go to when you die?

But as I take in her shrunken frame, a shadow of the woman she was, the anger drains from my body. The mother I'd known would have fought to live. She would have calmly but firmly insisted that the doctors run more tests. That there couldn't possibly be anything they couldn't find a cure for. The fact this disease has taken the fight from her is almost more heart-breaking than seeing her body fail.

"Thank you, Doctor," I say stiffly, gently pulling my mother to her feet. "We'll be going now."

This time, she doesn't refuse the hover.

The taxi pod drops us back at the house. Thomas must have been watching for us as he immediately comes out to meet us. He lifts my mother into his arms and carries her up to her room. Her eyelids are already drooping with fatigue as he lays her down on the bed. Moments later, she's asleep.

I shake my head at Thomas's questioning glance, go to my own room and slump down on the bed, dropping my head into my hands. Numbness spreads through my veins, leaving me feeling empty and detached.

We live in one of the most luxurious houses in the country. I have all the money I could ever need.

Yet it is all for nothing.

My mother is dying, and there is nothing I can do to save her.

I hang my head, waiting for the tears to fall. But my eyes are dry. All I wanted was to be the son she deserved. The man my father wanted me to be.

But I've failed them both.

17

Aleesha

"Okay. Yer done."

My body sags in relief as Jake straightens to admire his handiwork. I never realized getting a tattoo took so *long*.

The smell of disinfectant fills the air. My bottom lip throbs where I've bitten down on it, and my back feels as if someone has carved ribbons of fire into my flesh.

Perhaps going for a full back tattoo wasn't the best idea. But anything less would have felt half-hearted, like I wasn't fully committed to the gang. Although the food Trey had given us eased the complaints, the sidelong glances when I walk through the main hall, the muttered conversations that stop as I approach, remind me that I still need to prove myself to these people.

The tattoo is a reminder – a rather *painful* reminder – that I have a responsibility to others now. That if I screw up, they will get hurt.

Carefully, I sit up, pressing my jacket to my chest to cover my nudity. "Can I see?"

"Sure."

Jake manoeuvres me between two mirrors he's set up. I twist

around to get a full view of my back and gasp.

A burning phoenix stares out at me. Its fiery wings spread across my shoulder blades framing a thin neck that winds up to the head, which nestles just under the nape of my neck. The bird's body curves around my lower back, ending in a fan of tail feathers. Its beauty snatches the breath from my lips.

We are the phoenix that rises from the ashes to burn more brightly than before. Because there is always hope.

Jake sprays something on my back and hands me the rest of the bottle. "Spray it twice a day. Don't scratch at it. In a couple of days, it'll start to peel. That's normal."

I thank him, pull on my vest and leave the small room. Rogue strides up to me.

"You okay?" he asks, eying me as if I'm about to faint.

"Fine." I realize I'm pushing my shoulders back and force myself to relax. "Fine. You going to get one done?"

Rogue shrugs. "Maybe at some point. He's got plenty of people waiting."

I glance at the queue outside his door and realize he's right. Danny had brought Jake to headquarters two days ago, without asking my permission. He'd stared at me defiantly, as if daring me to challenge him, but I'd let it go. Tattoos have always been part of a gang's identity, and I wasn't about to turn down anything that would help the two sides of my gang bond. Those who had been part of the Snakes were keen to embrace their new image, and while the ex-Metz officers were a little more cautious about inking their skin, many of them had been persuaded to take part in the ritual.

I follow Rogue into the room I've marked as my office. Megan, Danny and Anders wait inside, slouched around the table.

"Let's have a look," Danny says as I sit. He peers around my shoulder. "You know, it would look better if you took your vest off."

I roll my eyes. "That's not going to happen."

He shrugs, running a hand over the snake tattoo on his head. "A guy can always hope. What happened to yer boyfriend anyway?"

The smile falls from my face at the mention of Trey. "He's busy," I say shortly. "And he's *not* my boyfriend."

Rogue and Megan exchange a surprised look. A knot forms in my stomach, anticipating the confrontation that is to come. Not with them, but with Trey. But I've thought long and hard over the past few days, and it is the only way. There's nothing I want more in the world than to be able to have both Trey and my Phoenixes, but it's impossible.

I must choose. And my duty must be stronger than my heart.

My throat thickens. "Anders, how's our food supply looking?"

He raises an eyebrow, knowing that I know the answer to my own question. "Good. It's not particularly high-quality meat, but it's a hot bargaining tool. We've traded a third of it for flour, sweetener and other basics, as well as a reasonable number of chits. With what we have in the building, we should be good for the next week."

I give him a nod of thanks, then Danny, who looks smug. I'd put him in charge of the bartering – the ex-Metz officers don't have the first clue about what food is worth out here – and to his credit, he did a good job.

People haven't forgotten about the Bigland Boys' attack or my promise of reprisal, but regular meals have helped improve the mood. When we'd arrived on Saturday, headquarters had felt like one of Danny's firebombs – primed and ready to explode. Now it's more like smouldering embers.

But given the right fuel, even embers can be quick to burst into flame.

"Food prices are still sky-high, an' the government stores haven't

166

been getting supplies. Some problem at the factory, apparently." Megan shoots Rogue an anxious look. "With what we've got, every gang in the city'll be eyein' us up.

"Everyone's aware of that," I cut in before Rogue can answer. "We have extra guards on around the clock, and they know the consequences of slacking."

Her words add a further weight to my shoulders. Even miracles come at a price. Or, as the street hobies would say, "Don't look a free rat in the face. Always check up its arse." Poisoning was not uncommon in Area Four.

Was this what being a leader was like? Just one problem after another?

I feel like I'm being sucked into one of the whirlpools that lurk between the old buildings in the river. I wish I could ask my father for advice, but as far as I know, he's still in the Metz compound, and I don't fancy another trip through the sewers.

If only there was someone else I could go to …

I sit up straighter. Perhaps there is.

* * * *

It's almost as if Samson is expecting me. The Brotherhood doesn't seem to have a headquarters. Just a lot of properties scattered across the city. There's only one I know of, and when I knock on the door, a mousy woman lets me in without a word. I follow her up the stairs and through a large room to a doorway at the far end.

I spot Amber, the unofficial healer for Area Three, treating a man lying on one of the many beds packed into half the room. She dips her head and smiles at me, her red curls glowing in the glimmer of sunlight coming in through the window. Three of the other beds are occupied, but most of the people in the room are at the other end, sorting through piles of weapons or sitting with their heads bent over the large table. They're an odd mix. Most are Outsiders, I think, but their clothing is a cut above most people's in this part of the city. It makes me wonder, and not for the first time, just how far Samson's influence spreads.

In the small room that leads off the main space, I find the man himself, stretching. He nods at me to shut the door and motions to a pair of battered old chairs.

"How's the leg?" I ask, sitting.

"Almost as good as new." He grins wolfishly, flashing white teeth. "Managed to persuade that medic woman your father has to give me one of her magic pills. Say what you want about the outside world, but their medical technology is a step ahead of ours."

The smile falls from his face and he sighs. "Anyway, what can I help you with?"

"Whose side are you really on? If it comes down to it. The government or the Chain?"

Samson doesn't seem taken aback by the question. "I am on the side of the people."

I can't hide my exasperation. "What does that even mean? How are we supposed to trust you if we don't know what side you're on?"

"I could ask the same of you, Aleesha. Whose side are *you* on?" He rests his elbows on the arms of his chair. "If you had to choose between following your father or leading your gang, which would you choose?"

I don't give in to his baiting. "We're both on the same side."

"And if your father asked your gang to fight?"

I swallow, feeling his eyes bore into me. "Outsiders are no match for the government's or the Chain's fighters. My father has called in more people from overseas. He doesn't need our help."

"Then what makes you think he needs mine?"

"You said yourself that he did." I glance down at my hands and lick my lips. "Do you trust him?"

"Richard?" He snorts. "About as much as I trust the President."

My heart sinks.

Samson's voice softens. "But there are very few people I trust implicitly, Aleesha. I meant what I told your father. My trust has to be earned."

I peek up at him through my lashes. "Do you trust me?"

Samson throws back his head and laughs, a deep, belly laugh that echoes around the room. He chuckles for a full minute before composing himself. I frown, not seeing the humour in my question.

"Now, there's a question," he finally says, wiping his eyes. "You came here for my advice, yes?"

I give a small shrug of acknowledgment.

His face turns serious as he leans forward in his chair. "The *only* people you can trust are those who truly care about you. The people who would die to protect you. They don't expect perfection, but they understand your truth and trust your instinct. They will follow you through hell simply because they believe in you. Those are the people you want on your side."

My heart drops a little more. I'm not sure I have anyone who would do that for me. But Samson is right. I need to earn that level of trust. I suck in a breath and straighten my shoulders. I'm not sure I completely trust either my father or Samson, but sometimes you have to trust in something bigger than yourself. In people who have the power to do what you cannot.

"I promised the Phoenixes I'd keep them safe. You and Richard can fight it out between yourselves. As long as you get rid of the government, I don't care how you do it."

"Don't speak too hastily, Aleesha." Samson cocks his head to one side. "A city is like an organism. Every part of it is connected to something else. Often several things. You may not care, but when something breaks …" He snaps his fingers. "The repercussions are felt much wider than in that one place. You cannot guarantee the safety of every single person who looks to you for protection. And security comes at a price. Have you asked them if that is a price they're willing to pay?"

I ball my fists in frustration. The man talks in riddles about things I don't understand. What's a bloody organism anyway? And how dare he tell me I'm wrong? It's like he's deliberately trying to wind me up. I catch a glint of amusement in his eyes and realize he is doing exactly that.

The thought doesn't temper my anger.

I take a deep breath. "So, what's the plan for Thursday night?"

Samson raises a brow. "I thought you didn't want to be involved."

He has me there. "You said that if one thing snaps, others feel the effect." I shrug. "I reckon the President getting captured is a pretty big thing. Best way to stay safe out here is to know what's going on. Preferably before it happens."

"True." Samson pauses. "The Chain is planning to capture the President and some key players. As Richard mentioned, they're going to be at a small, private dinner. The President doesn't want to draw attention, so he'll only have a couple of guards for protection. Easy enough to take out. At the same time, I will lead the rest of the Chain's fighters and some of my own people to break into the government headquarters. If all goes according to plan, by Friday morning, London will be ours."

I chew my lip as I mull it over. My father must trust Samson more than I thought if he's willing to give him control of that part of the operation. With the government headquarters, they'll have control of the city – and the country.

"I have waited many years for this day." Samson stands and walks over to the small window overlooking the street below. "Many years for this city to become whole again."

I don't know if it's his words or tone of voice that calms my anger. He sounds so … sad.

"Why do you do this? You're an Insider, aren't you?"

He turns to me. "I *was* an Insider."

"Then why spend your life out here? Is it the power you have over the gangs? The fact you're stronger and smarter than them? Or did you get thrown out?"

Samson stills. For a moment, I think he's going to ignore my question or yell at me to leave, but after a minute, he turns back to the window and begins to speak in a low voice. "I was born Inside, though we didn't live there long. My parents bought me enhanced intelligence and strength. Mostly strength." He looks down at his giant hands. "They believed the division in our society was wrong and that while their generation still remembered what happened during the Dark Times and the reason the Wall was put up in the first place, my generation would be different. They believed I would be the one to heal the divide.

"But my father wasn't a patient man. He was soon accused of spreading lies and deceit and was taken to the Farms. We never heard from him again. My mother fled Outside with me, fearing for her own life and mine. But no one would employ her because of her connection with my father. My grandparents on both sides disowned her, but she persuaded hers to take me in. After all, I was only a child. They felt they'd be able to get rid of the *silly notions* my parents had put into my head."

He falls silent for a moment. I hold my breath, not wanting to interrupt. I wonder just how many people he has trusted with the truth about his past.

"When I was twelve, my grandparents told me my mother had

171

died. With no job or purpose, as well as little money, she'd fallen all the way down until she was just another tronk addict on the street." He clenches his hand into a fist. "There was no funeral.

"My grandparents paid for my schooling until I was eighteen. I would have run away sooner, but I knew I needed to learn as much as I could if I wanted to fulfil my parents' dream." His lips turn up in an ironic smile as he turns his head to look at me. "If I'd known how hard it was going to be, how much it would cost me, I don't think I would have ever set foot outside their door. But sometimes, lack of knowledge is a blessing in disguise."

"I'm sorry," I say quietly. "About your parents. I ... I know what it's like."

"Yes, I think you do," he says mildly, striding back to the chair and sitting. "Does that answer your question about which side I'm on?"

"I think so. But why did you trust the President? *He* doesn't care about Outsiders."

"Because I didn't want it to come to this. I hoped I could make him see sense. I do think he wants to help, perhaps even believes he *is* helping, but he is too proud to open his eyes to the reality of what his actions have caused." Samson's eyes bore into mine. "And your father forced his hand, drawing his attention away from what really matters."

I frown, sensing his words carry a deeper meaning.

He would always come back to London. He would always come back for me.

"This isn't just about who rules London, is it? What else is going on between them?"

"Perhaps you should ask your father that question."

"Fine. Talk in riddles."

I stand and make my way to the door, pausing with my hand on the handle. "You know, there's another reason my father may not

172

trust you."

"Just one?" Samson's lips twitch.

I roll my eyes. "Good point. But back before Richard arrived in London, when you were trying to unite the gangs … I think I understand why you killed a lot of the gang leaders, but why did you kill Lamar? You must have known the Chain wouldn't bow to you after that."

Samson's forehead creases. "Lamar?"

"Don't pretend innocence. You murdered him, or one of your people did. Big black guy, lots of tattoos. Ring any bells? Or have you killed so many people you don't remember their faces anymore?"

Samson's expression darkens, his eyes flashing a warning.

"He ran the Chain's operation in London before Milicent and Katya took over," I add quickly, wondering if I've gone too far.

"Ah, him." Samson crosses his meaty arms. "I heard he disappeared."

"He was murdered." I narrow my eyes. "Bryn told me you did it."

"He may have told you that, but I can assure you, I had nothing to do with his death."

"Are you saying he's lying?"

A flash of puzzlement crosses Samson's eyes. "No, I don't think he's lying," he says thoughtfully. "But that doesn't mean he's telling the truth."

As I leave the room, I glance back one final time to see him staring out of the window, a pensive look on his face.

Our conversation replays through my mind as I walk back to Phoenix headquarters. I'm so lost in thought I don't see Bryn until I'm practically on top of him. He pushes away from the wall he's leaning against.

"Chit for your thoughts?"

I smile at him. "They're not worth that much."

His expression turns serious. "Your father would like to speak to you." He hesitates. "It's about Thursday night. We need some extra assistance."

The smile falls from my face. *Was this what Samson was referring to? Did he know the Chain would ask for my help?*

The pull to help my father is strong. I owe him my life. But I owe my gang, too, and I will not break my promise.

"I'm not putting my people in danger again, Bryn. We can't help you."

"We don't need their help, Aleesha. Just yours."

18

Trey

"You're telling me you've known our mother is dying for weeks and didn't tell me?"

Ella quails under Anabel's gaze. Our older sister certainly knows how to intimidate. "I knew you were busy with work and Trey was busy with …" She glances at me. "Stuff. Mother didn't want me to worry you. Besides, they still had tests to run."

Anabel clenches her hands. "Yes, but if I'd have known—"

"What would you have done?" Ella glares up at her. "This isn't something you can fight your way out of or run away from."

"Run away from?" Anabel looks affronted.

It's rare that I agree with anything Anabel says, but part of me wants to join her in berating Ella. How dare she keep us in the dark about something this important?

But the guilt fuelling the anger inside me makes me hold my tongue.

I should have paid more attention. Should have asked the questions I was too afraid to ask. Like Anabel, I was too busy, too preoccupied with other concerns to see that my mother wasn't just ill. She was dying.

I heap the guilt of this on top of my other failures.

"It's easier to run away than face things, isn't it?" Ella snaps.

"I do *not* run away." Anabel's dark eyes flash as she takes a step closer to Ella.

"Stop it. Both of you!" I step between them. "Arguing with each other isn't going to change anything."

There's a tentative knock on the door.

"Yes?"

It opens and Thomas pokes his head in. "Are you ready for me to bring Mrs Goldsmith down?"

"Yes. Thank you, Thomas."

As the door closes, I look from one sister to the other. "Let's just keep things civil, shall we? For Mother."

Anabel steps back and runs a hand over her hair. Her shoulders sag as her anger evaporates. "Of course. I'm sorry. I just ... I didn't realize it was so serious. I thought she was just playing up her illness for attention."

"It's okay. We've all had other things on our minds lately." I pull out a chair and sit down at the dining table. "But I think we can all agree that whatever Mother wants from now on, she gets."

Both my sisters agree.

We eat dinner in silence, but no one's particularly hungry, despite the good food. Still, we draw the meal out, none of us wanting to start the conversation that needs to follow.

"I've had some time to think," my mother says eventually, folding her napkin delicately and placing it on the table. "I don't see there's any point in dragging this out. I'm not really up to a big farewell party." Her smile falters slightly. "All I want is for my family to be around me when I die. Ella, would you be able to make the arrangements with the crematorium?"

My sister swallows. "Of course."

"See how soon they can fit me in." She talks about it as if it were a routine medical appointment, not the end of her life. "Perhaps Thursday evening so you don't have to miss work?"

There's a sharp intake of breath beside me. "So soon?" Anabel whispers.

Mother gives a barely perceptible shrug. "There's not much to hang around for, is there?"

"Thursday is fine with me," Ella says quickly.

"And me," I echo. I glance at Anabel out of the corner of my eye. She looks torn.

"I have to accompany the President to a dinner on Thursday evening."

"I'm sure you can delegate that to someone else," Ella says tightly. She straightens the cutlery on her plate. "Just this once."

"Perhaps Friday would be better anyway, Mother?" Anabel says. "There's an extra hour before curfew, so we'll have more time."

Ella opens her mouth to reply, but I kick her gently under the table. "Would Friday be okay, Mum?"

She smiles fondly at us. "Of course. I didn't think about the curfew. That's very sensible, Anabel. We don't want to have to rush things. Ella, would you mind helping me go through my address book tomorrow? There are some friends I need to say goodbye to. Now, where is Thomas?"

After Thomas has helped her from the room, I turn to Anabel. "What was all that about?"

Her expression is blank, but there's an odd look in her eyes that I can't quite read. "I'm sorry. I'd normally be able to delegate, particularly as it's after hours, but the President insisted I attend with him. It's more than my job's worth to refuse. But you know Mother. She has so many friends who'll want to visit there's no way she'll get through them all before Thursday night."

"That's true," I admit. I can't believe we're discussing our mother's death so … clinically.

Anabel's comm band flashes. "Damn. I have to go." She glances at Ella. "Please let me know if there's anything I can do to help."

"Just make sure you're there," she replies acidly.

I frown at her as Anabel leaves the room. It isn't like Ella to be so hostile. "What's got into you?"

She glances at the open door, then walks over and closes it. Returning to the table, she lowers her voice. "I expected something more from Frankie, but I haven't heard anything. She hasn't replied to any of my messages. I'm worried she may have been caught."

"I told you to tell her to be careful." I clench my jaw.

"I know." Ella twists her hands together. "Have you managed to find anything about Project Griffin?"

Ella hadn't been home when I'd got back from the hospital yesterday, and I was so emotionally exhausted I couldn't face looking through the files I'd transferred onto the chip. And that's another problem I hadn't thought of. I don't have a holo pad that'll accept the chip. Ella does, but I don't want her getting any more involved.

I could buy one, but the shops will be shut by now, and I don't want to wait until tomorrow.

I glance at the tall grandfather clock in the corner, then stand. There's still time before curfew. "Maybe. I'm not sure yet."

"What about Frankie?" Ella follows me to the door.

"I told you this was dangerous, Ella." I yank open the door. "I told you not to get involved."

Thomas walks out from one of the back rooms as I pull on my boots in the hallway.

"I'm going out for a bit," I tell him, opening the front door. "I'll be back before curfew."

"Very good, sir."

"Trey, Thomas," I say between gritted teeth. "It's Trey."

Thomas gives a stiff nod, but he doesn't look happy.

Ella hops toward the door, trying to fasten her shoe. "Trey, wait!"

I let the door slam behind me and jog down the front steps. *This is my fault. I shouldn't have asked them to help. But what kind of idiot uses their comm to message secret information? If she's been caught, she'll lead them straight to …*

My feet slow to a halt as an icy chill flashes through me. I wheel around, almost crashing into Ella, who's run out after me. I grab her arm. "Give me your comm band."

She looks confused. "What?"

I try to loosen the band from around her wrist, but she pulls her arm away. "Just give me your comm band."

Puzzled, she unfastens it from her wrist and hands it over. I drop it onto the stone flag and stomp my foot down. It takes three sharp cracks of my heel before the casing gives. Ella stares down at the scattered scraps of plastic and metal.

"What the hell, Trey?"

"Pack a bag. You need to leave, now." I grab her arm and tug her back toward the house. "You can go to the house in Wales. That should be safe."

"Let me go!" Ella's voice is shrill as she digs her heels into the ground. I glance around anxiously. The curtains move behind an upper window in the house next door.

That's the last thing we need. Nosy neighbours.

"Keep your voice down," I mutter.

"Tell me what's going on then," she hisses. Her face is flushed, and there's a hardness in her eyes, an anger that my sister rarely displays.

"If Frankie has been caught, they'll know she messaged you. They'll come for you next. I should have told you not to use regular comm bands. You shouldn't even have sent me that message."

179

Comprehension dawns. "Trey, I'm sorry. I didn't realize ..." Her eyes widen. "Dexter." She lunges past me, but I grab her wrist.

"Tell me where he lives, and I'll go and see him. You're getting into a pod right now."

"Why did you smash my device? I could have just messaged him!"

"That's exactly *why* I smashed your device." My jaw clenches. "The less contact you have with him, the better."

The front door opens, and Thomas appears in the doorway. "Is everything all right?"

"Can you call a pod for Ella, please? A long-distance one."

"No!" Ella glares at me, then Thomas. "I'm *not* leaving."

Thomas looks uncertainly between us, then clears his throat as he glances around. "Perhaps you should come inside? The neighbours ... cameras ..."

Gods, I'd forgotten about the cameras in the street.

Ella allows me to guide her inside the house, but once the door closes, she yanks her arm away and turns to me, hands on her hips. "I'm not leaving."

"You have to. Please?" I try to change my approach. "Think about Mother. You don't want her worrying about you, do you?"

"Don't make this about her." Ella jabs me in the chest. "Anyway, I can't leave with her dying."

"Take her with you then."

My mind is running a million miles a minute. I need to get Ella away from London, find out what's on the chip in my pocket and figure out what to *do* about it.

"What? And have her die a slow, agonizing death away from home?" Ella's voice drips with scorn. "Besides, you know she'd hate to die in Wales. She's never liked that place. It reminds her of—" She bites her lip.

I raise an eyebrow. "Of me? Was that what you were going to say?"

Sourness burns my throat. Because I was an illegal child, my mother wasn't able to give birth to me in London. She'd been confined to our family's remote Welsh farmhouse for months to hide her pregnancy and my birth, with only a mechanical nanny bot for company.

"That's not what I meant, Trey. Anyway, if *I'm* in danger, *you're* in danger, too. It was your request she look for the information on that andro ... Whatever it is." Her jaw is set, determined, and for a second, she looks so much like our mother used to that I almost smile.

I glance up and see Thomas down the hallway, listening. He looks away when I catch his eye.

"Will you be wanting that pod, s— Trey?"

Ella gives me a look. "I'll only come straight back again. You're my brother, Trey. But that doesn't give you the right to control me."

"I just want you to be safe."

Doesn't she see? I failed Father and Mother. She's the only family I have left to protect.

She steps forward and reaches up to tug the collar of my shirt. "We'll be more careful, Trey. I promise. You're right. We didn't think things through properly. But we will from now on."

I wish I could believe her. But I can't help thinking all of us are treading on very thin ice.

Thomas clears his throat. "The pod?"

"We won't be needing it. Thank you."

I make Ella give me Dexter's address. As luck would have it, it's not far off the route I'd take to get to the pod point. I pull the chip blocker up over my forearm and leave the house, sticking to the shadows as I pad silently down the street.

* * * *

181

To my relief, I find Bryn at Abby's house. Alone.

"Abby got an emergency callout," he says as he lets me in. "It's good to see you."

"How are you?"

Bryn runs a hand through his sandy hair. There seems to be more grey in it these days. "I've been better," he mutters, then grins. "But I've also been worse. You hungry?" He grabs two mugs and dumps a spoonful of herbs into each.

"No. I'm fine. Thanks." I feel a pang of guilt that I didn't think to bring any of the leftovers from dinner with me.

"How's your mother?"

The kettle hisses on the hotplate.

"She ... She's dying, Bryn."

There's a yelp, followed by a curse. "Damn leaky thing," Bryn mutters under his breath as he slams a mug down in front of me, the hot water slopping onto the tabletop. He rummages through Abby's cupboards, eventually finding a burn plaster. An angry red mark already rises on his hand.

"The treatments didn't work. The doctors ..." I swallow. "They said there's nothing more they can do. It's on Friday evening."

"What is?" Bryn's voice is rough as he applies the plaster.

"She's going to the crematorium. No point hanging on any longer when she's in such pain." I stare down at the herbs swirling in my cup.

Bryn's chair scrapes against the floor. "I'm sorry, Trey. Is there anything I can do? Does she ... Would she want me to visit?"

"I'm not sure. Maybe?" I glance up to see him nod.

"I'll make time tomorrow morning."

I grip the mug a little tighter, the heat permeating my skin. "I thought with Milicent's money, everything would be okay." I swallow, my voice cracking. "I thought I could save her."

"I know it's tough to accept, but you can't protect everyone from everything, no matter how hard you try. I learned that lesson a long time ago." A trace of bitterness enters Bryn's voice.

I glance up at him, remembering what Abby had told me, back when I hadn't known Bryn was my biological father, about Bryn's other son who had died years earlier. "Daniel?"

"Yes. And his mother. I thought I could protect them both, but I wasn't there the day the bombs fell. You did everything you could for your mother, Trey. You have nothing to feel guilty about."

"I guess," I say, unconvinced. "There was another reason I wanted to see you. Do you have a holo pad I could use?"

"Of course." Bryn leaves the room, returning a few minutes later with a holo pad. "What do you need?"

I hold up the chip. "I managed to download some files on Project Griffin, which I think has something to do with the androcibus nanite the government has added to the lower-grade food lines."

Bryn unlocks the holo pad and sits next to me. "That's the stuff you think might be a tronk substitute?"

"That's what Barnes thinks. I'm not sure." I slip the chip into the pad and bring up the files.

We're halfway through reading them when Abby returns.

"Trey, what are you doing here? It's nearly curfew."

I glance out the window at the darkening sky and curse under my breath. "Can I stay here? I'll have to get up early to get back Inside and take a pod to work."

"Of course." Her face brightens, and she walks over to give me a hug. "Have you seen Aleesha? She's got the Phoenixes cooking. Honestly, that girl is a miracle worker. I don't think most of them knew a knife could be used for chopping."

"Yeah, I saw her."

Abby looks surprised at my unenthusiastic tone. I force a smile onto my face. Aleesha's quick dismissal of me had hurt. But she was probably just stressed. I'll go and see her this weekend. Hopefully we'll be able to have some proper time together.

Abby hangs up her green bag of medical supplies. "What are you looking at?"

"Just something I found in the factory."

"Trey. Look at this."

I turn back to the holo screen. So far, we've found a summary of what the androcibus nanite is, written in scientific terms neither of us understands, and a bunch of vague references to it in papers from board meetings. The document currently on the screen looks more promising. At the top is the header of the President's private office, and as I scan to the bottom, I see his signature.

"It's a private memo from the President to Coleman and Hendricks," Bryn says.

"The two food factories," I murmur.

Instead of being written in scientific terms, the memo is in political lingo, which means there's a lot of reading between the lines. Even so, what's there makes me stare at the screen in horror.

"Surely this can't be right."

Abby comes around and leans over our shoulders.

We all read it again.

The words blur in front of me as I remember back to my biology lessons at school. I should have figured part of it out from the name alone. We'd briefly studied nanotechnology and its application in medical science. Now that it's there in front of me, I don't understand why I didn't make the connection before.

Nanite. Nanobots. Microscopic bots carrying tiny amounts of cyanide able to cross the blood-brain barrier. Triggered by a specific radio frequency transmitted between the towers that make up the Wall. The ultimate weapon. Lethal, invisible and impossible to discover.

I think of the millions of Outsiders eating their pathetically small evening meals, never knowing that with every bite, more of the deadly nanobots enter their system.

I sink back into my chair. "How can they get away with this?"

"Because nobody knows about it," Bryn says flatly. "I bet the President has this tied up as tight as a rat's arse."

"Bryn!" Abby admonishes.

He shrugs, unrepentant.

"I thought the whole tronk issue was bad, but this is worse." Her voice shakes.

My brain tries to make sense of what I've read. "That explains why I could go through the Wall. As long as you don't eat Outsider food, *any* of us could go through."

"Apart from the inner barrier. That would be enough to put anyone off," Abby reminds me. "Plus, if they can detect when you go near it, the Metz would be on you like a shot."

I shiver at the memory of the pain that had shot up my arm when I'd approached the Wall. The memo describes the second set of towers as "a small precaution for any Insiders who get curious". The tiny amount of nerve agent in the chip embedded in every person's forearm isn't enough to kill, but it would make you think twice before trying to go through the Wall again.

"It doesn't explain why Aleesha can go through the Wall." I frown. "If the poison is in Outsider food, it must be in her system, too. We're missing something."

Bryn shakes his head. "She has a natural immunity. The President tested her when she was held in the lab. Seems he was curious as to how she could get through the Wall, too."

"Perhaps her body naturally expels the nanobots? The human body is so complex. There are always exceptions to any rule. That's

185

why one virus can never kill everyone. There are always a few people who will be naturally immune to it."

Abby's words don't reassure me.

We go through the rest of the documents, but only one other thing catches my eye. I point it out to Bryn.

"Look here. It says that if androcibus nanite is completely removed from the food, it will take between six and twelve months to be eradicated from citizens' bodies. That's why they had to put it in the lower-grade food lines at the factory when people stopped eating the government rations. If we can take it out of the production lines permanently, all we have to do is wait and the Wall will eventually become useless."

Bryn's expression darkens. "You may be right. It's good to know the situation is reversible. Once we have control of the government, we'll be able to act on this information."

I feel a flash of irritation. "And when will that be?"

"With any luck, by Friday morning."

Bryn refuses to elaborate on his cryptic remark.

That night, I replay his words as I lie on the thin mattress in Abby's spare bedroom. A pale moon shines in the cloudless sky, casting a wan light over the wooden floorboards. As I work it through in my head, it all makes sense. Remove the additive from the food supply, and within a year, Outsiders will have the power to demand change. Once the Wall is no longer an effective barrier, the government will be forced to listen. The change we all desire could be achieved just by a bit of subterfuge and patience.

I roll over and stare at the wall. Bryn sounded confident about their chances of taking over the city. Perhaps it is best to stay silent for now. But I won't be my father. I won't shy away from uncomfortable truths to fall in line with the system. If the Chain's plan doesn't work, I'll find some way of removing the additive from the food supply.

Whatever it takes.

19

Aleesha

The street below me is dark and deserted – as it should be. Even the moon is tucked away behind the clouds. It's a dark night for dark deeds.

I shift position slightly, my backside numb from two hours of sitting on roof tiles, and rest back against the chimney. Pitched roofs are not the most comfortable spot for waiting. At least it isn't raining. When they're wet, they go from merely dangerous to lethal.

The earbud in my right ear hisses, then an unfamiliar voice speaks. "In position. Two-minute countdown."

"Roger that," Bryn replies. "Aleesha, is the street still clear?"

"Street is clear," I whisper into the tiny mic clipped to my top.

Good. Something's finally happening.

I risk a glance at the house opposite. Despite my curiosity, I'd avoided looking at it so as not to ruin my night vision. Lights blaze out from three levels, illuminating smartly dressed figures inside. The only one I recognize from this distance is the President. I would know *him* from a mile away.

The figures occupy several rooms, drinking from fragile looking glasses and eating finger-sized food, but as I watch, they make their way to a huge dining room that stretches across three windows on the middle floor. Black-clad servers carrying steaming dishes pass by the windows.

"One minute," the voice in my ear says.

I move to a crouch, wincing at the prickle of pain that runs down my back. If my tattoo's not hurting, it itches like crazy. I draw a knife from my boot. My role in the mission is purely surveillance, and I was given strict instructions to stay on the rooftop and out of sight, but it pays to be prepared. Despite my reluctance to get involved, now I'm here, adrenaline surges through my veins and my skin tingles with anticipation.

Rogue and Anders are the only members of my gang who know I'm here tonight. To say they weren't happy about me joining the mission is an understatement. But the debt I owe my father gnaws at the back of my mind, and this seemed an easy, safe way to repay him. After this, we'll be even.

If I'm completely honest, there's also a part of me that feels proud that he needed *me*, someone who could scoot around the rooftops and stay unseen. This is my chance to prove myself.

Inside the house, I see the President sit, his back to the window. A dark-haired woman in a grey uniform steps forward to whisper something into his ear. He shoos her away with his hand, and she returns to her position beside the window.

One of his guards.

"Thirty seconds," the voice informs me.

Bryn told me practically nothing about the Chain's plan. Apparently, I didn't need to know. The first priority is to capture the President, then as many of his colleagues as possible. I think of Samson and his team, who must already be in position, ready to infiltrate the government headquarters. If all goes according to plan, by the morning, the Chain and Brotherhood will have control of the city – and the President.

If all goes according to plan.

"Ten seconds."

I glance up and down the street again. Still no sign of life. The windows of most houses are dark, their occupants retired for the night. It's after curfew, and there's work in the morning.

Movement on the wall opposite catches my attention. Black-clad figures descend on ropes, then hover next to the three large windows, like spiders waiting to pounce on an unsuspecting fly.

I had been warned about the explosions, but they still catch me by surprise. I slap my hands to my ears, too late to stop the ringing. The figures swing through the smashed windows and disappear in the cloud of smoke. A door opens down the street and a man peers out. I tense and grip my knife a little tighter, but he pulls back and slams the door. No doubt he'll alert the Metz, but by the time anyone gets here, we'll be gone.

As the smoke begins to clear, I make out fighting inside. Gunshots shatter the silence, and people slump to the floor, though I can't tell if they're the Chain's fighters or the guests. My earbud crackles, then cuts out.

Shit.

I tap my ear. Nothing. "My comm's out," I whisper into the mic, in case I can still be heard. "Street is still clear."

But as I look down from my rooftop perch, the door to the house flies open and two figures stumble down the steps. One is the dark-haired guard I'd noticed earlier. She looks up, scanning the street for danger, and as the light streaming from the upstairs window falls on her face, I stifle a gasp.

It's Anabel. Head of the Palace Guard – and Trey's sister.

She has her arm around the waist of a man who's bent double and clutching his thigh. His head is bowed, but there's no doubt who he is.

"The President's getting away," I hiss into my mic. "I repeat, the President is escaping."

There's no reply. Not even a hiss of static in my ear to confirm they've heard my message.

"Dammit." I glance around. The sound of fighting spills from the house, but no one follows the President and his guard. They mustn't have noticed him escaping in the confusion.

Anabel half carries, half drags the President down the street. I wonder how badly he's wounded.

He *can't* get away. Not now. Not when we're so close.

I balance the knife on the palm of my hand. I have a clear shot, and there's not a breath of wind, but it's a fair distance. If I miss, they'll know someone is after them. If my aim is off, I could kill Anabel.

If only she weren't Trey's sister ...

She may be Trey's sister, but right now, she is the enemy.

I let the knife fly.

There's a cry, and the figures lurch, falling to the ground. I scramble along the ridgeline of the roof, relying on my natural balance to stop me from plummeting to the street below. It had taken me half an hour to get into position, but I don't have that kind of time to spare now. I skirt around an old chimney and down to the edge of the roof, finding the top of a sturdy drainpipe. It holds as I shimmy down and drop the final few feet to the ground.

Anabel is already on her feet, hauling the President up. My knife lies on the ground beside her. I saw it embed in her left arm. She must have pulled it out.

When our eyes meet, she utters a low curse, releasing her hold on the President, who falls back to the ground. "What in ten hells are you doing here?"

She scowls and yanks a gun from her belt as I start running toward her, a second knife in my hand.

The first bullet flies over my shoulder, the second passing through the air where my leg had been a split-second before. I barrel into her, bringing us both crashing to the ground.

Anabel grunts as I land on top of her, but before I can take advantage of the situation, she bucks her body and knocks me off. A moment later, she's on top of me and pinning my arms to the ground.

Her grip is strong, but her left arm is weakened from where my knife had buried into it. Blood darkens her grey jacket. She tries to compensate by pushing her weight down through that arm, but I can see how much it pains her to do so.

Her gaze flicks to the side, perhaps looking for her gun. I bring my knee up into her back. A weak blow, but enough to make her shift. I twist my right arm out of her grip and punch her in the bicep, where the blood is darkest. She instinctively recoils, cursing, and I slash my blade across her arm before twisting my hips and wriggling out from under her.

I scramble to retrieve my throwing knife and roll to my feet. I've still got both knives and, except for a few bruises, I'm not hurt. I should have the advantage. But Anabel is stronger and a better fighter, even while wounded. She eyes me warily.

"Aleesha, you don't understand ..." she begins, but a shot from behind makes us both turn toward the house. There's a second shot and a puff of dust as the bullet ricochets off the ground in front of me.

Anabel curses under her breath. "Stop shooting!" she yells.

The shots come from an upstairs room where a figure leans out of the window, a long-barrelled weapon in his hands. I'm not an expert on guns, but it doesn't look like one of the Chain's weapons. A servant who managed to escape the bloodbath in the dining room perhaps?

I pull back into the shadows, wondering if he can tell the difference between me and Anabel from so far away. Does he even know who she is?

Anabel grabs her gun from the ground and fires a single shot up at the window. The figure pulls back. A flicker of movement further up the building catches my eye. A round face with wide eyes and shock of blond hair presses briefly against a window. A child's face.

Where is the Chain?

I mutter into my comm again, but it's well and truly dead. Surely they've noticed the President's missing by now.

I glance down the street and my heart skips a beat.

He's gone.

I start forward, straining to see in the dark, my vision blinded by the lights of the house.

Then I spot him – a shadow dragging himself along the street. He's made it a fair distance while Anabel and I have been fighting. All it would take would be for somebody to open their door and help him inside, or for the Metz to turn up, and everything would have been in vain.

Anabel has also seen him. For an instant, we lock eyes, each knowing what the other is thinking. Then we sprint down the street.

I'm faster.

I grab the stiff collar of the President's dinner jacket and whirl around, yanking him up. By the time Anabel skids to a halt, my knife is at his throat.

"Anabel ..." The President can barely wheeze.

She points her gun at me. "Let him go."

My mouth is dry, my arm straining to keep his head and shoulders up.

Damn, the man is heavy.

He must have lost a lot of blood from his leg wound as his struggles are weak, but even so, I'm not in a great position. Anabel has a clear shot of my upper body, and I'm not strong enough to completely pull the President to his feet.

Quickly, I drop down and press my back to a low wall fronting one of the houses, using him as a shield. My blade nicks the President's skin. He whimpers as blood trickles down to stain his white shirt. Now we're even.

A flash of irritation crosses Anabel's face. "Please, don't make me shoot you. I doubt my brother would be pleased."

"You can thank *him* for the fact you're still alive," I retort. "Otherwise, that knife would have ended up in your back."

Her eyes narrow. "Think about it, Aleesha. If there's anything left in your brain that tronk hasn't rotted. We need him alive."

The President coughs, causing the knife to nick his skin again. He rolls his eyes up to look at me. "She's right." His lips curl into a cruel smile. "Kill me if you want, but it'll make it harder for you to win."

"You lie," I say, wishing I knew if he actually was. "You just want to save your own skin."

"Maybe, but are you willing to risk it?" he rasps. "Kill her, Anabel."

The gun is steady in Anabel's hand, but her eyes dart to a commotion further up the street. People spill from the house and run toward us. I feel my body sag in relief. Backup at last.

I almost expect Anabel to turn and run, but she doesn't abandon her boss. I hope he appreciates her loyalty, but I doubt it.

The President also sees the approaching threat. His body tenses against mine. "Kill me."

For a second, I think he's talking to me, then I realize that the words are directed at Anabel. She doesn't react.

"Goddammit, woman. Shoot me! Don't let them take me."

He's scared, I realize. Scared of what the Chain will do to him.

When it comes down to it, he's not as brave as he likes to act. Saliva trickles from the corner of his mouth, and his face has taken on a greyish tinge. Blood from his leg wound soaks the ground beneath him.

"It's your *duty*," he says through gritted teeth.

To my surprise, Anabel shoves the gun back into her belt and crosses her arms. "Sorry, sir. I'm off duty."

I stare at her, confused. Bryn runs up, followed by another member of the Chain, then my father. Blood runs down from his hairline and he favours one leg. The expression on his face is grim.

"Everything okay?" Bryn pants, bending over.

"It would be a lot better if your lookout here hadn't interfered," Anabel says acidly. She glances around. "We need to move. He's lost a lot of blood. I hope you have a good medic."

Bryn nods. "Let him go, Aleesha."

I look from him to Anabel and back again. "But she—"

"She works for us," my father cuts in. He pushes past Bryn with a scowl and walks over to me. "You were told to stay on the rooftop. What the hell were you doing?" He grabs my forearm and pulls it away from the President's neck, then yanks the man away from me.

"Good to see you again, Tobias."

"Ricus," the President growls.

I don't catch the rest of his words. I'm too busy trying to make sense of my father's words

Anabel is working for the Chain?

Bryn comes over and crouches down in front of me. "Are you hurt?" he asks gently.

"What ..." I manage.

"She's our mole. It was stroke of luck when the job at the palace guard came up. Richard called in some favours and managed to get her over here. Now, are you hurt?"

I shake my head. "Does Trey know?"

Bryn's face is grim. "No. I couldn't risk telling either of you. If anyone had caught wind of what she was really doing here tonight, our plan would have been ruined. Besides, you weren't supposed to be involved."

I glance over his shoulder at Anabel, who's pressing a dressing to the wound on her arm. My father told me to trust him. I should have done what I was told for once. He's been planting the seeds for this plan all along.

Then I got in the way and almost ruined everything.

"You should have told me." I push Bryn away and get to my feet. "What did you expect me to do when I saw them escaping the house?" I tear the mic from my jacket and toss it to the ground. "And the comm you gave me broke."

A pod lands in the street, sending a rush of air toward us.

Anabel scowls at me. "If you had listened to me rather than attacking—"

"Shut up, you two," my father snarls, dragging the President to the pod. "Get in. We can discuss this later."

I follow Bryn down the street and into the pod, where I curl up in a corner. Two more black-clad figures push inside, then the doors close and the pod lifts off. Muscles ache and bruises begin to make themselves known as the adrenaline seeps from my body, leaving me feeling empty.

I turn my head to the wall. All I was trying to do was help, yet I nearly screwed up the entire mission. Out of the corner of my eye, I catch Anabel looking at me. I wonder who she really is, this sister of Trey's who hides so many secrets.

I feel like I don't know who anyone is anymore. Least of all myself.

20

Trey

On Friday, Barnes calls in sick.

"Has she ever called in sick before?" I ask Emilie as she places a pastry on my desk.

"Not that I can remember," she replies, carefully lifting a cup of steaming coffee from the tray in her hand and placing it next to me. "What did she say was wrong?"

I break off a piece of the pastry. "She didn't. She called the night foreman and said she'd be back in on Monday."

"It's probably just a bug she picked up." Emilie sits down at her desk and taps her holo screen to wake it up. "Let's hope we don't have any issues with the line today."

"It seems to be working fine at the moment." I chew on my pastry, mind whirring. Of course, I can't tell Emilie what's really bothering me. I'd bet half Milicent's fortune that Barnes isn't sick. She's staying away for a reason. I just wish I knew what that reason was.

If she's sabotaged the production line again, Louis will have my hide.

I doubt Barnes would care about that, though, or the fact Louis could be an ally. She's so dogmatic, she doesn't think about the bigger picture. I still haven't decided whether to tell her the truth about the androcibus nanite. The question has hung over me for the past few days, and every time I look down at the factory floor, I feel a renewed sense of guilt that I haven't done anything with the information. But until I can figure out a plan that has good odds of succeeding, it's best to do nothing. Acting rashly will only get me caught, and if they find out what I know ...

I shudder and take a sip of my coffee, wincing as the hot liquid burns the roof of my mouth.

A piercing alarm jolts me out of my thoughts. Coffee spills onto my hand. I curse, setting the cup on my desk. My first thought is that it's a fire alarm, but as soon as the thought hits me, the alarm stops and a robotic voice fills the room.

"Please return immediately to your desk for an emergency briefing. The briefing will commence in two minutes. Failure to attend will result in disciplinary procedures."

The message is repeated, then the voice cuts out. I glance over at Emilie.

Her eyes are wide. "What's happened?"

"I don't know." I glance out the window onto the factory floor. No one's stopped work or is even looking in this direction, making me think the alarm was restricted to this part of the building.

My holo screen beeps, announcing the emergency briefing. I press my thumb where indicated to register my attendance. As I wait for the briefing to start, Bryn's words come back to me.

Once we have control of the government, we'll be able to act on this information.

By Friday morning, he'd said.

What have they done?

After two minutes, the black screen fades, replaced by a projection of Coleman in his office.

"Thank you for your attention. Let me start by reassuring you that there are no immediate issues or concerns with the factory. However, our city – and country – is experiencing a wider disturbance, and we need to take immediate action to address this threat."

He lifts his hand, and the wall behind him fades into a giant holo screen. "This broadcast will be going out across all networks shortly."

The screen flickers, then Richard appears. I stifle a gasp. He's dressed in a light-coloured shirt, sleeves rolled up, and jeans, and sits at a table in a small room. The walls behind him are whitewashed and bare.

"Good morning, citizens of Britannia. You are probably wondering who I am and what I'm doing invading your news screens on this fine day. Well, I want to tell you a story ..."

I don't know how long he talks. It feels like hours but is probably only minutes. Whatever else he is, Richard has the gift of an orator. I find myself swept up by his words, carried on a roller coaster of emotions as he tells us about the world outside Britannia, a world our government has cut us off from for decades, leaving us a poor, inconsequential shadow of the world power our country once was. His face darkens as he talks about the division of London and other cities, the poisoning of innocent citizens to maintain law and order, the injustice of our society's segregation. Finally, he talks about change and how he will help us build better lives with the technology and benefits of a modern society.

The way he talks makes me feel as if we're some backward country stuck in the Dark Times. His face is replaced on the screen by futuristic cities populated by smiling adults and laughing children. We're told the images are of Paris, Tel Aviv and Bangkok.

"This is what your government has kept from you. And this is the man responsible."

The camera switches to an image of the President, his face ashen. He's sitting in another whitewashed room, clear cuffs binding his wrists to the chair arms. His lips move, but his words must have been cut from the footage as all we hear is Richard.

"Change is here. I have freed other cities from tyrannical dictators, and I will free London. I will help you build a country you are proud of. A country that will once again take its place on the world stage. A country where everyone can live the life they deserve."

The camera cuts back to Richard. His eyes seem to pierce my inner thoughts. "Some of you may distrust me, even fear me. I want to reassure you that my first priority is to keep *you* safe. There will be a short transition period while we fully establish control and set up a new government. For your own safety, I recommend you stay indoors this weekend and watch for updates on the news channels."

He smiles, but it doesn't reach his eyes. "This is the dawn of a new era for Britannia. An era of equality, prosperity and freedom."

The holo screen goes dark, then Coleman reappears.

"Sounds good, doesn't it?" he barks. "But this man, with his pretty words and promises, is the leader of the terrorist operation that gunned down innocent women and children just one week ago. The terrorists who took over the Metz compound, taking control of our law enforcement officers to use them against the people of this city."

He pauses for effect. "Our democratically elected leader has been captured," he continues quietly, his face grim. "I hope you'll join me in praying for his safety and that of all our leaders as they resist this attack on our city. The people of London depend on us for food. We cannot, *must not,* let the terrorists take over this factory. It is our duty to keep food supplies running."

I glance over at Emilie. Her face is tight, jaw set. Coleman's style is very different from Richard's – harder, more direct. But people here know him and trust him in a way that they will not trust a stranger.

"From this moment, the factory is in lockdown. We must keep the production lines running, our workers safe. We cannot risk being infiltrated by the terrorists. The rooftop transport decks are no longer operational. I understand you will be concerned about your families, but we cannot let anyone return home until we know more about how the situation will develop. You can contact them, but please be aware that all communication into and out of this building will be closely monitored. I thank you for your patience. And your loyalty."

The image cuts out.

I swallow and tug at my collar, the room suddenly stifling.

"What does he mean?" Emilie says in a soft voice, still staring at the screen. "Are we at war?"

"I don't know."

I wish I knew what the Chain was planning. I wish I trusted Richard to do the right thing – for everyone. But the faces of the panicked crowd trying to escape the bullets at Aleesha's execution still haunt me.

My comm band bleeps. It's Phillips, wanting me to report to his office immediately. I rush up and squeeze into the room with the other production managers, most of whom I've never met, to get a similar spiel from Phillips. He tells us to report back at three in the afternoon to find out what plans are for shift changeover. I hang around after the others have left.

"Yes, Goldsmith?"

"I … My mother is dying. We had planned on going to the crematorium tonight. I know Coleman said we weren't allowed to leave, but I thought perhaps …"

Phillips's face softens into a rare expression of sympathy. "I'm not sure the crematoriums will be running, son, but I'll put in a special request for you. You might be able to get out for a few hours."

I nod. "Thank you. Also, Barnes called in sick today."

Phillips's eyebrows shoot up. "She did?"

"Yes. She said it's a minor issue and she will be back in on Monday."

He frowns. "Seems a bit coincidental. Comm her to get more details. I want her back in this building as soon as possible."

"Yes, sir."

As I leave his office, I can't help but share his suspicions. It seems a little too convenient that Barnes is off. Did she know what was going to happen? And are Samson and his gang involved in the takeover?

* * * *

The tiled lobby of the crematorium feels cool after the evening heat of the city. A wave of déjà vu washes over me as I glance up at the glittering chandelier suspended from the ceiling. Had it only been ten days since I was here with Milicent?

Coleman had given me permission to leave the factory for the night, along with a message of sympathy and a note for my mother. She read it and smiled, though hadn't shown me the content. I suspected part of the reason I'd been permitted to leave was that Barnes hadn't responded to any of my comm messages. Phillips had grown more agitated as the day progressed and ordered me to find her and bring her in tomorrow – whatever it took.

As we'd flown toward the crematorium, the streets below us had been empty, far from the chaos Coleman had predicted. Whatever happens next is in the government's hands. I wonder if they'll surrender or try to fight the Chain. But I can't worry about that tonight.

Tonight is about my family. What's left of it.

I pluck at the hem of my suit jacket. It's the bright blue one I hate, but Mother asked me to wear it, saying it reflects the colour of my eyes. She's dressed in a silver evening gown that somehow manages to disguise her frailty. Her hair is elaborately coiled on top of her head, peppered with diamond pins, and makeup adds a flush of life to her cheeks. She looks like she's going to a formal party, not her death.

Ella wears a stylish summer dress, and even Anabel has made an effort. I almost didn't recognize her when she turned up at the house wearing a figure-hugging green dress and heels. Her hair hangs loose around her shoulders, softening the strong jawline she inherited from our father, and I realize that my older sister is just as beautiful as Ella, in a different way. When the buzzer sounded just a few minutes after I'd got home from the factory, a small part of me wondered if it was a messenger carrying news of her death. Perhaps she didn't go to the President's dinner after all, but I note that she hasn't removed her jacket, despite the hot weather, and the thick makeup on her cheek can't quite disguise the dark bruise underneath. Curiosity burns inside me, but as she hadn't left mother's side since she arrived, I haven't been able to question her.

A man in a tailcoat suit leads us to a room looking out over the gardens. In the centre is a dining table set for four.

"Would you like an aperitif, madam?" the man asks, addressing my mother.

She smiles. "No, thank you. We'll go straight into the meal."

I hadn't expected food, and my stomach clenches at the thought, though I don't remember eating lunch.

Anabel walks over to the window and looks out. "The gardens here are beautiful," she says softly. "Don't you think, Mother?"

"You know, your father and I used to come here when we were dating," Mother says, joining her. "There was a little glade between the trees where you couldn't see any of the buildings. It felt like you were in a private world of your own." She lays a hand on Anabel's arm and smiles up at her. "I'm so glad you were able to come back to us, Anabel. I couldn't bear to die without seeing you again."

Anabel smiles, but it seems strained. "I'm sorry I had to be away for so long."

The door opens. A waiter walks in, carrying a bottle of wine. As we sit, he pours it into crystal glasses. My mother takes a sip and closes her eyes, smiling dreamily. "Mmm, this is good. Your father always loved a good red."

The food is excellent, and Mother keeps up a bright patter of conversation during dinner, as if this were just a family night out. When she tires, Ella steps in and talks about stories from her and Anabel's childhood, before I was born, making us laugh. But what comes after dinner looms over us, like death's shadow is already there in the room.

After the waiter has cleared the dessert plates, Mother takes a sip of her wine and glances out the window at the setting sun. "It's a lovely evening, isn't it?" she says to no one in particular.

She turns back to us. "You know, when I was young, I never wanted to grow old. But now I think I can appreciate the peace and wisdom that age brings. I know I haven't always been the best mother to you all, or the best wife to your father. He loved me so much more than I deserved." Tears glisten in her eyes. "And even though he didn't get a chance to say goodbye to you, he was so proud of you all and what you've achieved. We both are."

A lump develops in my throat as memories of my father's final moments flash through my mind. What did he feel as Katya placed the gun to his head? Fear? Dread? It wasn't the peaceful death he had earned.

My mother turns to Anabel. "It was my selfishness that led to you having to go away, yet I cannot regret my actions, because they brought me Trey." She gives me a fond look and reaches out to squeeze both our hands. "When I am gone, I hope you can forget the past and just remember that you are brother and sister. Family."

"And, Ella …" She smiles at her across the table. "My sweet Ella. You carried the burden of the truth all these years and never let us down."

She hesitates, looking at all of us. "I don't have the inheritance I would have liked to have given you. But there is the house in Wales if any of you want it. And I kept a small amount of money aside for each of you, so that is something."

There's a quiet knock on the door.

My mother stiffens and releases our hands. "It is time. I thought I had prepared for this, but now …" Her voice falters and a stricken expression crosses her face as the man in the tailcoat suit enters. "Now I am not so sure."

Anabel pushes back her chair. She takes Mother's arm gently, as if lifting a child from the ground, and when she speaks, her voice is raw with pain. "We're here. We will be with you to the end."

Her words stir me to action. I take my mother's other arm and we help her across the room. "Would you like the hover?"

Mother shakes her head. "No. I will walk."

The chamber is in the adjoining room. The windows are covered with heavy curtains, and soft lamps warm the pale walls. As her gaze falls on the narrow bed in the corner, I feel my mother's legs fail, so I wrap an arm around her waist to stop her from falling. Together, Anabel and I carry her over and help her sit on the edge of the bed.

"Stay strong," Anabel whispers into her ear.

My mother wraps her arms around Anabel's neck. Her words are a whisper, not meant for me, but I catch them all the same. "Look after them."

"I promise," Anabel says, kissing the top of her head. "I love you."

She pulls back as Ella approaches, carrying a single white rose plucked from the display in the room next door. Her lower lip trembles as she holds it out. "Your favourite."

205

Mother nods. "I noticed. I didn't realize they grew here."

Ella tries to smile. "I managed to get them from Wales."

"You're always so thoughtful," Mother murmurs. She reaches up to brush away the tear that runs down Ella's cheek. "No tears now, my love." But her own eyes shimmer.

I dig my fingernails into my thigh, blinking hard. I'm the man of the family. I can't cry.

Gently, Ella helps my mother lie back. Then she steps away, and my mother reaches out to me. "Darwin Trey. My baby. How have you grown up so fast?"

I take her hand and kneel by the bed. Her skin feels cool and clammy. I want to tell her I'm sorry for failing her, sorry the money came too late and wasn't enough, sorry I couldn't work the miracle she needed. I press my lips to the back of her hand and take a deep, shuddering breath, forcing a smile onto my face.

"We'll be fine. We have everything we need." My voice catches. "I love you, Mum."

She beams up at me. "I know. You have such a big heart." Her eyes search mine, and for the first time, I feel like my mother sees me for who I truly am. Sees how I've battled against myself to be the son she wanted me to be. Sees the shame I've hidden inside when I failed again and again.

She gently pulls her hand from mine and places her palm flat against my chest. "You know in here what is right," she whispers, almost too quietly for me to hear. "Trust yourself, Trey, and you will do the right thing."

I know if I try to say anything, I will cry, so I bend over and kiss her on the forehead, then stand and nod to the man waiting silently by the door.

As the domed lid closes over the bed, my mother smiles at us once more, then closes her eyes. Moments later, she is gone.

21

Aleesha

A knock on the door to the small room I've been using as a bedroom interrupts my train of thought. "Come in!"

The door opens, and Tommy sticks his head in. As usual, his scruffy hair falls into his eyes and there's a smudge of dirt on his nose. Even if someone let the kid into a posh Insider school, I reckon he'd still have dirt permanently smeared on his face.

"That Insider boy's waitin' outside. Want us to let 'im in?"

Something flutters in my belly. "Trey? Yes." When he starts to duck out again, I stop him. "Actually, tell him to wait there. I'll come out to him."

I push myself up off the bed and follow him from the room. In the corridor, I pause for a moment and lean against the wall, closing my eyes to try and plan what I'm going to say. But no words come to mind. Only memories.

Memories of his lips brushing mine. The heat of his body pressed against me. The way he'd held me in the square so tightly I could barely breathe.

I force my eyes open. I'm stalling. I know what I need to do. I've gone over this again and again. It's the only way. But that doesn't mean I want to do it.

The morning air carries barely a hint of freshness. We're still some way off the heat of full summer, but already, I'm reminded of how unbearable it can be. The itching on my back is a welcome distraction. Yesterday, it seemed as if all the skin on my back was starting to peel. Danny laughed when I asked him about it, said it was normal. I find it oddly comforting, like I'm shedding my old skin to make way for the new.

Trey waits down the street. I observe him for a moment. His shoulders are slightly hunched and he looks older than his seventeen years.

He doesn't hear me approach. "Hey."

His head whips around and his face breaks into a smile. Inside me, something that was whole begins to slowly break apart.

"Hey yourself," he says, gesturing at the building behind me. "You don't want me to come in?"

"Things are a little ... tense." I choose my words carefully.

His face falls. "Oh. I came to see if you were okay. You know the Chain has captured the President?"

I nod. "I was there." I hesitate. "I'm not sure if you know, but Anabel's working for the Chain."

From the look on his face, he didn't know.

"I only found out on Thursday. She's the mole."

Trey's face hardens. "Well, that explains why she's still alive."

"I may have buried a knife in her arm," I admit. "Before I knew we were on the same side."

He stares at me for a moment, then laughs. "You fought her? Who won?"

My lips twitch. "I'm not sure." Then I remember why I'm here and the smile falls from my face. "Trey, I—"

He steps forward and reaches for my hands. I want to pull away, *should* pull away, but I can't.

"Aleesha," he murmurs as his arms wrap around me, tugging me in and—

Pain shoots down my back. "Ow!"

Trey jumps back, his eyes scanning me anxiously. "What's wrong? Are you hurt?"

I suck in air. "Sorry." I turn to show him the tips of the phoenix wings peeking out from beneath the straps of my vest, then lift my top to show him the bird's tail across my lower back. "It's still pretty sore."

He lets out a low whistle. "Wow ... That must have hurt."

"It did."

I decide to get the conversation onto a safer track. "Thanks for the food. You pretty much saved us. If you have any more where that came from, just send it our way."

Trey's expression turns serious. He glances around before lowering his voice. "I managed to find out what the androcibus nanite is that's being put into Outsiders' food. Bryn and Abby already know, but I wanted to tell you, as well, in case anything happens to me."

A chill trickles down my spine. "What do you mean? I thought you were safe Inside."

He smiles, but it seems forced. "I'll be fine. Anyway, remember I told you that the factory started adding androcibus nanite to the food supply after the tronk fiasco?"

I frown, sifting through my memories. "I think I remember you mentioning it."

"Barnes said it was also in the government rations when she worked at that factory, though she didn't think it was important then. The food is all chemicals anyway, so it's impossible to know what everything is unless you're a biochemist. But when it was introduced into the lower-grade products on our food line, she began to wonder if it was more than just another additive or preservative." He pauses.

"So, what is it?"

"A nanobot."

I stare at him blankly. "A *what*?"

"A nanobot. Or, rather, thousands of them. Millions. That's where the 'nanite' bit of the name comes from." He rubs his forehead. "I should have made the connection. We did a module on nanobots in class last year."

I dampen down a spark of irritation. It's not his fault he got to go to school when I didn't. "What the hell is a nanobot?"

"They're tiny robots so small you can only see them under a microscope." The confusion must show on my face because he adds, "They probably don't look like what you're thinking. Not like humanoid robots. Anyway, that's not important. What's important is that once you eat the food, they get into your bloodstream."

I look down at the blue veins on my wrists, trying to make sense of his words. The idea of thousands of tiny robots marching through my body sounds crazy.

Trey's fingers brush mine, and a spark of electricity shoots up my arm. "I know it sounds strange, but nanobots are used for lots of things, including medical treatments. They're not all bad."

"But these nanobots are," I say flatly. I look up into his blue eyes, searching for the truth. "What do they do?"

He hesitates for a second. "They stop Outsiders going through the Wall."

I look around. The two guys guarding the entrance to my headquarters are keeping a close eye on us. I pull Trey down a narrow side alley.

"What do you mean? Just tell me simply."

"I don't know the exact science behind it. It wasn't included in the briefing paper, and we haven't been able to ask a scientist—"

"Trey!" I glare at him.

His gaze darts to the side. "Sorry. The nanobots contain a tiny amount of poison. While it's contained in the nanobot, it won't harm you. But the more food you eat, the more they build up in your system. The Wall emits a signal to the nanobots, triggering them to release the poison. When someone with a lot of the nanobots in their system comes into contact with the Wall, all the poison is released at once ..." He trails off.

"And they die," I breathe.

I take a step back and lean against the alley wall, my legs feeling weak. A poison ... in all the food we eat. In the food I've been telling the gang to eat.

Trey nods. "It's only in the food Outsiders eat, and the poorer people at that. Those who are dependent on the government rations. I don't know why they don't give it to everyone. Perhaps they were worried about side effects or something. But theoretically, people who haven't eaten the food *should* be able to pass through the Wall unharmed." His brow furrows. "Bryn said the President told you that you had a natural immunity. I think your body must attack or reject the nanobots so they don't build up in your bloodstream."

I snort. "So I'm just a lucky freak."

A faint smile brightens Trey's face, making him look like a young boy again. "I guess there are worse things to be."

I try to process this information. I don't understand half of what he's said, what these nanobot things are, but it's clear what they do. A poison, lurking in our blood, waiting for a signal to be released. We are walking bombs, primed to die. All to control us. To make sure we don't step on their territory, don't protest about our pathetic lives, don't realize other people in this city have more than us.

My fingernails dig into my palms.

You can't get involved. You promised the gang to put their safety first.

Thursday night was enough.

But if I don't get involved, then I'm harming my people anyway. What kind of leader would I be if I stood aside and let them get poisoned, all the time knowing I'm immune?

Trey steps closer and runs his hands up my arms. I breathe him in, cool spring air and needled trees, and my heart pulls me forward. But my head holds me back, and today, my head is stronger.

"The food you gave me—"

"Was safe."

I jerk my head up.

"I was supposed to destroy it after Barnes removed the androcibus nanite from the production line. It's clean, but I wouldn't rely on anything else. I need to figure out a way of removing it from the production lines without anyone finding out. If we can do that, the files say the nanite will naturally get expelled from people's bodies in six to twelve months."

"So if we stopped eating that food today, within a year, we'd be able to walk through the Wall?"

"Yes. The second set of barriers transmits a signal to your chip. When it connects, it releases a tiny amount of nerve agent. It's not enough to kill you, but it hurts like hell." He sighs. "I told Bryn. I thought perhaps the Chain could just wait a bit longer rather than attacking ..."

I shake my head. "We can't wait a year, Trey. There's no other food, and people out here are already half-starved."

"But if I could find a way of getting it out of the system—"

"And how are you going to do that without getting caught?" I pull back. "Let the Chain do their stuff. They have the President *and* the government headquarters. Once they get the rest of the city under control, they'll be able to get rid of this drug and take down the Wall."

"I guess." He doesn't sound convinced.

There's an awkward pause, then Trey steps closer. "Aleesha ..." His voice is husky.

My heartbeat quickens and I swallow, knowing that this is it. It's now or never.

And it has to be now.

"You have to go," I whisper, staring at the ground so I don't have to see the hurt in his eyes. "I need to get back inside."

He grasps my hips, careful not to touch my back, and pulls me toward him. I place my hands over his and close my eyes, committing this moment to memory. Then I gently remove his hands from my waist and step away.

"Aleesha, what is this? What's wrong?"

My throat thickens as I try to find the right words, but I know whatever I say won't be what he wants to hear. "You have to go, Trey. We need to end this."

He stills. "But we've barely started."

The pain in his voice is a blow that sends cracks rippling out from my core.

"I know. I'm sorry."

It's not enough. I owe him more, but the thickness in my throat chokes my words, and I dare not risk looking up in case he sees the tears pooling in my eyes.

"Rogue." His voice is monotone, emotionless. "That's it, isn't it? He's strong, handsome and everything ... everything I'm not."

He turns away. Despite my previous resolve, I reach out and grab his arm. "No, Trey. This has nothing to do with Rogue."

He glances back. This time, I meet his gaze. Tears shimmer in his eyes as he swallows, and I know that if he cries now, I will cry, too. I drop my hand from his arm.

"It's not anyone else." I glance back at the headquarters. "I have a duty to them now. I'm their leader."

"But you don't have to choose between us. I would never ask you to do that."

I try to force a smile onto my face, failing miserably. "Don't you see, Trey? I always run to you. I will *always* come to save you. That's the problem. It was okay when it was just me. But now I have to think of them, too. I have to *live* for them."

And I need you to be safe. You can't be if I'm in your life.

My chest tightens as I destroy our relationship, our happiness, before it's even begun.

"Haven't you always talked to me about duty? About doing what's right? I nearly died last week, and if I had, they would have fallen apart again. Everything I fought Primo for would have been lost." I reach up. I can't help myself. I just need to touch him one last time. His cheek is warm under my palm. "It doesn't matter what I want, Trey. What matters is that they need me."

I stand on my tiptoes and press my lips gently against his for one final, sweet kiss. Then I pull back, staring at his face, memorizing the faint creases on his forehead, the colour of his eyes, the way his lips twitch at the corners. I drink him in as if he were a life-giving drug, creating a photograph in my mind that I will never forget.

"I'm sorry," I whisper.

Then I drop my hand, turn and walk away.

He calls after me, his footsteps trailing me up the street, but when I don't turn, they stop.

Finally, as I step back inside the building, I let my tears fall.

Inside me, the cracks widen. I know this is the right thing to do – for both of us. So why does it feel like my heart has been torn from my chest?

22

Trey

I watch as Aleesha walks back up the street, waiting for her to come back and tell me I'd misunderstood what she'd said. That it isn't over. But she doesn't even look back.

Am I supposed to run after her? Beg her to change her mind? Is this some game girls play to make you chase after them?

I shake my head, running trembling fingers through my hair. Aleesha's not like that. If she says something, she means it. And that look she gave me just before she'd walked away ... It feels as if she pulled out my heart, broke off a corner of it and shoved it back in to keep beating.

Maybe one day, I'll be able to understand why. But for now, all I can think about is how much her rejection hurts.

I shoot a malevolent glare at the box-like building with its painted, blue snake coiling over the entrance. "I hope you appreciate her."

When the chip blocker on my right forearm itches, I have a sudden urge to rip it off and throw my arms into the air, shouting to the government to come get me.

But I don't.

Instead, I stalk through the streets, knowing that I need to go home to talk to my sisters, need to get back to the factory. These are the things I *should* do, but right now, I don't care about any of it. My hands ball into fists, and when a drugged-up hobie totters into me, I shove him away. The man stumbles into a pile of trash. His curses follow me as I stride down a narrow alley and onto a wide street lined with warehouses.

And then it is in front of me.

The Wall.

Curiosity filters through my anger, numbing the pain. I grasp it like a drowning sailor clinging to a raft. A distraction. Exactly what I need.

I run over the details of the files in my mind. If I'm right, the Wall itself shouldn't harm me. It was the invisible barrier on the other side that triggered the shock of pain I'd felt the one time I'd tried to approach it from the other side. I hadn't dared try since, even with the chip blocker, instead relying on pods and the fake chip Louis had given me.

The surge of recklessness I'd felt before returns, and before I can stop myself, I plunge my right arm into the swirling mass of colour.

Nothing happens.

Relaxing, I draw my hand back and inspect it. Nothing. I reach out again. It's an odd sight, watching your arm get swallowed up in front of your eyes, but there's no pain. Just a slight tingling sensation.

I step forward and stand half in, half out of the barrier. Green swirls dance at the edge of my vision. In front of me, tall office blocks rise up, separated from the Wall by half a street. About ten metres to my left, there's a metal tower, an identical tower further down the street to my right. The second barrier that triggers a small amount of acid to leak from your chip when it comes into range, warning off any Insiders who get too close. No wonder everyone assumes it will kill you. A chill runs down my spine as I remember the pain.

Stepping back, I wrinkle my nose. The smell is one thing I don't miss about living Outside.

"Are you a ghost?"

I turn to see a young girl watching me. She's a grubby little thing, but her expression is alert.

"Da says people can only go through the Wall when they're dead," she clarifies.

"I'm not a ghost." I move toward her. She flinches but doesn't run. I hold out my hand. "See. I'm real."

Cautiously, she reaches out and prods the back of my hand. "You don't *feel* like a ghost. Yer too warm." She looks back at the Wall. "How come you can go through it if yer not a ghost?"

"Because I have special powers," I lie. "But you mustn't go near it. It will kill you."

"How d'ya know?"

"Because I do."

She looks disgruntled. "That's what me da says." She glances curiously at the Wall.

I stifle a grin. "Well, your da is right." I search for something to distract her, not wanting to leave in case curiosity gets the better of her. "What's your name?"

The girl eyes me for a moment before replying. "Helen. Helen Gollin. What's yours?"

"Trey. Can I ask you a favour, Helen?"

She cocks her head. "What's a favour?"

"It's a thing you do to help someone. I don't know these streets very well. Could you show me the best way to Area Five?"

"Mebbe."

Inwardly, I breathe a sigh of relief. Once we're away from the Wall, hopefully she'll forget what she's seen. "Great. Let's go then."

"It'll cost you."

I frown. "What?"

The girl sticks out her chin defiantly. "Said it'll cost you." She holds out her hand. "Half a chit."

"I don't have any chits."

She shrugs and turns away.

"Oh, come on ... Fine. Just give me directions."

The girl wrings her hands. "Not until you giv' me summit. Tommy says I shouldn't do stuff for nothin'."

"Tommy? You mean Aleesha's little friend? One of the Sn— Phoenixes?"

Helen looks up in surprise, then affects a casual tone. "Mebbe."

I cross my arms and look down at her. "Well, Tommy owes *me* a favour. I saved his life when Aleesha was fighting Primo. So if you help me out, I reckon that means Tommy owes *you* a favour in return."

This is too much for Helen to comprehend. "Huh?" She narrows her eyes suspiciously. "Are you tryin' to trick me?"

"No." I think for a moment. "Let's say I saved Tommy's life and he was going to give me a chit, but he didn't have one. That means he owes me one, right?"

Helen frowns, then nods.

"If you help me, that means I owe you a chit. If Tommy had given me his, I'd have one to give to you, but as he hasn't given me the chit, I can't give it to you. But we can *pretend* that he has, right? So if you show me the way to Area Five, you can ask Tommy for the chit he'd have given to me."

There's a long pause.

"So ... Tommy will give me a chit?"

"Well, you can ask him. Or you could ask him for a favour, which is what this is really about."

"Reckon a chit is worth more than a favour." The girl spits on her hand and holds it out. "Deal."

I shake it solemnly, then gesture down the alley. "Lead the way."

In a few minutes, we're back on a street I recognize, but I let Helen lead me up to the boundary with Area Five.

"Here you go," she says proudly, pointing across the street. "Area Five."

"Thank you, Helen. I reckon it's time for you to head home. Your da will be wondering where you are."

"He'll still be at the food factory." She flashes me a shy smile. "I'm goin' to find Tommy now an' get me chit."

"Nice to meet you!" I call after her as she disappears around a corner.

The encounter leaves me feeling a little lighter, but as I walk up through Area Five to find a pod point, my footsteps get slower and the weight in my chest heavier.

I always run to you. I will always come to save you. That's the problem.

Is that all I am to her? A burden? Yet when her life had been in danger from the sniper on the roof, *I* had been the one to save *her*.

When I get back to the house, Anabel and Ella are just finishing breakfast.

"Where have you been?" Ella asks as I slump into a chair and reach for the coffee pot. Dark circles ring her red-rimmed eyes.

"None of your business." I pour a cup of coffee and take a gulp. It's tepid at best.

"Someone got out of bed on the wrong side," Anabel says acidly. She eyes the plate of bacon. "You hungry?"

I shake my head. The coffee churns in my empty stomach, but I can't face food right now.

"Shame. You've got a great cook here." Anabel shovels the remaining two rashers of bacon onto her plate. If she's been crying, you wouldn't know. But she is more like Aleesha than Ella. She keeps her grief locked inside, disguised by her barbed comments. My eyes are drawn to a thin, plastic bandage wrapped around her upper arm.

"So, when were you going to tell us you were working for the Chain?"

The piece of bacon pauses halfway to Anabel's mouth. But only for a second. She shrugs as she chews. "When you needed to know. Guess you've been to see Aleesha then. Can you remind her to not play with pointy things when I'm around?"

My chest tightens, and I take another gulp of coffee. Normally, I'd add cream and sugar, but I welcome the bitterness today.

"You're working for the Chain?" Ella stares at our older sister in disbelief.

Anabel grabs another piece of bacon. "Yup. It seems to be quite a family affair for us Goldsmiths, getting involved in rebel causes. Father *would* be surprised. I've been working for Richard for the past eight years, mostly undercover. Part of his strategy is to infiltrate governments or dictatorships at the highest level. A personal security guard has the closest access to a premier of anyone."

"I don't believe it." Ella's voice sounds strangled. "I thought you came back to be with us. How can you work for *him*? He killed our father!"

Anabel's face darkens. "*Katya* killed our father. That bitch is even more ruthless than Richard. And yes, I've thought about quitting. But without me, they wouldn't have been able to get access to the government headquarters and it would have been a hell of a lot harder to take the President alive. Besides, Father wanted change, too. He just went about it a different way." She reaches for a piece of toast. "Unsuccessfully."

"But *ethically*," Ella snaps. "He didn't *kill* people."

"Neither do I, if I can help it."

I interrupt before Ella can speak again. "What are you doing now the President's been captured."

Anabel shrugs. "Whatever Richard needs me to do."

"Well, if you haven't anything better to do today, you can help me go through Mother's things." Ella stretches to pick up her mug of coffee. The liquid spills, and she pulls back, wiping her hand on her napkin. A tear leaks from beneath her closed eyelids as she draws in a shuddering breath.

Anabel looks at her, then down at her plate. "I can do it if you don't feel up to it," she says, picking at the half-eaten toast.

"It's fine," Ella says stiffly. "You won't know what she'd have wanted to do with anything anyway."

Anabel's gaze is still fixated on her plate. "Let's do it together." She looks up at Ella. "Please?"

Ella reaches for her coffee again. She takes a large gulp, then wipes her eyes. "Fine."

I narrow my eyes at her arm. "You have a new comm band."

"Well, *someone* smashed my old one." Ella holds out her wrist. "It's a modified version. All messages are encrypted. Even the government won't be able to read them."

Anabel frowns. "That doesn't sound legal."

"It's not." Ella sounds defensive.

"You don't need to justify it to me, sister." Anabel grins wickedly. "Just wait until you see some of *my* toys."

My comm band vibrates. It's Phillips, wondering where I am. "I have to get back to the factory."

"If you find out anything about Project Griffin, you'll let me know, won't you?"

I hesitate, wondering whether to confide in Ella. The more she knows, the more danger she'll be in, but I still haven't figured out a way to get the androcibus nanite out of the production line without anyone noticing. Having some more input on the problem can't hurt.

Anabel narrows her eyes. "He already knows something. What's Project Griffin?"

I stand and pull the chip out of my pocket, tossing it to her. "I presume you have a secure holo pad?"

She nods.

"Everything's on there. Bryn already knows about it, but he doesn't think Richard will be interested. If you can think of a way I can get the drug out of the system, I'd love to hear it." I head for the door. "I'm not sure when I'll be back. The factory is in lockdown, and no one's allowed to leave unless it's an emergency."

As I start pulling on my boots by the front door, I hear footsteps approaching. Thomas stops in front of me.

"Before you go, sir, we need to talk."

I straighten in surprise. "Talk?"

His face is impassive. "Perhaps we could step into the front room?"

We squeeze into the sitting room, which is still piled high with my mother's furniture. "What is it?" I ask impatiently. "Do you need money for something?"

"No. We have sufficient funds to keep the house running." He clears his throat. "The staff are worried. We knew the mistress was involved in something that wasn't quite lawful, but she was discreet about it. It was bad enough that she departed so suddenly, but with all the comings and goings recently, as well as the arguments, well … The neighbours are starting to talk."

"Milicent left the house to me. I didn't ask for it."

"I know, sir, but that in itself has caused gossip. This boy, barely a man, if you'll beg my pardon, suddenly inherits once of the most valuable homes in the city. Then strange people turn up in the dead of night. People who don't *belong* in this neighbourhood ..."

Irritation flashes through me. "Is that what they're worried about? That I'm lowering standards? That's the problem with this city, Thomas. Insiders hide away from the reality of the world. They close their eyes to the injustice out there because they don't want to risk anything that could spoil their perfect little lives. Perhaps it's time they got a wakeup call."

I step toward the door, but Thomas blocks my path, looming over me. "This is our home, too, Master Trey." His voice is low, almost a growl. "And right now, you're putting us all in danger. Every day we don't report what's happening here is a day we risk getting dragged off by the Metz ourselves. It's a miracle they haven't been back since they dragged that girl off the night Milicent passed."

"You mean the girl you let them take to be executed?"

"I only did what my mistress ordered."

"But you won't do what *I* order?"

Anger burns inside me. Part of me realizes I'm being irrational. I didn't *want* to be master of this house. But I find myself falling more and more into that role, bossing Thomas and Dana around as if ... as if they were servants.

Thomas stiffens. "Perhaps you should consider if you still require our services." His voice carries a warning.

"Or what? You'll report me? To whom?" I smirk. "Didn't you hear? The President's been arrested."

I push past him and yank open the door, not caring that my boots leave a trail of dust on the floor. At the garden gate, I turn and look back at the tall townhouse. Thomas stands in the open doorway, looking after me. His face is sad as he turns back inside, closing the door behind him.

I lean against a stone pillar and close my eyes. He is right. This house might be mine in name, but it's their home.

And my actions have put them at risk.

A shiver runs down my back. *How did I come to be this person?*

23

Aleesha

"Have you seen Anders?"

I glance up at Danny. "Not since last night. Why?"

Danny frowns. "He's missing." His face drops.

I can see he wants to say something more but is struggling to get it out. I sigh and rub my temples. Since I walked away from Trey this morning, things have gone from bad to worse. The Bigland Boys attacked at lunchtime, and though the guards I'd placed around our precious food supply managed to fend them off, four were wounded. I can't put off speaking to Denzel much longer.

"Missing?"

Danny pulls up a chair and leans in. I force myself not to wrinkle my nose, making a mental note to talk about hygiene next time I call a meeting.

"We had a bit of a row. He's been moping over that friend of his."

"Giles?" My heart strains. "He died in his arms, Danny. What do you expect?"

His gaze shifts to the corner of the room. I wait for him to speak, patience seeping from my body as I stifle a yawn.

"Do you think ..." He pauses. "When Giles and Anders were in the

Metz, were they, y'know … *together?*"

I cross my arms. "Would it matter if they were? Don't tell me you have a problem with two guys being together."

"No, it's not that." Danny looks at me helplessly.

"So what is it?" I take in his shifting gaze, the way his hands move restlessly over the table. "Do *you* like Anders that way?" I ask gently.

Danny shakes his head vehemently. "No! I mean, I ain't got nothin' against that kind of thing, but he's just me mate, y'know?"

"So does it matter what his relationship was with Giles?"

His shoulders slump. "I guess not."

"Why don't you ask Anders about it? He might like to talk about him."

"Yeah. Mebbe." He sounds uncertain. "I was just … I just thought that mebbe seeing Giles die made him think about his friends in the Metz. And the city Inside, well … It's posh, innit? I figured he might want to go back and not hang around with us anymore." He pauses. "I mean, who would?"

My chest tightens. Danny is a strange character. I used to think he was just another swaggering toughie – happier fighting then keeping the peace. But he uses his bravado to hide his insecurities. To hide how much he cares, though he'd die sooner than admit it. Danny was never one of the more popular gang members, never had many friends. But Anders paid attention to him, *listened* to him, made him feel important.

"You know, just because Anders is friends with other people doesn't mean he's not your friend."

Danny mumbles something under his breath.

"What did you say?"

He raises his voice slightly. "He'snotmyfriendanymore."

"Did he say that?"

A red flush works its way up Danny's neck. "Na. But I said some bad stuff."

"Well, maybe you should apologize to him." I glance at the door, almost expecting Anders to stroll in. "Did he say where he was going? Maybe he just needed some time alone."

"Yeah, but it's not safe for 'im to walk around here at night. You know a lot of people still see them as the Metz – the bad guys." Danny twists his hands. "He should be back by now."

There's a knock on the door. "Come in!"

Megan sticks her head in, asking if she and Rogue can go to barter with the monks for more vegetables.

"Have you seen Anders?" I ask her as she turns to leave.

"Not since last night." Her brow creases. "He headed out late. Asked me for directions to the concrete jungle."

I meet Danny's gaze. "He wanted to see where Giles lived. I'd promised to take him, but I've been so busy …"

Face grim, Danny stands and strides to the door. "He shouldn't have gone alone."

"He may be fine. Probably just holed up in Giles's place overnight." My words lack conviction. "Wait!"

He pauses and turns. "If you're going to tell me not to go …" The threat in his voice is unmistakable.

I push back my chair and stand. "I'm coming with you."

* * * *

The streets of Area Four are busy as we weave our way through the crowd to the concrete jungle. Street hobies have already moved into the burnt-out buildings that were casualties of the Battle of Rose Square. I still don't know if the fires were set by the Metz or the people fighting them. As far as I know, no one has come to inspect the blackened buildings, and no effort has been made to cordon them off for safety. But over the past few weeks, the weakened parts of the structures have come down under the probing of the hobies, for whom a broken building is accommodation worth fighting for.

I turn and spit onto the ground, causing a man with a lined face and dirt-encrusted hair to step back and curse at me. Danny glances at me, surprised.

"You all right, boss?"

I nod, tightening my lips. Soon, these people will get the life they deserve.

Danny stops in front of the buildings that mark the edge of the wasteland separating the pile of rubble called the concrete jungle from the built-up part of Area Four. To our right, the Wall shimmers, shades of blue and green merging into the clear sky above. His hand twitches at his side as he eyes the barren area in front of us.

"An' you told me to leave my gun behind."

I don't admit I'm starting to regret my decision. I'd thought walking through Area Four with a gun would be asking for trouble but clambering around the jungle in broad daylight with only a couple of knives for protection is asking for trouble of a different kind. I should have at least brought more people, but I didn't want to raise an alarm or pull people away from guarding the food supply.

I take a deep breath and start across the cracked concrete. There's no point trying to be sneaky. Anyone watching will see us coming from a mile away.

I lead us on a weaving path around the towering concrete blocks. Rusted metal bars that have withstood the efforts of generations of Outsiders to remove them from their concrete casing plant crisscrossed shadows on the shifting rubble. I walk carefully, knowing all too well the dangers of loose stones and hidden holes. Danny follows my footsteps carefully, the smell of his fear filling my nostrils.

I glance around as we approach the entrance to the tunnel that leads to Giles's home, but there's no sign anyone's noticed us. No sign of Anders, either. Maybe I was wrong. Or perhaps he was ambushed on his way here – if he could even remember the route through the pile of rubble. He's only been here once before. That time, he'd waited outside while I went in to speak to Giles alone. I wonder what would have happened if he'd come in with me and their reunion had happened earlier.

"Stay here," I tell Danny, then duck into the dark, low tunnel.

"Not on yer life," he mutters behind me.

I sigh, but truth be told, I'm glad he's at my back. I don't know if any of the hobies who call the jungle home have taken over Giles's place.

Silently, I lower myself down the drop in the tunnel floor, knife in hand. A chink of light at the corner of the curtain that covers the entrance to the cavern beyond illuminates my final steps. I slowly stretch out a hand and freeze at a scuffling sound from within. Danny's breath warms my neck. I stand on my toes and place my eye to the chink of light.

Lights burn brightly in the colourful cave that Giles called home. Through the gap in the curtain, I can see the table, the kitchen unit behind and a section of floor. Whoever is moving around is out of my line of sight. I chew my lip and wait. A moment later, Anders appears, slipping into and out of my vision as he paces the room. I let out a breath and pull the curtain aside.

Anders whirls around, settling into a fighting stance. He relaxes when he sees us. I'm not sure whether to hug him in relief or berate him for heading off on his own.

Danny beats me to it. "You idiot! You could 'ave been killed coming here." He steps out from behind me and scowls. "I'd 'ave come with you if you'd asked."

Anders casts him an inquiring glance. "Would you?" His face is pale, eyes red and puffy.

"Danny's right," I say, replacing my knife in my belt. "The jungle's one of the most dangerous parts of the city. And to not even tell someone where you were going ..." I let my words hang in the air.

Anders looks abashed. "Sorry. I just needed some time alone."

We fall silent. Danny stares around the room at the brightly coloured cloths hanging over the ceiling, the neatly stacked shelves filled with paper books, the table, still piled high with the tools and components Giles had used to build his creations. His face, usually so easy to read, is closed and guarded.

"He made it a proper home, didn't he?" I say.

Anders bows his head. He holds a jar in his hand, turning it around and around.

"What's that?"

He starts and looks down, a small smile lifting the corner of his lips. "Honey. You don't seem to have much of it out here."

"It's expensive," I reply with a shrug. "I don't even know where he got it. Must have been up in Six where the rich Outsiders live."

"I wonder why he bought it," Anders muses. "I didn't think he liked it. When we were trainees, we were given some for a treat on Sundays. Just enough to spread on a piece of toast. I loved it, but Giles always gave his portion to me. Said he didn't want it."

My throat tightens. "He gave me a bit once when I came to him for help. He said ..." I swallow. "He said it reminded him of someone ..."

A shadow passes over Anders' eyes. "He begged me to stay out here with him." His face spasms, and I turn away, embarrassed by his grief. People had nicknamed Giles "The Ghost" – partly for his pale skin and hair, but also for the way he hid from the world, seeming to care about no one. Yet he had spent all those chits on a tiny pot of honey.

"Giles said his parents sent him to the Métz compound when he was young because they couldn't find a cure for his condition," I say quietly.

"He was barely five when he arrived. His parents abandoned him. Not because they *couldn't* look after him – unlike the people out here, they had plenty of money – but because they didn't *want* him." Anders' fingers tighten on the jar of honey. "They were ashamed of him. He was locked away with only a nanny bot for company. The one time he tried to get out, to follow a bird he saw in the garden, he was beaten. After that, they shuttered up the windows so he couldn't look out. Is it any wonder he hated being outdoors?"

Nausea turns my stomach. The conditions kids grew up in out here were bad. Many parents were forced to give up their children if they couldn't feed them or, if they were illegal, they were taken by the Population Control Officers. But for a rich Insider family to treat their child that way?

They do not deserve their privilege.

"Poor kid," Danny mutters. He runs a finger across a cushion covered in a soft, fluffy material, as if he's never felt anything like it before. He probably hasn't.

"Once they stopped trying to force him to become an officer, Giles blossomed in the Metz compound. He was a genius with anything mechanical, and he had such a thirst for knowledge. The Professor was like a father to him. Sometimes I'd come to see Giles in the morning, and he'd have been up all night, trying to solve a problem." A smile touches Anders' lips. "He was happy. Until he realized what Metz officers were made to do when they were outside the compound."

"And then he left."

"Yes." Anders turns to me. "Does your father still have the

Professor prisoner?"

I sigh. "No. He swallowed a suicide pill before they could question him."

"Coward. He deserved a worse death than that." Danny spits and pulls out a knife, inspecting the blade. "Anyone else we can skin instead?"

"Giles would have wanted us to forgive him," Anders says thoughtfully.

Danny stares at him, uncomprehending. "What? The man *killed* him."

Anders sighs and rubs his forehead. "I know. But one death should not beget another. And Giles hated violence more than anything. He always tried to see the good in people. That's one thing he taught me."

Or perhaps one thing you taught him, I think, remembering my conversation with Giles in the Metz compound shortly before his death.

Anders' words remind me of something Giles had said to me when I'd been focused on killing Andrew Goldsmith. I'd wanted justice for my mother's death, but he made me realize that I actually wanted revenge. It took Andrew Goldsmith's death for me to learn that killing someone for revenge doesn't bring back the person you love. It just taints your memory of them even more.

"The only way we could have saved Giles was by forcing him to not do what he believed to be right." Anders shakes his head. "That's no way for someone to live."

"What are you goin' to do with all this?" Danny waves his hand around the room. "Won't be long before people figure out The Ghost ain't comin' back."

Anders looks at me, but I shrug. "What do you think he'd want done with it?"

He looks wretched. "I don't know. I only knew him in the Metz compound when we had nothing." He looks around the room. "This is a different Giles than the man I knew. But I think he'd want his things to go to someone who'd look after them. There are so many pieces of history here." He waves at the books.

"We could block the entrance for now," I suggest. "Give us some time to figure it out."

Anders gives a slow nod. "Yes."

We crawl back up the tunnel, Anders grunting as he tries to manoeuvre his huge body in the cramped space. I blink as we emerge into the light. Danny disappears behind some blocks to take a piss, while Anders uses his weight to push a giant block in front of the tunnel entrance. Veins bulge on his arms with the effort. After adding a second block to the first, I'm pretty sure none of the miscreants living in this part of Four will be able to disturb Giles's home.

Anders stands there, panting, dusting off his hands, when the scuttle of pebbles makes me turn. I catch a glimpse of movement just as a knife embeds itself in Anders' shoulder.

He drops to the ground, letting out a grunt. I yank a knife from my pocket and move toward him, but before I've taken two paces, a weight lands on my back.

My knife flies from my grip as I stumble forward under the weight of my attacker. An overpowering stench chokes the breath from my throat. I try to twist him off, but his arm wraps around my neck and my legs collapse under me, bringing us both to the ground.

I try to roll as I land, kicking out even as pain shoots up my back. The man jumps nimbly to his feet, barring what's left of his rotting teeth in a feral grin. Dark, greasy hair hangs around a pasty face.

The Boots Brothers.

My heart sinks as I scramble to my feet, looking around for my knife. It must have fallen between two of the concrete blocks.

"Back 'ere again, are ye?" The man is unarmed – at least as far as I can see. "Ghost's gone, ain't he?" He glances back at Anders, who's reaching for the knife on his belt, and aims a kick at his chest.

Anders isn't quite quick enough to escape the blow and he sways, biting his lip against the pain.

"Where's your brother?" I scan the surrounding rubble, searching for the man's twin.

He ignores me and shifts position so he can keep an eye on both me and Anders. "Why don't you pull back those blocks now an' let us in. Then you can run off home."

"Your strategy's poor," I reply, not letting him see the fear bubbling inside me. Anders looks *very* pale. "You've just injured the only person with the strength to move them."

The man hisses in anger. "Shut it, girl."

"I've already faced you two once, and I'm pretty sure you lost that time." I look him in the eye and keep my voice level. "Besides, you owe me a favour. I could have had you killed by that Metz officer, but I let you go. Let us go now, and we'll call it even."

A globule of saliva lands at my feet. A faint breeze hits me, making me gag. Compared to the Boots Brothers, Danny smells like an Insider's flower garden. "Favour?" He leers. "*Favours* carry no weight 'ere."

"Reckon your brother might disagree."

Danny hauls the second brother out from behind a block, a knife held to the man's throat. Relief floods through me.

"Here's how this is goin' to work. You're goin' to let Aleesha tie your hands, then we'll take your brother with us." A gurgle escapes the man's lips as Danny's blade nicks his skin. "*If* you cooperate, we'll let him go at the edge of the jungle. If not …" The implied threat hangs in the air.

For a moment, I think he is going to agree. A slight twitch of his eyebrow is the only warning I get. I start toward him. "Da—"

There's a grunt as Danny's captive thumps him in the groin and twists away. A thin, red slash across his neck trickles blood. The knife was within millimetres of his jugular.

They really are mad.

I start forward, but I'm not sure which twin poses the biggest threat. My hesitation is costly. The first twin has already reached Anders and yanks his knife out of my friend's shoulder. Anders screams in pain and pitches forward, but the man grabs him by the hair and pulls his head back.

"Reckon not," he hisses.

Shit.

I'm not sure if Danny would have killed the man, but I'm damn sure the Boots Brothers won't hesitate to kill us to get what they want. I was truthful when I said Anders is the only one strong enough to push aside the rocks blocking the tunnel entrance, but Danny and I are expendable.

The brother holding Anders glances at his twin, trying to figure out what their next move should be. His twin watches me. Which means neither see Danny send his knife flying through the air to embed in the right eye of the man holding a knife to Anders' throat. The man falls back, his blade clattering to the ground. His brother lets out a keening wail and runs toward him. I stick out my foot to trip him, sending him flailing into a block. He hits his head and crumples to the ground, lying still.

Danny and I rush to Anders and help him up. "Better get out of here before he wakes up." I glance at Anders anxiously. "Reckon you can make it back to the main street before we patch you up?"

He nods, his lips tight.

Danny retrieves his knife and the Boots Brothers' weapon. I

quickly search and find my knife slotted in a narrow gap between two concrete blocks, the blade slightly nicked.

Before we leave, I bend and press my fingers to the neck of the man I'd tripped. His pulse is strong. I debate slitting his throat, but I can't bring myself to do it.

"Let's get out of here," Danny mutters.

Back in the relative safety of the streets of Area Four, I sit Anders down. Danny pulls a rag from his pocket and tries to stem the blood pouring from his friend's shoulder. The rag is filthy, but likely no worse than what was on the blade.

"Let's get you back to headquarters, then I'll see if Mika and her pod are around." I try to sound reassuring.

Anders swallows and closes his eyes. For a moment, I think he's going to puke, but he manages to contain it. When he opens his eyes again, he stares at Danny. "Thank you," he rasps.

Danny brushes off his thanks but gives me a dark look. "Here's the thing about forgiveness," he says. "Some people it's best not to forgive. Else they'll just come back to bite you in the arse."

I can't disagree with him as the three of us make our way through the streets and back to Phoenix headquarters.

24

Trey

A shadow crosses the sky as I hurry to the pod point. I glance up and my footsteps slow.

"What's that?" a girl ahead of me asks her mother as they stop and stare at the huge ovoid skimming the tops of the towers.

"I don't know, love." The woman's voice is tense as she grabs the girl's hand, pulling her forward. "Come on. We need to get home."

"You're hurting me," the girl complains as she struggles to keep up with her mother's clipped footsteps.

My mouth goes dry as the shadow continues to move slowly overhead. It's by far the largest pod I've ever seen – if it can even be called a pod. It must be two hundred metres long, at least. The deep bluish-black paint on its hull shimmers in the sunlight but must make the pod almost invisible at night. Finally, it passes over me, heading north. I can't imagine how you could even build something that size, let alone where it would land. It is like nothing I have ever seen before.

A bright flash ricochets off the dark vessel, followed by a staccato burst. There's another flash, then the pod is suddenly surrounded by smaller flying machines that buzz around it like flies. The noise of the fight cuts through the peaceful quiet of the weekend morning, but whatever weapons they're using seem to bounce off the strange pod without damaging it. It doesn't retaliate, just continues to move slowly, inexorably, across the sky.

Changing my mind about taking a pod out to Area Six, I switch direction to the East Gate. By the time I finally make it into the factory, via one of the entrances the factory workers use, and report to Phillips, my boss is livid.

"Where have you been? I messaged you hours ago."

I explain about the giant pod and not wanting to risk flying in. Phillips grunts.

"Well, Barnes has still not turned up, and Emilie's reported that there's an issue with the line again. I thought I told you to speak to her?"

"Yes, sir." I realize that with everything else going on yesterday, I'd forgotten to contact Barnes. "I'll follow up with her right away."

"She must come in. The workers are getting tetchy about being kept in, and for some reason, they seem to respect her. I don't care if she's on her deathbed. Get her in here by the end of the day or you'll both be out of a job."

I swallow. "But, sir—"

Phillips scowls, his face bright red. "Just get it done."

He turns back to his holo screen as I back out of the room.

When I walk into my office, Louis is lounging in my chair with his feet on my desk, talking to Emilie. He waves. "Good. You're back. I'm about to die of boredom." He flashes Emilie a smile. "No offence."

She rolls her eyes and stretches. "Another coffee?"

Louis holds out his cup. "Please. And cake. Chocolate if they have it."

"What did your last slave die of?" Emilie drops her voice to a whisper. "I've had to talk to him for the past two hours. Your turn."

Behind her, Louis snorts. "You love it!"

Emilie smirks and steps out of the room.

I try to call Barnes on the comm, but she doesn't answer, so I send her a quick message before turning to Louis.

He removes his feet from my desk and leans forward, his face serious. "I read the Project Griffin files." He gives me a knowing look. "All of them."

So he knows about the additional files I added onto the email. I meet his gaze levelly. "And?"

He blows out a breath. "I don't know what to think," he admits. "They're pretty damning, but at the same time, it's not as if we're actually poisoning people. If Outsiders stay away from the Wall, the nanobots won't hurt them."

"We don't know that for certain. It could just be that the side-effects take decades to show." I pace over to the window overlooking the factory floor. "If it were harmless, why wouldn't they add it to all the food?"

"Good point." Louis pauses. "So, what do you want to do about it?"

I stare down at the workers checking the production line and monitoring the vats, none of them aware that the food they're producing, the food they eat, has the potential to kill them. "Find a way of removing it from the production lines."

Louis starts to rise from the chair. "I told you. I'm not doing anything that'll put the factory in jeopardy."

I wave him back down. "I know. But this isn't about stopping food production. It's just removing one ingredient."

"And how do you think you'll do that without quality control noticing?"

"That's what I need to figure out."

The door pings as it opens and Emilie walks back in, balancing coffee and cake. "They're out of chocolate, I'm afraid. I brought you lemon instead."

"It'll do," Louis replies, picking up a piece. "Looks like they've started rationing us already." He sighs theatrically. "Let's hope the reinforcements the government is bringing in can get the situation under control as soon as possible."

My pulse spikes. "Reinforcements?"

"I heard on the news that they're using freight trains to bring in security officers from across the country," Emilie says, handing me a coffee. "And they have aerial fighters. I never even knew they existed. Hopefully everything will get back to normal soon and we can go home."

I take a sip of my coffee, my mind whirring. This isn't good news for the Chain. But if the government forces are coming in by train, then what was the gigantic pod doing over London?

I wonder if Richard has brought in some reinforcements of his own.

* * * *

When Barnes hasn't responded to any of my calls or messages by four in the afternoon, I don't know whether to be angry or worried. Either she's ignoring me or something's happened. Either way, my job's on the line, so I get permission to leave the factory to walk to her apartment in Area Seven.

There are few people on the streets. The heat of the day is setting in, and the air feels heavy, as if the whole city is holding its breath, waiting for something to happen.

By the time I reach Barnes's apartment, I'm sweating and wishing I'd taken a taxi pod. I lean against the cool wall of the building and press the buzzer next to her name. When the speaker crackles to life, I jump.

"Who is it?" Barnes slurs.

"It's Trey. Can—"

"Go away."

The speaker cuts out.

I press it again. For a moment, I think she's going to ignore me, but then her voice comes through again, stronger this time. "I said, *go away.*"

"If you don't let me in, I've been ordered to call the factory security team to drag you out. I think you'd rather speak to me than them."

There's a pause, followed by a click as the main door to the apartment block unlocks.

I push it open and step into the lobby. Cool air chills the sweat on my neck. I take the elevator up and knock on Barnes's door. A moment later, it opens.

She looks a mess. Her hair is greasy and tied in a knot at the nape of her neck. Dark bags hang under swollen eyes that droop with tiredness. From the look and smell of her clothes, she hasn't changed in days. But she doesn't look sick. Just exhausted.

"You'd better come in." She turns and walks into the apartment, leaving me to catch the door as it starts to swing shut. I follow her in.

"How are you feeling?" I ask as she slumps down onto the sofa, leans her head back and closes her eyes.

"How do I look?"

"Like hell."

"That pretty much sums it up." She cracks open an eye. "I'm not coming in. I don't have to work weekends. It's not in my contract."

I sigh and sit down next to her. "I wouldn't be too sure about that. I suspect this counts as 'emergency measures'. Phillips has ordered me to bring you in one way or another. If you don't come, we'll both lose our jobs. Coleman says it's our duty to keep the food lines running and get food out to people. He's paranoid about the Chain taking over the factory. Security is insane. The only reason I've been allowed out is to find you."

Barnes stares out the window. "I don't care. The job doesn't matter anymore … Not without him."

I frown at her. "Who? Samson?"

Barnes nods and tears well in her eyes. She scrubs them away. "What do you know about what happened the night the Chain took over?"

"Only what I've seen on the news."

She barks out a laugh. "Richard's lies then."

"What do you mean?" I'm confused. "Are you saying he doesn't have the President? Or the government?"

Her fingers tug at the hem of her vest. "No, he has them. Whether he can hold them is another matter."

She falls silent. I wait impatiently for her to speak again.

"Samson made a deal with him. Richard didn't have enough people to capture the President and infiltrate the government headquarters at the same time. The plan was for Richard to lead the operation to get the President, while Samson led the attack on the headquarters with his people and some of Richard's."

"You were involved?" I can't say I'm shocked.

She casts me a sideways glance. "Perhaps. Everyone who had a chip blocker or wasn't chipped was needed. Even then, there weren't enough of us. We banked on the fact that the palace guard would be depleted. Richard said he had a way to call them back, out of the building, but only after the President was captured." Barnes shrugs. "But he lied. They weren't depleted at all. We encountered a lot more resistance than we expected and ended up having to separate. Petal led our team to secure the perimeter, while Samson took a group of Richard's people to try to break through to the security control room."

She falls silent.

"It didn't work?"

"We managed to take the building in the early hours of Friday morning. Half of the team Samson had taken with him returned ..."

"But he didn't?" I ask gently. The pain is etched into every line on her face. Samson was not just her boss. He was her lover.

And perhaps the only person, save the President, who would stand up to Richard.

"They said he'd gone down fighting the palace guard. That he'd died bravely." She turns to me. Her eyes burn with such ferocity that I can't meet her gaze. "But I searched the *entire* building and he wasn't there. If he were dead, there would be a body."

"You think he escaped?"

Her fists tighten. "I *know* he escaped. He's alive somewhere. I just have to find him."

I bite my lip, not knowing what to say. Her grief makes me uncomfortable. This is not the Barnes I know – the stoic, sarcastic woman who always has a smart retort. I don't know how to respond to this Barnes. Does she see me as a friend, an ally or just an inconvenience?

"Have you spent all night searching?" I ask.

"And all day yesterday. Normally I wouldn't risk staying Inside so long. The cameras are set up to detect people who shouldn't be there. *Outsiders*. But I figured with the city in chaos, that wouldn't be an issue. Petal's been looking, too, but neither of us have found anything. I just don't know where else to look."

My mind races. "Did you search the tunnels?"

"We searched the route we use to get Inside through the old train lines ..."

She blinks and sits up, suddenly alert. "You're right. There's a way directly into the headquarters from the tunnels. Samson used it when he went to visit the President. We couldn't use that to break into the headquarters. He said he couldn't guarantee we could get through the security barriers, but *he* could."

She jumps up, her face flushed. "We have to go. He could be down there, injured."

I grab her arm. "Sit." When she doesn't respond, I yank her down next to me. "You're exhausted and not thinking straight. This is what we're going to do. You're going to go back to the factory—"

"B—"

"*Listen.* You're going to go back and pretend you're ill. You definitely look sick. Fix whatever's wrong with the line, then get some rest. We can't afford to lose our jobs."

Barnes opens her mouth to protest again, but I hold up my hand. "Just listen to me."

I tell her what I found in the files about the androcibus nanite. Her eyes widen.

"You see? If we get fired, we've got no chance of figuring out a way to remove it from the food supply."

Barnes stares out the window, her brow furrowed. "You're saying we all have these ... nanobots in our bloodstream? Carrying poison?"

"If you eat the government rations or lower-grade food, then yes. But they're only dangerous if you try to get through the Wall."

Barnes shakes her head. Her face drains of colour. "Not just if you try to get through the Wall."

I frown. "What do you mean? The nanobots need to be activated in order to—"

"Exactly!" She stands. This time, I don't stop her. "But if it's just a radio frequency that activates them, that doesn't have to come from the Wall." She turns to look at me, her green eyes wide with horror. "All the government would need to do is project a signal from a transmitter across the city and every Outsider with these nanobots in their system would die. It's a weapon of mass destruction, Trey. A weapon that only targets the people the government doesn't care about."

A chill ripples through me as her words hit home. *Why didn't I think of this? How did I let Louis convince me that the androcibus nanite was harmless?*

"I'm going back to the factory." Barnes shoves past me and heads into her bedroom. "I'm getting rid of that poison once and for all."

"Barnes, no." I run after her and stand in the doorway to her bedroom until she looks pointedly at me and holds up a clean jumpsuit, eyebrow raised. I turn my back to give her privacy, but don't move away from the door. "We need to work out a way of removing it from the system without quality control noticing. You getting caught isn't going to help anyone."

"Oh? And how many more people are you willing to poison before you figure out *your* plan?" There's the hiss of a cleaner unit.

I wait until I hear her dressing. "Think about what Samson would want. You've spent years to get yourself to this position. Don't blow your cover now."

From the silence behind me, she knows what I'm saying makes sense. She just doesn't want to admit it.

"Look. I'll make you a deal. You go back to the factory, keep the line running and your head down. I'll go find Samson. I've been through the tunnels into the government headquarters before. I've got a better chance of finding him than you."

I risk a peek over my shoulder. Aside from the lingering bags under her eyes, Barnes looks like a different woman. But the worry and fear is still on her face. "You'll find him?" Her voice cracks. "You promise?"

I meet her gaze, knowing that this city and its people need Samson as much as she does. "If he's in those tunnels, I'll find him. And I promise, we'll come up with a plan to get rid of the androcibus nanite. We just need a bit more time."

"Fine. No involving the Chain, though."

I nod and step back to let her out of the room.

So many promises to keep.

So many promises I might have to break.

Once outside, I send a message to Phillips, telling him Barnes is on her way. I add that I have a few things to sort out concerning my mother's death but will be back in tomorrow. He'll be mad, but he needs Barnes more than he needs me right now. If she meets her end of the bargain, I hope it'll buy me some time.

I walk south, my feet dragging as I steel myself for the confrontation to come. The last thing I want is to go crawling back to Aleesha, not when even the thought of seeing her makes my heart burn, but right now, I can't think of anyone else who can help. Even if I could find my way through the tunnels to the government headquarters, finding Samson on my own, not to mention getting him out if he is injured, feels like an impossible task.

I've just crossed the border into Area Five when my comm band buzzes. I glance at it, expecting to see Phillip's caller ID, but it's an unknown number. I answer it cautiously, voice only.

"Hello?"

"Trey? It's Dexter. Have you seen Ella?"

"Not since I left the house. She was there at breakfast. Why?"

There's a pause. "She messaged me three hours ago saying she had some important information. Even if she walked, she should have been here by now. I've tried her comm five times, but she's not answering." There's an edge of panic to his voice.

My mind freezes. "What are you thinking?"

"I think ..." I hear him swallow. "What if they've got her, Trey?"

25

Aleesha

"Let me see him."

My father glares at me. "Why? What can you possibly have to say to him?"

I jut my chin out defiantly. "I just want to ask him something."

"What?"

"None of your business."

My father lets out a small growl.

"Oh, come on, Richard. What harm can it do?" Katya asks from across the room. She's perched on the edge of a table, her legs swinging. Her blonde hair tied back, she's dressed in practical combat gear, which she somehow makes look like the latest fashion trend. "She needs closure. You may have moved on from Maria's death, but she obviously hasn't."

I grind my teeth. She can bloody well shut up about *closure*. I still haven't forgiven her for Andrew Goldsmith's death. Even if it had been my fault he'd ended up in her hands. If she thinks the only way I can come to terms with my mother's death is by killing more people – by *facing my demons*, as she'd told me when we'd sat on the steps of the monument stained by Trey's father's blood – she's wrong. Just because she hunted down every man and woman connected with the death of her parents and sister doesn't mean I want to do the same.

Katya once told me she didn't like killing people, that she never killed needlessly. But I can't help wondering just how many people she's killed and how many are yet to come.

My father's face darkens. "Leave Maria out of this," he says tightly.

It's been nearly two days since the President was captured. The news has spread, but people still aren't sure who Richard Masterton is. If you listen to the rumours spreading through Area Four, he's a war hero who's been sent to free Britannia, a thief who's telling us a pack of lies or a trumped-up Insider making a desperate grab for power.

I'm not sure if any of the rumours describe the man standing in front of me.

I cross my arms. "Nine days ago, *I* was the one who was prisoner and *he* was about to give the order for my execution. Surely I'm allowed a chance to gloat? Besides, I *did* help capture him."

This comment earns me a snort from my father.

"You can't blame me for attacking Anabel when *you* didn't tell me she was part of the plan."

My father looks at Katya, who shrugs. "She has a point."

He sighs. "Fine. You can have five minutes with him. But you're to stay behind the table, understand? There will be someone watching you – for your own safety."

And so you can listen in on our conversation.

"Behind the table. Got it."

I follow one of the guards down into a basement beneath the old house the Chain is using as their new headquarters. It smells musty and damp.

"Wait here," he tells me.

I do as he says, looking over the neatly labelled boxes stacked on one side of the room. Some seem to be food, others weapons. Enough for a small army.

How did they smuggle all this stuff in?

"You can come through now."

I straighten my shoulders and follow the man into the next room. At the far end is a low doorway. The door's ajar, and two guards wait beside it.

"We've secured him," one says, "but stay on this side of the table."

Nerves claw at my stomach, though I can't explain why. It's not as if he can do anything to me now. Twice, I've been at his mercy, and both times, I escaped. Now our situations are reversed.

He sits in a heavy, high-backed chair on the far side of the room. About a metre in front of him is a wide table with a smaller chair on the near side. I sink onto it, my legs suddenly weak.

We sit in silence for a moment. Now that I'm here, I'm not sure how to start the conversation.

The President eyes me curiously. His brown skin carries a greyish tinge, and there's a bandage wrapped across his forehead and one eye. The shirt he's wearing should be white, but it's stained with blood and dirt, a long tear running across one shoulder. Transparent cuffs bind his wrists to the arms of the chair, and with a sickening jolt, I notice that his right forefinger is missing.

"Well, this is a turn of events." The President's voice carries a trace of amusement, and I wonder how he can find anything funny about his situation.

"Have they tortured you?" I ask.

He gives a small shrug. "They took my eye and my finger." He tries to lift his right arm, seemingly forgetting it's secured to the arm of the chair. "But at least they gave me painkillers."

My stomach churns and I swallow down bile. "Why?"

"Well, I assume your father has plans to take over the government headquarters, if he hasn't already. Perhaps they thought bits of me might come in useful to access some of the more secure files."

His gaze hardens. "What are you doing here, Aleesha? Have you come to gloat?"

I swallow again and shake my head. The man is in pieces – literally – and tied up. A large, heavy table separates us. How can he still feel like a threat to me? "I wanted to ask you something. Two things, actually."

The President remains silent.

"I know about the Wall. How you put the nanobots in the food to stop us being able to go through it. But why? If you wanted to control us that much, why not just lock us up in some big compound and be done with it? Why make us think we're free?"

The President observes me for a minute. "You just answered the question yourself. What would happen if we created huge compounds Outside and locked all of you up?"

"People would try to escape."

He nods. "Exactly. Put a wire fence up and freedom suddenly jumps up people's priority list. Besides, I don't *want* to lock people up. That's never been what I've wanted."

"Then why have the Wall in the first place?" I lean forward, resting my arms on the table. "Why not just pull it down?"

A fleeting sadness crosses his face.

"Because it is not just my decision. People voted to keep the Wall in place."

"*Insiders* voted," I say, my voice sharp.

The President gives a small shrug. "Does it matter? My job is to keep people safe. The Wall may have been originally put up as an emergency measure, but it still fulfils that function today. You don't understand what people went through in the Dark Times. There

251

wasn't enough food for everyone, and innocent people got killed in riots every day. There was no law, no order. The government had to put something in place, and quickly, to stop people from killing each other. There was no time to build a concrete wall, so they came up with a technological barrier. A fake wall to provide a safe haven in the centre of the city. It was intended to be temporary, to be taken down once the situation stabilized."

"So why wasn't it?"

He sighs. "Because these things are never temporary. It wasn't long before people realized the holo projection was nothing more than a smokescreen. The nanobots were an experiment. I'm not sure anyone thought they'd work. But once Outsiders started dying, well … That quickly stopped them trying to get through the Wall. By then, food factories were up and running and supplies had started coming through. It was the first time in ten years that anyone – Insiders *or* Outsiders – had any kind of stability. After that, the Wall made Insiders feel safe. No one wanted to return to what life was like during the Dark Times."

"You said innocent people were killed then. But innocent people are killed today under *your* orders." A memory of Lily's pleading eyes springs into my mind, and I have to clench my hands on the seat of my chair to stop myself leaping across the table and slamming my fist into the President's nose.

"No one is truly innocent, Aleesha," he says softly.

I grind my teeth, unable to think of a response.

We sit in silence. A faint dripping comes from the corner of the room. Outside the door, one of the guards shuffles and mutters something to her companion.

"Anyway, there is more to this than you can fathom. Our country has changed a lot since the Great Flood. Before that time, we had a diverse economy with imports and exports from all over the world. After the government closed our borders and the flood and fighting happened, few businesses were left. Those who survived the upheaval were not so keen for things to change. Trust me, Aleesha. Having the Wall up is for the best."

I feel like he's talking in riddles. Or perhaps politics. That's what they do, isn't it? Talk around things without ever getting to the point.

"I don't understand."

The President gives a low chuckle. "Do you really think *I* am the one in control of this city? This country?"

I stare at him blankly. "You're the President."

He shakes his head. "God, you are so much like your mother. Everything is black or white, right or wrong ..." His voice trails off. "Or perhaps it's just too complex for you to understand. I guess you haven't had much in the way of an education."

Irritation flares in my belly. "No, because *you* made me an illegal citizen."

"Time!" a voice calls from the door.

I turn to see the guard who'd brought me down waiting by the door.

"Just a few more minutes."

He looks uncertain, shuffling his feet.

"Please? You're just outside."

"Okay ... Two more minutes."

I turn back to the President. A spasm of pain contorts his face and he twists in the chair, tugging at his bindings. His torn shirt flaps open, and I catch a glimpse of puckered skin on his shoulder. An old scar. It strikes me as odd that he never had it healed. I thought Insiders were obsessed with perfection.

"Tell me about my mother. And my father. What was he like when he was young?"

He pants, his head hanging, as the pain subsides. "Ricus? He came to London when we were fifteen. I remember him turning up at school partway through the year, wearing a second-hand uniform two sizes too small. Didn't even have a data pad. He was surly, defiant – he even resisted authority then – but he could turn on the charm when he needed to, so he mostly got away with it." He lifts his head to look at me. "He had this ... charisma about him. You've seen it. And he was bright enough in the classroom and strong enough on the rugby field that he could get away with numerous transgressions."

"But you were friends?"

"Yes. We got into some scrapes." His lips twitch. "I was always the one who got caught. Unfortunately, I didn't have his speed or knack for knowing when something was about to go wrong. But Ricus would turn on the charm and bail me out. We planned out our future together. He would be President, I'd be his Vice-President. Together, we'd fix the world."

"What happened?"

He looks down at his hands. "He changed. We were at university in London. He used to spend a lot of time Outside the Wall, just walking the streets. He got angry – at society and the political situation. He wanted to take action. *Violent* action. We had a confrontation. I told him his plan was wrong. That we had to try to change things from inside the government." He sighs heavily. "I stormed away. Two days later, Ricus tried to blow up the government headquarters. He was caught, but somehow managed to escape. Many of his allies did not. That was the last I saw of him for years."

I stare down at the table. The President leans forward in his chair. "Aleesha, I know you don't trust me, and I have done nothing to deserve that trust, but believe me, I loved your mother. I loved her more than it is possible to love someone." His voice cracks. When I drag my gaze up, I see raw emotion on his face for the first time. "He never loved her as she deserved. I would have given her anything she wanted, anything she asked for. We even dated a few times. But when Ricus showed up and turned on the charm, it was as if I didn't exist. I was just a shadow – the moon forced from her sky by the dazzling sun."

I look down, digging my fingernails into the tabletop. "Shut up," I whisper.

"Ricus was once my best friend. I *know* him. He is not the man you think he is. He's not the man Maria—" His voice breaks again. "He is not the man Maria fell in love with."

"I said, shut up!"

I hear movement behind me and whirl around. The guard stands in the doorway, eyebrow raised. "Is everything all right?"

I suck in air. "Yes. I'm done." I stand quickly, the chair clattering to the floor behind me.

"They were blanks, you know," the President says in a soft voice.

My chest tightens. "What do you mean?"

His face sags. "I could never have killed Maria's daughter. But I had to make you *think* I would. It was the only way to make *him* believe. That's why I gave you the tronk. It was supposed to knock you out, but I guess you must have built up a resistance to it. It was why I let you speak, spouting your nonsense to the crowd – to give Ricus time to act."

"But he didn't, and you still ordered them to shoot me."

"One of the firing squad had sedation darts. The rest were firing blanks. You'd have keeled over as if dead, then the Metz would have rushed in to take you away before people could note the lack of blood."

I shake my head. "You're making this up. Did you tell anyone else about this plan to *not* kill me?"

"Only the leader of the firing squad. He was killed by the Chain when they were attacked."

"Convenient. Did you tell him he was to be your sacrificial goat?"

He doesn't respond to my goading. "The Metz officers know there is risk and they accept that. Sacrifices have to be made."

"So you're happy to sacrifice the lives of dozens of people, expecting me to be okay with that because it was all to save me?" I rest my fists on the table and lean forward. "Your lies tie you in knots. You want me to feel sorry for you, to persuade my father to spare you. Well, I won't. I'm not the stupid Outsider you think I am."

"Don't be naïve, Aleesha." He holds my gaze. "Power can raise people up, but it can also corrupt. Remember that. There has always been something dark, something dangerous inside Ricus. I thought I could change him. I was wrong."

I turn away, sickened by his words. "Yes, power can corrupt, as *you* have proven. I don't need to listen to your lies any longer."

"Are they lies, Aleesha?" he asks quietly. "Or do you just not want to believe the truth?"

With one last look, I walk from the room, his words lingering in my ears. The guard falls into step beside me.

"You okay?"

I nod, not trusting myself to speak.

* * * *

I find my father talking with Bryn. Katya, to my relief, has gone.

"Are you okay? What did he do to you?" Frowning, my father pushes back his chair and walks over to me.

I swallow and stare down at the floor, tears pricking my eyes. Coming up here again was a mistake. I should have just walked out the front door.

He places his hands on my shoulders. His warmth spreads across my skin, numbing some of the chill filling my body. Something in my chest pulls me forward. A want, no, a *need* to close the distance between us.

I lick my lips and force my feet to stay where they are. I can't frighten him away. Not now he's finally accepted who I am.

But my father surprises me. Stepping forward, he pulls me into an awkward hug. I melt into him, his warmth rushing through my body. It makes me feel safe, secure. The moment is fleeting, though. I've barely had time to register what's happening before he pulls away again. But the warmth lingers, and I feel a little less cold.

A little less alone.

"What did he say to you?"

I manage to find my voice. "A pack of lies, mostly." I peek up at him, a smile drifting to my lips. "I asked him what you were like as a teenager. He said you were surly and defiant."

Bryn barks a laugh. "Well, some things don't change."

Even my father manages a brief smile before his face turns serious once again. "I have to admit, I was worried he would try to turn you against me. He's always been a convincing liar. I'm sorry. I should have trusted that you'd be able to see through him." He brushes a hand across my arm. "And I'm sorry I didn't tell you about Anabel. You did a good job the other night. I ... I'm proud of you."

Heat rises to my cheeks. I look down at the floor to hide my grin. *He's proud of me. My father is proud of me.*

"Did he tell you the reason I left London?"

I hesitate, not wanting to spoil this moment by saying the wrong thing. "He said you tried to blow up the government headquarters."

"I'm guessing he didn't tell you he betrayed us to the government. In return for a ministry position straight out of university, I suspect." His eyes darken. "I had many good friends killed that day. People who were also once friends of his. He betrayed us all."

"That's why you had to leave London? Leave my mother?"

Something flickers briefly in his eyes. "Yes. I left London that night."

I swallow, the words I want to say catching in my throat. "I ... I'm glad you came back. Glad I got to meet you."

He smiles down at me. "Me, too."

Bryn shuffles his feet, as if to remind us he's there.

"So, what's your plan now?" I ask.

My father walks back over to the table. "We had some reinforcements come in yesterday. Aerial fighters and some ground troops. They're camped in an old airfield just outside London. We have the Metz compound, the government headquarters and the President. I'm trying to open talks with the remaining government ministers to discuss the terms of their surrender, but so far, they have been uncooperative. If they don't respond by this evening, we plan to root them out."

"And kill them?"

"If we have to." He rubs a hand over his face, suddenly looking tired. "I'll be glad when this is all over."

"Won't we all," Bryn says fervently.

"Well, I'd better be getting back. Thanks for letting me speak to him."

"I hope it helped."

I nod and leave the room, heading toward the front door. Hearing footsteps behind me, I turn, seeing Bryn rushing down the hallway.

"Aleesha, have you and Trey had a row?"

I narrow my eyes. "Why?"

Bryn holds up his hands defensively. "Just something I heard on the street."

Great. Now all my personal issues are aired to everyone.

I take a deep breath. "We split up. I told him it couldn't work between us."

"Why do you think that?" His voice is surprisingly gentle.

I turn to pull open the door, but he leans against it, arms crossed. I sigh. "Come on, Bryn. You know as well as anyone it can't work. Wasn't it you who told me not to lead him on? You should be glad I listened to your advice."

"That's not what I meant. You care for him. I know you do."

I look pointedly at him until he moves out of my way. "I have responsibilities now. What would you have me do? Abandon my people again to play house with a boy I will never, *ever* be good enough for? He deserves better, Bryn."

I reach for the bolt above the door handle, but Bryn is quicker. He covers it with his hand, leaning over me. My jaw clenches.

"I know why you think that, but you're wrong, on both counts. He needs you, Aleesha, and I think you need him. I may have once given up love for what I believed was right, but I'm lucky. I got another chance. You may not be so lucky."

"And you're living proof you *can't* have both."

After gazing at me a few moments, he pulls back the bolt and lets his hand drop from the door. I yank it open and stride through, letting it slam shut behind me. Taking off at a run, I feel my lungs burn and the hot air tickle my face. I run down to the river, then back up to the Phoenix headquarters. By the time I walk through the door, I am composed again. The hard, fearless leader they need me to be.

26

Trey

I sink to the ground beside a low wall, my legs suddenly unable to hold my weight.

"Trey, are you there?"

Dexter's words bounce around inside my head, as if my brain's unwilling to hold onto them and compute what they mean.

The government can't have taken Ella. There has to be another explanation for this.

But what if they have?

"I'm here," I croak out. "What did she tell you?"

"Just that she had some new information we had to act on and she'd be over soon. But that was *three hours* ago."

The initial shock I'd felt dissipates, the fog in my brain clearing, leaving behind cold, hard reality. Ella is missing.

"Have you spoken to Anabel?"

"Your other sister? I don't have her number."

"Let me see if she knows anything. I'll get back to you."

I end the call and tell my comm device to call Anabel.

The heat of the late afternoon sun burns my skin. I force myself to stand, aware that I'm getting some odd looks from passersby.

Drawing attention to myself is the last thing I need right now.

"Trey?" Anabel sounds surprised. I guess it is the first time I've ever called her.

I get straight to the point. "Is Ella with you?"

"No. She left the house a few hours ago, leaving me to deal with all this junk." There's a scuffling noise in the background. "Can you believe Mother had three identical black diamante handbags? And she kept them *all*."

"Did she say where she was going?"

There's a pause. "I assumed she was going to her boyfriend's. She left in a hurry. Is everything all right?"

"I don't know." I take a deep breath. "She was going to Dexter's, but she never made it."

"What do you mean?" Anabel's voice is sharp.

I recount what Dexter told me. "Did she say anything else? Maybe that she needed to stop somewhere on the way?"

"We looked through the information. She seemed flustered about something. Had that bright, over-eager look she gets when she's hatching some plan. Then she grabbed the chip, said she had to show it to someone and ran out."

"And you didn't follow her?"

"I'm not her mother, Trey." She sounds exasperated. And worried. "Where do you think she went?"

"I don't know. But if they find that chip on her …" I can't continue. Voicing the words aloud will somehow make them seem more real. I massage my temples, wondering what to do. My heart tugs me Inside, insisting I have to search for Ella and make sure she's safe. But my head tells me it's more important that I find Samson. That time is running out.

Why does everything have to be so complicated?

"Look. There's not much you can do," Anabel says, as if she can read my mind. "Tell Dexter to call me. He'll be the one most likely to know who else she might have gone to see. If we still can't find her, I should be able to get into the city camera system at government headquarters and search for her that way."

Relief floods through me. "Thanks, Anabel." Then a thought occurs. "By the way, do you know what happened to the Brotherhood's leader, Samson, when the government headquarters was taken?"

"Why do you ask?"

I hesitate. "Someone was asking after him."

There's a pause. "I'm afraid he's dead."

My heart skips a beat. "But I don't think they found a body. Could he possibly have been injured but escaped?"

"Not from what Liza said. She was part of his team when they took the control room. They were ambushed by a group of palace guards and had to fight for their lives. Samson tried to draw them off, but he got shot in the chest."

"And they left him?"

Anabel sighs. "They were in a firefight, Trey. They had to prioritize the mission. That was Samson's order. I'm sorry."

I blow out a breath. "Okay. Thanks. You'll let me know if you hear from Ella?"

"Of course."

I cut the connection, send a message to Dexter with Anabel's comm code and stare down the street, a sense of foreboding washing over me. I wish I could split myself in two so part of me could run off to find and Ella and the other part Samson. But I can't. I just have to do what I can and trust others to do their part.

* * * *

"You know, a building plan would be really useful," Aleesha says for the fifth time.

"Barnes made me promise not to tell the Chain," I reply – again.

"Yeah, but asking Bryn for the plan isn't exactly telling them you're looking for Samson." Aleesha shines her flashlight down a rough, narrow tunnel with steps leading up. "Have we searched this already?"

I slump against the wall, about ready to admit defeat. "Maybe … I don't know."

To say things are awkward between us is an understatement. Having to walk up to Phoenix headquarters and beg an audience with her was bad enough, not to mention the stares and snickers of her gang as I walked in, but the fact she hasn't even mentioned our conversation the other day, hasn't even *acknowledged* we've gone from being in a relationship to nothing, hurts. It feels like we're back to getting to know each other. She is cold, aloof and one hundred percent focused on the mission.

We've been down here for hours and haven't found any trace of Samson. It feels like we've searched an area the size of London itself, but it's easy to get lost in the warren of passageways and rooms under the government headquarters. Without Aleesha's sense of direction, I'm not sure I'd ever find my way out.

I peer up the passageway. "Let's see where the stairs take us. If we don't find anything, we'll call it a day. Perhaps the Chain disposed of his body without telling Barnes or Petal."

We walk up the stairs and down another corridor, which divides into two.

"We've definitely been down that one," I say, shining my flashlight right. "I recognize that chip in the wall. Come on. Let's get out of here."

I start back down the corridor, suddenly impatient. I haven't heard anything from Anabel – being underground probably blocks the signal to my comm band – and my worry for Ella has overtaken my concern about Samson.

"Trey, wait."

The catch in Aleesha's voice stops me. She's kneeling at the divide in the passageway. I walk back to her and peer at the floor. "What is it?"

It's only when she points to the centre of the circle of light that I see it. "Blood."

I swing my light down the left passageway.

"There's another spot." She points to a faint, dark smear on the wall, her voice rising with excitement. "How did we miss this?"

Because it's barely visible.

"We can't have searched here. Look. There are footprints in the dust. It's hard to see them, but if you shine your light just so …" She demonstrates, running her finger across the floor so dust sparkles in the light. "I'm pretty sure these are recent."

We follow the passageway down into another basement room. It's empty, with a single corridor leading off from the far corner. I'm certain we haven't been in here before. In one corner, there's a dark stain on the floor, but there's no other sign that anyone has been here.

I pan my light around the room, searching for clues, as Aleesha heads off down one of the corridors.

After a few minutes, I hear her voice echo back to me.

"Trey, give me a hand."

Aleesha's light bobs further down the tunnel as I rush to her. There's the sound of metal scraping against brick.

"There's dried blood on this," she pants as she tries to haul the grate away from the wall.

"You think Samson could get through that?" I eye the opening dubiously. It's large enough for Aleesha or me to crawl through, but

Samson?

"If he were desperate. Are you going to help or what?"

I curl my fingers over the edge of the grate, and together, we pull it off the wall. It lands on the floor with a clatter. I shine my flashlight into the opening, my nose wrinkling as an unsavoury smell wafts out.

The low tunnel isn't quite big enough to crawl properly, so I lie on my belly and slither. From the smear marks I can see, it looks like someone else has been along here recently. Someone who was bleeding … a lot.

Not for the first time, I wonder if we're looking for an injured man or a body.

We emerge into another tunnel, this one tall enough to stand up in, though nothing like the size of the underground train tunnels. Patterned brickwork curves overhead, and there's a damp, fetid smell.

"Do you think there are rats down here?" Aleesha's voice wobbles and her face looks paler than usual, though that could just be the glow of the flashlight. She glances around nervously.

I find another patch of blood on the floor. "This way."

I cast my light ahead and freeze, seeing a dark mound a short distance down the tunnel. I begin to walk toward it, then break into a run as the mound resolves itself into legs, feet, a torso.

"Samson?"

There's no answer. He lies still, face down, arm outstretched, as if he stopped mid-crawl, too exhausted to continue. I reach out, but the thought of touching a dead body makes me hesitate. Aleesha has no such compunctions.

"Samson?" She drops to her knees and grabs his shoulder, trying to heave him over, but the giant man is a dead weight. "Give me a hand, Trey."

"Are you sure we should move him? His back might be injured or something."

She gives me an exasperated look. "Or he might be dead. Let's find that out first, shall we?"

Together, we roll the big man onto his back. His arm slaps the ground like a piece of meat on a butcher's slab. His eyes are closed, his skin covered in dust.

I swallow and gingerly press my fingers into his neck, feeling for a pulse.

"Is he dead?"

I push my fingers in harder. "I think—"

Was that a flicker of something underneath my fingers? A spasm? Or did I imagine it? The man's neck is so damn thick it's hard to know where to feel. I lean closer. A hand whistles past my face. There's a slap as Aleesha's palm connects with Samson's cheek.

I pull back, glaring at her. "What was that for?"

She shrugs. "Seeing if he responds to pain. Sometimes people do if they've been out a while."

"I'm not sure—"

A faint moan interrupts me. Samson's eyelids flutter briefly, his head lolling to the side.

"See!" she says triumphantly. She bends over him. "Samson, time to wake up! Rescue party's arrived."

I shine my flashlight into his eyes, but when his face scrunches up, she pushes it away. "Don't blind the man."

Samson's lips part, the tip of his tongue flicking out. "Water," he rasps.

Aleesha swings the backpack off her shoulder and pulls out a water bottle. I'm grateful for her forethought. I hadn't stopped to take anything with me when I'd left. A mistake my stomach has been reminding me of for the past two hours. She slowly dribbles a little water onto his cracked, swollen lips.

"More ..."

She increases the flow until he coughs and splutters. "You're supposed to swallow it, not choke on it, you idiot." She chews on her lip as Samson's eyelids flutter again, then finally open.

"Where are you injured?" I shine my light down his body. His black clothing is so covered in dust and dirt it's impossible to tell where he's wounded.

"Everywhere?" He gives what I think is an attempt at a laugh, which comes out more like a rasping cough, and closes his eyes again. When he opens them, they lock on Aleesha. "Don't ... trust ... him." His chest heaves, and his face spasms in pain.

Our eyes meet, and I frown. *Does he mean me?*

"Trey, we need to get help. If we can bring Mika down here, she'll have some drugs she can treat him with."

A hand grips my arm with surprising strength. "Not ... them."

I glance at Aleesha. "I don't think he wants the Chain involved."

"But he's half-dead! I'm not even sure Abby can do anything for him—"

"Amber," Samson interrupts. "Get Amber, Petal ... Rae ..." His head lolls to the side as he passes out again.

Aleesha peers down the tunnel before shucking off her light jacket, folding it and gently placing it under his head. She shoves the backpack at me. "There are some first aid supplies in there. See what you can do for him. I'm going to get help."

I look down at the hulk of a man in front of me. Nausea twists my gut, and I have to close my eyes. The fetid air in the tunnel doesn't help. "Are you sure you don't want me to go for help? You're much better with this stuff than me."

"I doubt you'd be able to find Petal. Besides, how long do you think you'll spend lost in these tunnels before you find the way out?"

She has a point. But the sharpness in her words hurts.

Will I ever be good enough to keep up with her?

Aleesha reaches out to squeeze my arm, her face softening. "You'll be fine, Trey. Just do what you can." She glances over her shoulder. "This tunnel's going in the right direction, and I reckon it should link into the larger ones at some point." She stands and starts walking.

"Be careful!" I call after her. But the only answer I get is the bobbing of her light in the blackness.

I shiver as a chill runs down my back. I hate being underground. It's cold, damp and unnerving.

I bet Aleesha was right about the rats.

As if on cue, a scratching sound comes from further down the tunnel. I jerk my light around and catch a flicker of movement. The beam of light trembles slightly.

I dim the light to its lowest setting to conserve power, then rummage around in Aleesha's backpack. Am I supposed to keep him awake or is it better to let him rest?

Aleesha's first aid supplies are minimal. A couple of folded bandages, sealed dressings and a half-empty pack of anti-infection pills. There's also a knife, a small blanket and a couple of protein bars. Figuring I may be here a while, I rip one open and bite into it.

Taking a deep breath, I get to work, using the knife to cut Samson's clothing. It feels wrong to be stripping a man, but there's no other way I can figure out where he's injured. My hands tremble as I do my best to clean his wounds.

There are many.

Some are shallow scratches, others are deep and weeping blood. When I touch his right side, he lets out a painful moan. But the wounds that most worry me are two small bullet wounds – one on his shoulder, the other on the side of his chest.

I can't move him by myself, so I don't know if the bullets are still lodged in him, but the flesh around the wounds is hot and swollen, puss mingling with the blood leaking out.

At one point, I stumble down the tunnel to vomit.

Hurry up, Aleesha.

I use up all the dressings and bandages and most of the bottle of water cleaning his wounds, then cover him with the blanket. Figuring he must be dehydrated, I try to get him to drink some of the remaining water, but he struggles to stay conscious long enough to swallow. He seems almost feverish, muttering words I can't make out. A couple of times, I pick out Barnes's name.

"Rae's fine, Samson," I say, gently squeezing his arm.

This seems to get through to him. His eyelids flutter open and his eyes find mine. "She's alive?"

"Yes. She's exhausted from looking for you, but she's okay. She's the only one who believed you were still alive. Everyone else thinks you're dead."

The corner of Samson's mouth twitches. "Hard ... to kill."

I smile. "Well, hang in there a bit longer. Help is on the way."

But as he slips back into unconsciousness, I can't help but wonder whether it will get here in time.

27

Aleesha

It must take me about two hours to find a way through the tunnels and out into Area Four. By the time I eventually emerge, my nerves are on edge from the dark, enclosed space and the skittering sound of rats. I swear, there must be enough of them down there to feed the whole city.

I hurry through the darkening streets to the apartment in Area Three that Samson uses as his base. The windows are dark, the door locked. I bang on it. When there's no answer, I return to the main street and throw stones at the windows. A couple of the street hobies peer up at me suspiciously.

"Whaddya want?" a voice calls from the alleyway. A surly looking man, probably in his twenties, leans against the wall with his arms crossed.

I hurry over to him. "Is Petal up there?"

A brief flicker in his eyes tells me he is. I move to push past him, but he sticks out his arm. "An' what d'ya want with Petal?"

"I need to speak to him." I lower my voice. "It's about Samson."

The man hesitates, then pulls back his arm. "You try anythin' funny and they'll be scraping yer skin off the pavement."

I ignore the threat and run up the staircase to the large room on the first floor. The windows are blacked out, the lighting dim. Some people are sprawled out, asleep, but a few sit around the large table, muttering in low voices.

My gaze falls on a man sitting on the far side of the room, his back to me, head in his hands. When the man behind me calls his name, Petal sits up slowly and turns, gaze locking on me. He looks exhausted. More than exhausted. He looks as if he's given up hope.

"What do you want?" he asks flatly, turning back to stare at the wall.

I weave my way through the people and beds toward him. No one bothers to move out my way.

They've already given up.

"We found him," I say in as low a voice as I can manage.

Petal's head jerks around, his thin braid whipping through the air. "What?"

"We found Samson. He's badly injured, though. I don't know how he's lasted this long, but he's alive."

I'm not sure what reaction I expected. Surprise, delight perhaps. What I don't expect is for him to fly out of the chair and grasp me around the throat, throwing me back against the wall.

Petal's face is set in a snarl. "If this is some game yer playin' to get us on yer side …" He grips my jacket and yanks me toward him. His breath stinks. "If yer father sent you to play a trick on us, I—"

I bring my knee up between his legs – hard.

He grunts and doubles over. I shove him backward. "This has nothing to do with him. Samson is lying wounded in a tunnel miles from here, and if you're not going to help him, I'll bloody well find someone who will."

Petal scowls up at me and straightens awkwardly, one hand clamped protectively over his groin. A murmur spreads around the room, and he glances at the faces turned toward us.

"Get back to what you were doin'!" he snarls, then grabs me and pulls me into the smaller room, slamming the door behind us.

"He's definitely alive?" Now that we're alone, the anger falls from his face. His hand twitches nervously. "We searched everywhere."

"He escaped into the tunnels below the building and into some kind of old sewer. It's a miracle we found him."

Petal searches my face, his eyes pleading. "How bad is he?"

"Bad." I swallow. "Honestly, I'm not sure he's going to make it. He's lost a lot of blood. If we can get him to a medic centre—"

Petal shakes his head unhappily. "He can't go to a medic centre." He turns and yanks open the door, barks out an order, then slams it again. "I've sent someone for Amber, the healer."

I bite my lip. Amber may be able to patch people up, but Samson's wounds aren't minor. If he's bleeding inside, I'm not sure there's anything she can do for him.

"I'll get a team together to carry him out."

"It needs to be small. And no one who's chipped. Even in the tunnels, it's not worth the risk they'll be tracked." I grab his arm as he turns to leave. "I'll get a couple of my guys – the ex-Metz officers. They've all had their chips removed, and they're the only ones strong enough to have a chance of carrying him out."

Petal looks reluctant.

"You know how big he is."

He grimaces. "Fine."

As I start to leave, a lithe woman rushes up. She gives me a curious glance before turning to Petal. "Amber says she can't come. She's delivering a baby an' won't be able to leave for a couple of hours."

I exchange a look with Petal. "I'll get Abby."

"Right." His face looks pinched. "Meet at the concrete jungle."

It takes me another hour to get back to Phoenix headquarters, send an excited Tommy to fetch Abby and persuade my leadership team that we should help. Or what's left of my leadership team. Anders and Danny are conspicuous by their absence.

"I don't see why we should put ourselves at risk," Megan pouts. "He was the one who killed Dane. An' he didn't help Jay, did he?"

I bite back my irritation. "No, but if it wasn't for him, we'd have never won the Battle of Rose Square. And without him, his gang will be at a loose end. How long do you think it'll be before they get out of control?"

Even Megan can see the sense in that. "Take Danny with you. He needs somethin' to do."

"Is he still with Anders?"

She nods, worry darkening her eyes. "It doesn't help Anders havin' him frettin' over him."

When I'd asked my father for Mika's help with Anders, he'd told me the medic pod was still needed to heal the prisoners they'd released from the Metz compound. They'd been evacuated to a building the Chain controlled in Area Eight, and Mika had been there ever since. Anders, he said, would have to wait his turn.

Abby had been more help, bringing clean bandages and antibiotics. At first, Anders had seemed okay, but when I returned from the Chain's headquarters and checked on him, I'd found him tossing and turning in bed, mumbling incoherently.

"He's burning up," Abby had said, touching his forehead. "The antibiotics might take a bit to kick in. Sometimes the fever just needs to run its course."

Her words had lacked conviction.

"Fine," I tell Megan. "But you know he won't leave Anders alone."

Megan exchanges a quick look with Rogue. "I'll stay with him until you get back."

"Great. Jax, you're in charge while we're gone. Rogue, get the makeshift stretcher that's in the storeroom. I need you, Leon and two others you trust."

Ten minutes later, we're ready to go. Danny is the last to arrive, the gun the Chain had given him slung over one shoulder. He's a bundle of barely contained energy, his hand twitching on the grip of the weapon.

"Didn't we take that from him?" I whisper to Rogue.

Rogue grins. "Yes. It took him a whole twenty-four hours to figure out where it was hidden."

I roll my eyes and sigh.

As soon as Abby arrives, breathless, we set off for the concrete jungle. Petal and two others are already waiting for us. They're stocky for Outsiders, but next to the ex-Metz officers, they look puny.

Petal inclines his head to Abby, then glances at Danny's gun. "You'd better have a safety on that."

Danny twirls it with a wicked grin. "Don't worry. I know how to use it."

"Ignore him," I mutter to Petal as we pick our way across the rubble to the tunnel entrance.

Part of me is afraid I won't remember the way back, but once we're below ground, it comes back to me. Finally, I see the dim light of Trey's flashlight and hurry forward.

He gets to his feet, his face full of relief. "You took your time."

"Sorry. How is he?"

"Still breathing." Trey glances at Abby, who's already placed her bag on the ground and is kneeling at Samson's head. "I cleaned his wounds as best I could, but I think some of them may be infected." His face pales. "He's got at least two bullets in him."

Abby sucks in a breath. "Has he had any water?"

"A little."

She pulls out a plastic case and shoves it at me. "Bryn gave me one of the medical kits the Chain takes on operations. I haven't even had a chance to look in it yet, but it may have something useful."

She pulls on a pair of transparent gloves and begins to feel around Samson's skull. She pinches his earlobe, and his eyelids flicker.

I open the medical kit. There are a couple of syringes in plastic tubes, gloves, a couple of large dressings and an oddly shaped package labelled with a word I can't read.

"What's this?" Petal grabs one of the syringes, his eyes flicking nervously to Samson.

"I think it's some kind of stimulant," I reply, examining the other one. The syringe is filled with a blue liquid, and there are various symbols on the packaging that I can't make head nor tail of. "It says only a medic should use it."

Abby pulls back the blanket covering Samson's torso and curses. *That doesn't sound good.*

I peer over her shoulder. Samson's chest is a mess. Dark red slashes cut across pale scars, deeper wounds topped by the dressings and bandages Trey has clumsily applied.

Petal moves closer, but the rest of the team hangs back. "Is he goin' to make it?"

Abby's lips are tight as she carefully peers under each of the dressings. "When did he receive these wounds?"

"Thursday night."

"Two days." She rests her hand on Samson's forehead. "He's burning up. These bullet wounds are infected, and it looks like he might have some serious internal bleeding, as well. He might hang on for a few more days …" She chews her lip and glances at me. "If we could get him to that medic pod of Richard's, they've got the best chance of saving him."

"No!"

Abby glances at Petal in surprise.

He looks torn. His gaze snaps to Samson, as if looking for guidance. "It's not what he'd want."

"Does he want to die?" I know Samson might not agree with everything my father does, but he can't do anything about it if he's dead. "Because that might be the alternative."

"Barnes didn't want the Chain involved, either." Trey glances over at me. "Let's just get him out of here first, shall we? If he wakes up, we can ask him what he wants."

Abby straightens. "There's nothing else I can do for him here anyway. Once we get him out, I can clean and look at his wounds properly. Who's got the stretcher?"

Rogue and Leon exchange a look, then Rogue glances at the men behind them.

I groan. "We *did* remember the stretcher, didn't we?"

Rogue looks shamefaced. "Sorry. I thought Leon had it."

"I thought Rogue had it." Leon heaves a sigh. "We could try and lift him by his shoulders."

I think of the miles of tunnels we have to navigate. Without a stretcher, it would take even longer to get Samson out, and carrying him like a sack of potatoes won't do his wounds any good. "Danny, do you remember the way out?"

"Course."

"You're the fastest of us. Take one of the others with you."

"It's all right. I can manage it myself."

I give him an exasperated look. "Two people will be quicker with the stretcher. Go!"

Danny swings the gun over his shoulder and grabs the arm of one of Petal's men. Their footsteps pound as they disappear into the dark.

"Shall we try to carry him?" Rogue looks to Abby for confirmation.

Her brows knit as she sits back on her heels. "I'd rather wait for the stretcher. Has he been conscious at all, Trey?"

"A slap woke him up last time," I volunteer. Abby gives me a look. I shrug. "What? It worked."

"We could try this." Petal holds up the syringe.

"I don't think that's a good idea," Abby begins, but she's too slow to stop him.

Petal plunges the needle into Samson's chest before any of us can react. "Big man can take it." He jerks it out and looks expectantly at his leader's face. "Come on, boss. Time to wake up."

For a moment, nothing happens. Then Samson's eyes fly open and he sucks in a huge breath. His eyeballs roll to the back of his head as he shifts and pushes himself up onto his elbows with a groan.

Petal gives Abby a triumphant look. "See?"

"What in ten hells ... was that?" Samson rasps. His eyes are feral, and when Abby tries to get him to lie back down, he shoves her, sending her sprawling to the ground with a grunt.

"Just a bit of medicine, boss." Even Petal looks slightly unnerved by Samson's wild appearance. "Let's get you on yer feet and out of here."

He bends over and loops his arms under Samson's shoulders. Rogue steps forward and grasps Samson's hands.

"Wait a minute—" Abby begins.

Rogue and Petal heave. Samson's arms bulge with the effort of pulling himself up, but nothing happens.

"You need to help us out and move your legs, big man," Petal says impatiently. "Come on. We ain't got all day."

He doesn't see the look of fear that passes across Samson's face, but Rogue does. He lets Samson's hands fall and looks mutely at Abby.

"What are you doing?" Petal gives him an angry look. "Give me a hand."

"Petal, put him down," Abby says gently. When he doesn't respond, she places a hand on his arm. "You need to put him down."

The expression on Petal's face turns from anger to puzzlement as he does as she asks. "What is it? What's wrong?" He glances down at Samson, whose eyes are closed. "Boss?"

"My legs," he croaks. His eyes flicker open and lock on Abby. It is the first time I have seen fear on Samson's face, and the sight sends an icy chill lancing down my spine. "I can't feel my legs."

* * * *

By the time we emerge from the tunnel, it's the dead of night. Samson has lapsed back into unconsciousness, and we're silent as we slowly make our way down the loose blocks of the concrete jungle.

Petal leads us in a different direction than I'd expected. "Goin' to take him to a different safe house," he says by way of explanation. "Don't want the rest of 'em seein' him like this."

We've just started up one of the main roads in Three when a flash of lightning brightens the sky. There's another, followed by a bang. I look up and frown. It can't be a thunderstorm. There's not a cloud in the sky. A moment later, the sky bursts into life, yellow and white lights zipping around accompanied by bursts of staccato sound, like the fireworks display Insiders have at the turn of the year.

"What's that?" Petal asks.

"Guns," Abby says grimly.

There's a deep grumble from some distance away, like a sound a building makes when it comes down. I glance over at Trey. His eyes are wide.

Rogue looks back at me. "Is that the Chain?"

"My father said he had brought in reinforcements." I swallow.

278

"Insiders gettin' a taste of their own medicine for once," Danny mutters.

He's right. The flashes in the sky are on the other side of the Wall. Despite that, the disturbance has woken people. Lights come on in the building next to us, and a door opens further down the street.

"Come on," Abby says briskly.

We take a right off the street. A few minutes later, Petal pushes open the door of a ground-floor apartment. I can almost feel the relief radiating off the men carrying Samson. They're exhausted, and trying to haul him up a couple of flights of stairs may have proven too much.

A man staggers out of a room, rubbing his eyes, as Abby directs the men to place Samson on a large table. Samson's feet hang off the end. "What's goin' on?"

Petal jerks his thumb toward the front door. "Scarper. And keep your mouth shut," he adds as the man's eyes fall on Samson and widen.

Abby is already pulling out pans from a cupboard and filling them with water. She flips the switch on the hotplate and breathes a sigh of relief when a light comes on.

"I need more water and some supplies. Aleesha, can you fetch them from my house?"

I wait until she's given me a list, then tell Rogue I'll meet them back at headquarters and head out. I'm partway up the street when footsteps run up behind me.

"Wait up!"

Trey.

My heart leaps, then sinks.

"Can I walk with you for a bit? I need to get back to the factory," he says, keeping pace. "Barnes will be keen to know Samson's alive."

I nod but don't reply.

"Thanks for coming to help. He'd have died if we hadn't found him."

"Maybe it would have been better if he had."

Trey frowns. "What do you mean?"

I stop and turn to him. "You saw him. How long do you think he'll be able to keep control of the Brotherhood when his legs don't work? That's assuming he survives the next few days. Believe me, a quick, clean death is preferable to slowly dying inside."

Uncertainty flickers across Trey's face. His throat bobs as he swallows. It takes every ounce of self-control I have not to reach out for him. The pull in my chest is so strong it's painful. But I dig my fingernails into my thighs and start walking again.

Breaking up was the right thing to do. The only thing to do.

"Can the Chain defeat the government forces by themselves?" Trey hurries after me. "They're bringing in reinforcements from across the country, you know."

"The government?"

"Yes. Emilie said they're bringing them in on the freight trains."

"Emilie?"

"My assistant."

Oh, right.

Anger flares in my belly. So much for feeling bad for him. "I'm sure my father has it under control," I say tightly.

We continue to walk, in silence, up the street.

"Are you sure they're doing the right thing?" he asks eventually. "I mean, I know the government is bad, but what if they're worse?"

"I don't think that's possible."

When he doesn't reply, I stop and turn to him. "What are you saying? You want to support the government now?"

Trey looks down at the ground. "No. At least not exactly."

"Not exactly?" I don't know why I'm so irritated. Perhaps it's

Trey's words. Or perhaps it's because I have to fight from reaching out to touch him. Being this close weakens my resolve.

Perhaps just one more time ...

My hand stretches out for him. I snap it back to my side. Trey doesn't seem to notice.

"I just don't want more people to die." His gaze flickers west. The aerial fighting has stopped, the night quiet again.

"You don't want *Insiders* to die, you mean."

"I don't want *anyone* to die, Aleesha." He looks miserable. "Maybe if they just talk about things with the President, there can be some compromise ..."

"Yeah, well, I talked to the President, and I'm pretty sure compromise is a word he doesn't understand." I wince inwardly as hurt flashes across Trey's face.

I take a step back as he reaches for me. "Look, I've got to run. Take care of yourself, okay? Stay away from the fighting."

I feel his gaze on my back as I hurry up the street. The further I walk from him, the easier it is to forget what it feels like to have him near.

But part of me wishes he was just that boy on the run again – lonely, lost and looking for someone to love – and I was just that girl – no home, nobody else to worry about.

28

Trey

I'm woken by the sound of raised voices outside my door. Light streams in through the open curtains, but it still takes me a moment to remember where I am. By the time I'm fully conscious, the voices fade down the corridor.

I sit bolt upright. *Was that Ella?*

I scramble out of bed, almost falling when the sheets get tangled around my legs, and rush to the door, yanking it open. The corridor is empty, but there are sounds of people moving around and the clinking of plates and cutlery from downstairs.

I run down the stairs and into the dining room to find Ella, Dexter and Anabel sitting at the table. Part of the weight in my chest lifts at the sight of my sister.

"When did you get back? Where have you been?"

"An excellent question," Anabel snaps. I match the scowl on her face and the tight set of Ella's lips to the voices I'd heard outside my room.

"Last night," Ella says, chewing her bacon with unnecessary force. "And I said I'd explain when Trey got up, Anabel."

Her face softens and she offers me a smile. "Where have *you* been?

282

You look as if you've been dragged up out of a mine."

I glance down at my dusty clothes, stained with blood, dirt and goodness knows what else, and feel a pang of guilt as I think of the crisp, white sheets I'd collapsed onto last night. I open my mouth, glance at Anabel, then close it again.

My older sister raises an eyebrow. "Don't want to tell me, huh? What's so secret?"

"It's nothing. I mean, it's complicated." My tongue feels tied in knots. A sour taste coats my mouth. "Let me go change. Then we can talk."

Ten minutes later, with clean clothes and brushed teeth, I feel a bit more human. There were three messages from Phillips and one from Emilie on my comm band asking me where I was. But I figure half an hour won't get me in any more trouble than I'm already in, and if they *are* rationing food in the factory, I might as well have a good meal now.

The coffee pot has been refilled in my absence, and I pour a mug, adding milk and sugar, then sit down. "Right then. Where have you been Ella? You had us all worried."

"Sorry." She looks guiltily at Dexter, then me. "I just wanted to follow-up on a hunch. I wasn't sure it would amount to anything, which was why I didn't tell you."

"Does this have to do with what was on the files? You do still have the microchip, right?"

Ella holds it up, then sends it skidding across the table toward me. I stop it before it flies off the edge and shove it into a pocket. "I went to speak to a friend of ours – Barney. He's an engineer at Hendricks' food factory. I figured if this was being added into the lower-grade production lines at Coleman's, the same would be true for Hendricks. Barney worked for Coleman before Hendricks poached him, and he says the factory lines are pretty much identical."

My heart leaps. "Does he know a way we can remove it from the system?"

Ella breaks into a smile. "Yes. It took us all afternoon to figure out the details, but he's come up with a plan that he thinks should work. And if it works for one factory, it should work for the other. Fooling quality control is the easy part. The final part of production before packaging is the quality check, right?"

I nod in confirmation, beginning to understand where this is going.

"Barney loaded a programme onto your chip. If you insert it into the control panel for that section of the line, it should override the code that tells the machine to check for the androcibus nanite. Even if the food going through doesn't have any trace of the drug in it, it tells quality control it does. You'll have to plug it into each of the production lines, but Barney said there are software updates all the time and the foremen don't tend to bat an eyelid."

I try to contain the excitement building inside me. "So the code will make quality control believe the products contain the drug. But how does he suggest removing the drug from the production line altogether?"

Ella makes a face. "That's the hard part. He said you could override the code to prevent the drug from being added, but it'll look suspicious if you're not loading new vials into the machine. The solution we came up with was to intercept the deliveries of androcibus nanite and replace them with identical vials containing a placebo. Barney is friends with the procurement manager at Hendricks' factory, so he thinks he might be able to do something there, but we don't have anyone at Coleman's …" She looks at me expectantly.

"Apart from me." My mind races. I don't know the procurement manager at Coleman's, but I have a feeling Louis will.

"Barney smuggled out one of the vials," Ella continues. "It'll take a couple of weeks, but we're pretty sure we can replicate them so they'll look identical to the vials you get from the labs."

"You know that once Richard's in charge this won't be an issue, right?" Anabel yawns. "He can just order it to be removed from the system."

"Perhaps. But what if he doesn't win?"

Anabel narrows her eyes at me. "Why so little faith? So far, everything has gone according to plan."

I swallow down my irritation. "Nothing wrong with having a backup plan."

She opens her mouth to reply, but a buzz from her comm band stops her. She glances down, frowns, then stands. "Got to run." She glances across the table at Ella. "Please stay out of trouble. Sounds like I'm going to be busy for the next few days."

Ella rolls her eyes at the closing door.

"She was worried about you." I grab a piece of toast and carve a generous lump of butter off the block. "We all were. Why didn't you reply to our messages?"

"I got pretty caught up in what I was discussing with Barney. Then I had a bit of a run-in with the Metz on my way over to Dexter's." She glances guiltily at her boyfriend.

His face is dark. Clearly, Anabel's not the only one Ella's been arguing with.

"What kind of run-in?"

She stares down at the table. "They stopped me. Wanted to know what I knew about Project Griffin."

I freeze.

"It's fine," Ella adds quickly. "I told them I didn't know anything and that my comm band had been taken from me." She glances up and adds, almost defensively, "It's not a lie. And they seemed to believe it."

"But they'll be watching you," Dexter says in a low voice. "You need to take a step back." He gives me a pleading look.

"I agree." I put the knife down. "If Anabel's right, the Chain will have control of the city in the next few days. If something goes wrong, we'll take a closer look at Barney's plan. It's not as if we can change anything overnight. Will you go out to the house in Wales? Please? Just for a few days."

Ella rolls her eyes. "And that won't look suspicious? Besides, I can't just take off from work with no notice. I'll be fine, Trey. *You're* the one I'm worried about. What if Coleman figures out you've been poking around in his files?"

"He won't. But I'll lay low for a few days, too. Wait and see what happens." Even as the words leave my lips, I feel a pang of guilt.

I should be out there with Bryn, fighting for the future of our city, not hiding away in luxury.

I put down my half-eaten toast. "I'd better be going."

I leave Ella and Dexter talking quietly in the dining room. As I pass the large, gilt-framed mirror in the hallway, I pause. The boy looking back at me appears to have aged five years. Purple shadows hang under eyes that don't quite mask what I feel inside. The constant fear that never quite goes away. Fear that someone else I love will die. Fear of getting caught by Coleman again. Fear I'm not doing the right thing. Fear that my action, or inaction, will harm others. I wish I could gaze into the future and see how all of this will end.

Most of all, I wish someone would tell me what I should do.

I suck in a deep breath, then let it whistle through my teeth. "You've got to make your own decisions now," I tell the boy in the mirror. My hand strays to my chest.

You know what is right ... in here. Trust yourself, Trey, and you will do the right thing.

I close my eyes and let my mother's words calm me.

Trust. That's all this comes down to. And there is one group of people whose trust I've betrayed. But I can do something about that right now.

I turn away from the mirror and stride down the hallway to the kitchen. The sound of chatter and clattering plates comes from within. Taking a deep breath, I push open the door.

The atmosphere immediately chills. The bustling noise descends into silence as they catch sight of me. Derek moves from the cleaner unit, where he's been stacking dishes, to stand next to his wife, and Dana slowly rises from the small table at the far side of the room.

Thomas walks over to me, blocking the others from sight. "Can I help you, Master Trey?"

"I-I'd like to apologize." I step forward. After a second, Thomas steps aside. "Please, sit down. I didn't mean to interrupt."

Derek and Lydia exchange a look. Dana glances at Thomas.

They don't trust me. And who can blame them?

"I appreciate the past few weeks have been a bit of an upheaval for you. I wanted to explain what's been happening and offer you a choice. Can ..." I gesture to the table. "Do you mind if I sit down?"

Dana sits and nudges a chair in my direction. Derek and Lydia take the chairs opposite. Despite their obvious reluctance, I sit, leaving Thomas standing. But my attempt to make them more comfortable seems to have the opposite effect. I can almost sense them having to force themselves not to lean away from me. I take a deep breath.

"I'm not sure if you're aware, but Milicent was involved with an organisation called the Chain. They're the people who captured the President. They want to take down the government and replace it with one that treats all citizens, Insiders and Outsiders, equally."

Lydia's arm twitches nervously. My words don't seem to be putting them at ease, but I continue regardless.

"I know you weren't expecting her to leave the house and everything to me. Believe me, no one was more shocked than I was. And I know I haven't been very … present over the past weeks." I smile weakly. "To be honest, most of the time, I don't know what I'm supposed to be doing. Three months ago, I was just a normal kid. Now I have this job I don't really know how to do, a house I don't know how to run and some uncomfortable truths I'm not sure how to deal with. I watched my father get executed, watched my girl—" I swallow, "my best friend nearly get executed, then lost my mother. I …" My voice cracks as emotion rises in my throat.

Both my parents – gone.

Strangely, that deep pain is more of a dull ache, masked by the sharper pain of Aleesha's disinterest. I'd hoped searching for Samson would bring us closer together, perhaps make her rethink things a bit, but she seems further away from me than ever.

I stare down at the table for a moment, unable to speak. Something brushes my hand and I glance up into Dana's eyes. She pushes a handkerchief in my direction, then looks away.

"Thank you. I just wanted to apologize to you all. I know Milicent's death must have been a huge shock to you, and my actions haven't helped reassure you. In fact, they may even have put you all in danger." I glance up at Thomas. His face is unreadable. "That wasn't my intention, and I don't want to put you at any more risk than you already are. I believe things in this city need to change. The government – not just this government, but previous ones – have done things I believe to be unforgivable. I couldn't live with myself if I stayed silent and did nothing to help, but I don't want anyone else to suffer for my actions. I don't want *you* to suffer for my actions."

I have their attention now. "I know this is your home. I'm not asking you to leave, but I am giving you a choice. If you stay here, I will do my best to protect you, but I can't guarantee you won't be in danger. Or you are free to leave, and I'll give you whatever money you need to set yourselves up in the life you choose." I look around at them. "It's your choice. You have no obligation to me. You owe me nothing. I just want you to feel safe and happy."

There's a pause as they all stare at me, then glance at each other. I push back my chair and stand.

"Think about it."

"Trey?"

Thomas's voice stops me at the door. I turn back to look at him.

"Thank you."

I duck my head and walk out, wondering if I've actually helped anything at all.

* * * *

Emilie calls me as I approach the factory. She sounds irritated. "Where are you? Phillips has been spitting feathers since yesterday evening. He's convinced you've run off."

I grimace. Phillips isn't the most patient of men, and I didn't mean for Emilie to bear the brunt of his anger at my absence.

"I'm two minutes away. All the pods are grounded, so I've had to walk."

"Great. The west entrance is closed off, though. You'll have to go around to the east." She reels off a set of directions. "I'll let the guards know you're coming."

"Thanks. Is Louis around?"

"I think so. He sent you a message an hour ago. Haven't you read it?"

"Not yet. I'll see you in a few minutes." I end the call and bring up Louis' message. It's just four words.

We need to talk.

I frown, wondering if this is good news or bad. Either he's been doing his own thinking on how we can remove the androcibus nanite from the system or he's getting cold feet.

When I find the entrance – an unassuming hangar door – I'm kept waiting in a high-ceilinged lobby while my identity is verified multiple times. Finally, I'm allowed to proceed to the elevator, which takes me down to a long, rough passageway with flickering white lights. The east entrance is identical to the west, the route I've been using to get into and out of the factory since the lockdown, and the route the Outsiders take into the East Wing every day. It's a far cry from the rooftop gardens and glass elevators Insiders use.

I bring up the building plan loaded onto my comm, manipulating the holo image in the air as I walk. The most direct way to my office takes me past the huge canteen I'd visited once before, but a slight diversion would take me in a more roundabout route that would bring me out close to Louis' office.

Most of the doors on this side of the factory are unlocked, and my Coleman Corporation chip lets me through the few with access panels. I know somewhere deep in the building, a machine tracks my movements, spitting out alerts, but I doubt I'll trigger any alarms. There's a tense, frantic atmosphere in the factory, and the strain of having to keep all production lines running and keeping the factory workers inside means the small security team has bigger things to worry about than the route I take to my office.

When I reach the door to Louis' office, I pause, my finger hovering over the buzzer. Perhaps I should report to Phillips first. But some sixth sense tells me that what Louis has to say is important.

I press the buzzer. A moment passes, then the door swishes open and I step inside.

The outer office where Elaine sits is empty, but the door to Louis' office is ajar. Odd. Doors are either open or closed. Perhaps the mechanism has jammed.

I take a step closer. "Louis?"

"Come in!" His voice sounds slightly strangled.

As I push the door aside and step into the room, there's a flash of movement. My eyes fall on the desk and empty chair. I frown. Turning, I come face to face with Coleman.

"Goldsmith. Good to have you back in the factory." His face is expressionless, but his dark eyes are hard, and he doesn't sound very pleased to see me.

I swallow. "I—"

I sense movement behind me a second before my arms are yanked back, cold metal closing around my wrists.

Nausea swirls in my gut. *So this is it. They found me out.*

"You think you can mess with my factory? That I wouldn't notice? I gave you a second chance, for your mother's sake, and this is how you repay it? *This* is how you honour her memory?"

I look down at the floor, unable to meet his eyes. Shame curdles my stomach. Bile rises in my throat and my knees suddenly feel weak.

Coleman gives a flick of his hand, dismissing me. "Lock him up. I've got enough to deal with at the moment without foolish boys playing games."

As I'm led away, I catch a glimpse of Louis lurking in the far corner of the room. I want to spit into his face, but the guard yanks my arms, causing me to stumble from the room. I curse myself for being so foolish as to trust him. He'd even warned me, hadn't he? But I had pushed him too far. Believed he would stand up to his father and risk everything just because *I* would risk everything.

Not all Insiders are like you.

Aleesha was right. Bryn was right. Trust is dangerous.

Trust can get you killed.

29

Aleesha

Anders' face is ghostly white, highlighting the dark circles ringing his eyes, and his brow glistens with sweat. He lies still, not tossing and turning as he has for the past twenty-four hours. I'm not sure if that's a good or bad sign. Beside me, Danny fidgets anxiously as Abby places a hand on Anders' forehead. The frown on her face relaxes slightly.

"I think the fever has broken," she says with a smile.

"So he's gonna be okay?"

Abby pulls back the blanket covering Anders' shoulder. "Help me roll him over."

I step forward, but Danny pushes me roughly to one side. I bite back the admonishment that springs to my lips. Danny's hands shake as he helps Abby roll him to his side. He's barely slept or eaten since we brought Anders back from the concrete jungle. Apart from helping us bring Samson out of the tunnels, he's kept an almost constant vigil at his friend's bedside.

"Hmm," is Abby's only comment when she pulls back the dressing covering the knife wound. She purses her lips.

"What does that mean?" Danny's voice carries more than a trace of panic. I shoot him a warning look, but he ignores me. "He's goin' to be okay, right?"

The desperation in his voice tugs at something deep inside me, and I have to bite my lip to keep tears from springing to my eyes.

We can't lose him. Not now.

Abby lowers Anders carefully onto his back, then turns to us. "The good news is, the antibiotics have helped. He's sleeping now, which is good. When he wakes, he should feel better. Try to get him to drink some soup made with the best ingredients you've got. Meat. Vegetables, if you've any left."

"Soup. Right." Danny twists his hands in front of him.

"Can you go and get me some hot water please, Danny?"

He rushes from the room.

"What's the bad news?" I ask as the door swings shut behind him.

"I think there may still be some infection inside the wound. The antibiotics I have can only do so much. Hopefully his body can fight it off ..."

I swallow. "What about that stuff you use to draw out infection?"

"I'll make up another poultice for you, but I'm not sure it can reach deep enough into the wound." Abby glances at me. "Mika may have something stronger. Herbal remedies can only do so much."

I look down at the pale face of my kind, generous friend, and my throat constricts. *Why Anders? He is the best of all of us.*

"If we can't get anything else, what are his odds?"

"Hard to say." Abby doesn't meet my eye. "He's strong. That goes in his favour."

Her words are an echo of what she'd said earlier this morning when we'd finally left the small apartment where Samson is resting. Petal had banished me from the room while they stripped him, then cleaned and dressed his wounds, but I'd waited outside for Abby. The sky had begun to lighten by the time we'd finally made it back to headquarters.

The door slams open and Danny rushes in, a bowl of water sloshing in his hands. Panting, he holds it out to Abby. "Here you go."

She manages a warm smile. "Thank you."

I push past Danny and leave the room. Even if I have to knock Mika out and carry her here myself, she *will* come. My father can't deny me this.

I will not let my friend die.

* * * *

The Chain's headquarters is surprisingly busy. There's a tension in the air as I press myself against the wall of the narrow hall to let two men hurry past carrying a large box between them. More people follow. No one questions my presence as I weave through them, searching for a familiar face.

In the kitchen, I find the female guard from the other day arguing with a tall man. When I ask if Mika's around, she gestures toward the basement with barely a glance in my direction.

Mika is busy sorting through crates and doesn't hear me approach until I'm standing in front of her.

She glances up. "Hi, Aleesha." Mika stands and stretches her back. "How are you?"

"What's going on?" I wave my hand vaguely to indicate the activity going on above us.

Her face pinches. "Didn't you hear? The President escaped."

My heart lurches. "What? When?" My gaze strays to the far end of the room and the door that stands open and unguarded.

"Last night. The government brought in an army. We lost the government headquarters, and Richard barely managed to hold the Metz compound. But all of that was just a distraction to draw us away from here." She stifles a yawn and brushes back a strand of dark hair.

"Is my— Richard okay? Bryn?"

She nods. "They're up in the conference room deciding what to do next. Did you come here for a reason or just to help out?"

I look around at the packages of medical supplies, then at Mika's tired, drawn face, and my heart sinks. But I ask anyway. "I was hoping you might be able to help me. One of my men got attacked yesterday and the wound's infected. If we could just use the medic pod for five minutes ..."

"Sorry, Aleesha, but I've already sent the pod to the Metz compound. Richard ordered me to prioritize the combatants, and he's right. I need to get them back on their feet or we won't have a chance." She gives me a sympathetic look. "I want to save everyone, but I only have the one pod and am nearly out of supplies for that."

"What about the reinforcements my father ordered? Did they not bring more medic pods?"

"Only what was in the main ship, and that isn't exactly mobile." Mika lifts a crate and dumps it onto the floor, then opens the box underneath and pulls out a plastic package about a foot square. She hands it to me and begins to rummage through another crate. "That's the best I can give you. It hasn't been field-tested yet, but it's designed to draw out infections and promote rapid healing. Similar to what a pod can do but in field conditions." She straightens and hands me a pair of syringes. "General antibiotics. Between those and the pad, he should be okay, as long as none of the internal organs are affected."

I swing the small backpack I'd brought with me off my shoulder and take the syringes from her. "Any chance I could have a few more of the pads and syringes? Just in case."

Mika tightens her lips, then reaches back into the crates, handing me a pack of syringes and three more wound pads. "Please, don't tell Richard. I'm not supposed to give out supplies."

I fill my backpack and tie it tight. "Thanks, Mika. I won't."

I leave the room and make my way through the hall and up the stairs of the townhouse. Raised voices draw me toward what must be the conference room. Two men stand outside the door. One of them moves to block my path.

"Sorry, miss. You can't go in."

"Fine." I lean back against the wall to wait, crossing my arms. The guards exchange a look, but neither attempts to move me on.

I strain my ears to pick up what's going on inside. It seems to be a heated argument, but they're talking over each other, so I can barely make out one word in ten. My father's calm voice rises over the hubbub.

"We're not making any progress here. We need more information. Let's see what we can find out in the next twenty-four hours, then we'll meet back here tomorrow."

The guards step aside as the door opens and people filter out. Bryn catches sight of me and frowns, walking over. I don't think I've ever seen him look so exhausted.

"Is everything okay, Aleesha?"

I nod. "Just wanted to speak to Richard. Mika told me what happened. How did he escape?"

Bryn sighs. "They attacked the government headquarters and the compound simultaneously. We left Tomas and five guards here but pulled everyone else away to help with the fighting. They blew a hole right into the back of the basement, where the ground's lower."

"Were ... Were the guards killed?"

Bryn rubs his jaw. His stubble is getting longer. "Yes. All of them. They were good men and women. I'd worked with Tomas for many years." His expression tightens and he pats my shoulder. "Go on in now. He should be free." He walks off down the corridor.

The door to the meeting room is slightly ajar, and I pause outside at the sound of a heated conversation from within.

"This vendetta has got to stop, Richard." Katya's voice is sharp, very different from her usual purr. "You may fool the others into thinking you're just concerned about London, but not me. We can't risk everything for one man. We have to concentrate on the bigger picture."

"He *is* part of the bigger picture," my father says in a low growl. "If we can make him surrender, then we can limit the fighting. We're never going to be able to overpower them through sheer force. You know that."

My blood runs cold at his words.

"We can't sacrifice all our people just to root him out again. Let me infiltrate their command. I can—"

"Sleep with them all?"

The sound of a slap causes me to jerk back, my heart pounding. *Did she just hit him?*

"Careful, Katya."

"That was uncalled for after what I've done to get us this far." There's a pause. When she continues, her voice is more like the calm, persuasive tone I'm used to hearing. "All I'm saying is that you need to put *your* emotions to one side. Let someone else take command."

"Not going to happen. Besides, we don't have time for you to infiltrate them. Now that we know about the nanobots, we can use that against them."

"You can't threaten something and not go through with it."

"Who says I won't go through with it?"

There's a pause. When Katya speaks, her voice carries a slight tremor. "You can't be serious, Richard. "It could kill—"

Footsteps sound behind me. I glance over my shoulder to see two men approaching up the staircase.

297

Best not get caught snooping.

I knock on the door and push it open. The room is small and filled by the chairs clustered around a wide table. At the far end, my father stands with Katya. For once, she doesn't look the picture of perfection. Her blonde hair is dulled and matted, hastily drawn into a knot at the nape of her neck. Her black combat suit is torn, the skin underneath bloody. She grips my father's arm, her fingers digging into his skin. He scowls down at her.

They break away as I walk in. Katya shoots my father a dark look. "Think about it, Richard, for all our sakes." She pushes past me and out of the room.

I squeeze around the chairs to approach my father. "Lovers' tiff?"

"Not exactly." He sighs. "What are you doing here?"

I open my mouth to reply, then remember what Mika had said. "I wanted to talk with you more about my mother," I say quickly. "But I realize this is not a good time."

He waves me to a seat. "I have ten minutes." He yawns. "Then I need to get whatever sleep I can."

I run my gaze over him. He looks uninjured. The tight knot in my stomach relaxes a little. "How bad is it?"

"It could be better. Last night was rough, but they've backed off now they've got what they wanted." He grimaces.

"The President."

"And the government headquarters. I anticipated them pulling in reinforcements, but I underestimated how many reserves they would be able to call on. They must have left the other cities almost unguarded." His eyes stray to a set of maps and documents laid out on the table and he frowns.

"Do you have more people who can help?"

"Perhaps. I'll make some calls this afternoon. There are a few favours I can call in." The frown relaxes as he reaches forward to rest a hand on my arm. "Don't worry. We will free London. Whatever it takes, I won't let him win."

I try to smile but can't quite make it work. My stomach churns with indecision. Should I offer to help? But if the Chain's fighters, with their armour, guns and genetic enhancements, can't beat the government army, what chance do my people have? We'd be slaughtered.

But if the Chain loses, how long will we survive? Whatever claims he made about not wanting to kill me, I don't think the President would be happy letting me walk free.

"Now, what did you want to know about Maria?"

I shake myself, tuning back into my father's words. I had used my mother as an excuse to disguise my real reason for coming here – to get help for Anders. But now I'm here with him, just the two of us, perhaps he'll finally answer some of my questions.

I take a deep breath. "Were you there the day she died?"

His smile falters. He searches my face for a moment before answering. "I was in London, yes."

My breath catches. I swallow, my mouth as dry as the baked earth on the street outside. "What happened?" I whisper.

Something flickers in his eyes. "You know what happened. You saw the Metz report."

"That only showed me part of the story. Why didn't you …" I take a deep breath, trying to keep my voice calm. "Was she meeting you that day?"

My father looks down, then reaches out to take my hand. His touch is warm, though it doesn't relieve the tension in my body. "She thought she was," he says quietly. "The President faked a message from me to draw her out. I'd spent three days in London searching for her. The government found out I was in the city and set a trap, using Maria as bait."

"Why didn't you take her with you when you first left London?"

"I tried." He glances up at me. "She refused to come. I spent too many years feeling hurt and bitter over that. Perhaps if I'd swallowed my pride and gone back sooner, well ..."

He gives a short laugh. "All this time, I can't believe I didn't know you existed. But I knew your mother. I know how much she would have loved you. How she would have wanted a better life for you. Even if that meant sacrificing her own."

A flush of heat courses through my body. My chest tightens. "You mean ... She went to Rose Square because of me?" My voice comes out small and weak.

My father doesn't meet my eye. "Maria and I didn't part on the best of terms. But she knew that all children were genetically tested for their parentage and that any child of mine ... Well, you wouldn't have had the life she wanted for you – if you'd have had any life at all. There was no other reason for her to give up her life Inside. From what you've told me, they were closing in on her. She must have thought I offered your best chance of survival. And if I'd known, if I'd found her sooner, I would have found a way to get you both out of London." He hangs his head. "But I was too late."

I remember the final words she'd said to me on the morning she left. *It's all going to be okay. Everything will be okay.*

I've sought to blame other people for her death – Andrew Goldsmith, the Metz, the President, even my father. But if it hadn't been for me, my mother would have never been in that situation in the first place. The weight of this knowledge presses down on my shoulders and squeezes my ribcage against my lungs.

It was all for me.

"I ..." The words catch in my throat, my windpipe constricting as emotion threatens to burst from my chest. "I understand." I pull my hand from his grasp and push back my chair.

"Aleesha, wait!"

But I don't stop, and he doesn't follow as I rush from the room and down the stairs, pushing past people to escape the building.

It was my fault. My fault.

Head down, I plough through the streets, tears blurring my vision. Angrily, I scrub my eyes. *Damn waterworks.*

I duck into a small side alley and lean against the wall, sucking in deep breaths. The summer heat intensifies the smell of decay and rotting trash, which catches at the back of my throat. I need to get myself under control. I can't go back to Phoenix headquarters like this.

Breathe in for four, out for four.

I focus on my breathing, pushing down those two words lingering in my head, storing them in that deep part of my mind that I'd so recently purged. There are still some secrets in there that I've not been able to face yet, so I add this one to them and close the door until a time when I feel strong enough to face them again.

For now, though, I need to get back to Anders.

I walk slowly through the streets, giving myself time to calm down. As I get closer, I sense people watching. I glance around, but the street hobies quickly look away, refusing to meet my gaze. I frown, wondering if they know something I don't. Or perhaps word has spread that Richard Masterton is my father. Would they take his side if the fighting reached Area Four? Would they stand with me, or do they still fear the government too much?

I wonder what the role of the gangs will be in this new city my father's trying to create. If there will even be a place for us at all.

These questions fill my mind as I turn the corner and see the arch of the main entrance to our headquarters. The blue snake still extends along the wall. Jax hasn't had time to replace it with the gold phoenix I requested. I get halfway up the street before I see who is on guard at the gate.

I slip behind the shelter of a nearby trash can, my heart pounding. *How can this be?*

I peer out from behind the bin just in time to see a man come out of the building and walk over to the two guards lounging against the arched gateway. He is not one of my gang, but a man I've faced only once before. I'm not close enough to see his pudgy, acne-scarred cheeks and flat nose, but his size betrays him, as well as the way he moves. He swaggers, like a bully.

He says something to the guards, who wear yellow bandannas around their heads. Their gazes turn in my direction. I pull back, feeling their eyes bore through the bin. My body feels as if it's turned to ice, my brain frozen, unable to comprehend what has happened.

But there is only one explanation.

The Bigland Boys have taken over Phoenix headquarters.

30

Trey

The numbers on the elevator screen whiz past. We stop at -3, and I wonder how far underground the factory extends. I test my cuffs, but there's no give to the metal. Even if I could get loose, there are two guards, both armed, and the chances of me being able to take down even one of them are slim to none. Luck doesn't seem to be on my side lately.

The guards escort me down a short corridor, which divides at the end. I glance to my left, but a shove from behind indicates that we're to go right. I crane my neck to look back, but one of the guards pokes me in the back.

"Keep your eyes forward. Wouldn't want to slip now, would you?"

His tone implies that the slip might not be entirely accidental. Asking him why two armed men guard an inconspicuous metal door in the deep basement of the factory is only likely to get me into more trouble, so I stay silent, even as I mull over the possibilities in my mind. What does Coleman have down here that requires guards?

The corridor opens up into a long, narrow room that smells slightly damp. Identical, transparent cubes sit against the long side of the room, each about two and a half metres by two and a half metres, linked by what seems to be a ventilation tube. There are six in total, all empty apart from one.

Barnes stares out at me from inside the fifth cube, her expression blank. A purple bruise mottles the left side of her face, a cut still oozing blood. My breath hitches.

One of the guards places his palm on the access panel to the final cube. The other uncuffs my hands and pushes me forward. I whirl around as the door swishes shut behind me. The guards' footsteps echo around the chamber as I run my fingers around the edge of the door, searching for an opening, a crack, anything.

"Don't waste your energy."

Shoulders hunched, Barnes sits on a long, white bed that bears a disturbing resemblance to the coffins my mother and Milicent had lain in at the crematorium. Her face and voice are sullen.

"How long have you been here?"

"A day perhaps. They got me to fix the production line, then dragged me down here. Seems they think I'm involved in your fun and games." She gives me a pointed look, but there's no malice in her words.

"I—"

"Careful," she warns, pointing up to the ceiling. "They may be watching, listening. What took you so long to come in?"

I sense the question she wants to ask but can't. Not if Coleman's people are listening.

The layout of my cube is identical to hers. There's no chair, so I perch on the bed, thinking about how best to reply. "For one thing, the pods are down, but I was late leaving home. There was a blackbird in the garden that looked like it had been attacked by a pack of crows. Poor thing was broken. At first, I thought it was dead. But I managed to revive it. I took it in and gave it to the servants to care for. Hopefully it'll get a second chance at life."

Barnes is silent. When I risk a peek over my shoulder, I see her eyes are closed, her lips pressed together. A single tear trickles down her swollen cheek.

I look around the cube, then out at the bare, concrete room. "I don't think they *are* listening," I say. "There's a camera over the entrance, but it looks about twenty years old. What do you think they use these cells for anyway?"

"Rows break out in the canteen sometimes." Barnes shrugs. "Guess they put the perpetrators in here until the Metz can come and collect them. Or until they're suitably terrified and can be thrown back out onto the street. I doubt they get that much use. They could easily fill any job here. Anyone makes a fuss, they're fired."

"Exactly. So why waste time putting high-tech monitoring equipment in here? It's not as if we can escape."

"True."

I scratch my wrist absentmindedly. They had taken my comm band and were probably searching it for incriminating messages. "What did they do to you?"

Barnes is silent a moment. "They questioned me. When they didn't like the answers I gave, they beat me up a bit."

"What were they questioning you about?"

A smile ghosts across her face. "You."

I open my mouth to reply, then close it again at the sound of footsteps. I push myself up off the bed, but the person following the guards is not someone I expected to see.

"Emilie?"

My assistant clutches a data pad. It trembles in her hands as she approaches.

"Want us to cuff him, miss?" one of the guards asks.

"No, thank you. I'm sure I'll be fine."

"Well, we searched him. He's clean. And we'll be right here if he tries anything," the other guard says encouragingly.

They had searched me. Thoroughly. And were disappointed to find I didn't even have a toothpick on me.

I stand back as the door swishes open and Emilie steps inside. The guards wave their guns threateningly to make sure I don't try anything. The door closes behind her.

"Are you okay?" Her voice is almost a whisper. She casts a nervous glance at the next cell. Barnes refuses to meet her gaze.

"Fine. Well, apart from being stuck in here, of course." I pause, waiting for her to explain what she's doing here, but she just stares down at the data pad. *My* data pad. "How's the production line going?"

"It's working now." Emilie hesitates, then adds, "I need you to give me access to your files. So that someone can pick up your work while you're … absent."

"Coleman replaced me already then?" I joke.

Emilie doesn't seem to find it funny. Her cheeks darken slightly, and she looks at the floor.

I sigh and take the data pad from her. "What do I need to do?"

She opens up the screen and shows me where to press my thumb and enter my passcode. As my computer screen appears on the data pad, a thought strikes me. If Coleman reports me to the Metz, the first thing they'll do is go to the house. They'll almost certainly arrest Ella, perhaps even the servants. I remember Bryn's description of the prisoners they'd freed from the underground lab at the Metz compound, and my stomach clenches.

It may already be too late. But I have to try.

I glance over Emilie's shoulder at the guards. They're talking in low voices, barely glancing our way. I keep my voice at a whisper and my face downturned in case the cameras can pick up the movement of my lips.

"Could you do me a favour? I need to get a private message to my sister."

Emilie's eyebrows raise a fraction, but she gives a slight nod.

Can I trust her?

I don't have a choice. I must get a message out. And there's no one in the building I trust more than Emilie, Barnes included.

I bring up the notes app and type a short message into it, then tilt the data pad so Emilie can read it.

Ella, leave London immediately. Barnes and I have been taken prisoner. DO NOT try to rescue us. Tell Thomas that he and the others may want to leave the house. If you can get a message to Bryn, do so, but not if it prevents you leaving. I love you. Trey.

I add Ella's comm code, then turn the data pad back to Emilie. Her brow furrows as she scans the lines.

"Memorized it?"

"Except the number. I'll need that."

I delete the message, leaving Ella's comm number, then return the data pad to my assistant. Former assistant now, I guess. "Thanks. And I'm sorry. I hope you're not in any trouble because of me."

Emilie shrugs. "I still have a job. That's the main thing."

I back away as Emilie walks toward the door, just so the guards don't think I'm going to try anything. As she steps out, she turns.

"I'm sorry—"

Her words are cut off when the door closes.

"It's okay," I reply, though I'm not sure if she hears me. She gives me a sad smile and turns to leave.

"What was all that about?" Barnes asks once we're alone again.

"I guess they need to keep the factory running while we're locked up here." I thump my fist against the wall, frustration welling inside me. "Damn Louis. You were right. I should never have trusted him."

"So he betrayed you." Barnes doesn't sound surprised.

"Yes. Couldn't risk his daddy's ire, I guess. I thought that if I could persuade *him* of all people to do what's right, then we might have a chance." I kick the coffin-like bed. "Guess I was wrong."

She snorts a laugh. "Insiders don't care about anybody else. They just think about themselves. Especially Insiders like him. When they can take everything they want, why would they want anything to change?"

I don't answer, not wanting to admit that she's right.

Hours pass. It's impossible to keep track of time down here where there's no daylight or clock. At some point, there's a rattle and a cardboard box shoots down a tube that connects the cell to the concrete wall. Inside is a lukewarm burger. Barnes devours hers with obvious relish, but to me, the fake meat tastes like the cardboard it came in.

Perhaps an hour later, the lights go out. The darkness is absolute. Having nothing else to do, I lie down on the bed, trying not to think about how much it resembles a coffin. My muscles tense, my mind almost expecting a domed lid to rise and encase me, followed by the hissing sound of gas. I force myself to breathe steadily. Soft snores filter through the tube connecting my cell with Barnes's.

Still, I cannot sleep.

At some point, I must doze off, because I awake with a start, almost blinded by a bright light. Blinking, I raise my hand to ward off the intrusion. The door swishes open. Terror freezes my limbs. The only thought that percolates the fog of sleep is that being dragged from my cell in the middle of the night cannot have a good outcome.

When a hand grabs my arm, I pull away, lashing out, my foot connecting with hard muscle and bone. There's a grunt and a muttered curse.

"Stop that," the person hisses. "I'm trying to help you."

My muscles go limp. "Louis?"

"Come on. I don't know how long we've got. Here. Put this over your arm."

I nearly drop the slippery sheath before I realize what it is. A chip blocker.

I pull the rubber tube over my forearm and let Louis drag me from the bed, my mind still struggling to comprehend what's happening. "What's going on? Why are you—"

"Shut up. Just ... Let's get out of here first, then I'll explain."

I plant my feet and yank my arm from his grasp. "Not until you tell me where you're taking me."

Louis' face is ghostly in the white light, his jaw clenched. "I am trying to help you escape."

"Escape? You're the one who got me locked up."

Anger flickers in his eyes. "We need to go or they'll pick us up on the cameras. Follow me or stay locked up. Your choice."

He strides out of the cell. I stumble after him, my thoughts a web of confusion. Halfway down the cavern, a voice stops me in my tracks.

"Hey! What about me?"

Barnes. Of course.

"Louis, come back," I hiss. His light bobs ahead, then turns to shine directly on Barnes's cell. She's standing with her hands pressed to the door. "Come on. Let her out."

Louis doesn't move. "When she was caught sabotaging the production line? Not likely."

I stare at Barnes, who doesn't meet my eyes. "I thought you were locked up because of me."

She mutters something under her breath.

"Trey, come *on*," Louis growls.

But I stand firm. "I'm not going without her."

He curses and strides up to her cell. "Fine. But you do exactly what I say." He presses his hand to the access panel and opens the door to Barnes's cell. She tries to push past him, but he holds his arm out. "You're going to have to cut out your chip. It'll sound an alert in the guardroom as soon as you step out of the cell." He pulls out a pocketknife.

"No need." She reaches down the front of her overalls and pulls out a tiny box, placing it onto the bed. "There are some places even your father's guards won't look."

"A biobox?"

She nods.

"You crafty minx." Louis sounds impressed.

Barnes gives him a disparaging look. "Can we go now?"

Louis steps aside to let her out of the cell. "We need to be quiet," he tells us in a low voice as we approach the corridor leading out of the room. "I managed to slip something into the guards' coffee, but it may not completely knock them out. Follow me and do exactly as I tell you."

He switches off his flashlight, plunging us into darkness. We creep up the corridor, my hand on Louis' shoulder, Barnes's hand on mine. A faint light shines around a corner ahead.

Louis peers around, then whispers into my ear. "We go one at a time. Stick to the shadows as their eyes will be blinded by the light. Left up ahead. I'll wait for you around the corner."

He disappears before I can reply. I repeat the message to Barnes, then take a step forward and peek around the corner.

Louis is a shadow against the faint light as he moves silently up the corridor, sticking close to the wall. Further up, dim emergency lights illuminate the door I'd noticed when I was led to my cell, the two figures slumped outside it. One of them turns his head and mutters something. Louis freezes. The other guard lets out a grunt, his head lolling back against the wall. After a moment, Louis resumes his pacing, and a moment later, he disappears.

I take a deep breath and step out into the corridor, my eyes never leaving the guards. But they give no sign they've noticed me. I let out a breath as I turn into the larger access corridor and find Louis waiting. A minute later, Barnes joins us.

"Don't they have cameras here?" I whisper.

"Yes, but I set them on a loop."

We follow him in silence as he leads us past the elevator to a rough staircase that smells damp. "No one ever comes this way," is his only comment as we ascend two levels, then walk down another dark corridor.

Finally, Louis opens a nondescript door and ushers us inside. He closes it and switches on his flashlight, resting it on top of a pile of boxes. He sinks onto another box with a sigh.

"Thank goodness that's over. I never knew creeping around could be so *stressful*."

The room feels vast, rows of boxes leading into the darkness. The ones nearest me are stamped with a code that I think relates to one of the distribution centres. I open my mouth to ask Louis what the hell's going on, but Barnes beats me to it.

"So you betray us, then free us. What's the deal?"

Louis scowls. "I didn't betray you."

Barnes's gaze flickers to me.

His scowl deepens. "You think I told my father about our conversations?"

I shrug noncommittally.

He snorts. "Do you know what my father would do if he found out I'd freed you? Do you know what I've risked?"

"No one else had access to our messages or knew we'd been talking. No one else knew what we did," I say flatly.

Louis runs his hand through his hair. "I can't believe you thought

I would do that." He almost sounds ... hurt.

I push down the twinge of guilt. *There isn't anyone else it can be.*

"If you didn't mention it to Daddy, then who did?" Barnes snaps, her words echoing the question in my head.

Louis sucks in a long breath, then looks at me. "I believe Emilie requested a confidential meeting with my father yesterday afternoon."

Emilie ...

His words hang in the silence.

Efficient Emilie, who is the first to pick up my messages and check my email. She must have seen the one I had Louis send me with the Project Griffin attachments. All this time, she's known about it.

Barnes curses under her breath and glances over at me. "Didn't think she had it in her. I thought she was sweet on you."

"I think she was worried about losing her job," Louis says quietly.

My head begins to throb, my chest tight, lungs burning. Realizing I'm holding my breath, I let it out in a rush, sucking in fresh air. "She was saving up to help her sister go to university. It was so important to her."

"Clearly more important than our lives," Barnes says bitterly.

But I can't feel bitterness. Just guilt. I was the one who put her in that position, forced her to make that choice. Of course, she chose her sister over me.

But her betrayal still hurts.

"I thought you knew," Louis says. "Dad sent her down to see you this afternoon, didn't he?"

I collapse onto one of the boxes, my legs suddenly weak.

Her words had been cut off by the door closing. Had she been apologizing for what she'd done ... or what she was *about* to do?

I bend over, my fingers raking my hair. "No," I whisper. "No."

No, no, no.

If I say it enough, think it enough, perhaps it won't be true.

"Trey, what's wrong?" Barnes sounds alarmed.

I can't speak. The throbbing in my head gets louder, drowning out whatever she says next. My brain focuses on the words I can't bring myself to voice.

The Metz had questioned Ella, letting her go. They had no evidence she was involved with anything. But the message I'd asked Emilie to pass to Ella ... That clearly implicated her. And not just her, but Thomas and the servants. Even if they swore they didn't know anything, why else would I have told them to leave?

Coleman had probably already acted on the message. Had the Metz caught them in their beds? Were they torturing them at another one of their underground labs? And if they did interrogate Ella, how long would it take them to make the connections to Bryn, to Aleesha, to Samson?

I shudder, trying to push the painful thoughts from my mind.

I'd wanted to protect my sister and the servants. Instead, I'd condemned them all.

31

Aleesha

I climb up onto the rooftops and circle Phoenix headquarters. Unfamiliar guards stand outside every entrance. There is no sign of my people.

Is Denzel holding them hostage? Or did they fight and lose, their bodies growing stiff and cold as the Bigland Boys feast on our food, drain our water tanks?

Bile rises in my throat. This is my fault. Danny had warned me that Denzel would act. And I had ignored him because I didn't want to deal with the problem.

I pace the rooftop, then slowly lower myself down a drainpipe, hand over hand, to the street below, a plan forming in my mind.

They may be on my patch, but if I challenge Denzel and beat him, they'll have no choice but to leave. Gang rules.

Denzel is twice my size, probably three times my weight and a good fighter. But not as good as me. I know I can win this fight.

I *have* to win this fight.

I stride up to the main gate, stopping ten paces from the guards. "I want to speak to your boss," I call out.

They look me up and down. One of them leers and lets out a

high-pitched whistle. They know who I am.

A moment later, a young kid runs up. The guard says something to him, and he runs back inside the building. Sweat beads on the back of my neck, but I don't move. Ten minutes he keeps me waiting, but finally, the huge figure of Denzel swaggers through the gate.

"Aleesha. What d'ya want?" He sounds cocky, overconfident.

"You have something of mine. I want it back."

Denzel leers at me. "Finders keepers."

I raise my voice so everyone in the street can hear. "I challenge you to a leadership fight."

He doesn't react, almost as if he was expecting it. "Fine. Make the arrangements. I'll see you in the square next week."

"Not next week or in the square. Here. Now." I jab my finger toward the ground.

Surprise flickers in his eyes. "That's not how things are done."

"Sneaking in to take over someone else's territory is not how things are done, either." My voice is dangerously low. "Send one of your runners for the ref. If you've got any of my people in there, they can sit on the jury."

It's a gamble on my part, but I need to find out if my friends are in there. Unfortunately, Denzel doesn't take the bait.

"Fine. But we can't fight in the street. Come in."

I shake my head. "And let your morons jump me? No thanks."

Denzel rolls his eyes, then shouts a name. The kid comes running. "Go find the ref." He pulls some chits from his pocket and presses them into the boy's hand. "Tell 'er to come *now*."

I saunter over to the windowless building that lines the alley and lean back against it, twirling my knife in my hand. The gesture makes me seem confident, as if I take part in leadership challenges every day, but the real reason I'd moved was to get into the shade. It's hot today. High risk of fires, especially as there haven't been any

Cleanings lately to clear the build-up of trash in the streets.

Now I have more time to think through the situation, I curse myself for being so hasty. I could have gone to speak to Samson, or Petal if Samson's still unconscious. I'm pretty sure the Bigland Boys answer to the Brotherhood. But I'm not certain Petal would offer any help without the authority of his boss.

A feeling of dread settles in my stomach as the full implication of Samson's injuries sinks in. Even if he survives, if he can't walk, he won't be in a position to command the respect of the gangs anymore. They only respect one thing – strength.

And what does that mean for Area Four? For all Outsiders?

After perhaps twenty minutes, Denzel's boy returns, followed by the woman who presides over leadership challenges. She stalks up the street, four men and women flanking her, her face set in a permanent frown. I'm not sure how she got her role or who she took over from, but she's perhaps the only person in the city who every single gang respects.

As long as she's here, Denzel will play fair.

I straighten as she approaches. The ref pauses when she reaches me and purses her lips. "What's all this about then?"

Denzel closes the distance between us. He doesn't want to be left out of this conversation.

"Bigland Boys have taken over Phoenix headquarters," I say. "I've challenged Denzel to a leadership fight to get it back."

The woman's gaze rakes over me. "You've recovered quickly. It must be only two weeks since you were lying on the ground, beaten to a pulp."

I shrug off the challenge in her voice.

"I told 'er this wasn't how things were done, but she insisted," Denzel mutters. "And she'll be the one payin' your fee when she loses."

"This is most … irregular."

"So is him taking over my patch. I've done more in the past week to help the people around here get food than anyone's done for months." I jerk my thumb at Denzel. "If I wait a few days, they'll have eaten the lot."

She casts me a sharp glance. "Maybe you should have defended it better."

There is no sisterliness in her attitude. In her eyes, I am the annoyance to be dealt with, not Denzel. But as long as she does her job, I don't care.

Denzel looks smug. "Told you," he says to me. "We'll have to do it the proper way, in a week's time."

"No need for that. You've both stated you're happy to go ahead now, so let's not waste any more time," the ref says briskly. "Shall we go inside?"

For a moment, I think Denzel's going to refuse. But he can't back down now. He'd lose too much respect. "Yeah. Whatever."

A thread of unease tightens in my chest as I follow Denzel under the arched gateway. I'm gambling that the ref and her bodyguards will make sure the fight is fair. As for winning … That's up to me.

When we enter the main hall, I scan the people sprawled around it, my heart sinking as I see only unfamiliar faces. The golden phoenix Jax had painted on the far wall has already been defaced. It makes my blood boil. Not that they've marked this place as their own, but that they ruined something so beautiful. Yet, despite the black and yellow paint scrawled over it, the phoenix shines through, still proud. It knows its own worth, even when defeated.

I lower my eyes, too ashamed to look at it.

The Bigland Boys are a motley crew. They couldn't have been here more than an hour or two, but the place already stinks. Blood leaks from fresh wounds, and many sport dirty bandages, evidence of older wounds. I wonder how many of them were part of the mob who'd come to our rescue when we'd been attacked by Primo and his officers.

Now they've taken what they felt was owed.

I knew Denzel was unscrupulous, but the arrogance of the move still surprises me. Phoenix headquarters is a fortress. The only time it's been broken into was when the Metz raided it before the Battle of Rose Square. How had the Bigland Boys, a pack of barely trained fighters with homemade weapons, taken it?

My gaze alights on one of the older members of the gang, a gaunt man with scraggly, grey hair, slouched in the corner. He strokes something in his lap as if it's a pet, and well it might be. It's probably the most valuable thing he's ever touched. The matte grey metal barrel absorbs the light that blazes through the skylights above.

My blood runs cold.

I look around again, more closely this time. The knife Denzel's wingman holds looks new, the blade smooth and sharp, the handle familiar.

One of the alcoves on the far side of the room is partially curtained over. A short man jumps to his feet to pull the curtain across as I approach, but I catch a glimpse of what's inside. Crates of weapons.

I stalk back over to Denzel. "Where did you get those?"

"Filched 'em." He gestures to the fighting ring – a roped-off area with a padded floor that we use for sparring. "Ready?"

"In a minute."

No one stops me as I veer away from the curtained alcove and stride to the door leading to the room where I'd left Anders and Danny. The smell stops me two paces away, the acrid, iron tang making my nostrils flare. Unwillingly, I turn my gaze to the floor. A dull, reddish stain spreads across the stone, extending out from under the door.

I lurch backward and close my eyes, but the smell fills my nostrils, my body, my mind.

What have they done?

My hand trembles as I reach for the handle and open the door.

Empty.

There's the bed where I'd last seen Anders. The top sheet is missing, the lower one rumpled and torn. The chair Danny had been slumped in lies toppled on the floor.

I close the door and march back over to the ring. "Where are they?" Denzel shrugs.

I step closer and press the tip of my knife to his flabby belly. To his credit, he doesn't even flinch. "Where. Are. They?"

"Hey. No weapons." The ref steps between us and pushes me back, scowling. "You want a challenge? We do it the proper way." She holds out her hand. Reluctantly, I place my knife into it. "And the others."

I retrieve the other blades I have hidden and hand them over.

"Search them," the ref orders.

Two of her guards step forward and pat us down. Their search is thorough, and Denzel glowers when they find a thin scalpel concealed in the fastening of his boot.

I glance around the small ring. I've fought here before, though only once. This was where I'd fought Vihaan and won. But Vihaan was short and slight, whereas Denzel is big and heavy-set. I need to run him ragged and tire him out, using my speed to avoid his strength. That would work in the large arena usually used for leadership challenges, but this one is a fraction of the size. I chew my lip, wondering if I've made a fatal mistake.

Too late to back out now.

The ref's guards take their places, one at each corner. The Bigland Boys move closer, leaving a respectable half-metre between them and the rope.

"You both know the rules," the ref says. She drops her voice so only Denzel and I can hear. "Please don't kill each other. Your pride is not worth your lives."

Leadership fights go on until one party yields or is knocked out cold. But the last few have ended in death. Jay killed Rich. Primo killed Jay. I killed Primo. A shiver runs through me. Denzel smiles. Does he think me weak? But he must have seen me fight Primo, or at least heard that I bested him. I do not think he will underestimate me.

The first round involves no weapons. The ref bangs a metal spoon against a pan to signify the start of the fight, then backs out of the arena.

Denzel is the first to move, charging at me like a bulldog. I dodge him easily, dancing out of reach of his outstretched arm. Adrenaline pulses through my veins, sending my heart racing. He comes at me again, and once again, I duck out of the way.

For perhaps two minutes, we stand there staring at each other, waiting for the other to move. The Bigland Boys become impatient. There are shouts, jeers – aimed mainly at me, of course. My thoughts stray to Anders and Danny, Rogue, Megan and Tommy. The headquarters is big enough to hide a hundred people. How many were here when the Bigland Boys struck?

There's a blur of movement before a heavy blow catches me on my left cheek, sending me reeling. I stagger backward, but not fast enough. A second blow catches me on the chin, snapping my head back.

I see stars.

Blindly, I duck and plunge forward, sensing Denzel's arm slicing the air above me.

At the far side of the ring, I stop, swaying on my feet.

You idiot. Focus.

I try to gather myself, but he's already coming at me again, pressing his advantage.

I dive to the side, twisting around him, but I know I'm running out of time. The ring is too small. There is limited space to move, nowhere for me to grab a breather. I can't win this round by being defensive. I must attack.

Again, Denzel charges. I dodge to one side. Expecting it, he moves to block my path. Flicking my leg up and kicking out, I catch him in the stomach.

He doubles over, giving me the opportunity I need. I jump in the air and spin, kicking out again. My foot slams into his head. Bone crunches.

Denzel grunts and sways. I move quickly, knowing that if I give him even a second to recover, he'll turn the tables. I ram my shoulder into him. He lurches back, then falls to the floor.

His hand grasps my vest as he falls, pulling me down on top of him. I yank free, hearing the fabric rip, and bring my knee up between his legs, then aim a punch at his jaw. Still reeling from the knock to his head, his reactions are dulled.

Again and again, I lash out until I manage to get behind him and wrap my legs around his neck, squeezing.

"Yield," I pant.

Denzel doesn't answer. I squeeze a little tighter, causing his eyes to bulge. His hands claw at my legs, but my boots come halfway up my calves, and he can't reach higher than that.

"Yield," I say again, glancing across at the ref.

She steps forward, looking relieved.

But Denzel still doesn't yield.

His eyes roll as he looks to the side and gives an imperceptible nod.

Before I can react, chaos erupts.

People spill into the ring. The ref's guards fight, but go down under a pile of Denzel's people. I see the ref collapse to her knees and fall forward, eyes wide with shock, throat slit from ear to ear.

Rough hands grab me and drag me to my feet, Denzel wriggling free of my hold. He looks triumphant as he raises his fist, panting. I anticipate the blow and move with it, but it still makes my ears ring. A tooth loosens at the back of my jaw.

"You thought you were bein' so clever," he sneers. "You thought you could beat *me*."

I did beat you, I want to say, but figure now is not the right time. Someone yanks my arms back behind me, and I draw in a sharp breath as something twinges in my shoulder.

Denzel leans in so close I can smell his rancid breath. "Always thought yerself clever, didn't you, Aleesha? With your Insider friends. Well, they didn't come to help the rest of your gang, did they? An' Daddy won't help you now."

"Are they alive?" I fight to free my arms, though I know it's useless. I get a jab in the back for my efforts.

"It's always fun to keep a few to play with." Denzel leers at me. "I think *you* might be fun to play with, Aleesha."

I feel a sudden urge to vomit.

Denzel turns to the man holding me. "Lock her up. Then clean up this mess." He waves his hand vaguely at the fresh blood creeping across the floor. "I need a beer."

The man holding me shoves me forward. I twist my head to glance back at the bodies on the floor, my eyes finding the vacant stare of the woman who had been so respected, so feared. Even I had not considered that the Bigland Boys would so gruesomely flaunt their power. To kill the ref is to send a message to all the other gangs that they are above gang law. And that will make them every gang's target.

But they are armed like no other gang I know of. Even the Brotherhood doesn't have weapons like this. And that is where their confidence lies – in the cold, hard barrel of a gun.

Only two men accompany me from the hall. I feign an injury to my right leg and moan as they push me to walk faster. They seem to buy it. Denzel chooses his gang members for their muscle, not their intelligence.

As the sounds of the hall fade, my captors seem to relax. I draw in slow, steady breaths. They think they have me trapped, but there is another way out. I hadn't even known it existed until Bryn and Murdoch had broken into the building to rescue me from Primo. From inside, the door looks like a boarded-up wall.

I wait until I'm jerked to a halt. When the man holding my hands slackens his grip to push open a door, I kick out at the man with the gun. He holds it casually, not looped around his neck.

Before the gun hits the floor, I twist and wrench my hands out of the first man's grasp, then kick out, catching him on the kneecap. He yells in pain, falling back. The other man moves to grab me. He's blocking my way, his bulk filling most of the corridor. I kick out at him again, but he anticipates it and grabs my foot, twisting it painfully. Instead of pulling away, I lean forward and grab his arm. I've always been flexible but have never been more grateful for it than now.

I bite down on his hand – hard. He curses, but his grip relaxes just enough for me to slither from his grasp. I sprint down the corridor, their footsteps pounding on the floor behind me. They start closing in, but I finally see the door at the end of the corridor.

I burst through it, daylight blinding me.

And I run.

* * * *

Only when I reach the river do I slow to a stop. Then the guilt hits me.

I ran.

I saw my chance to escape and took it. But what about the people Denzel captured? I left them behind to deal with his fury.

You wouldn't have been able to help them if you had stayed, the small voice in my head reminds me.

I push it away. Guilt tears at my insides, burning away the ache in my jaw and the pain in my shoulder.

I abandoned them.

How many are even still alive?

My torn vest flaps around me, exposing half my back. The sun hovers above the towers Inside the Wall, the air stiflingly warm. Bugs swarm around me. I swat them away half-heartedly.

I walk along the water's edge. The slab of rock is still there, the water lapping around it now the tide is in. I blink, and for a moment, I see her body lying there, the pieces of firewood stacked up around it. The hum of the crowd singing fills my ears. When I close my eyes, I can smell the fire again, smell Lily's body burning.

"I failed them, Lily," I murmur. "Just like I failed you."

I keep moving, the weight dragging me down with every step. By the time I reach Denham Street, I feel as bowed over as the old woman who crouches in the doorway near my building, her muscles so distorted that she can barely lift her eyes from the ground to say thank you when I give her a half-empty bottle of Chaz.

It takes me a minute to realize that someone is shouting my name.

I drag my gaze up and catch sight of Mitch leaning in a doorway. I haven't seen him since he was released from the Metz compound. He's already regained some of the weight he'd lost, though the scars are still there, and his hair is thinner and greyer than it was before. He stands in the doorway of the half-constructed building he uses as a headquarters and drug den for the many people who come to him for tronk.

I feel my body turning, my feet carrying me toward him.

Leave him. You promised Lily you wouldn't go back. You promised Trey.

But they are both gone. Lily's dead. Trey is alive, but he is better off without me. All I seem to do is hurt him.

Mitch grins as I approach. "What's up with you?"

I wonder whether to tell him about the Bigland Boys, then decide against it. Just because he talked to me when we were prisoners doesn't mean we're friends.

"Come inside. I've got something for you."

I follow him numbly, past the guards at the door and the people slumped, semi-conscious, in various poses, into his office.

"Not turning over a new leaf then?" I manage to say as he opens a cupboard and rummages inside.

"Thinkin' of it. But you need money to do that, so I figured I might as well carry on while I move on to other lines of work." He pulls back and holds out his hand. "What do you think?"

A knife sits on his upturned palm. It's a fine blade.

"Take it," Mitch says, nodding at it. "It's yours."

Slowly, I reach out and pick it up. It's perfectly balanced for throwing and the blade is dulled, so it doesn't glint in the light. I brush my thumb across the edge, wincing when it easily slices my skin. I've never had a blade this sharp.

"Good, isn't it?" Mitch waits for my appreciation.

"It's beautiful. Where did you get it?"

He shrugs. "Seems there's some new stuff floating around." He hesitates, then gruffly adds, "Just wanted to say thanks, y'know, for getting me out of there."

I slide the knife into my boot. It feels good to be armed again. "Thanks."

I turn to leave, then stop. The pull of tronk is so strong in this room. My gaze strays to the cupboard in the corner. It calls to me.

Mitch catches the direction of my glance and frowns. "You should be going, Aleesha."

"I want some. You owe me."

I sound like a whiny child. I feel strangely detached from the voice and the words leaving my lips. My mind still seems to be focused on listing my failures, reminding me of everyone I've let down. It tells me I have no one left.

If it wasn't for me, my mother would have never gone to Rose Square that day.

My father had sounded so sad when he'd said it, like it was something he wanted to protect me from but knew he couldn't.

I suddenly know there's only one person I need to see right now. I need her to pull me onto her lap, press her cool face to mine and tell me she forgives me for everything. For the person I became and the mess I have made of my life.

"Give me some tronk. The good stuff, no messing. Enough for a long sleep."

Mitch's jaw tightens. "You don't want this, Aleesha. You quit, remember?"

What has my life come to when *Mitch* is trying to stop me from taking tronk? I pull the knife he just gave me from my boot.

He narrows his eyes. "Don't threaten me, Aleesha."

"Then just give me the tronk. Please?" My voice catches on the last word. I hate how I sound. Like a damn addict. "I saved your life. You owe me."

This seems to do the trick. Mitch hates being in debt. His face sags and he slowly walks over to the cupboard in the corner of the room. I watch carefully as he pulls out a large packet and decants some of the white powder into a smaller one.

"More," I say when he pauses, barely giving me enough to knock me out for a couple of hours. Reluctantly, he continues.

"A life for a life," he murmurs under his breath. Then he turns and holds it out. There's a sadness in his eyes that I haven't seen before. My fingers close over the packet, but he doesn't release it. "You don't have to do this, you know."

I stare into his eyes until, finally, he releases his grip.

"My debt is paid."

He doesn't phrase it as a question, but I nod anyway and turn to leave the room.

32

Trey

Louis' plan to get us out of the factory does not meet with Barnes's approval.

"You want us to hide in these crates, hope the distribution machines don't pick up on the fact that we're not pre-packed burgers, then somehow cut our way out when we reach the food depot, presuming we haven't suffocated along the way?" She crosses her arms. "No thanks."

Louis glares at her. "Do you always have to be so negative? I'm beginning to wish I'd left you in your cell."

"At least back in the cell, I wasn't in imminent danger of death."

"Once they find out you've escaped, I'm pretty sure they're not going to bother locking you up again," Louis retorts. "This is the final shipment that's going out. Father's orders. It's become too dangerous to send out the pods with all the shooting. If you don't get out now, you're stuck in here. It'll only be a matter of time before you're caught again."

"You're right," I say before Barnes can protest again. "We need to get out of here, and this seems like the best way." I glance helplessly at the crates surrounding us. "Do any of them have ventilation holes?"

"These do." Louis hurries over to a lower stack of crates. "Get in. I'll stack some of the other crates on top of you."

Barnes eyes the empty box in front of her, then reluctantly climbs inside, glaring at Louis. "If you betray us, I will personally come back and slice off your most precious body part." Her eyes drop meaningfully to Louis' trousers. "*If* I can find it."

I stifle a smile as she lies down, her legs bent, feet pressed against the end of the crate. Despite her bravado, her jaw is clenched, and she looks as nervous as I feel.

"Trey?" Louis gestures toward the second box.

I swallow and step into it. "Will you be all right? What if they find out you helped us?"

Louis' brows furrow. "I'll be fine."

"You could come with us?"

He shakes his head. "I covered my tracks. Besides, you might need someone on the inside." The corners of his lips tilt up. "Now, are you getting in or what?"

I drop to my knees. Unlike Barnes, there's no room to stretch out my legs. I huddle in a foetal position, feeling my heart begin to race as Louis gives us each a black baton that he says will cut clean through the crates. We have no time to test it before he closes, then seals the lids. Pinpricks of light leak into the crate through the ventilation strips that encircle the box.

Despite my many misgivings, Louis' plan actually works. After a few cramped hours, my crate is loaded onto a pod. But rather than being left at the distribution centre, I feel myself being moved onto a land vehicle for a short, bumpy ride, which comes within a hair's breadth of making me vomit all over the inside of the crate. I'm carried into what sounds like a store and unceremoniously dumped onto the floor.

I barely have time to catch my breath before something slices through the seal on the top of my crate and the lid opens. My limbs are stiff, my muscles slow to react, but the man isn't expecting to find a person inside the box, so his reactions are even slower. I swing weakly, catching him on the side of his head, and follow the punch up with a second, stronger one that sends him reeling back. My legs collapse under me as I try to push myself out of the crate, and I curse in a way that would make Bryn proud.

The man looks at me from the other side of the room, one hand clutching his jaw. "What the hell?"

I hold up my hands to show I'm not armed. "I'm not going to hurt you." I look around the small storeroom, and my heart sinks. There are only six crates, including mine. Four are already open.

"Who are you, and where are my burgers?" The man regains his composure and holds out a short-bladed knife. I eye it warily, my hands still in the air.

"I'll be out of here in just a minute," I say, trying to keep my voice calm. "Can you please open those other crates?"

The man looks suspicious but complies. Packed neatly into the crates are rows upon rows of coloured boxes. He peers inside. "At least some of my stuff's arrived."

"Dammit." I glance around. "Where are we? Which area are we in?"

The man looks at me as if I've gone mad. "Four."

"Were these the only crates you were given?"

"Yes. Wh—"

I run out of the storeroom, through a small shop, then out into the street. The noise and smell of Area Four overwhelm my senses, and for a moment, I just stand there, staring mutely at the street hobies and people shuffling around me, as I try to think what to do next.

Barnes could be back at the food depot or any of a hundred shops. It could take me hours, days, to find her, and that's time I don't have.

Not when other lives might be at stake.

I hurry north, through Area Five and into the southern part of Area Six, only stopping when I reach an inconspicuous millinery shop in a back street not far from the Wall. The sign on the door says closed, but I keep banging on it until a tall, elderly woman with steel-grey hair pulls it open. She jerks her head and steps aside to let me in, then closes and bars the door behind me.

"Try some discretion, boy. It's supposed to be a *secret* passage."

"Sorry," I call over my shoulder as I slip down a dusty aisle to the back of the room. "I should be back soon."

The woman lets out a snort, watching as I pull back the rug that conceals the trapdoor leading down to the cellar and the passageway that links the shop to Milicent's house. I race through it, panting, and push open the door to the cellar, finally emerging into the hall of my home.

Immediately, I know something is wrong.

The house feels empty, the ticking of the huge grandfather clock and my footsteps on the marble floor the only things to break the silence. But it's not the emptiness that worries me.

It's the destruction.

Glass crunches under my feet as I slowly walk down the hall toward the kitchen. The door is ajar, the room ransacked.

Palms clammy, I move on to the dining room and the large sitting room at the back, which overlooks the garden. Paintings have been torn from the walls and slashed, drawers hang open, their contents scattered across the floor. Milicent's favourite chair – the same one my mother had loved – is upended in one corner.

I lean against the wall in the hallway and sink to the floor.

I'm too late.

From somewhere upstairs, I hear the faint click of a door.

I freeze, my breath stilling.

331

Light footsteps sound. "Hello?"

Thomas. His voice is strained.

Slowly, I ease myself up off the floor and pad across to the staircase, wincing as I crush a tiny piece of glass underfoot.

The footsteps begin to descend the stairs. "Hello? Who's there?"

I wonder whose side Thomas is on. Pressing my back to the staircase, I look around for a weapon. There's nothing at hand, but I do have the element of surprise. Plus, I'm younger and faster. If need be, I can make it back into the cellar and through the tunnel before he can catch me.

His head comes into view first, his gaze darting around nervously. I step out from my hiding place.

"Thomas. What's going on?"

Thomas whips around, his face slackening in relief as he catches sight of me. "Trey. Thank goodness. Are you all right? Did they hurt you?"

He knows then. My jaw tightens. "Where's Ella?"

"She left as soon as we got your message," Thomas replies, descending the final few stairs to the floor. "She said it wasn't safe to tell me where, but in case you turned up, she gave me this to give to you. It's encrypted. The password is ACAOR." He holds out a thin comm band.

I step forward to take it. I don't think he's lying. Only Ella would have thought of that password. My lips twitch as I remember the nanny bot that looked after us when we were children in Wales. The acronym was emblazoned across its domed head, defining the model: Automated Childcare And Observation Robot. Of course, at the time, I didn't know that's what it stood for. I had thought it was our nanny's name.

"What message?" I ask, recalling Thomas's words.

His brow creases. "Didn't you send it? Ella said it was signed by you, though it didn't come from your band number. You told us you'd been taken prisoner and we should leave. It came just in time, too. An hour after Ella left, the Metz arrived."

So Emilie had passed on the message. But was that before or after she reported back to Coleman? "Did Ella reply to the message?"

Thomas shakes his head. "No. The message said not to." He gives me a strange look. "What's going on?"

I take a deep breath and look around.

"You can trust me, Trey," he says quietly.

I let out the breath slowly, suspecting that the manservant is more loyal than I've given him credit for. I explain my incarceration in the cell and how I escaped, though I leave Louis and Barnes out of my story. "Did everyone manage to get out before the Metz arrived?"

"Dana went to stay with her mother. Derek, Lydia and I hid in the tunnel while the Metz were here, ransacking the place." He runs a hand through his hair, his face sagging as he looks up at an oil painting ripped from corner to corner. "I'm sorry we couldn't stop them."

A lump forms in my throat. "You have nothing to be sorry about," I say fiercely. "This is my fault."

I leave Thomas to start clearing up the mess and head to my bedroom. After closing the curtains against prying eyes, I strap the comm band Ella had left me around my wrist, change out of my suit and pack a small backpack. Then I enter the password to access the comm. There is only one number saved in the contacts. I call it.

Ella answers, her holo springing into life above the device. "Trey?" Her face relaxes as I activate the holo at my end. "Thank God. I've been so worried. Are you at the house? What happened?"

I explain again about my imprisonment and escape. "Are you somewhere safe?"

"Yes. I—"

"Don't tell me. Just in case they capture me again."

Ella looks surprised, then worried. "What are you going to do?"

I hadn't thought any further than making sure the people I cared about were safe, but as I ponder the question, an answer crystallizes in my mind. "Coleman said they're stopping shipments of food from the factory. I assume Hendricks will be doing the same, which means that unless the fighting ends soon, people are going to begin to starve."

"The shelves are almost bare in the shops we've been to, and it must be worse Outside."

"You shouldn't be going out." I try not to let annoyance colour my voice, failing miserably. "Even if you have a chip blocker, they can still track you using the cameras."

Ella rolls her eyes. "They've got better things to do than chase me. The government may not have lost the fight yet, but they haven't won it, either. I think all the Metz efforts are focused on that."

"Perhaps. Just be careful, okay?"

She smiles. "I will. And don't forget that we're here to help." She holds up a hand as I open my mouth to protest. "No, Trey. We have skills your Outsider friends don't. You may need us to win this war. This has to end soon."

I sigh, knowing she's right, but promise myself I'll explore every other alternative first. "Fine, but right now, the best thing you can do is keep yourself out of harm's way so I don't have to worry about you."

"And what about you, Trey?" She cocks her head to one side, her gaze troubled. "Will *you* stay out of harm's way? You and Anabel are all the family I have left. I love you, little brother. Don't forget that."

She cuts the connection before I can reply

* * * *

Abby and Bryn look up from their seats at the table in her kitchen when I push open the back door.

"Trey!" Abby comes over to give me a hug. I squeeze her gently, feeling the bones of her shoulder blades. She should be putting on weight now that Bryn's buying her better food, but if anything, she feels thinner.

I sit down at the table, and Bryn squeezes my shoulder. "How are things going?"

"Not great."

I fill them in as Abby pours hot water into a mug and places the tea in front of me.

"So Coleman knows you've been working with us," Bryn says when I finish. "Well, that can't be helped, and as long as you stay out of his way, I don't think there's anything he can do about it." He frowns. "Tell me more about this door you saw down in the basement."

"Not much to tell. There was no sign or label on it. It was solidly built, and the fact it was guarded indicates it's probably important. Part of the factory power plant perhaps?"

"Perhaps," Bryn says, though he doesn't sound sure. He eyes my backpack. "You planning to stay here for a while?"

"Maybe, though I don't want to put you at any more risk."

"Nonsense," Abby says. "You know you're always welcome here."

I smile my thanks, then turn back to Bryn. "Tell me honestly. How is the fight going?"

Bryn looks down at the table. "Not great. The government has called troops in from around the country, so we're outnumbered. The President's escaped, and we had to give up the government headquarters. The only good news is that it didn't contain what we were looking for anyway. We managed to get all the information we needed from the systems before pulling out."

I blow on my tea to cool it. The smell of mint fills my nostrils.

"What were you looking for?"

Bryn hesitates. Then he sighs. "You might as well know. We thought the mechanism to take down the Wall would most likely be in the government headquarters. Turns out, it's a bit more complicated than we thought."

"What you mean?"

"Richard's team is still working on breaking the encryption on some of the files, but from what we've got so far, and what he managed to get out of the President before his escape, the system has two parts that need to be activated simultaneously in order to bring a section of the Wall down. One part is in the Metz headquarters, but the other is Outside."

"So what happens now?"

"We've got a meeting tomorrow morning to decide that. Richard's calling in some favours, trying to get us more support from overseas, but I'm not sure we can match the government's numbers." A crease furrows his brow. "In other missions, I've been more involved and he's bounced ideas off me, but he's kept to himself during this operation. But I'm sure he has a plan. It's not the first time we've faced poor odds and triumphed."

"I want to help."

Bryn stiffens, his knuckles whitening as he grips his mug of tea. "It's too dangerous. Stay here with Abby until all of this is over."

"You mean let other people fight for me?"

I stare at him until he looks up, but there is such fear and pain in his eyes that I am the one who looks away.

"Yes. That is exactly what you should do."

Slowly, I shake my head. Previously, I would have done what he asked. Part of me still wants to. It's an easy way out. I can say that I wanted to protect Abby or blame Bryn for not wanting the distraction of having me around. The memories of the Battle of

Rose Square still haunt me. I still see their faces, still see the bullets rip through their bodies, still taste the smoke and blood, still see the pale face of the boy who had sacrificed himself to save me.

I still see my father's death.

But while it may be the easy way out, while I may be able to persuade others that my actions were out of consideration for Bryn, deep inside, I can't conceal the real reason I would be hiding. That I'm scared of what might happen. Scared of death and the pain that precedes it. Scared that I'll have to watch my friends die and not be able to protect them. Scared that I'll let people down.

I hide my hands underneath the table so they don't see how much they tremble.

"No."

Bryn's jaw tenses. "Trey—"

"Don't make me feel guilty, Bryn. Don't say I need to stay safe for you or Abby or Ella or my parents. It's *my* decision. And I want to help. I may be a weedy non-fighter, but there must be something useful I can do."

Bryn deflates. "I didn't *say* you were a weedy non-fighter. You don't have to prove anything to me." His gaze darts to me. "Or Aleesha."

"This isn't about Aleesha." It's not a complete lie. It's not *all* about Aleesha, but how could I ever look her in the eye again if I chose to hide rather than fight?

When I read about past wars in my history class, I'd always thought soldiers were stupid for going to fight, that patriotism wasn't worth losing your life over. But I understand now. Most people fight not for their country, but for the people they love. To protect them or prove themselves worthy of their love.

Bryn glances up at Abby, who's been silently staring out of the window throughout our conversation. "Aren't you going to say anything?"

She turns slowly, her eyes glinting in the dying light. "How many times have I tried to persuade *you* not to go, Bryn? If it were up to me, neither of you would be fighting. But it's not up to me, and Trey is old enough to make his own decisions."

Her words strike a chord deep inside me. I know Abby loves me like a son. Yet she trusts me to my make own decisions.

Abby stands and pulls down her medical bag from its hook on the wall, shrugging when Bryn gives her a pointed look. "I'm just being prepared."

I remember the last time Abby had gone to help the wounded at the Battle of Rose Square. She'd almost died. My stomach lurches. "Abby—"

"Are you going to tell me to stay out of it, too, Trey?" She shoves a packet of dressings into the bag with unnecessary force. The unspoken words hang between us. I swallow down the lump in my throat.

What gives me the right to help and not her?

Bryn lets out a heavy sigh. "I don't know why you two have to be so bloody stubborn."

I look at Abby. The twitch at the corner of her lips sets me off, then we both start laughing hysterically.

Bryn looks at us as if we've gone mad.

"You call us stubborn?" Abby finally manages to say, wiping her eyes.

He looks unimpressed. "Well, you are." He pushes his chair back and stomps from the room, muttering something under his breath.

Abby sits and leans her elbows on the table. "Oh, that man ..." She smiles softly, a faraway look in her eyes.

I push my chair back and stand, draining the last of the tea. Abby moves to stand, but I wave her to stay seated. "Can you not even stay for dinner?"

I pull my backpack on. "Thanks, but I want to get down to Area Four before it gets dark."

I now understand why Aleesha pushed me away. It's not that she doesn't care for me, but maybe that she cares too much. She's also trying to protect the people she cares about, just like I wanted to protect my mother and Ella.

Perhaps we have both been making the same mistakes all along.

33

Aleesha

I pull myself up onto the rooftop as the sun dips behind the white towers Inside, turning the sky a brilliant red. It bounces off the Wall, intensifying the swirls of colour that range from a dusky pink to a deep crimson. The divide between Inside and Outside runs with blood. Remembering my dream, I wonder if it is an omen for what is to come.

Exhaustion washes over me as I slump down in front of a gap in the parapet where the old concrete has crumbled away. I sit and watch the sky as the red fades to pink, then grey. The packet of tronk rests in my hand, but I don't take it. Not yet.

At what point, I wonder, did it all start going wrong? Was it when I started thinking about others and not just my own survival? When I met Trey and learned that perhaps a guy could like me for me, and not just my body? Or when Abby invited me into her home, again and again, even after I had done awful, terrible things?

I never knew caring for other people could hurt so much.

For years, I have sat here looking out over the rooftops of Area Four, hoping that, one day, I would find my father and he would be the Insider who could save me from my life of poverty. When he did turn up, when he was the rich man I'd dreamed of and offered to take me away from this city, this life, I chose to stay.

The universe gave me exactly what I'd asked for, and I turned my back on it.

Fate has a cruel sense of humour.

The dark memories inside me push against the bars of their cage, their taunts filling my head. All the bad things that have been said about me – and there are many – swirl around, and however much I tell myself that I was only a child, that *they* were the bad people and the things they did to me were wrong, I still can't let the memories go.

"What do I do now, Mama?" I whisper, closing my eyes and trying to picture her face. It gets harder every year, time leaching the colours and smells from my memory. For the first year after she'd left, I could pretend she was still there. I would ask a question, then close my eyes and hear her answer. Then, slowly, I lost the ability to see her and had to learn to make my own decisions.

I was twelve the first time I took tronk. I'd seen enough addicts by then to know it was bad, but I'd been sick and was so weak from hunger I could barely climb down from my rooftop to scrounge for food. A hobie took pity on me and shared a rat he'd caught and roasted over a fire. He didn't even ask for anything in return. But I was still so hungry. Then a woman shuffled closer and showed us the packet of powder she carried up her sleeve. The man had shook his head, but the woman told me that just a little could take away the hunger. I had hesitated, but she'd been insistent, and the man had melted away into the shadows, leaving me alone with her.

"I don't want to go to sleep," I'd told her.

The woman had smiled kindly. "I know." She held my hand gently and tipped a small amount of the powder into it.

I paused with it halfway to my mouth. "What d'ya want for it?"

"Nothing." She saw the wary look on my face and sighed. "Honest. But if you want to give me something ... How about a smile? I had a daughter once." Her face softened, her eyes heavy with grief.

I forced a grin onto my face and thanked her. I even let her hold my hand as I tipped the powder into my mouth. The woman had been right. The growling in my belly faded almost as soon as the tronk touched my tongue. But she'd also lied, or perhaps not realized the effect even a small amount would have on a child's body. The tronk had quickly dragged me down.

But in that drug-induced stupor, I had seen *her*, as clearly as the day she'd left. I'd felt her arms around me and pressed my face into her hair, smelling the cheap soap that never quite made you feel clean. I felt safe, happy.

When I awoke, the woman was snoring next to me and the alleyway was dark and cold.

I didn't see her the second time I took tronk, nor the third. But I did the fourth. I was careful not to take it too often – I couldn't afford it and didn't want to become addicted – but if I hadn't seen her for a while, the desire for it became overwhelming.

Now, more than ever, I need to see her. Even if I know in my heart that she is just a figment of my imagination, I still need to feel her touch and have her whisper into my ear that she loves me.

My hands shake as I open the packet of tronk, but as the first grain of powder hits my palm, a scuffling noise from the far side of the roof stops me.

I slowly right the packet and silently get to my feet. The scuffling gets louder, and I pull the knife Mitch had given me from my boot. In all the years I've lived up here, no one has found the way up. No one should be *able* to get up. I curse inwardly, realizing that in my hurry to get up here I must have failed to lock the trapdoors behind me.

Now I will have to fight, maybe even kill. And there has already been too much violence today.

As if on cue, the swelling on my jaw begins to throb.

I pad over to the small building at the centre of the roof and duck underneath the rough shelter that extends out on one side. There's a muttered curse, then a head appears, topped with hair so blond it seems to reflect the light of the moon.

"Trey?" I step out from behind the wall as he hauls himself onto the roof, panting with exertion. "What ... How did you get up here?"

He glances up at me and grins. "I remembered the way. Are you proud of me?" When I don't reply, the smile slides from his face. "Are you okay?"

I turn my back and walk to the far side of the roof, my throat too thick and choked to speak. Anger flares in my belly that he dares come here of all places and interrupt me. I work my jaw as his footsteps draw closer.

"Do you want me to leave?" His voice is a whisper on the breeze.

I shake my head, then nod, then shake it again. Even that decision is too much right now.

"I went to your headquarters, but the guards wore yellow bandannas. Someone told me the Bigland Boys had taken over." Trey pauses. "Rogue, everyone ... Are they okay?"

The lump in my throat swells when I open my mouth to speak. I close it again soundlessly.

"Aleesha?" His fingertips touch my shoulder. I flinch instinctively and step away, not wanting to admit what happened. I swallow down the lump and try to compose myself.

Trey grabs my arm, jerking me around. Pain flashes up my shoulder and a cry escapes my lips before I can clamp it down.

"I'm sorry. I ..." Trey's voice trails off as he sees my face. "What happened to you?"

"Challenged Denzel to a fight." I try to keep my voice light, but emotion chases the words up my throat. "Beat him, too, but the bastard cheated and—" I choke on the words and turn away again, not wanting to see the pity in his eyes.

Trey curses. "What are you going to do?"

I close my eyes. *That is the question.*

He steps closer, and his scent fills my nostrils. He's so close I could lean back into him and let him wrap his arms around me. Every part of me yearns for that contact, and I have to ball my hands into fists to stop myself from reaching for him.

You sent him away for a reason.

To keep him safe. And protect my Phoenixes.

My nostrils flare. For a moment, I can smell the dirt, the blood that stained the fighting ring and the floor of the room where Anders had lain. My heart throbs in my chest.

"Talk to me, Aleesha. What happened?"

He doesn't touch me, perhaps waiting for me to make the first move. It makes sense. After all, I've pushed him away so many times. Yet he still comes back.

I wonder why. Why he came up here at night to a barren rooftop in one of the roughest parts of the city rather than relaxing in his new home. I guess I could ask him, but I don't. I just turn and stalk over to the sheltered area.

Send him away. Keep him safe.

Behind me, Trey lets out a soft sigh.

I stop in front of the building and sit down. "Thanks for checking on me. As you can see, I'm still alive. I'm sure you can find your own way back down."

Trey sits down beside me. "What if I don't want to leave?"

I nearly grind my teeth. "Why stay?"

"The stars look nice from up here. You don't get to see them much

Inside." He lies back and folds his arms behind his head.

My body is stiff with tension. The tronk burns a hole in my pocket, and heat pulses through my body, carrying with it anger, fear, despair. With every passing minute, it becomes harder to hold back the dark thoughts that swirl inside me. Only the tronk whispers of release.

Please leave, Trey.

I'm not sure why I can't say the words out loud.

"You can't protect everyone, you know. I made that mistake. I thought I could do my father's job and protect my family." His voice is quiet, thoughtful, as he stares up at the sky. "But if you try to look after people too much, you risk taking away their free will, their ability to make their own decisions and lead their own lives. A baby bird coddled in the nest will never learn how to fly."

He pauses. "I thought that if I earned enough money, I'd be able to make Mother well again. I thought if I could just keep Ella away from Samson and the Chain, she would be safe. But money can't cure everything, and my sister ..." He chuckles softly. "Well, we all know my sister has a mind of her own."

Trey tilts his head to look at me. "You know what I've learned? To truly love someone, you must be prepared to let them go. To allow them to fly on their own and let them decide if they will return."

Somehow, I don't think it's just Ella he's speaking about.

A tear escapes from the corner of my eye and runs down my cheek. I dare not lift a finger to wipe it away for fear that the trickle will turn into a flood.

I owe Trey an apology. Actually, I owe him a lot more than that. But for now, an apology will have to do.

I draw in a lungful of air and slowly release it. After two more, I feel calm enough to speak. "What I said when we spoke outside Phoenix headquarters ... I'm sorry."

"About which part?"

"All of it. I shouldn't have blamed you for the Metz capturing me. And it's not your fault I let my gang down. I seem to be doing that perfectly well on my own." I can't hide the bitterness in my voice.

He sits up. His hand brushes the back of mine, sending a small tingle up my arm. "What happened, Aleesha?"

Slowly, haltingly, I tell him. It's easier this way – sitting in the dark, staring into the night, pretending he can't see the expression on my face. I can almost imagine that I'm alone, telling my story to the wind and the stars.

When I finish, we sit in silence for a moment. "So you didn't see any of them in the headquarters?"

"No."

"If Denzel did have them prisoner, he'd have used them against you. The fact he didn't suggests they escaped."

I shake my head. "The blood on the floor—"

"Doesn't mean they're dead. Besides, you don't know whose blood it was. It could have been from one of the Bigland Boys."

His words make sense. *But if they're not at the headquarters, where are they?*

I file the thought away for a time when my mind isn't churning and battling with itself. The darkness sucks at me, the memories banging against the door of their cage so hard that I fear they might break through any minute. My stomach knots at the idea of facing them, of being pulled down into that pit of despair.

Trey's scent brings me back. Fresh pine fills my nostrils as he leans in. "Aleesha?"

He grasps my hand. I want to pull away, in case he could become infected by my darkness. My shoulders sag, my body caving as the weight pulls me down.

I let my fingers stray to my pocket and the packet of tronk.

It's the only way I can stop the darkness from taking over.

"Please, you have to go," I choke out. "Now."

"Tell me." Trey's voice is firm. Where has the frightened boy gone? Who is this confident, caring man who's replaced him? "Whatever it is, you'll feel better after speaking it out loud."

I shake my head. How can I tell him, of all people? He already knows some of it – a tiny portion of my past that I carved off and gave to him weeks ago when we stood on this very rooftop. But that was just a glimpse of the darkness I carry inside. If he knows the whole truth, he will run far away and never come back.

To truly love someone, you must be prepared to let them go.

But he couldn't have meant this. Could he? My head pounds from the effort of holding back. I try to focus on my breathing, counting in and out. Even tears won't come.

"You don't know what I've done," I finally manage. "Please, just leave me."

He doesn't leave. Instead, he wraps an arm gently around my shoulders, somehow remembering not to press on the tattoo on my back, and pulls me close. His voice is quiet in my ear. "I can't promise to get rid of the darkness, but I won't leave you to face it alone."

I don't know if it's his words, the warmth of his body or the smell of him, but part of me finally gives way. The cage door bursts open, and this time, I cannot close it.

"Tell me."

And because I have no choice, because it is either that or let myself be sucked down into that black void I am so afraid of, I tell him everything. I tell him what happened the day my mother left, then the days, months and years after that. I tell him about everyone I have hurt, everyone I have wronged, knowing he will hate me for it. In a way, it is a relief, because there will be no more pretence between us. He will know who I really am, and he will know I am not worthy of his friendship, his lo—

I can't even think the word.

When I finish, I pull away, giving him permission to leave. But he tightens his grip and pulls me close again. He does not comment on what I've just said, instead beginning to talk about another girl, a woman who is the bravest person he's ever known, who loves so fiercely and cares far more than she admits. A woman who's strong, beautiful and full of light and hope.

It is only when he reaches the end that I realize he's talking about me.

I struggle against his grip, but he just holds me tighter. "You've got it wrong! Weren't you listening to what I said?" Tears prick at my eyes as I lower my voice to a whisper. "Weren't you listening?"

Trey's eyes glint in the moonlight as he turns to look at me. "I heard every word. But what you told me was just one part of you. Have you forgotten all the good things you've done just to cling to the bad?"

"What do they matter? It's not them I need forgiveness for. It's the people I've lied to, the people I've hurt, the people I've ..." I swallow, barely able to utter the word. "Killed."

Trey places his hand on my chest. It rests on the amulet hanging around my neck, pressing the metal into my skin. "You talk about needing forgiveness from others, but it seems to me the person you need forgiveness from is yourself," he says quietly. "You are a good person, Aleesha. I see that. Your friends see that. Now *you* need to see that."

You are a good person.

Warmth blossoms in my chest. Not the fire of anger and repressed emotion, but a gentle, soothing warmth, like the early morning sun before the heat of the day sets in.

I let myself sag against Trey, feeling his heart beating in his chest, steadfast and sure. I let out a long breath, imagining that the air leaving my body carries the darkest memories with it. With every breath, I feel a little lighter inside. The memories are still there, but some of the weight I've been carrying is gone.

"You don't have to do everything alone, you know."

I smile, even though he can't see my face. "Do you always say the right thing?"

"No. When you broke up with me, I should have told you that you were being stupid and self-centred."

I lift my head and punch him lightly. "That's no way to talk to—"

His hand cups my neck, gently pulling me forward until our faces are inches apart. His breath is warm on my lips.

Then I do what I've been wanting to do ever since the day in the street when I told him we could never be together. When I kidded myself that I could be happy without him.

I kiss him.

Blood pulses in my ears as he pulls me down so I'm lying on top of him, our bodies pressed together. My lips tingle, my nerves sensitive to every touch. His hands roam down my sides, and I arch my back, wanting every part of me to touch him.

He pulls back to kiss my cheek, then my jaw, trailing his mouth down to nip the soft skin of my neck. A moan escapes my lips. Then his mouth comes back to mine, his hands moving lower. All I can taste, all I can feel, is him. I am drowning in him, yet I don't want to come up for air.

But I can't lose myself completely – not yet.

I pull away, the night air cool on my lips. His gaze is questioning, and I see the shadow of doubt in his eyes. I kiss him again, but this time, I don't allow myself to linger.

"I have to do something," I whisper.

I push myself up and sit back on my heels, fingering the amulet around my neck – the gift from a woman who loved me enough to give up her life for me. She didn't deserve to die, but that doesn't mean I don't deserve to live. I don't need to see her to know she would forgive me – has already forgiven me – for everything I've done.

She loved me more than her own life, and that is a gift I cannot waste.

Standing, I stride across the roof to the far parapet. I pull the packet of tronk from my pocket and open it. Light footsteps approach from behind.

"More tronk?" Trey asks sadly.

I shake my head, then tip the packet and let the wind carry the powder away. When it's almost empty, a thought strikes me, and I jerk the packet upright. I lick my pinkie and dip it into the packet, then touch the powder to my tongue. I close my eyes, waiting for the drug to hit.

But it doesn't.

"That bastard." A giggle bubbles up, erupting from my lips, then I'm laughing so hard tears run down my cheeks. "That bastard," I say again. Trey just looks confused. I hold up the packet. "There's no tronk in here. It's just a mixer." I wipe my eyes. "A debt paid indeed."

I tip the packet again and a gust of wind catches the remnants of the powder, carrying it out over the city. It reminds me of when I'd scattered Lily's ashes, and for a moment, I am silent.

Trey was right. I had been so afraid of losing my friends that I didn't give them the trust they deserved. I had wanted to protect them, not accepting that one person cannot always be by the side of a hundred others.

You cannot guarantee the safety of every single person who looks to you for protection. And safety comes at a price.

As much as I hate to admit it, Samson was right.

To care means accepting the fear of loss or betrayal.

To love someone is to give them the freedom to choose.

To lead is to give others power.

If my Phoenixes are still alive and still want me as their leader, I will give them a choice. To make what life they can out of the dregs the city has to offer, or to fight with my father and the Chain for more. For a better life. For freedom. Whatever they decide, I will respect that decision.

But I also have to respect my heart.

If they choose not to fight with him, I will go alone.

"The food factories are suspending supplies out into the city," Trey says. "Coleman said it was because of the risk of the pods being shot down, but I wonder if it's to force the Chain's hand. If the government blames them for the fact that food supplies have been cut, Outsiders won't sympathize with them for long."

"We need to end this." I stare at the Wall. "The longer this fighting goes on, the more people will die."

"I know."

"Do you trust him? My father?"

Trey shrugs. "Whatever he's offering can't be worse than the way things are now." He glances over at me. "You're not going to keep me out of this one. I'm a wanted fugitive – again." His lips quirk into a smile.

I grin over at him. "Well, I figure the best way to make sure I don't have to run off and save your arse is to keep you close."

He takes my hand and squeezes it. "I'd like that."

Inside my chest, the cage that has held for so long crumbles. The bad memories float around my mind like dust on a summer breeze, always present, yet not as invasive as they were. I am not the same girl I was twelve years ago, but for the first time since my mother walked out that door, I feel that maybe, one day, I will be whole again.

When you open your heart to someone, you risk fear, loss, betrayal. But I'll choose love over fear any day.

34

Trey

The night I spend on the rooftop has to be one of the most uncomfortable night's sleep I've ever had. Not that I slept much. By the time the sky begins to lighten, I give up and push myself upright, wrapping the thin blanket Aleesha had given me around my shoulders.

She hadn't wanted to stay here, but she'd been so exhausted she could barely walk in a straight line. In the end, she gave in and agreed to rest for a few hours before resuming the search for the remnants of her gang. I'd helped clean her wounds, made her drink and eat something, then curled up around her, cocooning her in my arms.

I offer up a silent prayer that I'm right and Rogue and the others escaped the headquarters. That I haven't raised her hopes only to have them smashed once again.

I'm not sure how long I sit, just watching her chest rise and fall. Watching her sleep feels more intimate than all our embraces, all our kisses. In sleep, the hardness and watchfulness that I've come to associate with her are stripped away, leaving the vulnerable girl behind. The urge to reach out and brush her hair back from her face almost overwhelms me, but I resist. She needs to rest.

If you exist, God, please keep her safe.

Last night, when she'd told me what had happened, I had to fight to retain my composure and not show the horror and disgust I'd felt, just in case she thought it was for what she'd done rather than what had been done to her. I'd wanted to slam my fist into the concrete, but instead, I just held her as she talked. Of all the gifts she could have given me, this one, telling me the truth about her past, is the greatest.

The first rays of the morning sun bathe the surrounding rooftops in a warm light. Aleesha stretches and yawns, then sits up, brushing her hair back.

"Sleep well?" I ask.

"When you weren't keeping me awake with your snoring." She gives me a mock scowl.

"*My* snoring?"

"I know for a fact I don't snore." She smiles impishly, then sobers. "How long have I been asleep?"

"A few hours."

She looks around at the warm glow of the sun, then gives me a wry look. "More like six."

"You needed it."

"Perhaps." She stretches, wincing, then stands. "I feel like I've been used as a punch bag."

"You were," I point out. I reach for my backpack and pull out a couple of carefully wrapped cakes Thomas had given me, holding one out to Aleesha. "Breakfast."

Her eyes light up as she unwraps the treat and takes a huge bite. "You can come more often if you bring these," she mumbles around a mouthful.

I know she's joking, but her comment causes my stomach to twist with guilt. Why had Milicent picked me to be her heir? I didn't need all her money, her wealth. Perhaps she hadn't meant it for me at all, but wanted me to be custodian of it. I ponder this for a moment while we eat.

"So, what now?" I ask, brushing crumbs off my legs and standing. My body is stiff and unresponsive.

"I need to find out what's happened to the gang." She draws in a deep breath. "If they've survived, I'll ask them if they will fight with the Chain."

I'm surprised. "You don't want to take back your headquarters first?"

Aleesha shakes her head. "The Bigland Boys have too much of an advantage. They somehow got their hands on some high-tech weapons. Denzel says they stole them, but only the government and the Chain have weapons like that." She stops suddenly, a frown flashing across her face, before she continues. "Anyway, the headquarters is a fortress. We don't stand a chance against them at the moment. But if we help the Chain, they'll owe us. They can help us take our home back."

"How can I help?"

She looks thoughtful, seeming to take my offer seriously rather than dismissing me. "The Chain needs all the help they can get." She takes a couple of steps over to her backpack and unfastens it. "Mika gave me some strong antibiotics and some kind of special dressing. I got some spares." She hands me a set of syringes in a plastic box and two square, plastic packages. "Take these to Samson and see if the Brotherhood will help us. We saved his life. They owe us."

We shoulder our backpacks and toss the blankets into a corner under the roof. Before we leave, Aleesha slips her arms around my waist, pulling me to her and resting her head against my chest. "Thanks for not giving up on me, Trey."

I wrap my arms around her, wondering if this means we're

officially back together. But this isn't the time to ask. There are more important things we have to do right now. After all this is over, there will be time for talking.

We're friends again at least, and that's enough for now.

But as I close my eyes and breathe in her sweet, vanilla scent, I wish that this moment, when there is just her and me, could last forever.

* * * *

The streets of Area Four are quiet. Aleesha gives me directions to get to the apartment where we'd left Samson and is about to veer off down a side alley when she stops and begins to sprint down the street. I run after her, my heart lurching.

What now?

Then I catch sight of a small figure perched on top of a large dumpster, peering in. He jumps and turns as Aleesha approaches, then his face breaks into a toothy grin.

Aleesha grabs him around the waist and pulls him down, squeezing him to her. "Tommy? You're alive. You're—" Her voice cracks, and she plants a kiss on his forehead.

"Hey, gerrof." Tommy squirms. Reluctantly, she lets him go. He wipes the back of his hand over his forehead, smearing it with dirt. "Eww."

"What are you doing here? Where are the others?"

"Lookin' for you, ain't I? Most of the others gave up when we heard you'd gone in to fight Denzel and not come out. They thought you was dead." He thumbs his chest. "But I know you *always* win. Anders an' Rogue thought so, too."

"Did everyone get out?"

Tommy scrunches up his face. "Most people. They attacked one of the shops to draw us out, then hit the headquarters. When Megan saw they had guns and stuff, she told everyone to get out the back way. Everyone scarpered, but I fink most ended up with the monks or in the jungle."

"They left headquarters …" Aleesha's voice trails off.

Tommy shrugs. "It's just a building. Not worth dyin' for." He catches sight of me. "Hey, Trey."

"Hi, Tommy." I smile at the boy, then remember something. It's unimportant now, but Aleesha still looks like she needs a few seconds to process everything. "Did a girl named Helen ask you for a chit?"

"Yeah, she did." His face twists into an expression that's half disgruntled, half grudging respect. "I bargained her down to half a chit."

I stifle my amusement. At least she got something out of it, and I suspect Tommy's lesson on bargaining was worth more than the half a chit she ended up with.

I place a hand on Aleesha's shoulder. "You okay?"

She nods, then takes a deep breath. "Come on, Tommy. Let's go." Glancing at me, she adds, "I'll see you for the meeting?"

"See you later."

I watch them walk down the street, then head off in the opposite direction, toward Area Three. I'm already sweating under the light jacket I wear, but I keep the hood up to hide my hair. Dressed in jeans and a black jacket, I might just about pass for an Outsider from Five or Six with business in Four. If I keep moving and make it look as if I know where I'm going, hopefully no one will stop me. I mentally recite the directions Aleesha had given me until I reach a street that looks familiar. Glancing around, I approach the door of the apartment we carried Samson into a couple of nights ago and knock twice.

I hear footsteps behind the door, but there's a pause before it finally opens a crack. A glinting, brown eye peeks out at me. "What d'ya want?"

"I have medical supplies for Samson."

The eye surveys me. "Who are you?"

"My name's Trey. He knows me."

The eye pulls back and the door slams shut. I'm about to knock again when it opens, a short man beckoning me in. The windows are boarded up, so when the man closes the door behind me, we're plunged into darkness. I blink as my eyes adjust to the dim light.

"This way." The man pushes past me and opens another door.

I follow him, drawn by the soft, warm glow of a lamp from within. A bed fills most of the room. Samson lies there, apparently asleep, but even in the dim light, I can see his skin is ashen. His huge frame makes the double bed seem like a single. Barnes sits beside him, clasping his hand in both of hers.

"You managed to escape then?" She doesn't look up.

I nod. "They delivered my crate to a shop in Area Four. Gave the shopkeeper the fright of his life when I didn't turn out to be twenty packs of burgers."

Her lips twitch, but she can't even manage a small smile. Her gaze lingers on Samson's face. "Similar story, except I got taken to Five."

"How is he?"

"I don't know. He hasn't woken up since I've been here, though the others said he was conscious a few times during the night." She glances up, tears glistening in her eyes. "Thank you for finding him. For believing me."

I pull the syringes from my backpack and hand them to her. "These are from the Chain's medic. They're stronger than whatever Abby gave him."

Barnes stiffens at the mention of the Chain and glares down at the syringes, as if they contain poison.

"Mika didn't know who they were for," I add hurriedly. "The meds they have are far superior to anything you'll get out here." I hesitate. "If he won't go to a medic, it's the next best thing. Surely it's better than letting him—"

"Don't!" Barnes brushes at her eyes angrily as her voice breaks. She coughs in an attempt to disguise her emotion. "Don't say it. He'll be fine. He has to be."

But both of us can see that he is far from fine.

I pull out the plastic packages and rip one open. There are instructions on the inside. "This should help draw out the infection from inside his body and heal the wound. I only have two."

Together, we unwrap the bandages covering the two bullet wounds on Samson's body. I try not to look at the red, angry skin surrounding each wound as I stick the pads over them. Samson barely stirs as we tend to him. When we're done, Barnes pulls the sheet back up to his shoulders.

"Richard, the Chain's leader, has a meeting scheduled this morning. The government has called in reinforcements. The Chain has lost the government headquarters and the President's escaped."

Barnes's shoulders stiffen. She turns and washes her hands in a bowl of water, drying them on a towel.

"They need your help."

"You think *we're* going to help him? He's the one who did this!" She throws the towel down on the table.

"You don't know that. The sooner this ends, the better the chances we can get Samson to a medic – a proper surgeon who can make sure those bullets are removed and heal his internal wounds. Do you really want to let him die?"

Barnes whirls around, her green eyes flashing. "Get. Out."

I glance toward the door, wondering if Petal is around and if he'll be more open to reason. But as I turn to leave, a small moan comes

359

from the bed.

Barnes leans over Samson, her anger forgotten as she presses a hand to his cheek. "Samson?"

A lump rises in my throat at the tenderness in her voice.

Samson's eyelids flicker, then open, his gaze looking past her to me. "Trey ..." His voice is barely audible, but I find myself walking the few steps to the bed as if it were an order.

Barnes fumbles with a jug of water. "Here. Drink this." She places her arm under Samson's head and manages to heave his shoulders high enough for him to take a sip.

When she lowers him back to the bed, his eyes met mine. "Tell me ... what Richard ... is planning. We may ... help." His eyes close and he sinks back against the pillow, exhausted.

An anguished expression crosses Barnes's face. "You can't mean that," she whispers, staring down at him. I've never seen her look so torn.

"Look, I'll go to the meeting. I won't make any promises on your behalf, but I will come back and tell you what the plan is. Then you can decide whether you want to be involved."

"Fine." Barnes sounds reluctant, and I can understand why. She picks up one of the syringes. "Any instructions?"

"The packet says to give him one dose every other day."

Barnes places her hand back on Samson's cheek. "He's burning up," she murmurs.

I back slowly toward the door. "I'll come back later."

"Wait." Samson's voice halts me. His eyelids flutter, then open again. The fingers on his left hand slowly curl into a fist. "Don't tell Richard I'm alive. If you can't lie ... tell him I'm ... incapacitated." A grimace ripples across his face as a shudder racks his body. "That's pretty much ... the truth."

"Why don't you want him to know you're alive?" I ask.

Samson turns his head to stare at me. His dark eyes bore through mine, and I take an involuntary step back, even though he can't move from the bed.

He raises an eyebrow in amusement. "So he doesn't ... send someone ... to finish the job."

* * * *

I wait at the corner of the street leading to the Chain's new headquarters. It isn't long before I see Aleesha striding up the street, Rogue's tall figure beside her. She favours me with a smile as they come closer, which I return, then give Rogue an awkward nod. He looks exhausted.

"Is everyone okay?"

Aleesha's face tightens. "We've accounted for most people. Some have taken refuge at the church, others at Giles's old home."

After knocking on the door of the tall townhouse the Chain has taken as their headquarters, we're kept waiting for over a minute. Finally, Katya opens the door.

"Bryn said you might be coming," she says to me, then glances at Aleesha. "Though I wasn't expecting you."

Aleesha pushes past her, Rogue following with an apologetic frown.

"Upstairs, second room on your left," Katya calls after us.

The room isn't as large as the conference room at the Chain's former headquarters in Area Six, and it's already full. Richard sits at the head of the table, Bryn and Mika to his left. To his right is an empty chair, then Anabel and a man I don't recognize. My sister gives me a brief smile before turning back to her boss.

Katya shuts the door and takes the seat next to Richard. There's one chair left. I gesture for Aleesha to take it, but she ignores me and shoves a pile of films off a small table in the corner before hopping up onto it. Rogue stands like a statue beside her.

I shrug and sit down in the chair.

Dark circles rim Richard's eyes and his shirt is rumpled and stained, as if he hasn't changed it in days. I look around the room, wondering where Murdoch is. He's the only senior member of the Chain who isn't present. The man to my left stifles a yawn and slips a pill into his mouth. A stimulant perhaps? How long have they been fighting now? Days? Weeks? Time is taking its toll, draining them of energy, of the will to keep fighting.

"Thank you for coming," Richard begins. "This engagement has gone on longer than any of us hoped it would. You know I don't like to admit failure ..." His eye twitches, momentarily distorting the scar next to it. "But I admit, I underestimated the strength of the government's response and their coordination in the President's absence. We are not defeated yet, nor do I intend to be. But the longer this goes on, the more our troops will tire. The government knows that. Their strategy is to wear us down."

He pauses and looks around the room. "They have more fighters, but their people aren't used to working together. They are less coordinated than us – at the moment. Which is why we must act now. One final push and we will take this city."

He places a black box on the table, and the holos of four figures appear in the air. "Our aim is to take out the President, plus his three remaining advisers."

"You mean kill them?" I blurt out. "Even the President?"

Richard lifts his gaze. "Yes. If we can capture the President alive, we will do so. We may be able to persuade him to surrender. As for the others, we can't afford the resources to look after prisoners. Once they're out of the picture, the government's coordination and defence will crumble."

As much as I'd rather no one got killed, I'm not convinced by his hope that the President will surrender. He didn't when the Chain had him prisoner, and the government must know they have the upper hand now.

"Where are they at this moment?" Bryn asks.

"Three are at various strongholds across the city. We believe one is leading their troops on the ground."

Bryn rubs his chin. "We're going to be spreading ourselves thin, even if our information is accurate. Air strikes?"

Richard shakes his head. "They have control of the airspace, not to mention we're almost out of the M360s that are the only missiles they can't stop. We'll try, but we can't rely on them."

He gestures to Anabel, who produces a large roll of film. She unrolls it on the table, weighing down the corners with mugs of coffee. It's a map of the city, sectioned off into the different areas. The Wall is a red line running around three sides of the inner part of the city, the southern side bounded by the river.

"Whatever happens, we cannot lose the Metz compound. It's only a matter of time before they find or create a weakness, breaking through our defences. Murdoch's there now, and he reports that they're not letting up. But there's not much we can do from inside the compound to weaken their army." He draws a circle on the map. "We need to draw them away, create enough of a distraction that they're forced to move some of their fighters elsewhere. Then we have small teams infiltrate the areas we know the leaders to be and take them out."

"That makes sense, but do we have enough people to do all that?" the man next to me asks.

"We do now." Richard looks at Aleesha, who meets his gaze steadily. My heart sinks.

What does he have planned for her?

"We need to divide their troops. Get some of them out of the picture." Richard leans forward across the map. "At the moment, they're protected by the Wall. But if we draw them Outside ..." He draws an arrow across the Wall into Area Four. "The Wall will trap them, splitting their force in two."

"But to do that you'd need to take down the Wall," Aleesha says.

"Then put it up again," I add.

Richard meets my gaze. "Exactly. That's the risky part of the plan."

Every part of his plan sounds risky to me, but I don't question him.

"Before we lost the government headquarters, our techs managed to hack into the main infrastructure system and find out how the Wall works. The information tallied with what we got out of the President. There are two control centres, which both need to be accessed to take down the Wall. One is in the Metz headquarters."

"The secret room," Rogue murmurs behind me.

Richard glances at him sharply. "You know of it?"

"Not much. We weren't told what it was for. Only that if the compound was ever compromised, we must defend it above all else. If unable to do that, we were to smash the access panel to keep it locked."

"Which your ex-colleagues dutifully did when we broke in." Richard's mouth quirks. "Fortunately, our technology is rather more advanced than what you have here in Britannia. We managed to gain access the other day."

"And the second centre?" Anabel asks.

"That's a little trickier. The government wanted to make sure no single person would be able to take down the Wall. I don't think they ever believed the compound could be taken but they wanted a failsafe in case anyone who did have access decided to take matters into their own hands. For that reason, the second part of the mechanism is located in a different building – one Outside the Wall that nobody in the Metz would have reason to access."

The man next to me frowns. "That should be a piece of cake after taking the compound. The government buildings Outside are generally small and undefended."

"True, but the mechanism isn't located in a government building. And, unfortunately, it's very well defended." Richard looks at me. "In fact, from what we know, it's currently in lockdown."

The pieces of the puzzle click together in my mind. "Coleman's factory," I whisper.

Richard nods. "Our intelligence indicated it was in one of the two factories. When Bryn mentioned that you'd seen a heavily guarded door in the basement, Coleman's refusal to open discussions with us began to make sense." His gaze flicks to Katya, whose lips twist.

"When we have control of both parts of the mechanism, we can switch sections of the Wall off and on as we please." He glances at me, then Aleesha, his face grim. "I didn't want to involve either of you in this. You're young and inexperienced, and it's dangerous."

I sense Aleesha stiffen behind me.

"But I have no choice," Richard continues. "Trey, you're the only one who's been inside the factory and knows where the mechanism is likely to be located. Plus, I believe you still have contacts inside who may be able to help."

He doesn't wait for my reply before he turns to Aleesha, his face softening. "I would much rather keep you safe until it's all over, but it's clear to me that you have a better knowledge of this part of the city than any of us. While I wouldn't normally pitch your gang against trained fighters, I believe that if you have time to prepare, you can set enough traps to keep the enemy contained. Only a small number of them will be Metz officers, and as their implant system is no longer working, they won't be as coordinated as they have been in the past. The other fighters are mostly from security forces in other parts of the country and don't know London's streets."

Aleesha crosses her arms. "You haven't asked me if we're willing to help you yet."

Richard's brow creases. "I presumed your presence here indicated your willingness to help."

"Sure, but we need something in return. Given that we're such a key part of your plan." She stares at her father, daring him to disagree.

"And what's that?"

"The Bigland Boys have taken over my headquarters. They've got themselves some fancy new weapons." Aleesha's eyes flick to the knife sheath on his belt. "Weapons like yours. Weapons we'll need if you want us to help you."

Richard frowns. "We did have some crates stolen from one of our warehouses last week. We've been too busy to track them down. But we don't have time to get involved in gang disputes."

Aleesha bristles. "It's not just a *gang dispute*. Do you really think it's a good thing for the people out here to have a trigger-happy bully armed to the teeth in control of the streets? If you help us, we can root them out today and still be ready to put your plan into action tomorrow."

Anger flashes in Richard's eyes. I get the feeling he doesn't like people, even his daughter, disagreeing with him. "I told you we don't have the time. Every person I have is working to get ready for this final push. We need every fighter we've got, and I can't risk losing more people trying to settle your personal vendetta."

Aleesha's face darkens. For a moment, I think she's going to storm from the room. Then Richard's expression softens.

"Once we have control of the city, we'll get your headquarters back. I promise."

They stare at each other for a long moment. "Fine," Aleesha says finally. "I'll ask them if they'll help. But it's their decision, not mine."

Richard's frown deepens. "It's a leader's responsibility to make decisions for their people."

Her hands tighten on the edge of the table. "Not this leader."

She pushes herself off the table and peers down at the map. "So, how do we get them Outside?"

Richard traces a line along the Wall adjacent to Area Four and glances at Anabel. "Once we have control of the Wall, we'll take down this section. Your team will go through and make your way to your designated target."

His gaze turns to Aleesha again. "Your gang will start creating trouble in this area." He circles several streets on the map. "Break windows, throw some bombs, threaten citizens. Do whatever you can to draw attention to yourselves. We will put the Wall up behind you, hopefully fast enough that they don't realize it's been down. They'll assume you got in through the tunnels. The government will be forced to divert some of its people to deal with you, allowing Schmidt and Murdoch to get their teams out of the Metz compound to deal with the other targets. Let them follow you back to the Wall, Aleesha. If you can, get some of your team behind them to drive them forward. Make them believe they have you trapped."

I glance at Aleesha. She's chewing her lip.

"I know it's a risk," Richard says quietly. "But I think they'll want to capture you, not kill you. They know you're my daughter and will want to use you for leverage. Once they think they have you trapped, we'll lower the Wall again, allowing you to escape back Outside. Draw them out into Area Four. Once they're through, we'll put the Wall up again, and *they* will be the ones trapped."

There's silence as each of us works through the plan in our heads.

But there's one thing they've forgotten. "You say putting the Wall up will trap them Outside, but Insiders can pass through without being killed. What's to stop them from just running back through?"

Katya leans back in her chair. "Until you read those top-secret documents, did you know that was the case, Trey?"

I shake my head.

She smiles. "There you go then. As far as they're concerned, touching the Wall means death. They'll take their chances on the streets Outside."

Richard turns to Bryn. "You're in charge of the team breaking into the food factory. Take Liza, Harrison and Filip. You'll have to run it as a stealth mission. I'll get one of the techs to send you images of the control room in the compound so you know what you're looking for in the factory. In order for the Wall to come down, the control switches in both the Metz compound and the factory have to be off. Same for putting it back up again. If only one switch is moved, nothing will happen. It's not a complex system, but you need to make sure you only apply the change to this section of the Wall." He circles an area with his finger. "Got it?"

Bryn blows out a breath. "I could use more people."

Richard grimaces. "I know, but I don't have more people. You'll just have to do the best you can."

His words hold an ominous note. Bryn's gaze flicks to me, and I know what he's going to say. I speak quickly, before he can insist I stay behind. "With more people, we might be able to take over the food factory in its entirety. The security team isn't that big because the building's designed to be hard to access. If we take control of the security centre, that would mean we'd have control of the factory *and* the food supply."

"Yes, but we would need more people to do that. Didn't you hear what he said?"

Heat rises to my cheeks at Katya's retort. "The Brotherhood may help. Especially if you have spare weapons they could use. They're smart, and the Outsiders in the factory would be more likely to trust them than your people."

"I'm not working with that scum," Bryn growls. "They'll stab us in the back as soon as help us."

I flash him a sympathetic look, knowing he's thinking about Lamar. I'm not sure he'll ever forgive Samson for killing his friend, but this is not the time for grudges.

Richard raises an eyebrow. "That's actually an idea. Who's in charge now that Samson's dead?"

I ignore the warning look Aleesha flashes me and meet Richard's gaze. "I'll speak to them. If there's a chance we can gain control of the food supply, they may be willing to help."

"Fine, but don't tell them all the details. And remember, your first priority is to get to that basement room."

I bob my head, dropping my gaze to the table. Samson's words ring in my ears. Perhaps they were the confused ramblings of a sick man. But if he does believe Richard ordered his death, why is he so keen to play a part in the Chain's plan?

35

Aleesha

The plan is agreed upon. Tonight, we will make one final push against the government forces. I jokingly describe it as a "do-or-die effort", but nobody laughs.

I hang back as the others leave the room, waiting until my father looks up from his conversation with Bryn.

"If you want us to help you, we'll need weapons. We've barely got a knife a piece. If we're facing trained soldiers with guns, we'll be mowed down before we can even think about drawing them out."

"I'll see what we've got, but we're running out. Besides, looking vulnerable may be your best strategy." My father straightens and comes around the table to stand in front of me. "If the government forces see that you're armed with high-tech weapons, they will shoot you. If they don't see you as a threat, they'll be more confident. They will be reluctant to shoot unarmed citizens. Remember, your job isn't so much to engage them as to draw them Outside the Wall. Once it goes up behind them, your team can disperse into the streets and pick them off like flies."

He makes a good point, but I still don't like the idea of my people going up against heavily armed soldiers with what amounts to little more than cutlery. "If you wanted to keep me out of danger, why did you accept my offer of help?"

He searches my face, the small lines at the corners of his eyes softening. "If I asked you not to fight, would you listen?" When I don't answer, he reaches out and squeezes my shoulder. "I truly don't believe the government forces will kill you. You're too valuable to them."

I want to ask him about the rest of my gang, if the government sees them as valuable, as well, but I'm afraid of the answer, so I turn to leave.

"Aleesha."

I turn back. For a fleeting second, I think he's going to step forward and pull me into a hug, but the moment passes.

"Be careful."

I nod, swallowing past the lump in my throat, and walk out of the room.

Rogue is waiting on the street outside. "So, we are to be dangled as bait," he says as we walk down the street. "Like cattle to the slaughter."

I glance up at him. "You don't approve of the plan?"

His blue eyes stare straight ahead. "I do not like being in a position of weakness. And facing an armed enemy force with no weapons is the definition of a position of weakness."

"So why didn't you speak up when we were inside?"

"Because you're my cap— leader," he says, correcting himself.

"And you trust me?"

"I do."

Does he know how heavy that trust weighs on my shoulders? The lightness I'd felt this morning has evaporated with the realization that we could all be dead in less than twenty-four hours.

Or our city could be free.

I guess I should look on the positive side.

The concrete jungle is suspiciously quiet as we reach the entrance to Giles's cavern. I greet the guards sitting outside, then drop to my hands and knees to crawl in. Rogue follows, grunting with the effort of contorting his large shoulders through the narrow tunnel. I was surprised Anders had made it in with his injury, but Rogue told me they'd dragged him on a blanket most of the way.

We drop down into the taller section of the tunnel and someone pushes aside the curtain ahead of us. Light spills into the dark tunnel, along with the stench of unwashed bodies. I wrinkle my nose. Giles's transformation of the cavern was nothing short of miraculous, but he hadn't accounted for twenty people being crammed into the small space.

As Tommy had said, most of the gang sought sanctuary with the monks at the church, but Rogue didn't want to risk bringing more fighting to their door, so the people he thought the Bigland Boys would be most likely to target came here. When Tommy had brought me here a few hours ago and they'd welcomed me back as if I'd never left, as if I hadn't failed them, I thought my heart would burst.

Perhaps my biggest failure had been underestimating my friends. I thought they needed me to protect them, but they don't. They have each other.

"So, what did they say?" Megan stands, gesturing to Rogue to take the chair she's been sitting on. He does, then pulls her down onto his lap. She favours him with a coy glance. Their relationship seems to be progressing well, but I still carry a slight unease about how much Megan truly cares for him. Rogue is older than her, but in many ways, still very naïve.

Rogue leans in and nuzzles her neck.

"Will you two get a room?" Danny shouts from the other side of the room where he's perched on the end of the bed.

Rogue pulls back, raising a brow. "Well, if you wouldn't mind vacating this one …"

There's a chorus of jeers.

I smile and head over to Anders, who's sitting up in bed. "How are you doing?"

"Feeling better already." He grins at me and touches his shoulder. "Whatever this thing is works like a charm."

His face has more colour, the lines of pain faded. I squeeze his arm, then turn back to survey the room. Anders isn't the only one with injuries, though most of the others are less serious.

"Okay. Listen up!" The room quietens. "Getting our headquarters back is going to have to wait. The Bigland Boys managed to steal a bunch of weapons from the Chain. It would be a suicide mission to take the fight to them now, and as you know, my leadership challenge didn't exactly work out well. But there is another way. The Chain is planning a coordinated attack on the government forces. A final push. In return for helping them take the city, they'll help us get our headquarters back. With their expertise and weapons, the Bigland Boys won't stand a chance."

"Oh right. Once *they* have the city. An' what if they can't beat the gov'ment forces?" Danny narrows his eyes.

"It's a risk." I look around at the faces turned expectantly to me. "But so is everything out here. If the government wins, they will keep controlling our lives. Poisoning our food, sending the Metz in to set fire to our streets, killing whoever tries to stand up to them. Things will be the same as they always have been. But it doesn't have to be. Not if we choose to change it."

Some of them are already captivated by my words, but others wear cautious looks. I remember my promise to myself. My promise to them.

"This is not something I will order you to do. Whether you decide to fight or stay here is your choice, and yours alone. There is no shame if you choose to stay. I'm not going to lie to you. We may not all survive. But I believe we deserve more than the life the government has given us. So I will fight for a better future." I pull out the knife Mitch had given me and place it on the table in front of me. "And if need be, I will die to give you that future."

Silence follows. I count to five. Then Rogue gently lifts Megan from his lap and stands, placing his own knife beside mine. "I will fight with you. For the freedom to choose."

To my surprise, Megan is the next to step forward. She has no weapon – she is not a fighter – but she rests her hand on the table. "I'll help, too." She glances at Rogue and whispers, "For love."

Perhaps I have misjudged her.

"Well, I guess you'll need someone to watch your backs while you're bein' all brave and noble," Danny grumbles, heaving himself up off Anders' bed. "Yer not takin' my gun, though." His knife clatters to the table. "For friendship."

"And for those who have already died for us," Anders adds, swinging his legs off the bed. He sways slightly but stays upright, his face set in determination.

I open my mouth to tell him to lie back down, that he is too badly injured, but his eyes meet mine, the pleading look in them halting my words.

"I'm comin', too!"

I turn back to the table in alarm as a sharpened piece of metal is added to the pile. "No, Tommy. No one under sixteen is allowed to fight."

"Aww, Aleesha ..."

"I mean it." I take his homemade weapon and hand it back to him. "I need some brave people to stay behind and look after the monks. Can you do that?"

He gives me a begrudging nod, and I make a mental note to ask Jax to stay behind and keep him and the other kids in line. They respect him.

One by one, the others in the room add their promises to the pile. Only one person questions me. Connor, a gangly man in his early twenties.

"Can't you just get your da to help us? Why do we need to fight for them?"

"He might, Connor, if I asked him. But do we want that? To beg for help and be in their debt?"

Danny lets out a snort. "Not bloody likely."

"We don't take *favours*," another voice calls.

I smile. My people may be willing to fight and steal, they may have been born in the gutter, but they still have their pride.

The only people you can trust are those who truly care about you. They will follow you through hell simply because they believe in you.

Samson had spoken the truth. And to hell I will take them.

"Well, let's not waste any more time." I quickly outline the plan and the traps I think we can spring. "Let's show the government *and* the Bigland Boys who really rules Area Four."

The cavern bursts into life. As people begin to talk around me, improving on my plans, coming up with new ideas for traps, something still niggles at me. The one big thing I have no control over.

The Wall.

Our safety is dependent on my father and Trey being able to operate the mechanism to raise or lower the barrier. The Chain still holds the Metz compound, so that shouldn't be an issue, but Trey … He'll have to sneak into the very building he's just escaped from, knowing Coleman and his security force will be watching closely for any intrusion.

After all this time, you still doubt him?

I would trust Trey with my life. But it's not just my life I'm betting on.

* * * *

It's early evening when I walk through the narrow alley that runs along the back of Abby's house and push open the gate leading to her small yard. I wanted to see Trey again before he left for the food factory, and I have a feeling I'll find him here.

The garden is a vision of colour. When I'd first come here, the beds had been largely empty, the winter rains leaching the colour from the brown earth. Now, green shoots sprout from the seedbeds, flowers blossom between pointed leaves and the fragrant scent of herbs fills the air. I stop for a moment and close my eyes to breathe it in.

What if every garden Outside could be like this?

Perhaps they will be, when things change. I allow myself a minute of fantasy. A house like this of my own. Flowers growing in the garden. Trey sitting next to me on the back step, laughing as we drink mint tea.

I sigh and open my eyes. It is something to dream of, at least.

Sidling up to the kitchen window, I peek inside.

Trey stands at the kitchen worktop, stirring a steaming pot. He says something, and Abby walks over and wraps her arms around him, planting a motherly kiss on his shoulder. Then Bryn wraps his arms around them both, Abby squealing as she's sandwiched between them. A hard lump forms in my throat as they pull apart, laughing. They look so happy. So together. Like a family.

I pull back before they see me and press my back to the wall, pushing down a pang of envy. Then I take a deep breath and knock on the door.

Bryn opens it and motions me in with a grin.

"Aleesha!" Abby's face lights up, and my envy diminishes as she pulls me into a hug every bit as warm as the one she gave Trey. "It's so good to see you. I was hoping you'd drop by. You're just in time for dinner."

I grin and sniff. "Perfect timing. Whatever you're cooking smells amazing."

"Well, I figured you'd need a good meal to see you through tonight and tomorrow, so I managed to find some meat to make stew." Her voice catches. "A last supper of sorts."

Bryn plants a kiss on her forehead. "Now don't go getting all melancholic. This time, I'm definitely coming home."

Abby wrinkles her nose, laughter dancing in her eyes. "And how many times have you told me *that*, Bryn McNally?"

Bryn grins. "But this time, I mean it." Their lips meet in a long, slow kiss.

Embarrassed, I turn away and sit down next to Trey, who's taken a seat at the table. He finds my hand and squeezes it, rolling his eyes. "You'd think it was just the two of them in the room, wouldn't you?"

"They're as bad as Rogue and Megan."

Trey raises an eyebrow. "Oh?"

"They can't keep their hands off each other."

His hand slides off mine to rest on my thigh. Heat rushes through my body. He lowers his voice. "Don't take this the wrong way, but I'm really glad to hear that."

I throw him a surprised glance.

His cheeks redden slightly. "Well, it's nice to know I'm not going to have to fight him for you."

"Don't be stupid. You know I've never felt like that about Rogue."

"Haven't you?" He gives me a searching look, but it slides into a smile as he leans in and whispers into my ear. "Sure you won't stay here tonight? We're not heading off until the early hours."

Reluctantly, I shake my head. "I need to be with the gang. But I wanted to come and say good luck."

Trey gives a rueful grin. "Well, I'm glad you did."

He raises his voice. "I think that pot might be burning."

Abby pushes Bryn away, her face flushed. She grabs a spoon and stirs the stew. "Just in time. Bowls please, Bryn."

He hums tunelessly as he sets four bowls and spoons on the table. The bowls are colourful and imperfectly round – handmade by Abby. My mouth waters as she places the pot of stew in the centre of the table.

"Dig in."

"What are you going to do after this is over?" Trey asks Bryn, ladling food into a bowl.

"I thought we might take a holiday." Bryn glances at Abby. "I've told Richard this is my last job. In a few days, I'll be a retired man."

Abby smiles. "A holiday would be nice."

"After that, I was thinking we might find a quiet place in the country. Somewhere peaceful, with a big garden." He stretches his hand out to Abby, a flicker of uncertainty in his eyes. "What do you think?"

"Leave here?" She looks around the kitchen, then out the window. "I don't know. People need me ..."

"They won't once everyone can access proper medical facilities," Trey says, blowing to cool his food. "You know, Ella, Anabel and I have a big house out in Wales. Why don't you go out there for a bit? It needs someone to look after it. The garden must be completely overgrown by now."

Abby still looks unsure. "Well, it would be nice to visit ..."

"That's settled then," Bryn says cheerfully. "And you and Aleesha will come out, too, Trey."

"Sure." He grins at me. "Bet you've never seen forests and mountains. It'll be nice this time of year. There's a lake you can swim in." At my dubious look, he quickly adds, "The water's clean and fresh. And you don't have to swim. You could just paddle or something."

Forests. Mountains. Lakes. My only knowledge of such things is from the pictures in the few books my mother was able to get for me when I was small. Even those images have faded in my mind. "Sounds nice," I say noncommittally. I don't want to tell him I can't just leave London on a whim to travel hundreds of miles.

But if I don't go, will he forget about me, just like Bryn forgot about Abby? Will he decide that the city holds too many painful memories for him to return? Will I lose him forever?

A squeeze on my hand pulls me back to the present. Abby laughs at something Bryn whispers into her ear.

"It's okay," Trey says quietly. "I'll come back."

I look up into his eyes. Blue like the summer sky, they are a window to his heart. A window that is always open, because he has nothing to hide. There is no deceit in them. There never has been.

He runs his thumb across the back of my knuckles. "We *will* take down the Wall. I promise. I won't fail you."

It's as if he can read my mind.

"I know."

A bubble of emotion rises in my throat as I let my spoon clatter into the empty bowl and push my chair back, not wanting to spoil the light, happy mood of the room with tears. I hug Bryn and Abby, smile as they tell me to be careful, then stand in front of Trey.

I stand on my toes and kiss him lightly on the lips. "Don't do anything dumb, okay? I ... Be safe."

Before he can answer, I push open the door with shaky hands and leave, striding out of the yard and into the alley.

Partway down the alley, there's an old plastic crate, faded by the light. I sink down onto it and lean back against the wall, closing my eyes. Each breath feels like a struggle.

Footsteps get closer, and somehow, I know it's him.

I hold my hand out to tell him to stay away, that I just need a moment, but the words I want to say are stuck in my throat.

Trey doesn't say anything as he sits beside me. He presses his palm to mine, his fingers splaying out along its length. Then he curls his fingers between mine until our hands are locked together. Unbreakable.

Slowly, I twist around, keeping my face downturned. If I look at him, I know I'll cry, and I don't want to cry. Not when I spent so much of last night sobbing over him. I didn't think I had any tears left.

Trey leans forward and rests his forehead on mine. He doesn't tell me it's going to be okay. He doesn't promise a happy ending. He just sits with me until the pressure on my throat eases and I can speak again.

"Sorry. I just needed some air."

"We're going to survive this." The conviction in his voice surprises me. "Don't ask me how I know, but I do."

I duck my head.

He pulls back slightly and tilts my chin up. "We started this together, and we'll finish it together." His eyes search mine. "And whatever happens, whatever you need to do to survive, to win, it won't change how I feel about you."

I wonder how many times he'll need to tell me this before I truly believe it.

Trey stands and gently pulls me up. I rest my head against his chest, holding him fiercely as if my arms can convey all the words I cannot speak.

Trey has always been the light to my darkness. But I think I understand now why I pushed him away. When you've been sitting in the dark for such a long time, the light is so blinding that you have to retreat and let your eyes adjust. You need someone to reach out their hand and help you step out again.

He has helped chase away the shadows of the past. The future is in my hands. I can't change what has happened, but I don't have to be defined by it.

That is a choice that's in my power to make.

I lift my face to his and feel his hot breath on my lips as his mouth closes over mine. His lashes tickle my skin as his tongue slides over mine, and the little girl inside of me starts clawing at the floor of the cave, crawling toward the light. He lifts his hands to cup my face, his thumbs tracing my cheekbones.

"I love you," he whispers in the space between one kiss and the next.

I barely have time to breathe before his lips are on mine again. Softly, gently, he pulls me in until I am him and he is me and all I feel is his warmth, all I see is light.

The girl kneels at the mouth of the tunnel. She rises to her feet and slowly, hesitantly, steps out into the light of a new day.

36

Trey

The comm bud crackles in my ear. I work my jaw, trying to dislodge the feeling that there's a bug crawling in my head. It's dark outside, the deep, inky blackness that comes before the pre-dawn light.

"A dark night can hide many things," Petal had said with a grin. I get the impression he's looking forward to this.

Me? I just want it to be over.

Barnes shifts beside me, her posture oozing tension. She had wanted to stay with Samson, but he had ignored her pleas and put her in charge of the Brotherhood's fighters. There are fifteen of them, including Barnes and Petal. Petal had introduced them to Bryn as some of the best fighters in the city. I'm not sure if he meant it as a boast or a warning.

Samson was awake when I'd returned to speak to him after the Chain's meeting. For the first time since we'd dragged him from the tunnels, he looked as if he might survive his ordeal. He was also insistent the Brotherhood help with the Chain's operation, despite protest from Barnes and Petal.

"You need people and we have them. The longer this goes on, the more people will starve out here." He lowered his eyes. "Besides, I owe you a life debt."

"Your *priority* is to get better," Barnes had retorted.

"What do you think I'm doing?" Samson gestured impatiently to the blanket covering his lower body. "Trey, as far as everyone else knows, Barnes is now running the Brotherhood. No one must know I'm alive."

I glanced at Barnes out the corner of my eye. Her lips were pressed into a thin line, but she said nothing. I suspected they'd already argued about it.

"You said you didn't want Richard sending someone back to finish off the job. But I thought the palace guard had ..." My voice trailed off as Samson barked out a laugh.

"That's what he told you?" He fell silent for a moment. "I made a deal with Richard. Neither of us had enough people to take over the government headquarters, but with our combined forces, we had a chance. Richard said he had a mole in the palace guard who would make sure there was only a light guard on that night. Whether that happened or not, we met with more resistance than I'd anticipated. Our priority was to secure the main control room. From there, we could control the cameras, perimeter and access to secure parts of the building. Richard's people were better trained with superior weapons. It made sense that I took them and left my team to draw attention away from our efforts. But once the control room was taken, they turned on me."

A smile twisted the corner of his mouth. "It seems Richard saw me as a threat to his plans."

"I don't know why you're laughing about it," Barnes snapped, snatching her hand back from Samson's. He took it again and patted it, as if soothing a child.

"I fought my way out of the control room, but two of them followed me, cornering me in one of the meeting rooms. I killed one, but the other shot me twice. She left me, thinking I was dead. I managed to escape into one of the hidden passageways and down into the underground tunnels."

"But Richard must know there was no body. What if he suspects?"

"I told the Chain we had taken his body to be cremated," Petal said, studiously picking at his nails with the tip of his knife. Unlike most of the rough, functional weapons Outsiders carried, his knife had an ornate handle. "They don't know his body wasn't there."

I was silent for a moment, absorbing this. There had always been tension between Richard and Samson, but I'd thought Aleesha's rescue had brought them together. After all, by finding Giles and bringing him to the square, Samson had saved Aleesha, as well as many other members of the Chain. If I were to believe Samson, Richard repaid that debt by ordering his death. Now I understood why Barnes and Petal are reluctant to help him. But why was Samson willing to put his people under the Chain's command again?

"So why help him now?

"I'm not doing this to help *him*. I'm doing it for the people of this city." Samson's jaw tightened. "The food corporations have more power than the President himself. Coleman is a ruthless man. He won't hesitate to use his control over the food supply as a tool to get what he wants, even if it means innocent people suffer."

Bryn's hand on my arm pulls me back to the present. "Are you ready, Trey?"

I nod, but a shiver runs up my spine.

"Just stick with me, okay?" he says in a low voice. "Leave the hero stuff to the people who are trained for it."

"Sure." I try to smile, but it quickly falls from my lips. I now wish I'd told him about what Richard had done to Samson. Or does he already know? Is this another secret Bryn is keeping from me?

Bryn pulls up the factory blueprints and scans through them again, though I know he's memorized every possible route in and out. The basement rooms and corridors aren't labelled, and it took a while to figure out the best route to the guarded room. I'm still not a hundred percent sure I'm right. We'd discussed trying to make contact with Louis, but agreed it was too risky. After he helped us escape, I trust him not to betray us, but if anyone else intercepted the message, the operation would be over before we'd started.

No. Best that he stays out of it.

Next to me, Barnes flicks between the different settings on her gun. Bryn had come to our meeting spot with a small arsenal of weapons, which he'd passed around to the Brotherhood's fighters. From the way Petal's eyes gleamed, I hope Richard isn't planning on getting them back. Even I've got a small handgun tucked into my belt, though I hope I won't have to use it.

Bryn tilts his head, as if listening to something. The comm buds are high-tech with different channels controlled by a thin band on the user's wrist. Mine is set to the main channel, which everyone has access to, but there are a number of private channels. Bryn set up a separate group for him, Liza, Harrison and Filip – the Chain fighters Richard assigned to our team – and Barnes and Petal, but we agreed I'd keep mine set to the main channel in order to communicate with Aleesha.

Richard's plan can't be put into action until we reach the control room and figure out how to access the Wall controls. They depend on us.

"Time to go," Bryn says shortly. "From here on out, essential communication only. Keep the camera blockers going at all times."

I finger the small, black tube in my pocket – the same device Mikheil had used to hide our movements when we'd broken into the government headquarters. It will help mask our presence from the cameras inside the food factory. But with the factory in lockdown and entry controlled by employee passes, which are almost certainly being monitored, getting in is the first challenge.

The streets of Area Six are dark and deserted. I lick my lips as adrenaline rushes through my system, turning my mouth dry. My senses are alert, despite my lack of sleep.

Silently, our group divides. I follow Bryn, slinking through the smaller side streets that lead us around to the entrance of the factory. A single light illuminates the doors, which are wide enough that ten men could walk abreast into the tunnel beyond. A smaller door is cut into one side, two guards concealed in cut-out sections of the wall nearby. One shifts his weight from foot to foot, glancing down at his wrist. He's ready for the end of his shift.

So are we.

Right on schedule, the small door opens and the two more guards step out. Bryn gestures with his hand, and he and the other three members of the Chain creep forward. Dressed all in black, they blend into the shadows perfectly. I hang back with half a dozen of Samson's fighters, waiting to see if we're needed. My thumb taps the camera blocker repeatedly.

A commotion from further up the street causes the guards to snap to attention. In that moment, Bryn springs forward. They are equally matched in numbers, but our fighters have the element of surprise. Only one of the guards has time to cry out before they're all knocked unconscious. Quickly, they're stripped, and Liza cuts the Coleman Corporation chips from their hands, quickly placing each one into a gel-like band that simulates the body's environment, preventing the chips from triggering an alert.

Bryn beckons again, and the rest of us move to join him. Four of Samson's fighters dress themselves in the guards' uniforms, strapping the bands containing the chips to their wrists. Two take up positions in the recessed sections of the wall. A third presses his hand to the access panel, opening the door into the factory.

We're joined by the other members of the Brotherhood. So far, everything is going to plan.

I follow Bryn through the door and into a short tunnel. At the far end is an elevator, and next to it, a door leading to the stairwell. Neither Barnes nor I were able to tell Bryn where the guards were likely to go once they were off duty, so Bryn had decided that the two fake guards would make their way to the security control room. They take the elevator, while the rest of us take the stairs.

Two floors down, the rest of the Brotherhood fighters peel off. Their job is to follow the two fake guards to the control room and take it over, or at least provide a distraction. Bryn, the three Chain fighters and I continue down another level.

The stairs end at a long tunnel that leads into the factory. It smells cool and slightly damp, a faint dripping sound quickly masked by our footsteps. I glance around, realizing the others all have their weapons drawn. My hand hovers over the gun on my belt, but I can't bring myself to pull it out.

Not unless the worst happens.

My palms are so slick with sweat that I'd probably drop the thing anyway.

The tension in my body ratchets up a notch as we draw closer to the end of the tunnel. Twice, I nearly jump out of my skin at an unexpected sound, but it's just someone tripping or the click of a safety. Part of me would almost rather the ghostly shadows in front of us evolve into flesh-and-blood people, just so we could start the fight and get it over with.

Glancing back at the people following me, I suspect some of them feel the same.

If we've interpreted the blueprints correctly, it isn't far from here to the room where Barnes and I were kept prisoner. The tunnel divides ahead of us, and we take the left-hand branch, which ends in a nondescript door. Bryn tries it. Locked. He steps aside and gestures to one of the men – Filip, I think. He pulls something from his jacket and kneels in front of the access panel.

Minutes tick by. I fight the urge to glance at my wrist to check the time. Bryn had estimated it would take us thirty minutes to reach the room, giving us another thirty to figure out the control mechanism. Aleesha will be getting her gang into position by now, but they can't act until we complete our part of the operation.

Filip curses under his breath and sits back on his heels, his face set in a frown. I glance at Bryn.

"Give him time," his whispers. "He's never let us down before."

I nod but can't help thinking that there's a first time for everything.

Filip spends a full minute staring at the access panel. Then he utters a low exclamation and reaches inside his jacket, pulling out a compact folding tool. A minute later, the door clicks open.

We file through it into a short corridor, Filip bringing up the rear after packing up his tools. The next door isn't secured and opens into a long tunnel lit with blue emergency lighting. There's a door about thirty metres ahead of us on the right, and beside that, a set of elevator doors.

My stomach lurches in recognition. I move to the front and tap Bryn on the shoulder. He raises an eyebrow questioningly, and I point down the tunnel and give him a thumbs up. In my pocket, I press the button on the camera-blocking device with fervent regularity. The boots Bryn had given me crush my toes, but the special rubber soles make little noise on the concrete floor.

The next part of the plan is the most dangerous. When Louis had helped Barnes and me escape, he'd put something in the guards' coffee to dull their senses so they wouldn't hear us. Today, we have no such option. Despite the rubber-soled boots, our footsteps seem loud in the silence of the tunnel. We're about twenty metres away from where the tunnel divides – the corridor to the cells to the right, the room with the guards to the left – when a cough stops us in our tracks. I barrel into Bryn's back, my foot scuffing the floor.

"Did you hear that noise?"

I hold my breath at the voice, frozen with one foot out, my hand clutching Bryn's shoulder. His body tenses.

"What? You coughing your lungs out? You should get that seen to."

"Not that, you idiot. Something else."

The voices of the guards bounce off the walls of the tunnel. Slowly, Bryn places his hand over mine and eases it off his shoulder. I wobble, a hand grabbing me from behind as I catch my balance. My mouth is so dry I can feel my throat wanting to spasm, but I'm scared to even swallow.

"Probably just a rat."

"Maybe. I'll check it out, though. Never had rats down here before."

Bryn reaches into a pouch on his belt and pulls out what looks like a small rubber ball. He squeezes it, then bends down and rolls it along the tunnel. The concrete floor is rough and uneven, but finally, the ball bounces off the end wall and comes to rest.

"Hey. What's that?"

The ball begins to hiss. Bryn waves at me to retreat and slaps a hand over his mouth and nose. I suck in a deep breath and repeat the gesture, following him back down the corridor.

The guards' voices fade into incoherent babble, then silence.

We wait for a count of ten before Bryn removes his hand from his mouth, then another minute before he motions Harrison to move forward. Gun out, Harrison creeps down the corridor and peers around the corner. He pulls back, grinning, and waves us forward.

The two guards lie motionless on the floor. Filip gets to work on the door while Bryn, Liza and Harrison strip the guards of their uniforms and chips. Harrison strips down and begins pulling on the larger of the two uniforms. The fabric bulges, and I hope the cameras won't pick up just how tight the uniform is on him. Fortunately, the hat the guards wear should hide his face.

I stand to one side, feeling useless. I'm beginning to wonder if Bryn gave me the camera blocker just so I'd feel like I was contributing.

There are two access panels on this door. Filip gets past the first one quickly, but the second takes more time. I catch Bryn glancing up at the pinpoint cameras in the ceiling. Outwardly, he looks calm, but I wonder what he's thinking. The camera blocker works by looping the footage. The sooner we can have the two "guards" back outside the door, the less likely anyone will notice anything odd.

I check the time. We've already used up the thirty minutes Bryn had allocated for getting into the room.

Filip breaks the second lock and the door swings open. The automatic light comes on as I follow Bryn inside, illuminating a small room with two doors leading off it. I try them. One is locked, with no access panel on this side. The other opens into an empty storage room.

"In here," I hiss as Harrison drags one of the unconscious guards into the room. He grins at me as he pulls the man into the storage room, then returns for the second guard. Within two minutes, Bryn, Liza and I are inside the room, the door closed, Filip and Harrison posing as the guards outside.

I let out a long breath and look around. Bare, hastily plastered, whitewashed walls and no furniture, save for a single chair that creaks ominously under Bryn's weight. A screen sits in front of him, a narrow shelf below it. In the wall beside the screen is a metal knob, it's bulbous base tapering like the stubby needle of a compass. If it were a compass, it would be pointing north.

Bryn runs a finger across the shelf, leaving a trail in the dust. "For a food factory, housekeeping leaves something to be desired. Tell them we're in, Trey."

I check the channel on the thin band on my wrist and set it to transmit. "We've found the second part of the mechanism. Bryn's working on it now."

There's a pause, then Richard's voice comes on the line. "Good job. Aleesha?"

"We're ready and in position." She sounds calm and collected, not a tremor of fear in her voice.

Richard comes back on the line. "Excellent. Any casualties?"

"None so far."

There's a longer pause, and I wonder if I'm supposed to cut the connection. I'm itching to talk to Aleesha, to make sure she's okay, but I know protocol – essential communication only.

After a moment, Richard comes back on the line. "We're under attack here. I'm going to need to leave the basement and get up to the main control room. How long is Bryn going to be?"

I look over. Somehow, Bryn has managed to get the system up and running. The tech looks ancient, like something from the history books. "Bryn? How long's it going to take to get it down?"

Bryn glances down from the screen to the film map of the city. "Two minutes. Maybe three. Just making sure I've got the right section."

I relay this back to Richard.

"Tell me when you're about to switch it." Richard sounds terse, and he cuts the connection without another word.

I join Liza, who's looking over Bryn's shoulder. He types in some numbers, and part of the line on the screen begins to flash blue.

"Trey, double check that's the correct section."

I glance down at the red line drawn on the film along the section of the Wall bounding Area Four. The individual towers are labelled with numbers in tiny print. I compare the numbers to those on the screen. "Looks the same to me."

Bryn adjusts something on his wristband and reaches out to the metal knob. "Ready when you are, Aleesha."

"We're ready."

Bryn turns the knob. The blue flashing line turns red.

I hold my breath. The room and the comm bud in my ear are silent. The moment stretches out, and I begin to wonder if there's been a breakdown in our comms.

Finally, I hear Aleesha's voice in my ear. "The Wall is down. We're going through."

I meet Bryn's gaze, a grin spreading across my face. "We did it!"

"Sure did." His grin matches mine. "Oops. Sorry, Richard. Didn't realize we were transmitting ... What?" The smile slides off his face. "Sure thing. We're good here. No resistance so far."

He glances up at me. "Trey, make sure you're not transmitting."

I change the setting on my band. "What's wrong?"

"Slight change of plans. The government has attacked the Metz compound. Richard's had to go deal with it, but he's turned the switch on his side to up, so we just need to wait until Aleesha's lot are through, then we can put the Wall back up from here. Liza, can you check in with Harrison and Filip?"

Liza moves a step away and speaks into her comm.

"What if he can't get back down to switch it again?" I ask. "If we can't take the Wall down, Aleesha will be trapped."

"Don't worry. Richard knows that, but it'll be at least an hour before it needs switching again." He flashes me a smile. "Richard w—"

"Sir, they're not responding." Liza looks across at us. "Permission to open the door."

"Granted." Bryn springs to his feet. "Trey, you've got the cameras?"

I fumble for the black device in my pocket and depress the button. "Yes."

Liza pulls open the door. At first, I think the corridor is empty. Then I look down and see the two still forms on the floor, dark blood spreading out underneath them.

"Shit!" She slams the door shut and yanks her gun from its holster.

There's a soft click behind us. I tear my gaze from the door and whirl around. I just have time to register the open door, the armed guards spilling through, before Liza fires. One of the men goes down, but before she can fire again, she collapses to the floor. Bryn goes down heavily, taking the chair with him. Belatedly, I remember the gun in my belt. I move to draw it, but two guards cross the room and grab my arms, yanking them painfully behind my back. My gun is tossed to the floor.

More guards spill into the space. Following them, striding into the room as if he owns the place, which I guess he does, is Coleman. His eyes settle on me, then flick to the lit screen.

"Well, what have we here," he says softly, walking over to it. "I knew you were a traitor, boy, but I didn't realize quite how far your ambitions stretched."

I struggle against the men holding me but know it's useless. Everything happened so quickly, it's only now that the shock hits, carving a hole in my gut. Guards surround Bryn's and Liza's still forms. I need to transmit a warning to Aleesha and Richard, but the band on my wrist is out of reach.

Coleman places his hand on the metal knob. He strokes it delicately, all the while watching me. I swallow down the thick lump in my throat, trying to disguise my fear.

I imagine Aleesha and her Phoenixes creeping through the gap in the Wall and pray they are already Inside.

"I'm not sure this should be in this position," Coleman says, raising a brow. "Are you, Mr Goldsmith?"

"Wait. I—"

Coleman twists the knob.

The line on the screen turns from red to blue. There's a fizzle of static in my ear, then Aleesha's voice comes through. "Trey, what the hell is going on? We're not ready—"

The comm bud is ripped from my ear. A hand forces me down to the floor, and the impact on my knees sends rods of pain lancing up my thighs.

I look up to see Coleman standing over me, a cold smile on his face.

37

Aleesha

"Trey?"

There's no answer. I curse under my breath and turn to survey the damage. About half of my team got through the Wall before it went back up. From the scream I'd heard behind me, at least one person had been directly in its path. The team of Chain fighters led by Anabel, who'd gone through ahead of us, has already disappeared.

Rogue jogs up to me, his face dark. "Clayton's dead. What's happened?"

Clayton was one of the ex-Metz officers. So the nanobots from the food they'd eaten in the few weeks they'd been Outside must have built up in their system enough to kill him.

"I don't know. Trey's not responding." I flick the transmitter on again. "Fa— Richard? What's going on?"

There's a pause, then my father's voice speaks in my ear. "Not sure. Bryn's not responding. It could be that there's interference with the signal. Or they've been caught." He snaps out a command that clearly isn't meant for me, then comes back on the comm. "Sorry, Aleesha. We're dealing with a situation here. Continue as per the plan."

My gut twists. "I only have half my team. How the hell are we supposed to get back out if Trey's been caught?"

There's a pause. "I'll see if I can get some reinforcements to you. Keep trying Trey. Remember, *you* can escape through the Wall." Another barked order. "I have to go. The government is hitting us hard. I need you to draw them away. If we lose the compound, everything is lost."

He cuts the connection.

Rogue looks at me, eyebrow raised. I sigh. "Richard thinks Trey's struggling to transmit as he's underground. I'll keep trying him, but for now, we're to continue with the plan. He's going to send some extra people to help."

I glance around at my motley bunch of fighters, trying to fight the dread that's seeping into my stomach. Richard had given us three sets of secure comms, so I split the gang into three groups led by me, Rogue and Anders. My group had gone first and are all accounted for. I estimate about half of Rogue's are here, but Anders is nowhere to be seen.

I switch the channel on the thin band around my wrist. "Anders?"

"Aleesha. What's happened?" Relief floods his voice.

Whatever had been in those healing pads had worked wonders. But Anders isn't back to full strength yet, which was one reason I'd put him in charge of the team tasked with setting the traps for the government fighters. It's a role requiring calmness, strategic thinking and nerve. Aside from Rogue, I can't think of anyone better suited for the job.

"We're not sure. Can you take charge out there? Let Rogue know if any issues come up and be ready to come through if the Wall goes down again."

"Got that."

I switch my channel and try Trey again. Still no answer.

I push down the worry gnawing at my insides. *He will be fine. Trust him. He won't let you down.*

We slip through the empty streets as the pre-dawn light rolls across the sky. The people who live here will be in bed or, if they're awake, observing curfew. There are cameras everywhere. I wonder if the government is still watching them. I hope so. Our plan depends on it.

My group is made up of equal numbers of ex-Metz officers and Outsiders. It's a tactical decision. The ex-Metz officers have greater strength and speed, more expertise with fighting. But my Outsiders know how to fight dirty and bear more of a grudge against Insiders. That might be useful, if it doesn't overrule their common sense. They look around with wide eyes, taking in the sights and smells of this part of the city. Another good reason to be doing this when it's still dark. In the daytime, they'd be so distracted by the sculpted buildings and beautiful gardens they wouldn't see a Metz officer if one stood right in front of them.

I've had perhaps three hours of fitful sleep. Exhaustion tugs at my eyelids, and I wish I'd thought to ask Mika for some stimulants.

I need you to draw them away. If we lose the compound, everything is lost.

I tighten my grip on the nailed club I'd brought in with me. For destruction, not fighting. I can't let him down. Not now.

When we get to a small square, our group splits into two. Rogue's team heads south, quickly disappearing between the tall office buildings. I take my group in the opposite direction, down a street lined with low-rise apartment blocks. After a short distance, I stop, lower my backpack carefully to the ground and beckon Danny over.

"This'll do. Let's hand them out."

Danny sets his pack down next to mine with equal care. Inside are the explosives he spent most of yesterday making. As he hands them out, I wave my hand for attention. Time for a reminder of the rules.

"It looks quiet at the moment, but with any luck, it soon won't be. Stick together. *No one* is to go off on their own. No attacking Insiders unless they're a threat, and no looting."

That's a bit like taking a bunch of kids into a sweet shop and telling them not to touch anything. I can already see my Phoenixes' eyes roving the buildings around us, no doubt wondering what treasures lie inside.

"If I find that anyone's thieved anything, you'll be left behind for the Metz to deal with." That quietens the murmurs. I grin. "Let's go and make hell."

Now *that* is something my gang understands.

My father had told us to make a scene, to draw attention to ourselves and force the government fighters to confront us. And no one makes a scene like people who've spent their whole lives being pushed down, starved and forgotten about finally being let loose to destroy the homes of those they've harboured resentment against for years.

Danny is the first to throw his home-made bomb, the device landing in the middle of a garden separating an apartment block from the road. The explosion cracks the windows and throws dirt up to speckle the gleaming white walls. Someone else sets light to one of the trash cans lining the street. A moment later, there's a muffled boom. The air is filled with plastic wrappers and scraps of cloth, which fall to the ground like brightly coloured snowflakes. I smile and heft my club, walking to the opposite side of the street. Perhaps this will be fun after all.

Unlike the buildings in Area Four, these apartment blocks are well constructed. My first few strikes create only hairline cracks on the Plexiglass windows, but by the fifth blow, the window gives way with a satisfying crash. There's a scream from inside. I pull back, not wanting to frighten the occupants.

Or at least not wanting to frighten them too much.

I wonder if the people who live here have ever been Outside. Do they care about the millions who don't have enough to eat? The kids who never get to go to school? Those who are carted away to the Labs and Farms before they've even had a chance to live?

Do they even think about us at all?

I imagine not. They go to work every day, come home, sit down for dinner with their kids. Two parents, two children – a perfect family. They wear clean, colourful clothes and eat wholesome food. And never, as they talk about what's happened during their day, will they mention what lies on the other side of the Wall. Never will they appreciate that in order for them to have everything, we have nothing.

The thought ignites a fire inside me. It burns fiercely, and I feel the pressure building, so I channel it out through my arms, moving methodically from window to window, swinging my club. In the distance, I hear more explosions and wailing alarms. Sounds like Rogue's team is having fun.

Lights come on in the apartments above us. Someone yells from a window that they're calling the Metz. Good. Only one man comes out to confront us. He's obviously dressed hurriedly – the fly of his jeans is undone and his t-shirt's inside out. He carries a metal rod, but when two of my gang make a move toward him, he quickly retreats inside.

Sweat builds on the back of my neck as I smash through a children's playhouse and the wooden fence behind it. Splintered wood flies around me. I'm at the centre of a whirlwind of debris. The eye of the storm.

It feels good.

"Aleesha!"

I whirl around to find Danny standing with his hands outstretched. His gaze flicks to the club in my hand, and I let it drop to the ground.

His face creases into a frown. "You all right, boss?"

"Fine," I pant.

"Good. Because I was beginning to wonder just what that fence did to make you so mad. And whether you're trying to smash us out of here." He glances down at my boots.

I haven't just destroyed the fence. I've taken the wooden boards clean out of the ground. My trousers are splattered with dirt, and I taste earth in my mouth.

I look up at Danny, reading the question in his eyes. "I'm good. Everyone out of bombs?"

"I've kept a couple back just in case we need 'em, but I reckon we're about done here."

I look up the street. Smoke curls lazily from burnt-out trash cans. Glass and debris are scattered across the ground, and terror-stricken faces press against the upper apartment windows. It looks like a war zone. Or like Area Four on a bad day.

"Any sign of government forces?"

"Not that I've seen."

I check in with Rogue on the comm. "How are you getting on?"

"We're out of explosives and going through the office blocks destroying anything that seems breakable. No sign of any opposition yet."

"Give it another five minutes, then get everyone back out onto the street. I don't want you getting trapped in the buildings."

"Got that."

"It's nice here, isn't it?" Danny looks around at the destruction. "Everythin's so clean an' colourful. There was a couple of birds in that tree over there. They flew away when we got near, though.

Seems a shame to wreck it all."

There's a wistfulness in his voice that strikes me as odd. I'd have thought Danny would be the first to resent these people. "Getting cold feet?"

He straightens. "No, boss."

But before I turn my back, I catch him picking something up from the ground. A toy soldier. He rubs it clean with his thumb, then slips it into his pocket.

I call my team over. "Split into pairs and start spreading out. If you see any sign of the government fighters, pull back immediately. We want to draw them to us, not get ourselves killed." There are nods and murmurs of assent. The ex-Metz officers look grim, as if this is just another military-style operation, but the Outsiders' eyes shine.

I watch them as they head off up the street, wondering what will happen when all this is over, if my father succeeds in uniting the city and bringing down the Wall. How long will it take to mend that bridge between Insiders and Outsiders?

I wonder if there are some resentments that run so deep they can never be fixed.

"What's your plan?" Danny appears at my shoulder.

I switch channels and try Trey again. Still no answer. I try my father.

"Yes?" He sounds out of breath and distracted.

"We've placed the bait," I say. "Just waiting to see if they bite."

"Good. Any news from Trey?"

"No."

A pause. "Keep going with the plan." For the first time, I hear a trace of concern in his voice.

I cut the connection and chew my lip, trying to think. We need another way out. If we manage to draw out the government forces and the Wall doesn't come down, we'll be trapped. I curse inwardly, wishing we'd had more time to prepare for this, to scout the area. I stare down at the hole in the ground my blows to the fence have made, an idea forming in my mind.

I begin to walk back down the street, in the direction of the square, then break into a run. I'm not sure how much time we have left.

"Hey, where are you going?" Danny shouts after me. "I thought we were going that way." He sprints to catch up.

"Not yet. We're going to find Plan B."

"And what's that?"

I flash him a smile. "We go underground."

Comprehension dawns in his eyes. "The tunnels?"

"They're all across the city. The main entrances have been blocked and built on top of, but I bet there are access shafts." I glance around, trying to place the mental map I have of the tunnel system on top of the city around us. "I'm pretty sure we're right on top of one of the tunnels now."

Danny stops and looks at the ground as if it might open up beneath him. "Okay ... So where do we start lookin'?"

"Basements of old buildings. Or anything that looks out of place, like it's built around something." I gaze around at the office blocks lining the square, and my heart sinks. I'm sure there are access points to the tunnels, but how long will it take us to find them? "Let's meet back here in twenty."

Ten minutes later, the band on my wrist vibrates, indicating someone's trying to get through to me on a different channel. I switch to what I'd nicknamed Channel Phoenix, and Rogue's voice sounds in my ear. "One of your team reported back. They couldn't find you. We've got government forces incoming. Where are you?"

"On my way. Meet at the square." I curse and aim a kick at the door I've spent the last five minutes breaking open. It slams smugly back into its frame. All I'd found on the other side was an empty storeroom. So much for Plan B.

Rogue is already at the square, with his team and half of mine. I scan their faces. A girl steps forward to report, but as she opens her mouth, an explosion sounds, near at hand. I instinctively duck and raise my arm to protect my head, then straighten and turn to look up the street. Danny explodes out of an alleyway and skids on a piece of trash. He recovers his balance and begins to sprint down the street, two other Outsiders hot on his tail.

Following them is the government's army.

They seem to come from all directions, flooding the street. The biggest fighters are the Metz officers in their black, impenetrable armour. There are more of them than I'd thought. Something about them strikes me as odd, but I don't have time to pin down what it is.

"Rogue, take the lead. I'll bring up the rear." I raise my voice to a holler. "Get back to the Wall!"

Our retreat is chaotic. The strength of the government's response sends fear lancing into the hearts of my brave Phoenixes. I see two duck into side alleys to wait out the confrontation. I make a note of who they are to talk to later. Most of my gang make me proud, following Rogue as he leads them back through the streets to the Wall and the spot we'd picked to make our stand.

I slow and wait for Danny to catch up. His face is red, cheeks puffed out from exertion. "Hundreds of 'em," he gasps.

"Did you find any entrances to the tunnels?"

He shakes his head.

Shit.

I clap him on the back and let him pass me, tagging onto the end of the retreating group. I stand alone for a moment, waiting for the first of the government fighters to round the corner.

They'll want to capture you, not kill you.

"So many of you just to deal with a few Outsiders?" I taunt as the first of the grey-uniformed palace guards appears on the street. One raises his gun and takes aim. "Catch me if you can!"

I turn and run. Something flies over my shoulder, causing a faint movement of air close to my ear. My mouth goes dry. Maybe they're not so fussed about capture after all.

Even in these unknown streets, we move faster than the government fighters. The size and coordination of their army make them slow. As I run, I switch the channel on my comm.

"Where are our reinforcements? The government has sent everything they've got after us."

It's a moment before my father replies. "They're on their way. The Wall mechanism here is down. I've sent a message to Bryn to be ready to switch the lever at their end."

Hope surges in my chest. "You got through to him?"

"Not to speak to, no." There's a pause. "You cannot let them take you, Aleesha. Understand? Escape if you must, but *do not* let them take you."

Hearing the anguish in his voice, warmth fills my chest. "I'll be fine," I lie.

My people stand in front of the Wall as I burst out from between two office blocks and cross the empty space between them and the Wall. I slow to a walk and turn my back so none of them catch the horror on my face. There are so few of us. So many of them. The cold dread of certainty seeps through me.

We are all going to die.

But you can't let them see that. They think the Wall will drop any second.

I compose myself and turn back to face my people. "Everyone ready?" I get a ragged cheer as I take up position next to Rogue at the front of the group.

I touch the band on my wrist, trying to get through first to Bryn, then Trey. All I get is static. I try my father, but he doesn't respond, either.

We will take the Wall down. I promise. I won't fail you.

Bryn wouldn't have let their communications get compromised. Both he and Trey know the consequences of leaving the Wall up. The fact they haven't switched the mechanism at their end can only mean one thing. They've been captured.

Which means we are on our own.

A hand squeezes my arm. I look up into Rogue's inquiring eyes. I bite my lip, giving a slight shake of my head, and watch the hope in his eyes harden into resignation. Then he looks out across the area in front of us.

"They're here."

I follow his gaze to see black-clad Metz officers blocking the street, standing five deep. They spill out to form a semi-circle around us, backed by the palace guard. The blue glow that had surrounded us fades into red as the Wall changes colour, and part of me wonders if this is an ironic coincidence or a deliberate ploy. Whispers ripple to me from the remnants of my gang.

"Isn't the Wall supposed to be down?"

"How much longer do we have to wait?"

"It's a trap. We're going to die."

My heart aches – for Trey and for us. Was this what all the planning was for? Were we always destined to die like this?

"Go," Rogue whispers.

The word jolts me from my daze. "What?"

"Go." His jaw is tight, his gaze set firmly forward. "You can get through the Wall. You don't have to stay here."

I pull my gun – one of the few the Chain had given us – from my belt. "Don't be an idiot."

"It's what he would want."

I'm about to retort, but something in Rogue's voice makes me pause.

Remember, you can escape through the Wall.

Anger burns through my fear. Did my father seriously think I would just leave them all behind?

My grip tightens on the gun. "I'm not leaving."

Rogue glances at me, a flicker of a smile crossing his lips before his face sobers. "Now who's an idiot?"

"I never claimed to be a genius."

"I don't suppose you've got some miracle up your sleeve?"

"'Fraid not."

He sighs. "This is it then." He turns to me again. "I don't think I ever thanked you for freeing me."

I shrug. "I'm not sure now is a good time to be thanking me."

My joke falls flat. Rogue stares out again. "Thank you anyway. At least I have had the chance to atone for what I've done in the past. Believe it or not, I would rather be here than in their shoes." He jerks his head toward the Metz officers watching us from behind their featureless masks.

"You weren't to blame," I say quietly.

"Does it make a difference now?"

"I guess not."

Scanning their ranks, it finally hits me what is different about these officers. "Rogue, the helmets ... The colours are different." The Metz's helmets have two yellow lines slashed down the side. There are a few of them in the army lined up in front of us, but there are other colours, too. Blue, green, purple.

"They're from outside London."

I wonder how we ever thought we could win this battle. If I had realized the size of their force, I would have never offered to help.

Behind me, the Wall stretches up into the lightening sky, bloodier than any sunrise I've ever seen. It is as opaque as the Wall in my nightmare. Then, I was trapped on one side, powerless to help my friends. Now, we are all trapped. But I am not quite as powerless as I was in my dream.

They will hate me for what I am about to do. But at least they will live.

I step forward two paces and bend down to place my gun on the ground, the club beside it. When I stand, I raise my hands into the air.

All my life, I have had to fight for survival. But sometimes the only way to survive is to not fight.

My voice cuts across the whispers of my gang, the sounds of enemy guns being raised, the silence of the space between us.

"We surrender."

38

Trey

I strain against the cuffs binding me to the heavy chair. I'm sitting in Coleman's office, a spacious room with windows along one wall, high enough that I see the Wall shimmering above the rooftops. It's an unbreakable sea of blue.

Without my comm, I have no clue as to what's going on. I don't know whether my sister's and Aleesha's teams made it through the Wall. I don't know where they are now or when they'll need the Wall lowered again.

The thought of them being trapped Inside with their backs to the Wall, trusting in me to save them, makes my stomach churn. How much time has already passed since Coleman caught us? Ten minutes? Twenty?

A slap across my face drags me back to the present. The blow makes my ears ring.

"I was talking to you," Coleman says.

I blink groggily at him. The guard raises his hand to strike me again, but Coleman stops him with a look. "That is enough. For now." He takes a seat in a high-backed, leather chair he'd pulled out from behind his desk and placed in front of me, resting the ankle of his right leg on the knee of his left. "Now, Darwin, I would like you to tell me what Richard Masterton is planning."

"I'm not going to tell you anything."

The guard steps forward again, but Coleman waves him away. "That's a shame. A real shame, Darwin."

The use of my first name makes me feel as if he's talking to a different person. Darwin was the boy who was scared of his own shadow, who spent his life trying to live up to his family's expectations, who didn't know or care about anything Outside the Wall.

I am Trey now.

And what good is Trey doing right now?

"Do you not feel ashamed of what you've done? Do you think this is what your parents wanted for you?" He leans forward, his gaze cutting into me. "Is this how you honour their memory, *Darwin?*"

Breath hisses between my teeth. Tendrils of shame swirl through me, polluting my thoughts with their sticky blackness and clouding my ability to think. I close my eyes, drawing on the memory of my mother's face and the feel of her hand on my chest.

Trust yourself, Trey, and you will do the right thing.

My parents hadn't wanted me to help the Chain because they wanted to protect me, not because helping them wasn't right. I know this. Then why do I still feel that I'm not good enough?

"Darwin?"

My eyes snap to his as an idea comes to me. Coleman thinks I am Darwin. What little he knows of me comes from conversations with my mother. What would she have said about me? That I am easily led. That I'm not that bright, but I try hard. That I trust too easily.

Perhaps I can use that to my advantage.

I cast my eyes down and slump in the chair, not having to feign the shame that still rolls through me. I'm not foolish enough to hope

Coleman will think I'm guiltless, but maybe I can make him believe I was led. If I can get him to underestimate me, perhaps even free me from these cuffs, I've got a better chance of escaping.

Having a plan focuses my thoughts and helps calm my fear.

"Please, don't hurt me." I sound pathetic. Let him think that.

Coleman's voice softens. "If you help us, then there's no reason to hurt you. Now, tell me how you came to be involved with these terrorists?"

That's an easy one, at least.

"You know I was my parents' third child?"

Coleman nods, his face expressionless.

"Well, when the government activated my chip, I went on the run and ended up Outside the Wall. The Chain saved my life and gave me sanctuary. I guess ..." I glance up through my lashes. "I guess I was maybe a bit naïve to believe what they told me. But they said if I didn't help them, they'd hand me over to the Metz. What choice did I have?"

"We always have a choice, Darwin." Coleman's voice is patronizing. Good. This may have a chance of working.

I let my gaze stray to the corner of the room, where Bryn and Liza lie in a heap, two armed guards in front of them. They appear to be unconscious, but as I turn back, I catch sight of Bryn's finger twitching. It *could* just be an involuntary movement, or perhaps he's not quite as out of it as he looks.

"Are they ... Are they dead?" I let my voice rise to a squeak.

Coleman chuckles. "Not yet. We'll question them when they come around. First, though, I want to show you something." He picks up a holo pad from his desk and runs his finger over it. "I suspect your leader hasn't been entirely honest with you."

A holo appears between us. Coleman's office hangs in the air – a room within a room. Coleman and Richard sit around the small table

410

in the corner. The date timestamped on it is around four months back.

A nagging doubt centres in my stomach.

"Richard approached me some months back, seeking my help to take down the government and replace it with a new regime. For years, I've been campaigning to open our borders so we can import supplies and trade with other countries, but the President and Cabinet were strongly against the idea. They wanted us to remain isolated, an island, even if that meant people suffered for it. Richard seemed sincere, so I agreed to help him in exchange for certain trade advantages once he took control."

"You're lying."

"Am I?"

We listen to the recording in silence. I wonder if Richard knew about the nanobots and tronk in the food supply when he made this deal. I hope not. As much as I know Coleman is trying to manipulate us, to turn us away from the Chain's leader, two questions hang in my mind.

If Richard had a deal with Coleman, why did he never mention it? And why did we have to break into the factory to take down the Wall?

The holo image snaps out.

"As far as I was concerned, we had a deal," Coleman drawls. "But it seems Richard Masterton is not a man who keeps his word. Why else would he send assassins to break into my building?" He leans forward in his chair. "What has he promised you, Goldsmith?"

I don't answer. Is it possible he faked the holo recording? But why would he go to the effort to do so?

"Wh—"

Coleman breaks off as the heavy wooden door to his office slams open, banging against the wall. He twists in his chair. "I said I wasn't to be disturbed ..." His voice trails off as he sees Louis standing in the doorway, his face pale.

Louis' gaze flickers to me before returning to the man in front of me. "Sorry, Father. It's an emergency. Can I come in?"

Coleman gestures impatiently. Louis shuts the door behind him and walks over. Just before he reaches me, he trips on the corner of a rug and staggers forward, crashing into my chair and knocking us both to the floor. An involuntary cry escapes my lips as Louis sprawls on top of me.

"What can I do?" he whispers into my ear.

"Follow my lead," I reply, unable to think of anything else.

Louis heaves himself up with a grunt. "That rug will be the death of me." He straightens and scowls down at me, as if it's my fault he tripped. "Damn traitor."

"What did you come to tell me?" Coleman sounds calm, but a flicker in his eyes gives his irritation away.

Two guards heave me back up as Louis makes his report. "This wasn't the only group to break in. A larger group has managed to gain access to the security centre. They've locked themselves in and are shutting down sections of the building."

I'm careful to keep my expression neutral, but inside, my heart leaps.

Coleman's face darkens. "Start talking, Darwin. Who are they? What's the plan?"

"W-we were to take down the Wall. They needed me to guide them in." I swallow. "There was another group of Outsiders led by Barnes. You know, the one who ran my production line? They wanted to take over the factory. That's all I know."

And it's nothing you don't know already.

Coleman's gaze doesn't leave me as lifts his holo pad. "Avril, activate the emergency procedure for when the security centre has been compromised."

"That would be procedures 103 and 104, sir. Do you wish to activate the moderate or severe scenario?" The AI voice is female and has a strangely provocative tone.

"The severe scenario please, Avril."

Louis' eyes widen as he glances over his father's shoulder. "But what if our people are in there? They could be holding them hostage. They—"

"The severe scenario will exterminate any living beings in the centre. Would you like to proceed?" Avril sounds as if she's tempting him to bed, not discussing the murder of a dozen people.

"Proceed."

"Please re-enter your password."

Coleman clicks his tongue and raises his hand to the holo pad. Louis' eyes meet mine over the top of his father's head, begging me to do something.

"Wait!" I gasp. "You don't want to kill them. Not yet."

Coleman's hand pauses. "And why not?"

"I don't know much about what the Chain has planned, but Barnes may know more. Don't you at least want to question them first?"

I hold my breath as Coleman lowers his hand, his gaze never leaving mine. "Avril, cancel that request. Override security centre controls and lock all doors leading to it. Transfer all control of security systems to this office."

"Of course, sir. If you'll just enter your password to conf—"

Coleman types a code into the holo pad and hands it to Louis. "That will hold them for now."

He nods to the guards standing over Bryn and Liza. "Get those pair up and onto chairs. The tranquillizers must have worn off by now. They're just feigning unconsciousness."

Whether they're pretending or not, Bryn and Liza make the guards work to get them up. The two guards hovering next to my chair go over to help. They pull them up onto two chairs, one guard holding each of the captives upright while the other attempts to fasten their arms to the back of the chair.

My heart beats a little faster as I test my cuffs again. This may be the only chance we get.

Behind Coleman's back, Louis messes about with something behind the desk. I try to catch his eye.

Now would be a great time to help out, Louis.

Bryn's head lolls to one side. There's a flicker of movement from his right hand.

A signal?

Bryn explodes out of the chair. In a whirlwind of limbs, he attacks the two guards behind him. Somehow, he's broken free from his cuffs, and though the guards are armed, it's clear that Bryn is the better fighter.

Liza comes alert at the same time. She flings her head back and head-butts the guard checking her cuffs. The man reels backward, blood streaming from his nose. Swivelling on her chair, she kicks out at the second guard, sending his gun skidding across the floor before he can fire. The man backhands her and pulls a second gun from his belt.

I throw myself forward, my back straining against the weight of the chair as I stagger to my feet. I run forward and, more by luck than anything, hit the guard, the combined weight of me and the chair sending both of us toppling to the floor. The man curses and tries to push me off his legs.

"Stop!" Bryn's voice rings out above the chaos. The guard freezes.

I twist my head to look around. Liza is fighting the guard with the bloody nose. As he pauses, she delivers a kick to the stomach, followed by a second aimed squarely at his groin. I can't help wincing as the man doubles over, groaning. Louis is frozen halfway around the huge desk, his eyes wide.

Bryn stands behind Coleman, holding a gun to his head. A large bruise colours Bryn's jaw and his hair is plastered to his forehead, but his eyes are alert, scanning the room for any movement.

"One step and I'll shoot." He sounds as if he means it. "Place your weapons on the floor and lie down in the corner."

Coleman sits ramrod straight, but his voice is calm. "Do as he says."

The guard pushes himself out from under me. I lie on the floor like a beetle, one arm trapped painfully by the weight of the chair, unable to even get enough momentum to roll onto my stomach and stand.

Shiny black shoes step into my field of vision. There's a grunt as Louis heaves my chair up.

"I said don't move." Bryn's voice is tight.

"It's okay," I say when I'm upright again. "Louis is a—"

The barrel of a gun presses into my temple.

Time slows.

The only sound I can hear is the thumping of my heart, each beat sending blood pulsing through my arteries. Beads of sweat dampen the hair at the back of my neck. The cuffs around my wrists feel like fire against my skin. The barrel of Louis' gun is ice pushing into my skull.

Coleman's face relaxes. "It seems we're at an impasse. Let's see whose life is worth more – mine or your son's."

Bryn stiffens, his gaze meeting mine for a fraction of a second.

How does he know?

"My life doesn't matter," I say, trying to sound casual. "I'm just a boy. I don't have power or control over anything."

Coleman observes me for a moment. "I think you have power over

415

his heart," he says quietly.

One glance at Bryn's stricken face tells me he's right.

39

Aleesha

"What the hell are you doing, Aleesha?" My father's angry voice comes over the comm. "Get yourself out of there!"

"Unless you can work some miracle to bring the Wall down, we're trapped," I reply in a low voice. "What do you expect me to do?"

"I told you to avoid capture at all costs. Just go back through the bloody Wall."

"And leave my people here?" My voice is a whisper, but only so the people behind me can't hear my words. "Is that what you expect me to do?"

"Yes."

The word is heavy with the weight of two dozen lives. A small voice in my head tells me he's right.

You don't have to die for them. If you're captured, he'll come after you. The battle will be lost.

But even for the battle, even for the changes my father could bring to the city, even for the future benefit of the people of London, I cannot leave my gang here to die. Perhaps that makes me less of a leader, perhaps it makes me more of one. At this moment, I don't care.

"Aleesha, I *order* you to get your arse out of there. Do you copy?"

"As long as my people are here, I'm staying. Out." I switch channels so I'm on a line with Trey only.

The government army is silent, watching me. The front rows part to let a Metz officer through. It looks identical to all the other officers apart from one thing. It's unusually short.

"Put your weapons down and raise your hands in the air." The gravelly, toneless voice sends a shiver down my spine.

There's a murmur from behind me.

"Aleesha?" Rogue questions.

"Do as they say!" I call, my eyes not leaving the Metz officer. I tell myself it's so I can see if they try anything, but I know that's not true. It's so I don't have to look into the faces of my people. The people I've failed.

There's a clatter of movement as my fighters lower their weapons to the ground – their visible weapons, at least. I, myself, have three knives still concealed on my person.

"I want to discuss the terms of our surrender!" I call.

"The terms of your surrender?" The voice synthesizers in the helmets don't convey any emotion, but I could swear whoever is in that suit is smiling. "You're surrounded by a superior force. We have guns trained on every one of your people. With one order, I could kill you all. And you want to talk about the terms of your surrender?"

I swallow, dust drying my mouth. "Yes."

Of all the gambles I have taken, this is the biggest.

They want you alive.

I reach down and pick up the gun. Time slows as I click off the safety and press the barrel to my forehead. I take another step forward. "My terms are this. You let my friends leave this place without being accompanied or followed. In return, I'll come with you without protest. Oh, and take your helmet off. I want to see who I'm talking to."

There's a shocked silence, then the officer reaches up to its helmet. There's a sudden commotion, and a man pushes through the ranks of guards. He says a few words to the officer, who steps aside, almost reluctantly. The man is slightly built for an Insider and dressed in the grey uniform of the palace guard, though I suspect that's as a disguise rather than an indication of his true position. My heart beats a little faster as I take in his pale hair, the strong jaw. I've seen his face before, in a holo rotating above the table in the Chain's headquarters. This is one of the men my father wanted to kill.

The man steps forward. "What makes you think your life is so important that we should allow a group of armed rebels to rampage through our city?"

"They have put down their weapons. And they will return Outside immediately and by the most direct route." The emphasis I place on my words is for Rogue and Danny, not the government man. "You have my word. But if you're not that bothered about using me as leverage against my father ..."

I close my eyes and tighten my finger on the trigger. A hair's breadth separates me from instant death.

"Fine." There's a pause. "Put down the gun, let us take you into custody and your friends will walk free."

Whatever this man's job is, he can't be a government minister. He's too bad a liar.

I open my eyes, just in time to see the man's head explode in a spray of blood.

The shock almost makes me pull the gun's trigger. For a moment, I think it was Danny who fired the shot, and I whip around, only to see him staring blankly forward, his gun by his feet. Then more shots fill the air, and everything descends into chaos.

I step backward, still holding the gun. Bullets rain down on the government's army from the surrounding buildings. Windows shatter, though whether it's the government shooting or those inside the buildings blasting the glass out to give the snipers more firing positions, I don't know. Bullets hit the ground in front of me, puffing up dust. This close to the Wall, the street is rough, without the permeable layer that resists dust and lets the rainwater flow through it to the sewers beneath.

My foot catches on something and I look down. A metal panel set into the ground.

Rogue grabs my arm. "If we focus our attack close to the Wall, we might be able to cut a way through."

"There aren't enough of us." I glance around wildly. The remnants of my gang dart around like startled rats.

"There are people up on the roofs," Danny says, joining us. "They're—"

His next words are lost as the metal panel in front of me explodes into the air. Dust fills my lungs as I stagger backward, coughs racking my body. The panel clatters back to the ground narrowly missing Danny's head. I point my gun at the hole it reveals, the barrel shaking as my chest spasms.

A head pops up.

"That's some way to greet your friends," Anders says, eying my gun. "Fancy pointing that elsewhere?"

He pulls himself up, then reaches a hand back down into the hole to help someone up. My lungs, barely recovered from the dirt, are now hit by an overpowering stench.

Danny wrinkles his nose. "You smell like shit."

Anders looks offended. "Waded through it to get here. Thought you might need a few extra hands."

I want to throw my arms around him and kiss him, but I keep my distance. The stench helps. "Have you got weapons?"

"More than you left us with."

"They don't need weapons. They *are* a weapon." Danny wafts his hand in front of his face. "Just send 'em in. The Insiders will faint from the smell."

I roll my eyes. We're still vastly outnumbered, but at least now we have an escape route. "Rogue, get everyone with guns to form a shield around the sewer. Anders, I need one of your team to show people the route out. Danny, organize everyone else into some kind of orderly line so they don't block the hole."

All three of them turn to stare at me. "We're running away?" Anders asks.

"Tactical retreat." I gesture back at the chaos behind us. A sixth sense makes me duck, and something whizzes through the air above me. There's a scream as the bullet hits someone else. "If we stay here, we're going to get killed."

"If we go, we'll be leaving *them* to get killed."

"What do you mean?

Rogue points behind me. "Look."

I turn and try to make sense of the chaos. The government fighters have retreated to the shelter of the surrounding buildings. They fire up at the snipers, carefully and deliberately. Splintered doors and the dull sound of explosions suggests they've taken the fight inside. As I watch, a figure comes flying out of a window to land on the ground below with a sickening crunch. They don't move again.

A flashing light on my comm band catches my attention. Quickly, I switch channels. Murdoch's voice is loud in my ear. "Aleesha? About bloody time. If you're done standing around, we could use some help here."

I glance back at the hole in the ground, then out at the space stained red by the reflection of the Wall. "What do you need?"

"I've got people trapped on the roofs. We can rap down, but only if the landing zone is clear. Anabel's team has had to split. They'll be coming around the sides. Join with them and attack the front. We think they're low on ammo. That's why they aren't focused on you right now. Most of their guns are empty."

It's the first piece of good news I've had all day. I turn to Anders, Danny and Rogue. "Sure you want to stay?"

They nod.

"Separate back into three teams. We'll each take one of the buildings. We need to push the government forces back so Murdoch's team can get down. There may be more Chain fighters coming to help. Danny, you got the last of those bombs?"

"Yup."

"Let's take them by surprise."

Less than a minute later, I run full pelt toward a group of grey-uniformed guards, a hoard of screaming banshees at my back. I wonder what we must look like to them – these fighters, in name only, who signed up for an easy job patrolling the corridors of power. By the expression on their faces, we are a crazed bunch of suicidal madmen, risen from the depths of hell. A few of them fire shots, and I hear shouts as people behind me go down.

Later, I will think of them. Later, I will mourn them. Now we fight for survival.

I scream a war cry as we hit their front ranks. The gun in my belt, I wield the club with both hands, using momentum to smash legs, arms, chests. I try to disable, not kill, but in the melee, it's impossible to know what I'm hitting.

There are more of them than us, but they're unprepared for our style of fighting, which is wild and furious, without rhythm or strategy. Just hitting or kicking anything that moves.

This is how Outsiders fight. There are no rules.

We push them back down the alley between the buildings. Over the thrum of the fighting, I hear a light whistle and shouts from above. A moment later, Murdoch's voice sounds in my ear.

"We're down. Pull back to regroup."

I shout to my Phoenixes to pull back. Few listen, but as the palace guard rallies and begins to fight back, faces look to me for guidance. I wave my arm, and we retreat up the street, pulling our wounded with us, to regroup in the "dead zone" between the office buildings and the Wall. The palace guard watches us leave without giving chase, which seems odd. Why wouldn't they press their advantage?

I'm not kept waiting for an answer long.

A shadow swoops across the ground. In its wake comes death.

The pod's guns fire silently, but the ricochet of bullets hitting the concrete precedes the screams. There is nowhere to hide. Like a wave crashing to the sand, we go down hard.

Pain lances up my arm as I drop to the ground, yanking the gun from my belt and firing blindly into the air. My bullets bounce harmlessly off the pod's armoured underbelly. Until last week, I'd never seen an armoured pod before, never even knew they existed. Something else our government kept hidden away.

"Move to the buildings!" I yell, pushing myself to my feet and yanking up the person next to me. Half his weight falls on me and I stumble, nearly tripping over a prone figure, but manage to keep my footing. I glance back at the hole to the sewers. It's not an escape route now but a trap. We'd be sitting ducks queuing up to be shot.

"It's me other leg," the man leaning on me wheezes. He's bleeding from his chest, too, though I think it's just a surface wound. I switch sides and help him hop toward the shelter of the nearest office building. We reach it just as the sound of bullets starts up again behind me. I unhook his arm from my shoulders and turn to run back out again, but someone grabs my arm.

"Don't be stupid." Rogue's face is drawn as he clutches his thigh. "You'll get yourself killed."

I shrug off his hand. "Just get everyone inside."

Bodies litter the ground, some moving, some ominously still. I know I will see them in my head again, many times, in the days and weeks to come. I will wonder over and over how I could have saved them. But for now, the adrenaline pulsing through my body makes me act, not think.

"Aleesha?"

"Murdoch!"

I reach down to help him up, but he shakes off my hand and rolls to the side, revealing another, smaller figure.

My heart turns to stone. "Tommy?" I whisper. He's lying face down and is still.

"He's alive," Murdoch wheezes. "Knocked him out trying to protect him." A smile twitches the corner of his lips, and a thin line of blood runs down his chin. "Take him."

I grab Tommy's arm, preparing to hoist him up, then hesitate. "Follow me."

Murdoch shakes his head and glances back at the pod, which is readying itself for another pass. "Give me your gun. There's a weak spot ... in the belly."

I fumble with the gun at my waist and press it into his hand, then lift Tommy's thin body over my shoulder.

"Richard ..." Murdoch coughs, blood spraying over my leg. "He didn't send us. Anabel ..." He coughs again. "You can trust her."

I don't have time to process what he means by this. I open my mouth to tell him ... What? What do you say to someone in what might be their final moment?

Murdoch's eyes tighten in pain as he cocks the gun and gives me a small smile.

"Go!"

I stand, my legs straining under Tommy's weight, and run. The *rat-a-tat-tat* of bullets follows me, dust choking my lungs, but as I reach the shelter of the building, a cheer rises from the people pressed into its shadow. I turn to see the pod weaving overhead. It rises, then falls, bobbing like a bird with a broken wing, before plunging down to smash into the ground.

Hot air pulses out like a wave, the sound of the explosion hitting a split-second later. When I open my eyes and lower my hand from my mouth, the dust is settling. The pod lies, half-crushed, surrounded by the bodies of those it had already killed and those who could have been saved.

I want to fall to my knees, to scream my anger and grief. A hard lump forms in my throat as I gently lower Tommy to the ground. His eyelids flutter as I cradle his head.

"What's he doing here?"

I look up. Anders' face is smeared with dirt and blood. "I was going to ask you the same question."

Anders' jaw tightens. "He was supposed to be with Jax. I didn't see him here. I swear."

"Easy to stay hidden ... when yer little," Tommy gasps.

"Are you hurt?" I begin to probe around his skull, working my way down to his shoulders, but he pushes my hands away.

"Geroff. I'm fine. Just wanted t' help." He sits up and sways slightly. "Feelin' a bit ... sick." His eyes roll back in his head, and I catch him as he topples backward.

"Can you take him inside?" I ask Anders. "I think he'll be okay. Just a knock to the head. Murdoch—"

My voice breaks. I stare out at the flames flickering around the downed pod. Somewhere underneath that mass of metal and plastic

425

lies the man who got me into all of this in the first place. Without him, I wouldn't be here, but I also would never have found out the truth about my mother's death or that I had a father.

"He went down fighting," Anders says quietly.

I nod and turn away as he scoops Tommy up. Getting to my feet, I spot a tall figure dressed in black stalking through the wounded toward me. *Anabel.* A dark piece of fabric is wrapped around her arm, but otherwise, she looks uninjured.

"You okay?" Her eyes soften as she takes in the blood on my clothes.

Belatedly, I remember the sting of the bullet hitting my arm. It ripped through my top and grazed my arm, but the wound isn't deep. "Yeah. Murdoch's dead, though." I gesture to the pod. "He took that down."

Anabel's expression is grim. "I saw. I'm down to about fifteen fighters. How about you?"

I glance around. "I'm not sure. Perhaps twenty? But most are wounded."

"And there'll be some of Murdoch's team." She purses her lips. "The government forces are regrouping. They're short on ammo, but I reckon they'll outnumber us five to one."

"Does Richard have more people he can send?"

"He doesn't even know we're here."

I stare at her. "What? Aren't you the reinforcements?"

Anabel shakes her head. "He's got his hands full holding the compound. Murdoch and I were in position to attack the buildings we thought the government leaders were hiding in. Turns out we had bad information. Murdoch got one of the four, but the President was nowhere to be found. When we heard you were in trouble, we decided to split and help you out."

I try to absorb this. "So Richard never intended to help us?"

"I don't know." Anabel sounds exhausted. "Maybe he sent

Schmidt's team and they got waylaid. But I'm not going to count on anyone turning up to help. What's happened to Trey?"

I briefly recount what I'd heard over the comm. Anabel curses under her breath.

"Do you have a plan?" I ask.

"Try to hold out as long as possible." She sighs and lowers her voice so only I can hear. "Do you believe in miracles, Aleesha?"

I don't know what to say.

"I don't. But right now, I'm praying for one. They've got us surrounded. Unless my little brother can figure a way out of his situation and pull that lever, we are up the proverbial creek without a paddle."

The paddle reference confuses me, but I get the gist of what she's saying. Murdoch and Anabel bought us time, but not enough. The escape route through the sewers is now blocked by the downed pod. There is no one coming to save us.

I look around at the hopeful faces turned toward us. They expect us to figure out a way out of here. They want to believe the worst is over, that they will survive.

I can't tell them this is the beginning of the end.

You can't face death and win. We may have cheated him once today, but our names are on his ledger, and he's coming to collect the debt.

40

Trey

The barrel of the gun digs into my head. Bryn is silent, his face wracked with indecision. I think he's trying to work out if Louis will go through with his threat. Liza and Coleman's guards watch us, waiting to see how this will play out.

"Don't do this, Louis," I whisper, wishing I could see his face. "I thought you were on our side."

The barrel of the gun trembles.

"I *am* on your side," he says finally. "But I won't let you kill my dad."

Hope squeezes through the tightness in my chest. I try to catch Bryn's eye. "How about we just tie Coleman up for now? Just until all this is over?"

"I'm sorry, Trey." Bryn's voice is rough. "He has to die."

I wince as Louis pushes the gun into my head. "Why?"

"Those are my orders."

There was nothing said at the briefing about killing Coleman. Richard must have spoken to Bryn separately, given him additional instructions.

Coleman chuckles. For a man who's just been given a death

sentence, he seems remarkably relaxed. "Did you question Richard as to *why* he wants me dead?" He doesn't wait for an answer. "I presume you heard the recording of our meeting, given you weren't quite as unconscious as you pretended. But there is more. Do you want to see what will happen to our city if *he* takes control?"

I'm not sure whether his words are meant for Bryn or his son.

Bryn opens his mouth, then closes it again.

"What do you mean?" I ask.

"Louis, put down the gun and get my holo pad."

"But—"

"I'm sure Mr McNally isn't going to shoot me quite yet. There is some footage on the holo pad I'd like to show you. It relates to events in the other cities the Chain has *freed*. Paris, Dublin, Damascus." Coleman places a slight emphasis on the final name.

Bryn tenses, then seems to reach a decision. "Liza, cuffs."

Liza glances down at the guard sprawled on the floor next to her, one hand clutching his nose, the other his groin. "Release me."

The guard looks to Coleman. "Do it," he orders.

A few seconds later, Liza is free. She strides over and secures Coleman to the chair using the same pair of cuffs. Bryn lowers his gun. To my relief, I feel the barrel of Louis' gun fall away.

I crane my neck to look at him. His face is pale and his hand shakes as he shoves the gun – an odd, old-fashioned model – into his belt. "Any chance you could release me?"

Louis hesitates and looks to his father for guidance. Coleman shakes his head.

"Not yet," he says apologetically.

I bite back my irritation. I had trusted Louis. Was I always going to be let down? But I have to admit that if our roles had been reversed, if it had been Ella or Bryn in that chair, I would have done the same thing. Family is family.

Coleman seems to be playing a dangerous game. What worries me most is that he's so calm about it.

Liza cuffs the guards. Louis picks up Coleman's holo pad off the desk, then freezes as the barrel of Bryn's gun turns to him.

"Bring it over here, lad. I want to see what you're doing." Bryn steps out from behind Coleman. "Show us what it is you want us to see."

"Do you know why the second set of controls for the Wall was placed in the basement of this building? It was to ensure cooperation between government and business and to protect the people of this city from rash decisions. Richard knew I would never agree to take the Wall down in this manner." Coleman's gaze flicks to Bryn. "So he decided to break our agreement and have me killed. What he doesn't know is that I've done my own research on him and his organization over the past few months. As part of our bargain, he gave me a secure channel to the outside world. With that, I've been able to make my own contacts and find out what happens to the cities he claims to have freed."

Bryn snorts. "I've been with the Chain for decades and seen with my own eyes what these places were like before and after we freed them. I don't need to see whatever it is you've fabricated to distort the truth."

"Perhaps. Or perhaps you've just seen the afterglow of your efforts. The honeymoon period rather than the ten-year marriage."

Coleman nods to Louis and rattles off a set of instructions. A holo appears in the air, expanding to fill the space between us. For a moment, I think its footage of one of the areas Outside – Area Three perhaps – but the skyline is wrong. Sunken eyes stare out of the faces of the hobies huddled against the meagre shelter of a building as rain lashes down. A child walks haltingly down the street. He stumbles, falls and does not get up.

"These are the slums of Paris five years after the Chain took down the elected government and replaced it with a puppet president, who answers to Richard. Living conditions got better for a time, but the government didn't know what they were doing and squandered taxes on the Prime Minister's pet projects rather than tackling the bigger societal issues."

The image flickers, then a different city appears.

"Milan, two months ago. After the Chain, or *la Resistenza*, as they were known there, took the city, what used to be Southern Italy broke away from the rest of Europa and formed its own state. Meanwhile, Milan is ruled by a dictatorship. There's been a reduction in poverty, but is it worth giving up your voice for?"

Five figures are lined up on a raised platform. They're each tied to a stake and wear cloth bags over their heads. As we watch, someone barks an order and a volley of shots ring out. The figures slump, blood oozing through their rough clothes.

"All these people did was ask for the right to a free vote. The government Richard put in place refused that, under his orders. It seems your leader may be skilled at conquest, but he's not quite so good at democracy. He moves on to the next challenge, not caring about the cities he leaves behind."

"And what about what this government's done?" I say, gesturing to the frozen image. "How is this any different than sentencing people to the Farms or taking them to the Labs to be used as test subjects?"

Coleman shrugs. "At least we don't hide it under the banner of 'equality'. True equality is impossible. It's a dream young men like you want to believe in. There is always going to be inequality in society. It's up to each one of us to make the most of what we have and build the life we want for ourselves."

"That's easy to say when you start at the top," I retort, remembering what happened to any of the factory workers caught smuggling their lunch rations out. "Try telling that to the worker whose fingers you've broken because you don't pay him enough to feed his family."

Coleman ignores me and motions for Louis to move the holo on. "And this is Damascus. Eight years ago, I believe. I'm sure you'll correct me if I get the dates wrong, Mr McNally."

I glance at Bryn, puzzled. His face drains of colour.

The footage is taken from a rooftop, looking across a suburban area. The buildings are a little rundown and worn, though the streets are clean, the apartment balconies crammed with lemon trees and green vines. It would look like a normal city scene if not for the muffled explosions and the fighter pods overhead.

"The fall of Damascus," Coleman comments.

"That had nothing to do with the Chain." Bryn's voice is hoarse. "We had no control over the city at that time."

"No? Pause it, Louis."

The scene freezes.

"Then why does the pod that is about to drop a bomb on this small, inconsequential apartment block have your markings?" Coleman nods to Louis. "Play."

The low-rise apartment block explodes into a cloud of dust, which slowly settles to reveal a pile of rubble and twisted metal. The scene plays for a few more seconds, then freezes again. I stare at Bryn, whose expression has changed from horror to anger.

"No," he whispers.

"Richard didn't tell you that, did he? That he was responsible for their deaths?"

Liza stirs. "Bryn, we need to—"

Bryn raises his arm and slams the butt of his gun down on Coleman's head. He slumps in his chair. Louis starts and scrabbles for his weapon, but Bryn just stands back and raises his gun. "He's not dead. I just knocked him out. Now, are you going to cooperate,

432

or do I have to knock you out, too?"

Louis sucks in a breath. "As long as you don't kill anyone or destroy the factory, I'm on your side."

"Good." Bryn turns to Liza. "Free Trey. We have work to do."

Louis looks on, his jaw slack as Liza unfastens my cuffs. I rub my wrists. My shoulders ache from being pulled back, and my upper arm throbs where I landed on it.

"Can you reverse the lockdown of the security centre?" I ask Louis.

"I'm not sure. Maybe." He stares down at the holo pad, his blond hair falling over his forehead. I recognize the lost look in his eyes. I've been there. It's the moment you realize your whole world is built upon a fabric of lies and that the people you look up to most are not the people you thought they were. It's when you have to choose between right and wrong, and the only way to know which is the right choice is to jump and hope for the best.

I squeeze his shoulder. "It'll be okay."

Louis stares at his father, slumped in his high-backed chair. "Will it?"

I know what he needs to hear. The same thing I had needed to hear all those weeks ago when I'd wandered into the rundown bar of a brothel in a city that seemed to have sprung from a nightmare.

"Yes. It'll be okay."

I hope I'm not lying to him.

"Trey, can you get hold of Aleesha? Richard hasn't been able to get through to her." Bryn switches channels on his comm and begins talking in a low voice.

Aleesha ... I press my hand to my ear, suddenly remembering the comm bud being ripped out.

"Here." Liza straightens from where she's bent over searching the guards and tosses something to me.

I fumble to put it into my ear and breathe a sigh of relief as the band on my wrist flashes to show it's connected. I switch to Aleesha's channel.

"Aleesha? Can you hear me?"

I hold my breath. For a moment, all I hear is silence. Then there's a crackle of static.

"Trey?" Her relief is palpable. "Are you all right?"

"Yes. Sorry. We had some issues on this end, but it's under control now. How—"

"Trey, you need to get the Wall down now. We're trapped, surrounded by government forces. Anabel—" Her voice cuts out for a second, then returns. "I don't know how long we can hold out."

"I'm on my way." I bolt to the door, ignoring Bryn's yell. "I'm going to the basement." When I press my hand to the access panel to unlock the door, the small light at the top of the panel stays red. "Come on," I mumble.

"I'll come with you." Louis shakes himself out of his daze and walks over to me, pressing his hand against the access panel. The light changes to green. "I have unrestricted access. Father's elevator is the quickest way down."

"Great." I yank open the door.

"Wait!"

I turn to Bryn impatiently. He strides over and holds something out to me. It looks like a transparent glove. "You may need this to get back into the system. President's fingerprints." He grabs the gun from Louis' hand, giving him a dark look, before handing me his own gun. "Point and shoot, got it? Any problems from him, shoot him in the leg."

Louis looks offended. "I'm not—"

Bryn holds out his hand. "Holo pad. You don't need that now you've unlocked the security centre."

I glance at Louis. "You did?"

He nods and hands the pad to Bryn, eyes narrowed. "If you do anything to my father..."

"Yeah, yeah. You'll kick my arse. Now, get moving." Bryn waves his hand. "We'll come down once we've dealt with this lot. Be careful. There are still guards about."

We tear through the building, only slowing when we come across the occasional security patrol. I'm glad Louis is with me. They believe him when he tells them the building is in lockdown and they're to go back to the guard room. We take Coleman's private elevator as far as the sixteenth floor, then move through the factory to the East Wing. As we run, my mind goes back to the footage Coleman had shown us and the meeting he had with Richard. The images he claimed to be a result of the Chain's actions. He could have faked the images. But why?

I shake my head, not wanting to think of the alternative. Perhaps the Chain doesn't have the perfect solution I had hoped for, but they couldn't be worse than the government. Could they?

I try Aleesha on the comm, but there's no answer. I pray it's because she's occupied with fighting. I can't bear to think of the alternative.

"What's in the basement?" Louis asks. He's barely out of breath, though I'm panting.

"The control mechanism for the Wall. It's in the room near the cells. The one that was guarded."

Louis slows to a walk as we approach a door leading to a staircase and pushes it open. "This way."

A few minutes later, we're back in a familiar, long corridor. "I'm guessing your father has it guarded," I whisper, wishing I'd thought of this earlier.

"I'll see if I can draw them out."

Louis strides ahead of me, his footsteps ringing through the tunnel, disguising my softer footfall. He disappears around the corner. I

435

creep closer and flip off the safety of my gun, wondering if Bryn had thought of this and what he expected me to do. Shoot them, I suppose.

Adrenaline makes my stomach knot.

I don't want to kill anybody.

Louis' voice rises. A moment later, I hear footsteps coming toward me. When the guard rounds the corner and sees me, his hand instinctively reaches for his gun.

I tighten my finger on the trigger. The sound of the shot reverberates around the tunnel.

The guard falls back, clutching his shoulder, a dark stain blossoming on his uniform.

A second guard appears, his weapon already out in front of him. I don't have time to take aim, just fire and hope for the best. The bullet hits him in the leg.

Louis pokes his head around the corner, his face pale. Our eyes meet. I read shock in his expression. I don't have time to wonder what he thinks of me. But what else could I have done?

"Tie them up," I tell him as I shove past him toward the door to the control room. "And see if you can stop the bleeding."

The door is unlocked. Lights flicker to life as I race inside, but the control screen is dark. I run my fingers over the small shelf beneath it and hold my breath, releasing it when the screen lights up.

It seems Coleman hadn't bothered to exit the program. The same section of the Wall appears as a blue line on the screen. I reach out and yank down the handle. The blue line flashes and turns to red.

The Wall is down.

My comm band flashes. I switch channels to speak to Bryn. "The Wall's down."

"Good. I'll relay that to Richard. I've sent Barnes to replace you. When she arrives, come back up here." Bryn pauses. "There's something you need to see."

41

Aleesha

It seems miracles do happen.

There is no organized retreat, no plan, no strategy. When the Wall goes down, we run. The government forces follow us, probably more by instinct than order. They seem as disorganized as us. Which is one thing going in our favour. The second is that they seem to have run out of ammo. They haven't fired a shot for almost ten minutes.

Mind you, we're not much better off. I have a couple of rounds left, but you never know when a single bullet can change the course of a confrontation, so my gun is in my belt, the safety on.

Once we'd drawn them Outside, the plan was to separate and disappear into Area Four, allowing the people we'd left behind to spring their traps. Now the traps are unmanned, and many of the people who'd set them up are wounded or dead. I see Anders trying to give orders and direct people, but most are too busy trying to find shelter to listen.

Anabel follows me up onto the roof of an old, derelict warehouse that has an unobstructed view of the Wall.

"Richard's called for reinforcements," she pants as she hauls herself up onto the roof from the top of a rickety fire escape. "Can you deal with this lot alone?"

"I don't know." I sound about as tired as I feel. A sting in my arm reminds me that I still haven't had time to bandage the wound. It feels as if we've been fighting non-stop for hours.

Anabel notices the injury and pulls a dressing from a thigh pocket. "Here. Get that fixed." Her hard expression softens slightly. "You're doing a good job. I've had trained, seasoned fighters who would have fallen apart back there."

I manage a small smile as I wrap the dressing around my arm. "We'd have been screwed if you and Murdoch hadn't turned up, though. Thank you."

"Thank Trey. He'd never have forgiven me if I didn't come to your rescue."

This surprises me. "I didn't think you cared about him?"

"I promised Mother I'd look after him." She shrugs. "Besides, family is family, and mine seem to be rather prone to dying at the moment. I don't want him trying to play the hero and getting himself killed saving you."

We cross the roof to look out at the Wall. The gap in the barrier must be visible from miles around. As we approach the edge of the roof, the downed pod comes into sight, the bodies of the dead littered under and around it. There hadn't been time to bring them with us. We weren't even able to grab all the wounded. Those who couldn't walk had been left in one of the office buildings with a loaded gun and a promise that we'd come back for them. I had been the one to close the door. When I blink, I see their despairing eyes staring back at me.

The government's army mills around the pod. Perhaps thirty or so have crossed Outside, but rather than chasing us through the streets, they seem to be waiting for something.

"Dammit," Anabel mutters.

"Why are they just standing there?"

"I don't know. Perhaps they've realized it's a trap." She casts me a fleeting glance. "Or perhaps they just need some motivation."

"Me."

"Maybe. If they don't take the bait, the only other option is to try and get behind them and push them out." She looks thoughtful. "I wonder what they would do if the Wall came down completely. Would they spread out to guard it or focus on getting the compound and factory back?"

"I don't know," I reply honestly. I wish I could see inside the President's mind and understand his strategy so I can unravel it, thread by thread, until his plans fall apart in front of him. "I'll go down to the street and see if I can draw them out."

"Wait."

Anabel's voice stops me as I start walking away. She stands with one foot on the low parapet looking over the edge. Curious, I walk back to join her.

"It's too late," she says when I reach her. "They must have been called back Inside."

I watch the last of the government fighters disappear into the smoke around the pod. "Shit."

"My thoughts exactly."

Anabel's comm flashes and she puts a hand to her ear. Her face pales, and dread begins to pool in my stomach.

What's gone wrong now?

Anabel straightens, dropping her hand. "They're inside the Metz compound. Someone betrayed us and let them in. That's why they've been called back. They must be planning one final push to take the compound."

And when they do, everyone in there will die. Including my father.

"Can we help?" My voice is remarkably steady given the turmoil I feel inside.

"I'm to meet up with Schmidt's team and force as many of them as we can into the compound. They're contained in one of the outer rooms at the moment, and Richard thinks he has a way of turning the tables on them once we have them trapped. If you've got any uninjured people, I could use some more fighters."

My stomach feels sick at the thought of more fighting, but I know there is no going back now. "We'll come with you."

"No." Anabel grips my shoulder. "You're to stay out here. Richard forbade you from coming near the compound."

I open my mouth to protest.

"Don't make me have to leave people behind to guard you. Not when we're already outnumbered."

"So he's willing to risk my people but not me?" I can't stop the bitterness creeping into my voice.

"He's your father. What do you expect?"

What did I expect? I expected him to trust me to make my own decisions. To lead my people from the front, not send them out to fight and die while I stay safe. But it seems the only reason he was willing to let me be part of his plan in the first place was because he thought I would abandon my team and escape through the Wall if things didn't go according to plan.

Is that what he would have done? Does he see his own people as being expendable?

I cross my arms. "Fine. I'll stay here."

Anabel nods, then turns and breaks into a run across the roof.

"Then I'll follow you at a distance until you're close to the compound. At which point I'll catch up and join your team, and you won't be able to do anything to stop me."

Anabel stops. She turns slowly, a smile tugging at the corners of her mouth. "You are so much like your father."

My chest squeezes tight at the compliment.

Seeing the resolve on my face, she sighs. "Fine. But if he asks, you did it without my knowledge."

"Of course."

I run past her and jump down onto the fire escape. It rattles ominously as we race down.

As I round the corner of the alley onto the main street, a movement near the Wall catches my eye. A lone figure, silhouetted against the bright light of the Wall, creeps toward the gap, then disappears through it. A moment later, someone else approaches from the other direction. A third person joins them, then a fourth.

I wonder how long it'll be before word spreads and half of Area Four decides to try their luck Inside.

Anders and Rogue meet me at the Wall, the remnants of my fighters behind them. I direct Leon and two others to rescue the injured and take them to safety. Then I explain that I'm going to go back Inside, follow the government's army and attack them.

Surprisingly, most of them agree to come with me. Perhaps the chemicals in the food they've been eating are starting to affect their brains.

"Where you go, we go," Rogue says, as if this isn't up for debate.

We quickly catch up with Anabel and her team. I send Rogue forward to find out what the plan is. He gives me a surprised look but complies.

My people are silent as we race through the streets, not attempting to disguise our presence. Insiders scurry past, swerving to the sides of the street to keep as far away from us as possible. We must look like barbarians to them in our dark, bloodstained clothing, brandishing homemade weapons. Any other time, it would make me smile. How scared I'd been the first few times I'd come Inside, hiding from people.

Now they are the ones avoiding me.

Rogue reappears, cradling a handful of weapons. "Got us some extra guns and grenades. Most of the government forces are in the main bay of the compound where we used to suit up. We're to pick off as many as we can outside, then drive them inside and close the main door so they can't escape."

I hand out the spare guns, ammo and grenades. There aren't enough for everyone, and I have to swallow down my irritation at my father for not supplying us with proper equipment, not to mention Denzel and his gang sitting in *my* headquarters, armed to the teeth, while we fight for their freedom. If my father could just have spared some fighters to take back the headquarters, we could have had our pick of weapons.

Doesn't do any good wishing that now.

I force myself to come back to the present, though one thought lingers. It was odd that the Chain didn't have a better guard on their precious weapon supply. Denzel isn't exactly the smartest Outsider around.

"So, this is it then. Do or die." Danny sounds uncharacteristically gloomy. He still has the gun the Chain had given him when they'd disrupted my execution. He'd held it with pride then, but now it seems to weigh heavily in his hands. When even Danny is sick of fighting, you know the end has to be near.

"Let's *do*, not die," I reply. "Once we're inside the compound, we'll be in a confined space. They'll be less willing to shoot, so we'll have more of an advantage. But before we head in, let's see what havoc we can create out here, shall we?"

Danny perks up, giving me a wolfish grin. "Now *that's* what I'm talking about."

The government's army is spread out around the perimeter of the compound. We throw our grenades. They don't do much damage, but it rattles them, which is something. Once we run out, we circle to join back up with Anabel's group.

"They're getting ready to send in more people," she tells me in a low voice. "We'll follow behind—"

She breaks off and frowns, touching her ear. "That's odd ..." She turns back to me. "Schmidt says half the force is pulling away and heading back toward the gap in the Wall."

I think of the Outsiders sneaking through from Area Four, the wonder I'd felt the first time I stepped Inside the Wall, the desperation of half-starved people wandering around the playground of the rich. The government can't afford to let them rampage at will. Perhaps the people of Area Four are lowering the odds against us, giving us one final chance to win.

At the cost of their lives?

I squash the thought and flick off my gun's safety. "Time to go?"

Anabel gives me a cold smile. "Time to go."

We follow the government's force like a shadow, waiting until the column of fighters has disappeared inside the hangar door of the compound. Four guards stand just inside the entrance, wearing the black protective uniforms similar to the Metz, but with blue stripes instead of yellow.

Anabel raises her hand, and eight of the Chain's fighters peel off from the group, heading in opposite directions. They sneak up on the guards from either side. Only one of the guards gets off a shot before they're taken down.

The rest of the Chain's fighters surge forward, my team behind them. Blood pulses through my veins, adrenaline sharpening my senses as we sprint toward the yawning entrance to the compound.

There's a *rat-a-tat-tat* of gunfire from above. *Snipers.* Someone screams behind me, but I don't turn to see who. Safety lies ahead, in the belly of the compound.

Anabel's team reaches the entrance and disappears inside just as the hangar door begins to roll down. I put on an extra burst of speed, sensing Anders and Rogue at my shoulder. They easily have the speed and strength to overtake me, but they hold back, letting me lead.

I reach the door just as it lowers to head height, skidding inside. Rogue ducks to twist his bulk through, the others following behind. Bullets slam into the retractable door as it silently closes, cutting off the daylight – and our retreat. As much as I know that this was the plan, it still makes me uneasy. They are trapped. But so are we.

I look around the wide tunnel I remember from the day we'd taken the Metz compound. Low-level blue lights lead underground. I feel a sense of finality, like I'm stepping onto a tightrope and the only way is forward – to death or glory. The sounds of fighting leak up the tunnel toward us.

I take a step forward, then a second. With the final remnants of my gang around me, I walk into the heart of the storm.

The tunnel ends in a vast room filled with rows of pillars – stations where the Metz officers store their exoskeleton suits. I try to remember the layout of the room, but the sound of bullets striking walls and flesh mixes with screams and shouts to create a cacophony of noise that overwhelms my senses. I can barely make out who is on which side of the fight.

I motion for the others to follow as I skirt around the edge of the room and crouch behind a row of pillars. The inside of them glows blue, the empty, black suits standing like sentinels ready to spring into action. I try to reach Anabel, then my father on the comm, but all I get is a crackle of static.

I lean close to Rogue's ear. "Can you and the others make use of those suits?"

He jerks back, as if I'd slapped him. "Take someone else's suit?"

I resist the temptation to roll my eyes. "It's just some armour. It'll give you some protection. Plus, they won't be able to tell the difference between their fighters and you."

He looks at me, aghast. "It's not just *some armour*. Besides, the suits are made to their owner's precise fit. Most of them will be too small for me. And I don't exactly have the time to wander around, trying them on."

"Fine. Got a better idea?"

A stray bullet whistles through the air above us. Rogue swallows. "Our bullets may not pierce the armour. We'll need to take them down by force."

"Easy for you to say," I mutter. Me trying to take down a Metz officer would be like a fly trying to take down a spider. I glance down the line. "Everyone ready?"

A wave of nods comes back to me. I pair them off, one of the former Metz officers with one of the Outsiders, then set two pairs to take down one of the enemy. Trying to take them all down at once won't work, but by focusing on one at a time, we may have a chance.

Twenty minutes later, I wonder how I ever thought that possible.

Two of my team are dead. Two others are badly wounded, cornered by a pair of black-suited fighters. I've lost track of where everyone else is. Rogue and I manage to take one down, mainly by Rogue's sheer strength. He tackles the officer and knocks him to the floor, then sits on him while I release his helmet, pulling it off. The man's petrified eyes stare up at us. Rogue hesitates for a second before slamming his fist into the man's jaw, knocking him unconscious.

I look around, trying to find Anabel amongst the confusion. My gaze alights on one of the government fighters. It's dressed in the same black suit as most of the others, but there are no coloured markings on the helmet. The figure is shorter than average, but that's not the thing that draws my attention.

It's the fact the fighter isn't fighting. It's just standing there, watching the chaos.

Turns out we had bad information. Murdoch got one of the four, but the President was nowhere to be found.

I remember the short officer who'd stepped aside after confronting us when we were trapped in front of the Wall. I'd assumed it stood aside to let its superior through. What if I was wrong? What if the man Murdoch's team had shot had put himself in the line of fire to prevent his boss from revealing himself?

I'm out of bullets, but with a knife in each hand, I weave through the pillars toward the solitary figure. I hear Rogue shout my name, but I don't dare turn around in case the figure ducks out of my sight. Exhaustion makes me stumble.

It also saves my life.

The blow skims over the top of my head. Had it connected, I'd have been knocked off my feet. I lash out instinctively, my blade skittering along the fighter's protective armour. The tip finds the tiny crack in the elbow – its only weak point – and I drive my blade home.

A guttural cry explodes from the fighter, and it yanks its arm away. The handle of the knife slides from my grip. The fighter pulls it out, blood dripping to the floor, and slashes through the air. I stagger back, the blade coming within inches of my nose. He keeps advancing, weaving a pattern in the air with such speed, I know it will cut me to pieces if my focus wavers for an instant.

My back slams into a pillar. I twist to the side, but a glint of metal flashes blue in front of my eyes before a burning pain lances my cheek.

The officer pauses, the blade – *my* blade – held out in front of him. Hot blood runs down my face. Behind him, I glimpse Rogue wrestling another fighter to the floor. My stomach is clenched tight. I've been running on adrenaline too long. I need water, food and rest, in that order. Or perhaps one of the Chain's magic stim shots. But first, I must survive.

I glance to the left, my eyes widening, feigning shock.

It works.

For a fraction of a second, the officer's attention is diverted. I duck around its arm to sprint away.

But not quickly enough.

The fighter kicks out, tripping me. I flail my arms as I stumble, knocking into it, both of us sprawling to the floor, its armour knocking the breath from my body. With a sweep of its arm, it brushes me off. My head slams onto the concrete, stars exploding behind my eyes. Something drips onto my forehead. Blinking to clear my vision, I see the fighter looming over me, my knife in its hand.

I twist my aching body, reaching down to my boot for the blade I have stashed there. The only weapon I have left. My limbs feel sluggish, my brain slow. I can't quite reach. Out of the corner of my eye, I see Rogue take a blow to the face and fall to his knees.

Then I look up into the faceless mask of my opponent. It raises the blade and I close my eyes. But nothing happens. There's a roar and the pressure on my chest releases. My eyes snap open just in time to see the fighter flying backward. My father towers above me, the muscles on his arms bulging, a snarl distorting his face.

He grabs my uninjured arm and drags me to my feet. I lean against the wall, panting. He may have just saved my life, but covered with blood and sweat, he looks scarier than any Metz officer.

"What are you doing here? I told Anabel—"

"She didn't know," I say quickly. "What's this trap you've got?"

"Katya's working on it. Just stay out of the way and—"

He stiffens and begins to turn. A black figure appears behind him, then a second and a third. My father lashes out, but they grab his arms and drag him to the floor, pressing a knife to his neck. I watch helplessly as others grab me, pulling my arms behind my back.

The short, armour-clad figure steps forward. He reaches up to remove his helmet, and I stare into the brown eyes of the President.

The trap has turned.

42

Trey

I slam my fist onto the desk. "She's not answering."

Bryn looks grim. "Richard's team is taking a hammering at the compound. He's called for all available teams to rendezvous and attack the government forces from behind."

"You think Aleehsa's gone to help him?"

Bryn gives me a look. "You know what she's like."

My chest tightens as I glance at the holo image still frozen in the air. "She needs to see this. Needs to know what really happened."

"It may not change anything. He's still her father."

I swallow, knowing he's right. Part of me doesn't want to show her the footage Bryn found on Coleman's holo pad. She doesn't deserve any more pain. The video could be fake. But I know in my heart it's not.

Because now I've seen it, a lot of things begin to make sense.

I should feel a sense of relief. We have control of the factory and the food supply to the city. We've gone beyond what Richard expected of us. But our success feels inconsequential.

"What do you want to do? Stay here, or go help Richard?"

Bryn sinks into Coleman's black leather chair. He looks utterly exhausted. "I need to get to the compound. We can't lose now. Besides, I have some questions for Richard, and he can't answer them if he's dead." He squeezes his eyes shut and massages his temples. "He told me to kill Coleman because the man was a government sympathizer. I'm starting to wonder if that wasn't the only reason. You need to stay here. Take charge. We can't leave the factory under the Brotherhood's control."

I shake my head. "I'm coming with you. I need to know what's happened to Aleesha. I need to be with her when she sees that footage."

To my surprise, Bryn doesn't argue. He drops his hand and opens his eyes. "Then who do we leave in charge?"

I think through the options. Barnes won't stand for Louis being in charge, but Louis is perhaps the only one who can instil some confidence in the other managers. Without him, they may try to take matters into their own hands and attack the Brotherhood. Which will mean more deaths. What we need is a neutral intermediary to keep the peace.

I hate myself for what I'm about to suggest. But I can't think of an alternative.

"Ella."

Bryn's eyes widen.

I shrug. "She's bossy and a natural diplomat. Which seems like the exact thing we need right now. She's about the only person I know who may be able to stop Barnes and Louis from killing each other."

"It could be risky. Do you trust Barnes not to hurt her?"

"I don't know. But I think it's the least bad option for everyone."

Except for Ella.

I push the thought down. Time and time again, she's told me that she and her friends could help. She's not a fighter, but if anyone can mediate between Barnes and Louis, it's my sister.

I activate the comm band Ella had left for me and call her. She's surprised to hear from me, even more surprised at my request, but is eager to help.

I cut the connection and turn back to Bryn. "She's on her way."

"How long will it take her?"

"Maybe half an hour."

Bryn drums his fingers on the arm of the chair. "Fine."

We lapse into silence. The footage Coleman showed us still niggles at me. I don't want to believe it's real. Don't want to believe *this* is the organization Bryn works for. The organization I trusted to free my city.

"Is the footage real? What Coleman showed us from the other cities?"

Bryn's fingers pause. He frowns, staring at the floor. "I believe so. I don't know why Coleman would have faked it. He couldn't have known we were planning to break in."

"Why didn't you know what was happening in the cities you freed?" I realize my words sound accusatory, but I'm not sure how else to phrase the question.

Bryn sighs. "I'm one of Richard's inner circle, but I only oversee the operations to free cities. My role ends when whatever tyrant has been in power is removed. I knew Richard was involved in establishing the government moving forward, but he keeps that side of the operation separate."

"Who's in charge of that part of the organization?" I ask, suspecting I already know the answer.

"Katya."

Of course. Though I'm not surprised, something about this seems odd. From what Aleesha had told me of Katya's background, I couldn't imagine her being complicit in creating the scenes Coleman had shown us. Children starving in the streets. People being shot because they dared to voice a different opinion.

"Katya doesn't believe in democracy," Bryn says, as if reading my thoughts. "She's seen what happens when democracy is corrupted, so she doesn't believe it can work. She's an excellent spy and a ruthless assassin, but she's not the person who should oversee rebuilding cities."

"Do you know Richard's plans for London?"

"No." He leans forward and pinches the bridge of his nose between his forefinger and thumb. "As I said, I'm not involved in that part of the operation."

There's another question needling at me. One I want to ask but am afraid will open wounds in Bryn that have been healed. Or if not healed, at least hidden.

"The third city Coleman showed us …" I hesitate.

"Damascus? I never realized …" He seems to be talking to himself. The creases on his forehead deepen. "He told me the rebel forces had returned, sponsored by a different government."

He falls silent.

"Daniel was in that building?" I ask gently. "The one that was hit by the bomb."

Bryn nods. He looks up at me, his face ravaged by grief. It's not an emotion I'm used to seeing from him. Irritation, anger, occasionally tenderness – never anything this raw. His anguish hits me like a punch to the chest.

"I had bought the apartment for them just a month before. I promised her I'd leave the Chain, start a different line of work. I'd made some contacts in Damascus and put away some money. Richard wasn't happy when I told him, but he wished me well. I said I'd finish the job I was working on before leaving."

Bryn glances over at the holo pad, as if his memories are locked away in there, just waiting to be replayed. "A week later, while I was still away, the apartment block was destroyed. They couldn't even find enough of them to bury. I went to Richard and asked to lead an operation to expel all the rebel forces from Damascus. He refused. Said it was already being taken care of. He sent me to lead the takeover of Munich instead."

His jaw clenches, fingers sinking into the leather upholstery. For a moment, I think he's going to rip off the arm of the chair. "All a pack of lies I chose to believe because I had nothing else to live for. No one else to believe in."

The air between us is thick with emotion.

"I'm sorry," I say finally, knowing it is not enough.

Bryn pushes himself out of the chair and walks over to the window. "As for what happened in the other cities after we left, well … Perhaps part of me did wonder. Perhaps I chose to ignore it because I didn't want to believe he wasn't the man I thought he was. That I'd spent my life fighting for something, someone, that wasn't worth my blood."

I join him at the window and place my hand over his clenched fist. After a moment, he turns to face me, and I see a man who's tired of running and fighting and rebellion.

"Just one more day. Then you and Abby can leave this city and start your own life together." I force a smile onto my face. "I reckon a break in the country will do us all good."

Bryn's expression softens, and I know he's thinking of Abby. So when he pulls me into a hug, I stiffen in surprise. "If there's one good thing to come out of this mess, it's that I met you." His voice is gruff, and I can swear he sniffs. "I never believed I'd get another chance at being a father, and Abby, well … You're the son she never got to have."

I duck my head and pull back, but Bryn grasps my shoulder and pulls my forehead to his. "Remember, Trey. You still have a family."

* * * *

"Let me get this straight," Ella says, perching on the edge of Coleman's desk. "On one side of this building, you've got Insiders who know the inner workings of this factory, have access to all the infrastructure systems and are loyal to the factory owner, whom you've just locked up. On the other side, you have hundreds of Outsiders who likely won't hesitate to rise up against their masters, plus a bunch of armed fighters who may be a little trigger-happy. And you want *me* to keep everyone under control?"

I nod. "And make sure there's someone available to switch the Wall mechanism if needed."

"You really *do* trust me, don't you?"

"Can you do it?" Bryn asks, his face grim.

With every minute we've waited for Ella, he's grown more uneasy about my idea of putting her in charge. I can see he's torn between wanting to confront Richard and wanting to keep the factory under the Chain's control. But I need him to trust her and help me get into the compound because, deep in my bones, something tells me Aleesha needs us. And time is running out.

Ella lifts her chin and meets his gaze. "Yes." She glances across at Dexter, who's tapping away on a holo pad. "We can."

I hadn't asked her to bring Dexter, but I'm glad she did. Perhaps his technical expertise will come in handy.

We'd left the door to Coleman's office open, so I hear footsteps in the corridor, then a knock on the wall. Barnes walks in without waiting for permission. She looks unruffled, as if coming to report on production line figures, not the takeover of the factory.

"We've secured the remaining guards. They're squashed in the cells, but a bit of discomfort won't kill them. I've left Petal down there with orders to shoot if any of them so much as twitch."

"What about the factory workers?" I ask.

"That was my next thing. I'm pretty sure the Outsiders will do as they're told. Those who heard the shots are terrified, and most of the rest are exhausted from working double shifts and not having a proper place to sleep. If we can release some of the food supplies and get everyone fed, I don't think they'll cause us any trouble." She pauses. "It's the management I'm worried about. I don't know if any of them might try something stupid."

"I'm creating some fake footage of Coleman. It's safest for everybody if people believe he's still in charge," Dexter says, his fingers flying over the keypad.

Barnes looks from him to Ella. "Who are you?"

"Barnes, this is my sister, Ella, and her boyfriend, Dexter. We're leaving her in charge of the factory," I say in as authoritative a tone as I can muster.

Barnes's eyes flick to me. "You're leaving?"

"We need to get back to the compound," Bryn says. "It's a choice between having Ella or Louis in charge."

"And why should we have either?" Barnes stares at Bryn, and the tension in the room rises a notch. "*We're* the ones who took this factory."

I decide now is probably not the time to mention the fact Coleman nearly killed the lot of them. I grab Barnes's arm and draw her to one side, lowering my voice. "I know you don't trust the Chain, and I understand why. I'm not sure I trust Richard, either. Not anymore. But we both want the government taken down and the fighting to end, correct?"

She gives a reluctant nod.

"There are hundreds of people in this building. Insider or Outsider, they don't deserve to die. But unless we get this situation under control, some of those Insiders are going to take matters into their own hands. That's why we need Louis. If they find out Coleman isn't in charge, he's the only one they might listen to."

Barnes opens her mouth to speak, but I continue. "You don't like Louis, and he doesn't like you. I get it. That's why Ella's here. Neither of you has to lose face by answering to the other."

"And whose side is she on?"

"The side of the people. As am I. That's why we need to go to the compound. I need to find out who Richard really is. If he'll make things better or worse."

Her gaze is calculating as she considers the plan from all angles. She knows that with us gone, the Brotherhood could easily over-power Louis and put themselves in charge of the factory. But Barnes is not a leader. She doesn't *want* to be in charge. If Samson were here, her attitude would be different, but without him, she is out of her comfort zone.

I'm banking my sister's life on my judgment of her character. The thought makes me dizzy.

"And if you don't come back?" she asks.

"Then I trust you, Ella and Louis to do what is in the best interest of the people."

Barnes straightens. "Fine."

I try not to show my relief. "You promise you won't hurt my sister or Louis?"

Barnes rolls her eyes. "I promise."

As I turn, she grabs my arm and lowers her voice to a whisper. "I hope you know what you're doing, Trey. And as a friend, I suggest you and Bryn get out of here. Now."

Her voice carries no threat, but her words make my blood run cold. "What do you mean?"

But she's already pushed past me, heading over to Ella.

Louis is easier to convince. It probably helps that he's the only one who knows the code to access his father's holo pad. I get him to transfer the files we need onto two small holocubes, which Bryn shoves into his pocket.

"I've told Liza to meet us in the entrance tunnel. Let's go."

After making sure Coleman and the guards were secure in the cells, Liza had taken Petal's comm bud and gone to the control centre to see if she could help make sense of the factory's security systems. She should have been closer to the rendezvous point than us, but when we reach the tunnel, she's nowhere to be found.

Bryn frowns and checks his comm. "Nothing."

A feeling of unease begins in my toes, spreading upward and chilling my body. "Something's wrong."

Bryn gives me a sharp look. "What is it?"

"I don't know. It's just a feeling." I try to shrug it off. "Probably nothing."

"Gut feelings are rarely nothing," Bryn says grimly, drawing his gun. "You think Barnes betrayed us?"

"I don't know."

I thought I'd read Barnes correctly. That I knew her well enough to know when she was lying. But even if every word from her lips had been the truth, it means nothing if I didn't ask her the right questions.

I assumed the Brotherhood's fighters would listen to her.

I assumed Samson's only motive in helping take the factory was to secure the food supply.

What if I was wrong on both counts?

I suggest you and Bryn get out of here. Now.

My unease turns to dread. It creeps up me like a winter fog, curling around my legs and chest. Suddenly, the empty tunnel feels too big, too exposed.

"We need to go."

But it's already too late.

There's a flicker of movement further down the tunnel. Instinctively, I launch myself at Bryn, knocking us both to the ground. Something whistles through the air above us and clatters to the floor. Bryn fires blindly down the tunnel. As the sound of his shots dies away, there's the sound of running footsteps, then silence.

"You okay?" Bryn whispers.

I nod and get to my feet. A blue glint on the floor behind us catches my attention. I bend and pick up a thin knife with a delicately carved handle. The carvings form a pattern of vines around a single flower.

I push the knife into my belt, wondering whether its owner was aiming to kill me or Bryn.

We retreat to the relative safety of the staircase, and I bring up the blueprints of the building. Bryn tries to comm Liza again. Still no answer. His expression is grim as we head toward the security centre.

"If they've got any sense, they'll be watching the security cameras," Bryn whispers. "Be alert until we know what's happened to Liza."

As we round the corner into the final corridor, we both freeze. Liza lies face down in a spreading pool of blood in front of the door to the security control room.

Bryn walks up to her and bends down, pressing his fingers into her neck. He shakes his head, his expression grim, then straightens and tries the door. "They've locked us out."

The hairs on the back of my neck prickle. Someone is watching us, waiting to see what we do next. Fear curls up my throat, weaving its way around my windpipe like a serpent waiting to choke the air from my lungs.

Bryn rises and gestures for me to return the way we've come. I'm grateful for the excuse to turn my back. My blood flows sluggishly through my body, my fingers whitening around the gun in my hand as I stumble away.

Bryn joins me a minute later. "Can you get through to Ella?"

My fingers tremble on the comm band. Ella answers within seconds. She sounds in control, relaxed. A little of my fear seeps away.

"Is Barnes still there?" I ask.

She picks up on the tension in my voice. "Yes. What's wrong?"

"Put her on."

A moment later, Barnes's voice sounds in my ear. "What is it?

"You promised you'd help me," I hiss. "Why are you trying to kill us?"

There's a pause. "I promised I wouldn't hurt your sister. And I haven't."

"But what about—"

"I told you to leave, Trey." She sounds rattled. "I can't be everywhere at once." She cuts the connection.

I stare down at the comm band on my wrist.

"What was that about?" Bryn asks. "Is Ella all right?"

"Ella's fine," I say, remembering what Anabel had told me about the night Samson had been shot. Slowly, the pieces of the puzzle come together.

I don't think they found a body. Could he possibly have been injured but escaped?

Not from what Liza said. She was part of his team when they took the control room.

The serpent tightens its grip on my throat. "We need to get out of here."

"We can't leave. Not if they're going back on our deal."

I turn to look at him. "If they are, what can two of us do to stop them?"

Bryn's face sags as he realizes the truth of my words. He glances back in the direction of Liza's body.

"We have to leave her. Come on." I tug at his arm.

I can smell the sweat and blood on his skin as we race through the corridors and down to the main entrance tunnel. I don't know of a better way out of the building, so I just hope I'm right and they will let us go.

Still, I feel we are being watched.

We reach the door leading to the staircase out of the factory. I pause and turn, pulling the knife from my belt, then jog a couple paces back and lay it down on the rough, concrete floor. "No hard feelings, okay?"

My words echo in the dark.

I don't relax until we're three streets away from the factory. We get some odd looks from people in the street, but right now, I don't care what they think of us.

Bryn pulls me into a side alley. "Care to tell me what all that was about?"

I look around for somewhere to sit. Finding none, I slump against a nearby wall and pull an energy bar from my pocket, ripping it open and taking a bite. After swallowing, I look at him.

"Samson led the operation to take the government headquarters, but Richard betrayed him. Ordered the Chain's fighters to murder him. Somehow, Samson survived. We found him in the tunnels three nights ago."

Bryn sucks in a breath. "So they tried to kill us in revenge?"

"Tried to kill *you*," I say. "And killed Liza. I don't think they have anything against me. I helped save Samson's life." Perhaps that was why Barnes had given me that warning. "Anabel said Liza led the Chain's team that night. She must have known about Richard's plan to kill Samson. Hell, she was probably the one who shot him."

"But I didn't have anything to do with that."

I shrug and take another bite of the bar. "Does the Brotherhood know that? They know you're high up in the Chain. Besides, killing you would send a clear message to Richard that the Brotherhood isn't to be messed with. I don't think Barnes wanted to kill you. Liza would have been enough for her. But that knife I picked up? It was Petal's. He seems a bit … rogue. I think he'd follow Samson's orders without question, but Barnes? I'm not sure her orders would carry the same weight. I reckon he took matters into his own hands."

Bryn leans against the opposite wall and crosses his arms. "Why didn't you tell me Samson is alive?"

"I wasn't sure you wouldn't tell Richard. Samson's still recovering. If Richard knew he was alive and sent someone to finish him off, it'd be an easy job."

"Truthfully, I probably *would* have told Richard." Bryn blows out a breath, then smiles at me. "I'm sorry I ever underestimated you, Trey."

My cheeks flush at the compliment. "I don't think they'll give up the factory without a fight. But I believe what Samson cares about most are the people of this city. If Richard truly wants the same thing, they should be able to come to some sort of arrangement."

Bryn sighs. "I agree."

That feels like even more of a compliment than his earlier words. "What's the plan now?"

"We sneak into the Metz compound and see what the situation is. If they need our help, we'll join in the fight." He pulls the two holocubes from his pocket and holds them up to the light, then hands one to me. "Once this is over, it'll be time to ask Richard some hard questions."

43

Aleesha

My father lets out a low growl as he stares up at the President. Tensing, he heaves upward, but even he cannot match the strength of three genetically enhanced fighters.

"We meet again, Ricus," the President says mildly. "Now, will you call off your fighters, or shall I?"

Around us, the fighting continues, both sides too focused on their struggle for survival to notice what's going on in the corner of the room.

My father stops struggling. His eyes darken, and a cruel smile twists his lips. "You will be the one to surrender, Tobias."

The President looks momentarily taken aback, but he quickly regains his composure. "I think not. You are outnumbered and outwitted. Now, please ask your people to stand down. There has been enough death today."

I hold my breath. My father must have some plan up his sleeve, some way to get us out of this. We can't have come this far, lost this many people, for nothing.

Slowly, he shakes his head. "Outnumbered perhaps, but never

outwitted. At this very moment, our transport pod is over Area Four. Your people trying to keep order outside will see it, no?"

The President's gaze flicks to one of the officers holding my father down, who gives a slight nod. "What of it? It's empty. Your fighters are all deployed here. Or dead."

My father gives a low chuckle.

I let my breath out slowly. *Of course he has a plan. You just need to trust him.*

"Remember when we used to play chess, Tobias? Remember why I *always* won?"

The President shifts nervously.

"Because I was prepared to make sacrifices for the greater good. You always wanted to keep your pieces alive, whereas I knew the only way to win was to sacrifice my pawns."

The blood drains from the President's face. "What have you done, Ricus?"

"That's the wrong question, Tobias. You should be asking what I *can* do. One of my spies found some ... interesting information about those nanobots you've been feeding your citizens. My transport pod has multiple transmitters, all of which are currently tuned to one specific frequency. The same frequency you transmit between those masts that make up the Wall. All it will take is a push of a button."

"You wouldn't ..." The President swallows. "You'd murder hundreds, thousands of innocent people."

Thousands of people? My brain fights to make sense of their cryptic remarks. A cold dread seeps through my veins. I stare at Richard, willing him to look at me. "Wait. What are you going to do?"

He ignores me. "This is not *my* weapon, Tobias. You have set this up, fed the poison to the people you were supposed to protect."

"That was a deterrent to stop them from going through the Wall.

It was a way of keeping order. What you're talking about is mass murder!" The President shakes his head. "You can't do this."

"Can't I?" My father raises an eyebrow. "My second-in-command is listening to our conversation right now. Katya, please show the President how serious we are about his surrender."

I look around but see no sign of Katya. She must be somewhere else in the compound listening via Richard's comm or a hidden drone. It's only then that I realize the fighting has stopped. All eyes are on us, waiting to see what is going to happen.

The President jerks his hand to his ear, his face stricken. "What?"

"I told you not to underestimate me, Tobias," my father says quietly. "Still, you should be grateful. I've helped your guards secure the gap in the Wall."

My brain finally pieces things together. The argument I'd overheard between my father and Katya. The files Trey had accessed in the factory that described the nanobots. What had I told him?

We are walking bombs, primed to die.

My legs feel as if they're about to collapse under me, and I'm grateful for the fighters holding me up. "What's happened?"

Everyone ignores me. The President's face is frozen in shock. My father still wears his cold smile.

I repeat my question, louder this time.

Finally, the President turns to me, his voice heavy. "Your father has just killed twenty Outsiders. A directed radio wave, I presume?"

"Across a very small area. But our transporter is large and has numerous transmitters. Would it be more effective if I asked them to move north, over Area Five or Six? Whose lives are most important to you?"

Their eyes lock on one another. It feels as if the whole room, the whole city, is holding its breath.

Finally, the President drops his gaze. His hands tremble as he curls them into fists at his sides. "It seems I underestimated you, Ricus. Not so much your strength and cunning, but your ruthlessness. I will not let you blame me for the massacre you seem determined to enact." He swallows. "I surrender. We will stand down."

The fighters holding Richard look at one another. The President gestures sharply to them. "Let him go." His voice is thick as he struggles to get the words out.

My father shrugs off the hands pinning him down and stands. He flashes me a smile, but I cannot return it. I have an overwhelming urge to vomit.

Your father has just killed twenty Outsiders.

How many more would he have been willing to sacrifice?

But it worked, I remind myself. *It's over. They've surrendered. It was all for the greater good.*

Around the room, there's a clatter of guns being dropped to the floor. The Chain's fighters – those still standing – marshal the remainder of the government's army into an open area in the centre of the room, removing the helmets of the suited officers. I shake myself loose from the hands holding me. The officers don't seem to know what to do.

The President stands, stiff as a statue, until my father grabs his shoulder and shoves him forward. The man who has caused so much hardship and grief in this city, a man I have feared for years, looks lost as my father pushes him across the room. My father was right. Now that he is faced with his own failure, perhaps his own death, he is pitiful and weak.

"Did we win?"

I turn to see Rogue approaching, Anders and Danny just a few paces behind him. Danny drags one leg, his face pale and taut as he leans on his friend for support.

"I think so," I reply. The truth is, I'm not sure. If it is over – if we have won the battle and the Chain finally has control of the city – it feels rather anti-climactic. "You okay?"

"Never bloody better," Danny wheezes. He looks around. "Reckon I've earned a slot in that miracle pod, though. Damn giant sat on my leg."

"What's happened to the others? Are they …" My throat constricts.

"There are two of yours in that corner. They're pretty badly injured, but Mika should be able to save them."

I turn to see Anabel. Her face is bruised and bloody, and one arm hangs limply by her side. She gives me a small smile and holds out her other hand. "Thanks for not dying."

I shake, then release her hand. She pulls a brightly coloured tube from a belt pocket and hands it to me.

"Looks like you could do with this." She inclines her head to Rogue, Anders and Danny, then makes her way over to my father.

I squeeze the sickly energy gel into my mouth. The sugar hits my system almost instantly, sharpening my mind. I unfreeze my feet from the floor and, after sending Rogue to account for the rest of my Phoenixes, follow Anabel over to the centre of the room. Before I can get there, a pair of double doors to my right swings open and Mika strides into the room, a hover stretcher by her side. A young man follows her with a second stretcher.

I rush forward and grab her arm. "I've got two badly injured over here."

Mika glances around in surprise. "Aleesha? Are you all right?" She takes in the blood on my face and clothes.

"I'm fine. But they need your help."

She nods. "I need to do a quick triage, but I'll get to them as soon as I can."

I let her go, feeling helpless that I can't do more to help my people. I'm about to head over to Rogue and see what state the rest of my team is in when a shot rings out.

I jump, my hand automatically reaching for the gun at my waist before I remember I'm out of ammo. I peek out from behind the row of pillars blocking my view and catch a glimpse of my father. Relief rushes through me.

The President stands off to one side, two of the Chain's fighters holding his arms, another standing behind. But the fight has gone out of him. He stares at my father, a blank expression on his face.

My father stands in front of the government fighters, who are all on their knees, forming two parallel lines.

The body of a woman sprawls on the floor in front of him, a pool of blood spreading from her head. The man kneeling next to her looks up at my father, his face pleading.

"Please, we surrendered. Please don't—"

My father raises his gun and fires.

I start and stare in horror as the man topples to the floor, blood spilling from the hole on his forehead.

So much blood for such a little hole.

I squeeze my eyes shut and turn away, but the image of his wound sears the back of my eyelids. It's not his face I see, though. It's hers. *Mama.* A flash of pain accompanies the memory, followed by a dull ache and emptiness in my heart.

Will I ever be able to think of her without picturing her like that?

I force myself to breathe, though my throat is so dry and constricted I barely suck in any air. When I dare to open my eyes and look back at them, Anabel is staring at me, a curious expression on her face. My father is not.

He moves on to the next person in line and raises his gun.

"Stop!"

Anders pushes past me and strides over to my father. The floor is slick with blood. The copper tang of it fills the room, along with the stench of urine. The government fighters look terrified, and I don't blame them. Covered in blood and dirt, my father is a monster of war.

"Stop," Anders repeats, raising his hands as he inserts himself between my father and the next man in line. He's shorter than my father, but stockier. My breath freezes in my throat, wondering if he's going to fight him. Against my father, he can't possibly win. "They surrendered, which makes them prisoners of war. They do not deserve to die."

I wonder how many of the men and women lined up are Metz officers. People Anders had grown up with, trained with, fought with. The closest thing he had to a family before he joined my gang.

"I doubt you gave any of the people you arrested the same courtesy, *officer*." My father's voice carries a trace of irritation, nothing more.

Anders doesn't flinch. "You have a choice. I did not."

"Exactly. I have a choice."

"And you choose to kill them? In cold blood?" Anders' voice is tinged with disbelief.

I try to find my voice, to add my protest to his, but it's as if my vocal cords have been severed. I open my mouth, but no words come out. I try to move, but my feet are frozen in place. I have seen many horrors in my years on the street, but only once before have I seen this kind of mindless killing. The day Lily died.

They lined them up and shot them. As if they were animals, not people.

"You care about them that much? Fine. You can join them." My father raises his gun and places the barrel against Anders' chest.

"No!" I lunge forward, but strong hands grab my arms and pull them behind my back in a vice-like grip. I hadn't even noticed one of my father's men come up behind me.

But I'm not the only one who's jumped to Anders' defence.

Danny emerges from behind the dark bulk of a set of Metz armour.

He leans against the pillar for support, but his grip on the gun is firm and steady. "You shoot 'im, I shoot you."

Do something, Aleesha!

I try to tug my arms free, but my brain is still too busy absorbing the horror of the situation to think clearly.

Loud footsteps cut through my daze. Rogue crosses the room to stand next to Anders, and somehow, that small gesture, along with the realization that I might lose more of my friends to this madness, pierces through the fog in my mind.

My legs come to life. My voice returns.

"Let go of me," I snarl, scraping the heel of my boot down my captor's shin.

He grunts and relaxes his grip. I jab him in the stomach and yank my arms free. As I run across to where my father and Anders stare at each other, Anabel moves away from my father's side to stop the guard from following me.

My foot skids on a pool of blood and I nearly go down, but I throw my hand out and grab onto the nearest thing, which happens to be my father.

He barely moves as I drag myself upright.

His eyes have always been a cold shade of blue, but as I look into them now, I wonder how I ever saw any warmth in them at all. His face is a mask, as blank as any Metz officer.

Power can raise people up, but it can also corrupt. There has always been something dark, something dangerous inside Ricus. I thought I could change him. I was wrong.

I swallow down my fear. Perhaps the President couldn't change him, but I am his daughter.

"Stop," I tell him, placing my hand on his chest. A rush of dèjá vu washes over me. For a second, it's not my father I'm staring up at, but Rogue in his Metz uniform, before I knew he wasn't a monster.

470

"Stop."

Slowly, he lowers his gun.

Relief floods through me. "You don't need to kill them," I say in a low voice. "There are plenty of cells to put them in."

For a moment, I think he will relent, but his face morphs into an expression of such anger that I take an involuntary step backward, bumping into Rogue.

"You're questioning my decision?" His voice is dangerously low.

I swallow again, feeling my courage wilt. "No ... I mean, yes. Please, don't shoot them." I sound like a little girl begging for a toy.

"Do the right thing, Ricus," the President calls. "Prove to her that you've changed."

There's a long pause.

Then he steps back and jerks his head at a tall man standing beside Anabel. "Take them to the cells." His gaze drifts across Rogue, Anders and Danny, then settles on the President. "All except him."

"But my friends—" I begin.

He whirls around. "Do *not* test my patience, daughter," he hisses. "And if you ever, *ever* question my decisions in front of my people again, you will live to regret it."

A shiver runs through me as he turns away. He mutters something into his comm, then beckons Anabel over.

"I'll get you out," I whisper to Rogue as he's led past me. "Just do what they say until then."

A muscle twitches at the corner of his eye, but he gives a small nod.

We have won the war. London is ours. But as I watch my friends get led away, I can't help feeling that this is a hollow victory.

44

Trey

"He's on his way up." Katya looks across the room to where Bryn leans against the wall next to me. "Are you going to tell me what this is all about?"

"When Richard gets here," Bryn replies.

I'm not sure what his plan is. Confront Richard with the truth, then what?

The silence drags out as we wait. All Katya has told us is that the Chain has won and the President has ordered his forces to surrender. The large screens lining the control room play camera feeds from around the city. Outside the Metz compound, government fighters mill around uncertainly. Residents of a nearby apartment block peer cautiously through their windows, no doubt wondering when it will be safe to emerge. One screen shows the gap in the Wall, a giant pod crushed into the ground in front of it. My stomach twists at the number of bodies surrounding it.

I should feel elated. London is free. This is what I wanted, what I risked my life for. But having seen the footage of the other cities the Chain has "freed", it feels like perhaps winning this battle is only the start of the war.

"Is Aleesha all right?"

Katya eyes me coolly. "Despite Richard's best efforts to keep her away from the fighting, it seems your girlfriend has a death wish. But yes, she's alive."

Footsteps sound in the corridor. A moment later, Richard enters, followed by two guards dragging the President between them. Aleesha brings up the rear. She looks exhausted. Blood is smeared across one cheek, and a half-torn dressing hangs from her arm. But she's still able to offer me a small smile that makes my heart flutter.

Richard dismisses the guards and gestures to Katya, who crosses the room and wraps her arm around the President's neck, jerking him backward. She presses a gun to his temple and whispers something into his ear.

Richard turns to Bryn. "What are you doing here? Your job was to take over the factory. Have you failed?"

"No. We took over the factory. But I heard your request for backup over the comm. Figured you might need an extra pair of hands."

Richard raises an eyebrow. "So you left the factory in the hands of the Brotherhood? What about Coleman?"

"Coleman's dead. I left Liza in charge. The Brotherhood won't cause any problems."

Richard seems to accept the lie. "Good. So, what did you want to talk about?"

"We found this on Coleman's holo pad." Bryn activates the holocube, and an image of Coleman's office fills the air. A few seconds later, Richard enters the office and extends his hand to shake Coleman's.

Aleesha's breath hisses through her teeth, but she stays silent until the holo reel has played. Then she turns to Richard. "You made a deal with him?"

He looks nonplussed. "I had to. We needed certain information he had in order to take down the government."

"But those things you promised him ... About raising food prices, the mo-nopo-ly ..." She stumbles over the unfamiliar word. "Outsiders can't afford that."

"Which is why I told Bryn to kill him. Coleman was just a pawn in the game."

"Like the people of Area Four you just *murdered*?" Aleesha's hand twitches. Her knuckles are white on the knife she holds in her hand. "Like my friends?"

Richard's face darkens. "Whatever gives you that idea?"

"Oh, I don't know. How about the fact you sent no backup to help us when we were trapped against the Wall?"

"*You* weren't trapped. You could have escaped at any time."

"But my team couldn't!" Her eyes narrow, voice turning even more scathing. "You thought I'd leave them, didn't you?"

It's the first time I've seen Richard taken aback. But he quickly recovers. "You're a survivor, Aleesha, and that's what a survivor would do." He pauses, then adds, "I'm sorry."

His apology melts into the air. Aleesha's jaw clenches, and I realize that Richard has underestimated her. He thought she would be like him – willing to sacrifice the lives of others for the greater good. But Aleesha would sacrifice herself rather than see her friends suffer, and she would never betray their trust in her.

I reach into my pocket and finger the holocube Bryn had given me. I know if Aleesha sees the footage it contains, she may never reconcile with her father. Is it right for me to destroy her dream of having a family?

But can she ever be happy with him as a father?

Bryn meets my gaze and gives a slight shake of his head.

"Now, if I've answered all your questions, we have work to do." Richard spreads his hands in a gesture of supplication. "A city to free."

"And what do you plan to do once you've freed the city, Richard?" Bryn squeezes the holocube, and the image disappears. I wait for him to bring up the footage from the other cities, but he keeps his hand closed tightly around the data cube.

Richard's eyes narrow. "That doesn't concern you, Bryn. Your role ends once the government forces surrender. Which, I'm pleased to say, they have done."

The President utters a grunt but falls silent as Katya digs the barrel of her gun into his head.

Richard walks over to Bryn and clasps his shoulder. "You've done a good job, Bryn. London is free, in no small part due to you. You've earned retirement time and time again. Now's the time to take it. Take Abby off to France or Scandinavia and give her the life she's been waiting for."

He offers a small smile. Bryn does not return it but looks down at the holocube and turns it over in his hands, as if debating whether to reveal its secrets or let them lie hidden. My breath catches in my throat. I squeeze the holocube in my pocket, wishing our roles were reversed and I had the cube with the details of the cities, Bryn having this one. He had handed it to me so casually I'd assumed he just wanted to split them up in case one of us didn't make it. Now I wonder if perhaps his decision hadn't been quite as random as he made out. If he made sure each of us held the truth we would be reluctant to reveal to force us to be certain of our decision.

If Bryn reveals what is on his holocube, reveals that he knows about Damascus and what Richard has done to the other cities, he will have no choice but to stand against him. It would be so much easier for Bryn to stay silent and accept Richard's peace offering. I know how much he longs to take Abby away from her cramped house and tiny garden. How much he wants the three of us to be a

475

family.

I want to speak out, to tell him that he *must* reveal this truth, that we can't let London turn into another Paris or Milan, but I stay silent. This is Bryn's decision. I don't have the right to take that from him.

"Good man." Richard squeezes Bryn's shoulder, then turns and walks over to face the President.

"Wait."

For a moment, I don't think Richard hears Bryn. He reaches out to remove the comm bud from the President's ear.

"Why didn't you tell me the truth about Damascus?"

Richard's hands freeze. Then, as if Bryn had asked about yesterday's weather, he carries on. "I don't know what you mean. What's going on in Damascus?"

"Not what *is* going on. What *did* go on. Eight years ago. You told me that rebel forces attacked the city, dropping bombs on civilians."

"And they did." Richard turns, frowning. "I know what happened that night, Bryn. I know Daniel died, but why bring this up now?"

"There were only a few bombs dropped that night. One of them hit the apartment block they lived in. The one I'd bought for them weeks earlier." Bryn works his jaw. "I thought it was just bad luck."

"It *was* bad luck." Richard steps forward and reaches out an arm, as if to comfort him. "I just wish—"

"No!" Bryn lashes out, knocking Richard's arm aside. A flash of anger crosses Richard's face, almost too quick for me to catch. "No, it wasn't bad luck," Bryn adds quietly.

Aleesha sidles over to me. "What's going on?" she whispers.

"You'll see," I reply. "Where's everyone else?"

Her jaw tightens. "Taken prisoner."

I want to ask her more, but at that moment, Bryn activates his holocube.

The city of Damascus sprawls in front of us. Bryn fast-forwards to the moment before the apartment block explodes, then pauses the footage. He points to the pod hovering in the air.

"That is *not* a rebel pod," he spits. "There are *no* rebel pods. This attack on the city was for one reason, and one reason only." Anger chokes his voice. "To kill my family."

Beside me, Aleesha stiffens and sucks in a breath, her eyes locked on the pod markings. The same markings that were on the medic pod that had healed her after the fight with Primo. The same as the pods that had flown over our city to take down our government. The markings of the Chain.

"Calm down, Bryn. Why would I want to kill your family?" Richard's voice is calm, but his scar twitches, betraying him.

I look across the room at Katya, wondering what she's thinking, if she played any part in the operation. She observes the events unfolding in front of her like a cat, her face expressionless. How far, I wonder, does her loyalty to Richard go?

"You didn't want me to retire," Bryn says flatly. "You said you needed me. And you always get what you want, don't you?"

"What happened in Damascus was an accident. I've given you everything, Bryn. Purpose, drive, money, power. And now you accuse me of this?"

Tension fills the air, like a fuel can just waiting for a spark to ignite it.

Bryn shakes his head. "I trusted you. Thought I was helping to do some good in the world."

"You *have* done good in the world. How many cities have you been instrumental in freeing, Bryn? Seven? Eight? Millions of people who are better off because of what we did for them."

"Are they really better off? What happened in those cities after we left, Richard?"

Katya shifts, her eyes narrowing.

Bryn starts the holo at the beginning. We watch Damascus burn, Paris starve and the resistance in Milan get executed.

Aleesha watches in silence. When the reel finishes, she turns horrified eyes to her father. "What was that? Those cities …"

"They're the cities the Chain 'freed'." I look straight at Richard. "The cities where life is supposed to be better."

Aleesha's gaze flicks to the President.

"Now you see what I was trying to protect our country from." His words are choked off as Katya tightens her arm around his neck.

Aleesha's eyes darken. "Don't pretend you're better than him. This is no worse than what happens in this city every single day."

The President doesn't flinch. "I never said I was perfect."

"You're about as far from perfect as it's possible to be." Aleesha turns to her father, her voice softening. "Is this true? Are these the cities you told me about?" A trace of bitterness hardens her words. "The places where people have enough to eat, where they can speak freely?"

"These images are a point in time. Taken out of context, they mean nothing." Richard takes a step toward her. "Nothing changes overnight. You must see that."

His argument is persuasive, his tone of voice even more so. These *are* just snapshots. Snapshots Coleman wanted us to see to turn us against Richard. But even if that is true, it doesn't change the person he is.

"So what happens to London now we've won?"

Aleesha's words echo my own thoughts. I hold my breath, waiting for Richard's answer.

"Well, that depends on you."

Aleesha looks confused. "What do you mean?"

Richard closes the distance between them and takes her hand. "My work has always been my passion, and it's led me from city to city.

I've always been a wandering nomad. I know I talked about taking you with me, away from London ..." He hesitates. "But you've made it clear that this is your home. If that's the case, well, perhaps it's time for me to settle down and make a home, too."

Aleesha's brow furrows. Her hand sits limply in her father's, but she makes no effort to pull away. "I don't understand."

"In every other city, we've set up a new government with an appropriate leader. Then we move on to the next city that needs our help. But all of them, everything I've done over the past nineteen years, has led up to this. Freeing London." His gaze flicks momentarily to the President before returning to Aleesha. "If we settle here, I will take over as President of Britannia."

I look at Bryn, who's frowning. I don't know Richard well, but from what I do know, he's impetuous. He likes the thrill of conquering, not the mundane routine of democracy. I can't see any situation in which him being President ends well for the people of London.

Aleesha looks down at the floor, then up at her father. "Why don't you let the people decide who they want in charge?"

"Because they voted for Tobias." He drops Aleesha's hand and throws his arms wide. "People *voting* caused this problem in the first place."

"Not everyone voted for him. Outsiders weren't allowed to vote. If you put yourself in control, you're no better than *him*." She jabs a finger at the President, her voice growing stronger. "Let us decide who we want to lead. Give us the power you promised."

Richard stares down at his daughter, but Aleesha doesn't waver, and for once, he is the first to look away.

Across the room, the President stirs. "She's right, Ricus. Can't you set your pride aside and give people a choice? Can't you admit that you might not be the right type of leader for our country?"

With a growl, Richard closes the distance between them. He grips the front of the President's suit and drags him out of Katya's grasp, tossing him to the floor in the centre of the room. His display of strength is unnerving.

"I would be a better leader than you, Tobias."

"Would you?" the President says mildly as he gets to his feet. "You always knew how to destroy, Ricus, but you never learned to build. That is why I have worked so hard all these years to keep you away. I knew you would break this country, tear this city down like you have so many others. I could not allow that."

"It's easy to criticize, isn't it? But what have *you* achieved? We had a dream, you and I, and it was not this." My father gestures at the screens around us. "It was *not this.*"

The President's face sags. "We were young, naïve. It is easy to have dreams when you are ignorant of the realities of politics."

Richard spits, the globule of saliva landing on the President's scuffed boot. "That is what I think of politics."

The President doesn't flinch. "You can't just charge your way around the world, taking what you want. For years, the leaders of other nations have ignored your exploits in Europa. It suited them. European countries were so busy fighting you and each other that the rest of the world could focus on building their own empires. But now, Ricus, their eyes are on you. There's a big bounty on your head."

"So that was your ploy? Hand me over to the Chinese? Pack me off to South Africa?"

"No." The President sighs heavily. "I did not want to bring more war down on these streets. And you were my friend ... once. So I ask this, as the man who was your friend all those years ago. Leave London. Take all your wealth and hide away somewhere where you'll never be found. Live out your days in peace and let the cities you've destroyed rebuild themselves without you."

"I made a promise to my parents on the day I learned of their deaths that I would never stop fighting to free people from the tyranny of oppression. That I would never rest until every man was equal."

"There can never be true equality. Who makes the tough decisions when everyone is equal? Besides, you haven't freed anyone. There is still poverty, still injustice. Much of it at your hand. Your legacy is one of destruction, and it's about time you faced up to it."

The President swallows and looks Richard straight in the eye. "We had some grand dreams, Ricus, but they died a long time ago. They died when you decided that violence was the only route to power. When you sacrificed our friends to save yourself."

A dark look clouds Richard's face. I glance at Aleesha, unsure what they're referring to, but she's focused on the battle of wills unfolding in front of us. I reach into my pocket and finger the small holocube. Is it time?

"I was not the one who got them killed. *You* betrayed me. You betrayed us all, just so you could get your nice government job."

The President shakes his head. "No, I didn't."

"Liar."

"It wasn't me. What you were trying to achieve was wrong. It would have killed countless people. I should have reported you, but I couldn't do it." He looks away.

Richard snorts. "Well, if you didn't tip off the Metz, who did?"

The President turns back, and the two men stare at each other. Something flickers in Richard's eyes and his jaw stiffens.

"No."

"Yes."

"She would never have betrayed me."

"She always did what she thought was right. You never gave her enough credit for that, Ricus."

Their voices are calm, but there's a deep undercurrent of tension beneath their words. A dark vortex of broken promises and unfinished business that's lain dormant for years and is only now beginning to surface.

I'm not sure I want to be around when it explodes.

"Did you ever wonder why she didn't leave with you that day? She was scared of you – scared of the person you were becoming."

Richard takes a step forward. He looms over the President, bigger and stronger by far. But the President stands his ground.

"She loved me," Richard growls.

He raises an eyebrow. "Did she?"

I exchange a glance with Bryn. I'm not sure why Richard is even having this conversation. Why he hasn't just killed the man. It's like he's an itch he has to scratch, even if it makes his skin bleed.

"Stop!" Aleesha's voice cuts through the thickness in the air. Both men turn to look at her. Her face is pale. "I want to know the truth."

She looks at the President. "You told me my father was to blame for my mother's death." Her gaze travels to Richard. "And you told me he was to blame. Neither of you were lying, but you weren't telling the full truth, either. So which of you will be man enough to tell me what really happened that day?"

For a moment, there is silence. A weight settles on my heart as I pull the holocube from my pocket and step forward.

It is time.

"I can show you the truth, Aleesha. We found a recording in Coleman's files. I don't know how, but it's different than the one we saw in the Metz compound. It's, well ... It's best that you see for yourself."

45

Aleesha

The lights in the room refract off the holocube in Trey's hand, sending rainbows dancing across the ceiling. He rubs his thumb across it, and a holo of Rose Square fills the room. Dread seeps through my veins.

"No," I whisper. I find his eyes. "Please, Trey. I've already seen this."

But his face is hard, his voice as cold as my father's. "You haven't seen this. You haven't seen the truth."

The footage plays. It is not as immersive as the holo projection we'd accessed from the Metz files. We are observers, not part of the scene. But the knot in my stomach still tightens.

The square is empty, the market traders having abandoned their stalls. I can't see the Metz officers, but I know they're there. Waiting for the man she believed she was meeting. My father.

The image rotates around the monument at one end of the square. A man sits on the steps, his face turned away from the camera, fingers tapping his knee in agitation. My heart skips a beat. In the footage we'd seen in the Metz compound, my mother had run into an empty square.

I don't have time to think this through because then she is there, running down the street. This, at least, is the same. Her hair flying behind her, a huge smile lights up her face. She smiles at him – the man on the steps. He stands and walks toward her, his hands outstretched as the camera turns to focus on his face.

It's not my father.

It's the President.

Time stands still as the two of them stand there, looking at each other.

"Tobias, I ..."

He closes the distance and takes her hands. "Maria, you came." He's hesitant, the confidence and arrogance of the man he became not yet tainting this younger version. His hair is naturally dark, not dyed, face smooth and unlined. His eyes shine as he looks at my mother, a soft smile spreading across his lips. "I never stopped looking for you, you know."

"I'm sorry. I didn't know what you would do. Whether you were still ... my friend."

My heart pounds at the sound of her voice. A tear leaks from the corner of my eye, and I taste salt on my lips.

"I would be more than your friend if you'd let me, Maria."

My mother swallows and looks down. "For everything that happened, for how we ... I treated you, I'm sorry."

"Ricus never deserved you." His voice hardens, but he catches himself and shakes his head slightly. "But the past is in the past."

"He's here. In London." Her words are barely audible.

He stiffens. "Ricus? Here?"

My mother nods. "I'm scared, Tobias. If he finds me ..." She grips his hands. "There's something I need to tell you. The reason I've stayed hidden all these years. I—"

There's a loud crack, and Tobias lurches forward, as if some invisible fist has punched him in the back.

My mother frowns. "Tobias?"

His face twisted in pain, he spins around, pushing my mother behind him. A dark stain blossoms on his shoulder. A second shot sounds, kicking up dust from the ground next to them. A flicker of movement on one of the buildings catches my eye, but it's gone before I can make sense of it.

Then the square erupts into chaos. Metz officers spring from their hiding places, flooding the area in a sea of black. My mother and Tobias are pulled apart. He calls her name, but the sound is lost in the trampling of feet as he's dragged across the square, fighting the officers holding him. My mother disappears behind a wall of black uniforms. Some of the Metz turn their weapons to the rooftops. But the figure who fired the shots is gone.

"Stop! Rewind the footage." My voice sounds raw. "There. Stop." The moment before the President is shot, I point to a blip in the skyline. A small bump on a featureless parapet. "Zoom in."

The image blurs as it zooms in, then clears, the features rendered in perfect clarity. Dark hair, blue eyes, a tiny, curved scar by his left eye. A rifle rests on the parapet in front of him.

I squeeze my eyes shut. "No."

"Aleesha, I can explain."

I shake my head. I don't want my father's excuses, his lies. Why hadn't the President told me this? Told me the truth?

Because you didn't want to listen.

My eyes snap open at the sound of footsteps. My father stretches out a hand, but I stumble back. A flash of anger crosses his eyes. Have they always been that hard?

"Aleesha, please ..."

"You tried to kill her."

My father snorts. "I'm not that bad a shot. I would never have killed her."

"Me, on the other hand …" the President says icily.

"I *should* have killed you, Tobias," he spits. "It would have saved a lot of trouble."

My mind's in turmoil, still trying to make sense of what I've seen. "You knew she was meeting him?"

He nods. "I was searching for her. I didn't have anyone in London then. At least no one I could trust. On the fourth day of my search, I got my first proper lead. A street kid claimed to know a woman matching Maria's description. Said he was on his way to give her a message."

He falls silent.

"The message *he* sent her?"

"Yes." His voice carries a trace of bitterness. "If I'd been thinking straight, I'd have smashed the holo pad to smithereens, but I was so shocked to see Tobias's name on the message and his declaration of love that the kid ran off before I could do anything. I didn't even have time to ask him for Maria's address."

"So you came after me instead," the President sneers.

My father rounds on him. "And found Rose Square surrounded by Metz officers. I could see it was a trap, but I was too late to stop her running into it. Then I saw you, sitting there, the bait in the trap *you* had set for her."

The two men stare at each other across the room.

Finally, the President breaks away and looks down at the floor. "I had nothing to do with the trap. I didn't even know the Metz were there."

"Didn't know? How could you not have known? There were *dozens* of them."

"I swear. I didn't know." He glances up at me. "I'd never really been Outside. I didn't know Metz patrols rarely ventured into that part of the city or that the square being empty was a sign something was wrong. I was just so focused on the fact that I'd finally found her."

I swallow and find my voice. "Why were you there? What did you want with her?"

"When Ricus left London years earlier, Maria disappeared. I assumed she had gone with him. I got a job in the Foreign Office, the only government department permitted to study what was happening in the world outside Britannia. Every day after work, I searched the foreign news bulletins for signs that they were alive. In time, I began to catch glimpses of what Ricus was up to, but I never saw any sign of Maria. Then one day, I was watching some footage from the cameras here and saw her face in the crowd. It took me another year to find her." He smiles softly. "Your mother was good at staying hidden, but eventually, I tracked her down."

He pauses. I shift uncomfortably under his gaze, though there's no cruelty in it. He looks as if he's telling the truth. But I'm not sure if anyone is telling the truth anymore.

"The first time I saw her, she was out shopping. I had to grab her to stop her running away. She fought like a cat to get out of my grip. I think she believed I was there to capture her." He shakes his head. "But when she saw I was alone, what I'd risked as an Insider coming out to Area Four, she stopped to listen to me."

"What did you want with her?" I repeat.

"I wanted to offer her a better life," he says, meeting my gaze levelly. "I wanted her to be my wife."

Can this be the truth I've waited for all these years? The person my mother was so excited about meeting that day wasn't my father but the man who would later become my greatest enemy. The man who tried to kill me again and again.

Except he didn't kill you, did he? He chose to lock you in a cupboard in the government headquarters rather than handing you over to the Metz. He gave an order that you weren't to be experimented on in the lab. He delayed your execution, giving your father time to intervene.

But whether or not he wanted to kill me, he has no excuse for the thousands of Outsiders who have died under his rule. Whatever he says, he is still my enemy.

My father's hand lunges out and grabs the President's suit. "She would *never* have married you. She never loved you."

The President fights to free himself, but he has neither the size nor strength to match my father.

I clear my throat, and they both look at me. "Did she mention me?"

The President shakes his head. "She said she needed two chips. I assumed the second was for a friend. She assured me she had no lover. It never crossed my mind that it was for a child. I promised her I would find a way. It took me three weeks and a hefty bribe before I managed to get everything in place."

When she'd received the message that day, my mother had smiled and swung me up into the air.

It's all going to be okay. Everything will be okay.

Was her happiness just about securing a future for me, or was there more to it than that? Had she loved Tobias?

None of us will ever know.

"I had no idea Andrew Goldsmith knew Ricus was in London and had connected him to Maria. The trap in Rose Square was a trap for him. The Metz officers didn't expect me to be there, but once I was shot, they acted against the threat to my life."

My mind is a whirlwind. "So if he hadn't shot you, she would have lived?"

"I believe so," the President says. "At the very least, I believe I could have persuaded them to take her in for questioning rather than executing her. Then I could have found out what was going on and intervened."

My father lets out a hoarse laugh and releases his grip on the President. "Don't lay this blame at my feet, Tobias. You are as guilty as me or anyone else."

"Perhaps." The President steps backward and straightens his suit. "But at least I accept my share of the blame. And the guilt."

"You ordered them to edit the record of what happened so you wouldn't be implicated?"

Trey's voice makes me start. I'd almost forgotten there were others in the room.

"The footage was doctored, but not at my request. I was something of a rising star in the government. There were people who didn't want my future to be ruined because of a young fool's romantic mistakes. I don't know where Coleman found a copy of the original."

"But Mrs Grady told me what she saw that day," I say, still not quite able to believe the evidence in front of my eyes. "Why wouldn't she have mentioned you?"

The President shrugs. "She was probably threatened that if she told anyone, her or her family's life would be at risk."

That much makes sense.

I remember the scar on the President's shoulder and the words he'd said to me.

Do you really think I am the one in control of this city?

"Coleman blackmailed you?"

"He didn't need that footage to hold me hostage, but yes, I knew he had it." He sighs. "Coleman and Hendricks control the city's food supply. Even the head of the government food factory was under their thumb. I couldn't let the people starve, but I had little to counter with. The only thing that could have tempered their power was opening up the borders and exposing ourselves to the world.

But that risked exposing us to the Chain. And I felt they were the greater threat."

"You kept the scar," I say in a whisper. "All these years, you kept it."

His eyes are heavy with grief. "It was all I had to remember her by."

I did not cause Maria's death. But I have lived with the guilt of it for the past twelve years.

There are so many people I could blame for my mother's death. My father, for having been in London in the first place and catching the government's attention. The President, for being stupid enough to let his message get intercepted and not seeing the danger he was drawing her into. Andrew Goldsmith, for not having been more certain they were after the right person. Primo, for firing the shot that ended her life.

But the truth is, it was all just a big mess.

I feel no anger or hatred in my chest at what I've seen. Just sadness. Sadness for me, sadness for two men who both lost the woman they loved. But despite his grief and guilt, I cannot forgive the President for what he has done to the people of this city.

Slowly, I walk over to my father, who's staring at the floor. "Why didn't you tell me?" When he doesn't answer, I raise my voice. "Why didn't you tell me?"

My father drags his eyes up to meet mine. The shield that has always protected his inner thoughts is gone, and I can see the darkness and turmoil he holds inside, hides so deeply that few are aware it even exists. Perhaps no one, until now.

"Because I didn't want to lose you," he says quietly.

It is the first time I know, without a shadow of a doubt, that he is telling me the truth.

Through the thin fabric of my top, I finger the points of the amulet hanging around my neck. The amulet a woman gave to her son, knowing she may never see him again. The amulet a man gave to the woman he loved. The amulet a woman gave to her young daughter on the morning of her death.

I had thought she'd given me the amulet to lead me to my father. Perhaps I was wrong. Perhaps she hadn't wanted me to find him, but had wanted to protect me *from* him, from the man he had become.

I replay the footage of the other cities in my head, see the grief and betrayal on Bryn's face as he accused Richard of killing his lover and son. What would such a man do to my city, to the people I love?

You always get what you want.

"I'm sorry, Aleesha." He takes my hand. "I've made mistakes. Who hasn't? But I'll make it up to you. I swear. I'll give you anything you want."

I remember staring out at the Wall, night after night, dreaming of the day my father would find me and spirit me away to that magical place Inside, where I would have all the food I could eat, new clothes to wear, real friends. Bursting that bubble is the hardest thing I have ever had to do, but my father is *not* the right man to lead this country. I didn't need the footage of those faraway cities to convince me of that.

I thought I loved my father. But I realize now that what I feel is not love for the person he is, but for the person I *want* him to be. However hard I try to convince myself he is that person, I know, deep down, that he is not.

"Anything?" I wait for his nod. "Then leave London and never return."

For once, my father is at a loss for words. "I ... I don't understand."

"I want you to take your people and leave London. I want you to swear, for my sake, that you will never return."

His confusion quickly changes to disbelief. "You would leave *him* in charge? After everything he's done?"

"No." I turn to the President, who's looking at me curiously. "You've done enough damage, killed enough people. You will step down. There will be an election – a *real* election in which anyone can stand, and everyone, Insider *and* Outsider, can vote for a new leader and government."

I take a step back so I can look at both of them. "I don't care what role either of you played in my mother's death. She didn't live in hate. She lived for love. If this whole thing has been about revenge, it needs to end today, before you both end up with more blood on your hands."

In the long silence that follows, I catch Katya staring at me, a thoughtful expression on her face. When I meet her gaze, she looks away, no doubt waiting for her leader's response. I turn my focus back to the men in front of me. Will either of them be willing to set aside their pride?

"For her sake," I whisper, "let it go."

Finally, the President lets out a heavy sigh. "Perhaps she is right, Ricus. Neither of us managed to create the government we dreamed of. Maybe it is someone else's turn to try."

My father stares at him. "You would step down?"

The President meets his gaze. "Yes."

There's a long pause, then my father turns to me. "Then I will leave."

I feel a pang that he doesn't even try to persuade me to go with him, but that is overwhelmed by the relief I feel.

"I'm sorry it had to end this way." The President holds his hand out to my father.

My father stares down at it, then slowly shakes his head. "I'm sorry, too." His voice is unexpectedly gruff. He opens his arms wide.

After a slight hesitation, the President steps forward, and the two men embrace awkwardly.

I frown, taken aback by the suddenness of their making up.

Unease stirs in my stomach and I lift my knife. Something is not quite right.

The President tries to pull back, but my father's arm is tight on his old friend's back. He stiffens and lets out a small grunt. When my father finally releases him, the President stares at him, eyes wide. He holds one hand in the air, as if waiting to continue the hug. The other is on his stomach.

Blood leaks from between his fingers.

"You were never strong enough to do what needed to be done, Tobias," my father says. "That was always your greatest fault."

The President's eyes bulge as he staggers back and falls to his knees, both hands clutching his stomach as if by doing so, he can keep his blood in his body. My father leans over and wipes the thin blade of his knife on the man's sleeve before straightening and sliding it back into a hidden pocket.

I turn to meet Trey's horrified gaze. He starts forward, but I hold out a hand to stop him and shake my head. Perhaps a medic could save him, if it got here fast. But I suspect not. And while I can't feel sympathy for the man who has destroyed the lives of so many, I do feel a strange sense of sadness. Sadness that even now, at the end, my father had to win. He couldn't just let the past die.

"Ricus ..." the President wheezes. He reaches inside his jacket with a bloody, shaky hand. His eyes meet mine. "I never stopped loving her."

I nod, though my mouth is too dry to speak.

He pulls something out and fumbles with it, his fingers slippery with blood. "I'm sorry, Aleesha ..." The President's eyes flicker. "It's for ... the greater good."

The object in his hands jerks open, and a metal ball rolls across the floor.

I should have known he would have one final trick up his sleeve.
The ball comes to rest between my father and me. Our eyes meet.
"Run," he whispers.

But my feet seem frozen to the floor. Perhaps he's fast enough to make it out of the room before the grenade explodes.

But the rest of us won't.

46

Trey

I barely catch a glimpse of the silver ball rolling across the floor before Bryn pushes past me. For a second, I think he's going to throw himself at Richard, but Richard is already halfway to the door, dragging Aleesha with him. A tiny, red light on the silver ball blinks once, twice. Everyone in the room holds their breath.

Everyone except Bryn.

There's a click, and I fall to the floor, shielding my face with my arm. But the room doesn't explode around me as I expect. There's a dull *whoomph* that makes my ears tingle, followed by a grunt, then silence.

I blink and look around. On the opposite side of the room, Katya gets to her feet and bends to pick up her gun.

I sit up and glance down at my body, surprised to see I'm uninjured.

A few metres away, Aleesha shakes off her father's hand and sucks in a sharp breath. She stares past me, her mouth forming a single word, though no sound leaves her lips. "Bryn."

I turn to follow her gaze, seeing the President lying on the floor, blood still pouring from the wound in his stomach. Next to him, lying face down, is Bryn.

He's so still, as if …

But he can't be.

I won't let him be.

"No." Do I say it out loud? I don't hear it, but there's a strange ringing in my ears. It feels as if someone's suddenly ratchetted up the temperature in the room. Sweat beads on the back of my neck and my head spins. Each breath feels suffocating.

I crawl across the room and shake his shoulders. "Bryn?" His body is heavy, as if he's in a deep sleep, but there's no blood. *That's got to be a good sign, right?*

Aleesha falls to her knees beside me. "He must have thrown himself on top of it," she whispers. She presses her fingers into the side of Bryn's neck. I wait for her to tell me he's okay, that he's just unconscious, that Mika will load him into her magic pod and heal him.

But she doesn't say any of that. She just looks at me, her brown eyes heavy with sadness and pity as she shakes her head.

I slump back, letting my fingers trail across his shoulders.

After I watched Katya shoot my father, my brain had shut down, my senses numbed by shock. Bryn had pulled me away from the square and sat me down, shaking me so hard that my teeth had rattled in my jaw. If he hadn't been there, I would have been killed by Outsiders who saw me as the enemy.

He saved me the day I ran from the Metz and ended up Outside the Wall. Saved me from Milicent's wrath when I refused to hand over the chip containing the information Mikheil had downloaded inside the government headquarters. Saved me when he dived in front of the bullet Rogue had meant for me.

Every time I needed him, he'd saved me.

A thick bubble of silence surrounds me as I look down at Bryn's body, waiting for the blood to spread out from beneath him. I wonder if I should roll him over, but I can't bear to see the damage the grenade has done.

I was worried about Aleesha dying, about Ella getting hurt. I never thought about Bryn.

He seemed invincible.

Remember, Trey. You still have a family.

I never thanked him for saving me. Never told him I loved him. I didn't even get to say goodbye.

My head is heavy, my movements sluggish as I allow my hand to fall from Bryn's back. Out the corner of my eye, I catch sight of his gun. I reach for it, not really understanding what I'm doing.

"Trey..."

Aleesha says my name several times before I hear her. I shake off her hand. My entire body trembles as I stand and turn to face Richard, holding the gun out in front of me with both hands. "You did this."

My voice sounds like a stranger's.

Richard shakes his head. In a strangely detached way, I notice he still holds his gun.

"You did this." I take a step toward him. The gun in my hand wobbles. The bubble around me makes it hard to think, but I know I must do it now, before he can kill anyone else. Before he can destroy this city like he destroyed all the others.

My finger fumbles on the trigger.

A shot rips through the bubble of silence that surrounds me. Suddenly, I can hear clearly again. As my gun catapults from my grip, I stare down at the bloody stumps that used to be my fingers.

Why doesn't it hurt?

I look up into Richard's hard eyes, then at the gun still pointing at my hand.

He lowers it a fraction. "Don't be stupid, boy."

I totter forward one step, then a second. I'm dimly aware of someone shouting, but all my senses have narrowed to focus on this one person in front of me. The man who must be stopped.

I lunge at him, not caring that he is stronger and faster. Not caring that he holds a weapon while I have nothing but my empty, bloody hands. He has already taken so much from me that I have little left to lose.

I reach out, but I barely brush his skin before I'm sent flying across the room. Another shot sounds.

This time, the pain hits.

47

Aleesha

When Trey stands and points Bryn's gun at my father, I know this is going to end badly. But my mind is dulled by shock, still trying to process the fact that Bryn is dead.

"You did this."

My father shakes his head and opens his mouth to speak, but his gaze alights on the gun quivering in Trey's hand, and he closes it again without uttering a word.

"You did this."

"Trey …" I begin, but my words catch in my throat as my father raises his arm. Unlike Trey, his aim is steady.

I hold my breath.

Trey brings his other hand up to steady the first, the barrel of his gun weaving all over the place.

They are only a few metres apart. My father is fast. He could easily duck to the side or drop to the floor and kick the gun from Trey's weak grasp.

Instead, he fires.

The shot echoes around the room. My mouth is dry, my palms

slick.

He shot him. My father shot Trey.

Trey stares down at his hand disbelievingly. The bullet blew one finger clean off. A second hangs limply. The sight makes my stomach turn, and I've seen plenty of nasty wounds.

I lift my eyes to my father. He refuses to meet my gaze.

It is too much to take in. I thought we had reached the end of the fighting. The war was over. My father and the President had both agreed to step down.

What went wrong?

But I know the answer.

If my father had just been able to forgive ... No, he didn't even have to do that. All he had to do was walk away. Instead, he dealt his old friend one final blow. Not even a fast, killing strike, but a twist in the gut that ensured a painful, drawn-out death. A wound that gave the President time to act.

If my father had walked away, there would have been no grenade. Bryn would still be alive. Trey would be uninjured.

I wanted to believe in him so much.

Of all the betrayals I have experienced, this one cuts the deepest.

Slowly, I draw my knife out of my belt where I'd stashed it when I rushed to check on Bryn. It is the knife Mitch gave me, the same quality as the knives the Bigland Boys had stolen, the knives my father and his fighters carry.

What happens now?

Trey lets his hand fall. He totters forward, his eyes locked on my father.

"Trey, no!"

He doesn't seem to hear me. I draw back my arm, ready to throw the knife, but hesitate. Even now, even to protect Trey, I'm not sure I can strike my father.

"Stop!"

I don't know which of them I'm shouting at, but neither listen.

My hesitation is costly. As Trey reaches out for him, my father lashes out, knocking him clean off his feet.

He glances over at me, and for a moment, our eyes meet. Then, slowly, he turns back to Trey and raises his gun, aiming at his chest.

Finally, I let my knife fly. It hits him in the shoulder and his arm jerks, causing his fingers to tighten on the trigger of the gun.

My strike deflects my father's aim, but it's small comfort. The bullet slams into Trey's knee. He lets out a shriek and writhes on the floor, fingers scrabbling at his leg.

My heart hammers in my chest as my father turns to me. He reaches up to grip the handle of my knife and, with a roar like a wounded lion, pulls it from his flesh. Blood spills from the wound, soaking his shirt as he strides toward me, face twisted in a snarl of rage.

Suddenly, I am very, very afraid.

I stumble backward, but something trips me, and I sprawl on my arse. I look down to see Bryn's legs, and my gut clenches. I try to suck in air, but my lungs are tight, and it feels as if my body isn't working properly anymore. Boots skidding on the floor, I scrabble backward until I bump into another body.

The President lies still, staring sightlessly at the ceiling. His blood oozes under my right hand.

"You dare attack me?" My father sounds almost inhuman. He looms over me, gun in one hand, my knife in the other. Veins bulge on his neck, and a red flush colours his cheeks, but it's his eyes that scare me the most. They burn with a blue fire. "I would have given you everything. *Everything.*"

I remember the darkness and turmoil I'd seen in him. The emotions he buried so deeply beneath his cool exterior. But I know only too well that pushing emotions down only allows them to fester, to bubble away like one of Abby's cooking pots as the pressure builds, waiting for its moment of release.

When I look into his eyes, I don't recognize the person I see there. And I'm not sure he recognizes me, either.

I raise my hands and try to keep my voice calm. "Father, it's me. Aleesha. Your daughter. I ... I'm sorry. I didn't want to—" I break off as he raises the arm holding his gun.

There will be no reasoning with him.

It is him or me. And for all our sakes, I can't let him live.

I glance around, but the President had no weapon, save for the grenade, and Bryn's gun is on the opposite side of the room. There's a flash of blonde hair in the corner of my vision, and my heart plummets.

Shit.

I'd forgotten Katya was still in the room. Now it's not just me against my father. With him in front of me and her behind, I don't stand a chance.

On the other side of the room, Trey lets out a low moan. Blood pools around his leg. I bite my lip. He needs a medic, fast. Surely someone must have heard the shots. But even if Mika does arrive in time, will my father let him live?

I have one more knife. One final chance.

I reach down to my left boot, my eyes drawn to the barrel of the gun. My fingers close around the handle of my thinnest blade, easing it out. But as my father's finger tightens on the trigger, I know I'm too slow.

A gun fires.

My father's eyes widen in surprise. His jaw slackens as red blossoms on his chest, and he slowly tears his gaze from me to look behind me.

Hardly daring to breathe, I draw the knife from my boot and turn.

Katya fires again, the bullet slamming into my father's body just above the first.

His eyes are wide in shock, mouth open as the gun falls from his hand. He takes a step back, sways for a second, then lifts his arm as if reaching for a lifeline. His hand closes on thin air and he crashes to his knees, then to the floor.

For a moment, I'm frozen in place. Then, as if released from a spell, I lunge forward to grasp his gun. Twisting onto my back, I bring it around to point at Katya.

But she just raises her hands in the air, her gun already back on her belt. "I'm not going to hurt you." She sounds tired.

I stare into her green eyes, but as always, she is unreadable. Slowly, I push myself up to sitting, then stand, the gun steady in my hand.

Katya glances over at Richard's body, raising one eyebrow questioningly. I nod but follow her with my gun as she steps over the President's and Bryn's bodies and crouches next to my father. She closes his eyes and trails her fingers across her lover's cheek, her lips moving in silent words. Then she stands and walks to the door.

Pausing, she turns and looks back at me. "London is yours now. Don't let these deaths be for nothing."

There are so many questions I want to ask her, but before I can find my voice, she slips through the door and is gone.

My hand trembles uncontrollably as I flip the safety on and shove the gun into my belt. I fall to my knees beside my father. His shirt is soaked, the three wounds dark against the brighter blood surrounding them. Though his eyes are closed, his face is still twisted in anger.

He had so much anger in him. Perhaps that was his downfall.

I reach out and trace the scar by his eye. I never asked how it got it. Another mystery, like so many things about my father's life.

Tears spring to my eyes, but I don't think they're for him. Perhaps they are for Bryn, or perhaps they're just tears of relief. Relief that, finally, this is all over.

As I look around the room at the bodies of the three men who have played such a huge part in my life over these past months, it hits me. The air rushes from my body as I slump back, dazed by the enormity of what has happened.

It really is over.

There is no President, no dictator waiting in the wings.

London is free.

48

Trey

I never knew there was a pain so excruciating that it would stop
you from screaming. That's how I know the voice I hear isn't
mine. I can barely breathe, let alone scream.

My leg is on fire, then it's pierced with shards of ice. Then fire again
– a red-hot poker twisting through my knee. I black out. I wake up,
wishing I were still unconscious. I drift on a tide of agony, unable to
focus on anything but the darkness and the pain. It swells inside me,
filling up every cell of my body until I think I might explode from
it. I have to let it out, have to find some way of releasing it. When I
open my mouth, it rushes through me like a trapped wind seeking
to escape, erupting from my body in one long, agonized cry.

When it fades, I am left empty, gasping for air.

Then the pain begins again.

I'm dimly aware of Katya leaving the room, and I try to push myself
up, but the movement just sends another rush of agony through my
leg. A groan escapes my lips as the room spins.

Aleesha's face swims into view above me. "Trey? Stay with me.
You hear me?" Her words echo in my head, and I think that it would
be a shame to die just when we might get a chance to finally be

together.

But if I have to die, at least her face is the last thing I will see.

Blackness encroaches on my vision. It whispers sweetly about relief from the pain, and I can feel it sucking me down.

I don't have the strength to hold it back any longer.

* * * *

The darkness lied.

There is more pain – so much pain.

There are familiar voices, too, poking at my consciousness. I want to tell them to go away, to leave me to die in peace.

I dimly register a prick in my arm. Then slowly, miraculously, the pain begins to abate. The relief at it leaving is almost as overwhelming as the pain itself.

I let myself slip away.

* * * *

When I awake, I see Anabel sitting cross-legged on the floor beside me, one arm supported by a sling. The bright lights of the control room make my eyes water. My head is fogged, and a sour taste fills my mouth.

I try to push myself up, but my sister's hand on my chest stops me. "Steady there. Let me help you."

She gently lifts my shoulders so I can look around. Empty syringes and plastic wrappers litter the floor. Stained sheets cover three long mounds, blood discolouring the concrete around them.

There is a *lot* of blood.

Nausea rushes up, and I turn my head to one side just in time to vomit up the little food I had in my stomach. When I've finished, I sit up again and wipe my mouth.

"How long?" I croak.

"You've been out for a few hours. Mika suggested not moving you until the medic pod is free."

I look down at my leg. What looks like a bandage is wrapped around my knee, forming a rigid casing around the joint, though I feel no pressure on the shattered bone. Just a cool, numbing sensation. The pain in my hand has gone, as well, what remains of it hidden beneath a mass of bandages.

"I thought I was going to die."

Anabel lets out a soft snort. "There are others who are closer to dancing with death than you, little brother. Though you did lose a fair amount of blood, and that knee is going to need some serious repair work."

"So, I'm going to be okay?" I clarify, my brain still fuzzy.

"Minus a few fingers." Anabel pauses, swallowing. "I'm sorry about Bryn."

I look over at the nearest sheet. A voice in my head tells me Bryn lies under there, dead. I don't want to believe it. Perhaps if I deny it enough, I will wake up from this nightmare and Bryn will walk in with that gruff smile on his face.

If he's dead, I don't understand why I feel so numb.

"Trey?" Anabel gives me an anxious glance.

I should say something.

"Thanks." I feel as if I'm back at my father's funeral, thanking a polite mourner who had only come for the wine and food.

Thank you for your kind words. Yes, he was a great man. Yes, we are devastated.

Where is the sadness and anger that comes from losing someone you love? Does there come a point when you've witnessed so much death that it stops affecting you? Is this empty feeling your body's way of protecting you from pain and heartache?

I *want* to feel. I want the crushing ache of loss to squeeze my chest until I can barely breathe, until all I see is his face, all I feel is despair from the knowledge that I will never again see him laugh, see Abby's face light up when he walks into the room, feel his arms around me, holding me, protecting me. I want to feel all this because then, perhaps, his sacrifice would be worth something.

But I don't.

He died to save me, yet I feel nothing.

"It only killed him. I thought … I thought we were all going to die."

"Aleesha described the grenade to me. It's not quite what you thought it was." She pauses and looks away.

"What do you mean?" I ask.

When she turns back, pity hangs in her eyes. "It wasn't a grenade as such. More of a targeted assassination tool designed to take out a single person, whether they're alone or in a crowd. It contains lethal darts keyed to a specific person. In this case, Richard. His height, weight, everything down to that scar by his eye would have been programmed into the weapon. From what Aleesha said, it had locked on to its target and was primed to explode when …"

"When Bryn threw himself on top of it."

Anabel is silent.

"So the darts fired into him instead?"

She squeezes my shoulder. "I'm so sorry."

Her words add another layer of grief to my battered heart. I glance down at my shattered knee, then across at Bryn's shapeless body. *What a waste.*

Richard should have died at the President's hand, each having killed the other. *That* would have been a fitting end to their story.

But real life is not a novel in which all the endings are neatly wrapped up. Life is messy. In life, sometimes the wrong people end up dead.

Footsteps approach. I look up to see Aleesha standing in the doorway. Anabel eases out from underneath me, and I rest my weight on my elbows. "I need to go and help Katya sort this mess out," she tells me. "I'm glad you're safe, little brother. And I'm sorry I ever thought you a spoilt brat. You proved me wrong." She offers me a smile as she stands.

I can't return it.

Aleesha kneels beside me and holds out a water bottle. "Thought you might be thirsty. You can't have anything to eat, I'm afraid. Not until you've been in the pod."

My stomach clenches at the mention of food. I reach out with my left hand. The layers of dressings and bandage make it look as if I'm wearing a boxing glove. "I might struggle to get the lid off."

"Oh, sorry." Aleesha unscrews the cap and hands the bottle to me.

I let the cool liquid slide down my throat. It doesn't fully remove the taste of vomit, but it does ease the grating feeling in my throat. I can't bring myself to talk about Bryn, so I forestall her inevitable questions with one of my own.

"What's going on out there?" I hand the bottle back to her.

"The government forces have surrendered. All their leaders are dead, and the people below them don't seem inclined to fight the Chain. Katya's kind of in charge, but it's all pretty chaotic." She shrugs. "I've mostly been in here with you. Just left to check that Rogue and my people had been released and were getting the treatment they needed. I ... I had hoped to be here when you woke up."

"It's okay." I pause. "Katya said London is yours."

"*Ours*," Aleesha corrects. "I don't think she wants to stay. But someone has to create order, and she's probably as good a person as any. She promised to stay until after the election, then she'll leave."

She hesitates. "I think I believe her. I don't think she agreed with Richard about everything he was doing."

"But why did she kill him? To save you?"

Aleesha's gaze flicks up to where Katya had been standing when she'd fired those two shots. "Perhaps," she says softly. "Maybe my father went too far, even for her ruthless heart." She looks back down at me. "Or maybe she just wanted control of the Chain and saw an opportunity to get rid of him. Who knows.

"Anyway, I spoke to Ella to let her know you were okay. Sounds like she's got everything under control at the factory."

I nod my thanks.

"How's the pain? Do you need some more meds?"

"No. It's fine." I look past her to Richard's body. The sheet covering him seems to take up half the room. "I'm sorry about your father."

Aleesha's eyes tighten. "Me, too. But he wasn't the man I thought he was. The man I wanted him to be." She swallows and looks down. "I should have realized it sooner, but I wanted to have a father so badly. Someone who cared for me and would look out for me—" Her voice breaks, and she scrubs at her nose with a fist. "Anyway, what I wanted was a dream. And dreams don't always come true."

"You don't need him, you know. You've never needed him."

"I know."

"And you have me, Abby and—" My voice chokes as I almost say Bryn's name. I swallow. "And your Phoenixes. I mean, that's a pretty *big* family right there."

She chuckles softly and looks down at me, but behind the smile on her face is a deep sadness. I take her hand with my uninjured one.

"I won't leave you," I say quietly. "Unless you want me to."

Her eyes glint. "We've been there once, and I don't remember it turning out so well."

She pauses and glances back at the shapeless body under the sheet.

510

"He supplied the Bigland Boys with weapons, you know. He claimed they'd been stolen, but I should have seen through that lie. Denzel isn't smart enough to carry out that kind of operation." She idly taps the water bottle on the floor. "He must have thought it was the only way of getting my people to fight for him. He manipulated me, just like he manipulated everyone else."

I give her hand a squeeze. "It's over now. You'll get your headquarters back."

"It's just a building. It's only as important as the people in it." She pulls her hand from my grasp and wipes a tear from her eye.

"How many did you lose?" I ask quietly.

"Too many." She takes a deep breath. "But even one person would have been one too many."

I envy her tears, her grief, her ability to feel.

My gaze turns to the other sheet-covered bodies. I turn on my side and begin to drag myself across the floor.

"Stop, Trey. You're not supposed to—"

"I just need to see him."

Perhaps if I see him, I'll realize that he's really gone, and I can finally cry.

With Aleesha's help, I pull myself to sitting, then reach out to pull the sheet off his head. He's still face down. "Help me roll him over."

"Trey, I don't think—"

"Help. Me. Roll. Him. Over."

Aleesha falls silent and steps over Bryn's body. Together, we heave him onto his back. The sheet is large enough that it still covers his body, the underside spotted with blood. *Where the darts hit him.* I swallow and drag my gaze up to his face, which apart from a couple of scratches, is unscathed. His eyes are closed, but I brush my fingers over them anyway.

"Why did he do it?" I murmur.

"Because he loved you, Trey. More than he loved himself."

Something stirs in my core. A thorn of anger pierces the numbness gripping my body.

Anger that he is dead while I am alive.

Anger that he didn't get the happiness he deserved.

Anger that his death was for nothing.

A tear lands on Bryn's cheek. I brush it away, but it's followed by another, then a third. I reach up to my cheeks, but they are still dry, though my body feels heavy with grief.

I close my eyes and lean forward, resting my forehead against Aleesha's. Inside, I feel empty and cold, but her hand is warm as it finds mine. I cling to that, hoping I won't remain this numb shell of a person forever. I press my palm to hers, then intertwine our fingers knowing I will never – can never – let her go. Aleesha's salty tears wet my skin, caressing my lips before they fall.

My eyes may be dry, but she cries for both of us.

49

Aleesha

I look down from the rooftop I'm standing on as Samson wheels himself up onto the stage to get sworn in as President. Barnes follows him, looking uncomfortable in a dress suit and heels. In the crowd below, Anders and Danny jostle to get through to where Rogue and Megan stand. They'd invited me to join them, but I don't like crowds, and besides, I knew I'd get a better view from up here. If this were Outside, others would have thought the same, but Insiders are less imaginative when it comes to getting around. Beneath me, drone cameras hover over the heads of the people gathered to watch Samson officially become Prime Minster of Britannia.

Prime Minister, not President. A new title for a new era.

The election was held two days ago, less than three weeks after the government forces surrendered. It was the first election since the Wall was put up in which every citizen, Insider and Outsider, was able to vote.

Even in his wheelchair, Samson had cut an imposing figure, drawing both Outsiders and Insiders to his cause. His campaign had centred around a promise to take down the Wall within three months and, over the next five years, redistribute wealth to fund improvements to education and healthcare, while allowing Insiders to keep their existing privileges. He had promised to form a government made up of an equal number of Insiders and Outsiders.

He had won by a landslide. But I worry that perhaps he was too ambitious in his plans, too hasty in wanting to take down this barrier that has existed for people's lifetimes. I wonder if he has really gauged the strength of the hatred that still infuses so many Outsiders, if he is too trusting of them. I worry they will turn to violence when they see what's on the other side of the Wall.

But that is his problem to deal with now. Not mine.

Already, the colour of the Wall has been changed to a pale grey. No bright colours, no "this is what you're missing out on". Just grey to blend in with the buildings around it. Outsiders are allowed to go through the gates, but anyone who causes trouble is quickly captured and given a warning. The Metz are gone, but Anabel has gathered up the remaining palace guard and many of those who were Metz officers to form a new group of law keepers. Leon and a couple of the Metz officers I'd freed have already decided to sign up.

Although the nanobots have been removed from all food production lines, the truth about how the Wall works has not been revealed. Samson thought it too dangerous, both for Outsiders and Insiders alike. I agree with him. Best they still fear it for now.

Louis runs the Coleman factory now, with more than a little help from Ella. His father has retired to their country home. Louis doesn't like to talk about him, and I sense he, too, has lost his family, though in a different way than Trey. Hendricks fell in line, too, once he realized Samson was serious in his threat to close down the factory in favour of imported food if he didn't comply.

Ella's set up food lines Outside, hiring people to hand out soup and bread to the street hobies and anyone else who can't afford to buy their own. It's cheap food and hardly filling, but it's a start.

There's a ripple of applause as an official wearing ceremonial robes places a heavy chain around Samson's neck and shakes his hand. Samson waves his arm to thank the crowd, then wheels himself to the front of the stage and launches into a speech.

I wonder if Trey is watching this from his house in Wales. I'm sad he's not here with me. However busy I keep myself, however much I fill my days with, it still feels like part of me is missing. But I know he needed time away from London to heal. And Abby needed him more than me.

I turn at the sound of footsteps, then stiffen when I catch sight of a hooded figure moving between the cooling units and vents on the rooftop. Slowly, I draw a knife from a hidden pocket in the seam of my trousers. It's illegal to carry a knife Inside, but I'm not brave enough to walk the streets unarmed. It seems my paranoia was justified.

The hood shades the person's face, but there's something familiar about their gait, the swing of their hips. A tendril of blonde hair escapes the hood as they pause ten paces away.

"I thought I might find you up here." Katya reaches up and lifts the hood off her face. "You stand out like a sore thumb. A good target for a sniper."

Her voice is mild, but my pulse quickens, and I weigh the knife in my hand, poised to throw it if need be.

Katya's gaze drops to the blade. "I'm not here to hurt you, Aleesha. I just wanted to say goodbye."

She comes to stand next to me. I step to the side, putting a bit of extra distance between us.

"You're leaving then?"

She nods. "We'll be moving out tonight, back to one of our bases on the continent."

"And what will the Chain do next?"

"Recuperate. Build our strength. See where we are needed." Her voice sounds detached, her face as expressionless and beautiful as ever. I wonder what goes on in that mind of hers.

"Was that why you killed him? So you could become the Chain's leader?"

Katya is silent for a moment. "I will continue the good work he started. There are many wounds he inflicted in our organisation that need to heal."

It is not really an answer.

A breath of wind catches her hair as she looks out over the city. "He was good once, you know. But even when he met you, he was Richard Masterton. Ricus Meyer died a long time ago."

I bob my head, then ask a question that's been on my mind. "He killed Lamar, didn't he?"

Katya glances at me in surprise. "Yes ... Well, not directly, but he ordered his death. Lamar had gone rotten. He questioned Richard's orders, then refused to carry them out."

"You mean he didn't think what Richard was doing was right?"

Katya ignores the question. "How did you find out?"

"I assumed Samson had killed him, but when I asked him about it, he laughed it off. Plus, Lamar was too smart to get murdered in some random gang fight."

She gives a low chuckle. "You're clever, Aleesha. Smarter than I gave you credit for. But you *are* your father's daughter."

"And my mother's."

"Yes."

She falls silent for a moment, then turns, her emerald eyes appraising me. "I thought you were like him. Like me. But you're not. You're better than both of us. I know you wanted to fix him, but it wouldn't have worked. Don't ... Don't become like us, okay?"

I swallow and nod, not knowing what to say.

A smile ghosts across her face. "Goodbye, Aleesha. And don't take this the wrong way, but I hope we don't meet again."

I feel the corner of my mouth lift. "The feeling is mutual."

I wonder if she expects me to thank her for killing my father, for doing what I could not. But she just turns and walks away.

"Did you love him?" I call after her.

Katya pauses and turns back to me. "Love? I think I've forgotten what that is." She looks away, and her voice drops so I can barely pick up her next words. "Or perhaps I am just incapable of it."

I watch until she disappears behind a low wall, thinking back to what she'd told me about her childhood. My mind wanders down the route my life could have taken if I had never met Lily, Trey or Abby. If I'd never been offered friendship, compassion and unconditional love. A path where I continued doing what I needed to do in order to survive, using my looks and intelligence to manipulate the men around me while closing off my heart. Would I have ended up like her, sealing the cracks of my childhood trauma with an unending drive for vengeance and power?

It must be a lonely life.

I will never forgive Katya for killing Andrew Goldsmith, but I am grateful to her for showing me what I could have become.

And as I watch the crowd cheering Samson's speech below me – watch Rogue plant a long kiss on Megan's lips, watch Anders' face crease in puzzlement as Danny shows him the chit he'd picked from his pocket – I vow I will never become that person.

Not when I have a life to live, a city to help rebuild.

What has happened is in the past.

Now it's time to look to the future.

* * * *

I set the comm station up on my roof. It has been my only home for so many years, but now it's official. I have the deeds to the entire building in a safe box, which Rogue scavenged for me from the Metz compound, along with those to the warehouse that had been Phoenix headquarters.

Katya had made good on my father's promise to help me take back the building from the Bigland Boys. But the satisfaction of having Denzel trembling on his knees in front of me, my knife pressing against his throat, was brief and shallow. I felt little anger or hatred toward him. Just pity. Like all bullies, he was a coward when beaten. He'd pissed himself before I could throw him out of the building.

The roof I stand on will soon be torn down. The structure has been deemed unsound. Samson has promised that whatever is built in its place will be mine, and I already have big plans for it – a home for those who have no home. But part of me will be sad to see it go. It's only a crumbling piece of concrete, but it's *my* crumbling piece of concrete. My refuge. How many nights did I spend up here, staring out at the Wall, wondering if I'd ever see the other side of it?

"Boss?" A small voice pipes up from the side of the roof. "Here's the final bit."

"Thanks, Tommy."

He scurries over, clutching a scrap of wire. "I'll do it. Jameson showed me how." He bends over the comm station Jameson had built for me.

The corners of my lips twitch. Jameson's health has improved so much since I'd invited him to join us at Phoenix headquarters. He and Jax have formed a strong, if rather silent, friendship, and Tommy's interest in everything mechanical was enough of a distraction from the horrors of what had happened to him that he's slowly started coming out of his shell.

"Anders asked if you'd be comin' back to HQ for dinner. Got

somethin' he wants to chat to you about." Tommy tilts his head and grins at me. "An' Danny's carvin' faces into those pumpkins Megan found. They're awesome! He did one of the President and one of yer da. Made 'em look like monsters."

I roll my eyes. "Does he not have better things to do with his time?"

A pang of sadness tugs at my chest. I guess they seemed like monsters to Outsiders. One man destroyed their lives, the other tore their city apart. When I'd managed to get the remnants of my Phoenixes back together, it had shocked me how few of us there were. The memories of our friends are carved into our hearts, the scars of their loss much deeper than the scars visible on our skin. They died for us. For a better world.

However long it takes, I will create a world that's worthy of their sacrifice.

"There. Yer done." Tommy sits back and flexes his fingers, a gesture he's picked up from Anders. "Wanna test it?"

"If you've set it up, I'm sure it'll work fine."

Tommy's chest swells. "Should do," he says confidently, "but I can wait around if you have any trouble."

I give him a smile. "I think I'll be fine. Thank you. Tell Anders I'll be back in an hour or so."

"Sure thing." He jumps to his feet. "Say 'hi' to Trey for me."

"Will do."

I watch as he disappears over the edge of the roof to climb back down to the ground, then glance at the comm band on my wrist. Five minutes.

I walk over to the shelter in the centre of the roof. Kneeling at the back, I wiggle out the loose brick and retrieve my old lockbox. I open it. Inside is another box – the beautifully painted one Jay had bought me for Lily's ashes. I lift it out and rest it on my lap, running my hand over the pattern.

"I wish you were here to see this, Lily."

I lift the amulet from around my neck. It feels different now. For so long, I clung to it as a symbol of my past and my hopes for the future. But I don't need it anymore. My future is mine to determine. As for my mother, she's safe in my heart.

I rub my thumb over the three points of the triquetra. I used to think they represented my father, mother and me, but now I think they can represent many things. The government, the Prime Minister and the people. The three pillars of the democracy we're trying to build. Or perhaps it's just a piece of glass and metal bent into a pattern and has no greater meaning.

I place the amulet into Lily's box and close the lid, then place it back into my lockbox. At one time it held tronk and whatever chits I'd managed to scrounge. Now it holds something far more precious – memories.

As I slide the brick back into place, the scratches on the wall above catch my eye. I've got behind on my markings these past few months, so I draw my blade and scratch a couple more into the brick to bring it up to date. Soon, all too soon, these bricks will come crashing down and a new building will arise.

I will miss my rooftop. But I don't need it now. Not the way I once did.

I glance at my wristband. It is time.

Long-range comm units are almost exclusively reserved for government use, but Jameson cobbled together this one for me out of some spare parts we found in Giles's home. I type in the code I've memorized and wait. There's a crackle and hiss.

Come on.

The amber light turns to green and flashes once, twice. An image flickers in the air, then disappears. *No.* I reach out, but before I can twist the small dial, the image returns, clear and strong.

520

I close my eyes and feel hot tears prick at the back of them, though I do not know why. I should be happy to see him. I *am* happy. But sometimes I miss him so much it hurts.

Trey smiles at me. "What took you so long?"

I shrug, sniffing. "Oh, you know ... Sorting the city out and all that. Did you watch the ceremony?"

Trey nods. "I think he'll do a good job. I looked for you in the crowd but couldn't see you."

"I was on a rooftop." I don't tell him about Katya. "How's Wales?"

"Green. Beautiful. Peaceful. Abby loves it here. She's waged war against the garden, and I'm pretty sure she's winning." He smiles softly. "She misses you. We both do."

"I miss you, too."

I clear my throat. "I saw Ella yesterday. She said she might get out there at some point, once a pod becomes available."

"You should come out, too. You might like it."

"Soon. Once things are a bit more sorted."

We both know I'm lying. There is too much for me to do here to leave. This is my home. These people are my family. But perhaps a visit ...

I reach out, my fingers spread wide. Hundreds of miles away, Trey reaches out in a mirror image. Well, not quite a mirror image. Two fingers are missing on his left hand. It's a visual reminder of the hurt he has suffered, but I know the real wounds linger much deeper. Those will take longer to heal.

There is no warmth in the holo's touch, no tingle of excitement or spark of energy. But it makes me feel closer to him somehow, as if he really is here with me.

The holo image flickers, then stills again.

A tear runs down my cheek, then another. I allow them to fall as I smile through them so he can see that, despite the lies, despite the promises we have made and broken, despite the fact he is there and I am here, and that we have never been further apart, despite everything, I love him.

One day, I'll tell him that.

One day.

Epilogue

Aleesha (3 months later)

The grass is still wet as I walk across the garden and into the woods. Dew, Abby had called it, after I'd ventured outside on my first morning and returned with the legs of my jeans soaked, wishing I hadn't left my boots in London. Another new word. It seems the countryside has a language all its own. One I have yet to learn.

I know where I'll find Trey – perched on the flat boulder by the stream. It's hard to move silently through the woods when leaves rustle and twigs snap at every step, but the babbling of the water tumbling over its stony bed masks the sound of my approach. I step out into the clearing.

"Hey," Trey says, staring down at the water.

"Hey." I push myself up to sit beside him on the rock and wiggle closer, feeling the cold seep through my jeans. "Nightmares again?"

Trey jerks his head. "Sorry. Didn't mean to wake you."

"It's okay."

The first night I heard him screaming, I'd rushed into his room to find him tangled in the bedsheets, sweating. He'd bolted upright, his eyes focusing on the knife in my hand. I'd gone to push it back into my belt before realizing the pyjamas Abby had given me to wear didn't have a belt or pockets. Still, at least it had caused the briefest flicker of a smile to cross his face.

"You know we're in the middle of nowhere, right?" he had said, after he'd managed to stop his hands shaking. "There is literally no one out there to attack us."

I'd held him that night until he'd fallen back to sleep, and every night since. It hadn't stopped the nightmares, but Trey said it helped to have me there.

"Bryn again?"

"My father this time. I mean, my other father." He tries to smile. "I'm sure they'll eventually disappear. It just takes time."

I reach out and take his hand. It's cold. He's been sitting here a while. "I can send the pod back, stay longer."

He intertwines his remaining fingers through mine. "No, it's fine. You need to get back. The building comes down tomorrow, right?"

I nod. In twenty-four hours, the barren, concrete roof I'd spent so many nights on will be no more. I'm no longer sad to say goodbye to it, but excited about what will rise in its place. "Building work starts in two weeks, once they've cleared the site."

I approved the final plans with the architects ten days ago. Despite Samson ruling that all citizens were now legal, there were many children whose parents didn't come forward to claim them. Some of those children already have a home in Milicent's old house, the huge bedrooms having been converted into dormitories and the reception rooms into classrooms. Ella laughed when she described the expression on Thomas's face as she went through each room, ordering the priceless paintings and furnishings to be sold. But I've been there almost every day helping the kids, including Tommy and Helen, settle in, and all I see is a firm, yet kind man. A man the children adore who seems to have found a happiness many people would envy.

More children will be housed in the new children's home and school that will be built on the site of the old apartment block. It will be a place of safety, learning and happiness. A home for children who have never known a real home. I have already named it, the bold, bright letters curving above the arched entrance clear in my mind.

Lily's House.

"Perhaps I should go back, too ..." Trey sighs. "It just feels too soon. Here, I can forget about the rest of the world. I know it's not a long-term solution, but for now ... I just need a bit more time." He grimaces. "Sorry."

"Don't be."

Trey's changed. The man I found when I finally made the trip out to Wales at the beginning of the week was not the boy I knew in London. Though I'd spoken to him via the comm station twice a week, his holo image hadn't prepared me for seeing him. His eyes are still haunted by the horrors he's experienced, dark circles under them evidence of his disrupted sleep.

He's changed, but he is also still the Trey I love. In time, he will accept the scars of grief and learn how to carry them. I am more practiced than him at that, though I'm not sure how I would have responded to losing both my parents and the man I'd come to think of as a second father in the span of a few weeks.

He didn't speak about Bryn's death in the days immediately afterward. I think he was still in shock. When I arrived here, at the house in the woods, Abby took me to one side and begged me to get him to talk about it. She'd said he cries in private, but when she tries to talk about Bryn, he closes up and walks away. I guess people grieve in different ways.

Even with me, it was only after the second nightmare that he finally broke down and mentioned Bryn's name. It was like a dam had burst. He talked and talked until the faint glow of morning spread above the trees.

We have spent so much time this week talking, sitting together, talking some more. It feels like a luxury, having the time and space to just be.

I wish I could do something to take away his pain, but I know from bitter experience that I can only walk part of this journey with him. I can't remove the burden from his shoulders. But secretly, I carry a hope that when he finally does heal, he'll be able to return to London and join me at the school. He's patient, kind, understanding – everything a good teacher should be.

"You know, sometimes I wake up and, for a moment, forget all this has happened. The fact I've lost my parents, my home, everything. Then it hits me again like a tidal wave, crashing down and swallowing me up." He falls silent. "Then, when it recedes, I realize I'm still alive, and although I've lost many things, I've also gained some. What I still haven't figured out is whether it was worth the cost."

I squeeze his hand and rest my head on his shoulder. "It's not as simple as that. How can you measure what a life is worth? You can't weigh one person's life against another, or freedom against family."

He sighs. "You're right. Again."

"I love you. You know that, right?"

He kisses the top of my head. "And I love you."

My eyes stray to his knee. I know it causes him pain, though he rarely complains about it. The medics hadn't been able to piece together the fragments of bone, so they'd replaced it with an artificial one, but his rehabilitation hasn't gone as well as they'd hoped. The boulder we sit on is the furthest from the house he can comfortably walk at the moment. Sometimes, I catch him looking longingly up at the mountain that rises above the treetops, and I want to tell him that he will go up there again, but I worry that will only make him feel worse.

A small bird lands on a stone in the stream and bobs its head, chirruping as it washes itself. There is so much beauty out here, so much colour and life. Yet I feel a strange sense of unease walking through the woods or up to the small lake behind the house. I am a stranger in this unfamiliar land, so different in every way from the streets of Area Four. I think I could grow to like it, but I'm not sure it would ever feel like home.

"Is it time?"

"Yes." Reluctantly, I lift my head from his shoulder. I reach up and turn his face toward me so I can look into his eyes. "Promise you'll tell me if you need me to come out?"

"I promise."

I know he's telling the truth, but I still make a mental note to check in with Abby more often. "It's getting easier to get long-distance pods now. And if I tell Samson it's for you, he'll make it happen."

"I'm not sure you should be abusing your friendship with the President in that way." Trey smiles, but it fades before reaching his eyes.

"Prime Minister now. He felt the term President was too grand." I hop off the boulder. "Besides, you're a hero. That comes with privileges."

"I don't feel like a hero." Trey stiffly clambers down.

I wrap my arms around him and tilt my face up to his. "You are. And you will feel whole again. Happy again. I promise."

I have lost count of the number of lies and false promises I have made in my life. But this is one promise I will not break.

I lift up onto my toes and kiss him, putting every part of me into the touch of his lips against mine. I kiss him like it's the first time,

527

the last time and all the times in between, and for a wonderful, long moment, our world is this kiss, nothing else. There is no death, war or grief. No sorrow or longing for what could have been. There is only here and now, two people in love.

But, eventually, it has to end.

He is the first to pull away. In his eyes, behind the shadows, I see a spark of light and hope, and a certainty settles in my heart that he will be okay.

We will be okay. We just need time.

We walk hand in hand back through the birch trees and into the orchard. I remember sitting around Abby's kitchen table in London and Trey telling me about the apple trees here. He'd said they made something called cider from them. I have eaten two apples every day since I've been here, and last night, I picked enough to fill a bag to take back to London with me.

Abby has transformed the garden from the tangled mess of overgrown brambles Trey had said were here. Neat beds are cut into the lawn, and in the Plexiglas hothouse, seeds for winter crops already start to poke up. This garden has been her saviour, I think. She has poured all her grief into it, digging and building to create her and Bryn's dream.

In the kitchen, a pot of oats bubbles on the stove.

"They're here now. Can we eat?" Tommy jumps down from his chair and grabs his bowl, running over.

"You know yer supposed to wait, Tommy," Helen Gollin calls from the table. But she wriggles in her chair, clearly impatient to join him.

The kids had come out with me as a test for a new project Abby had thought up. A countryside school, where children from the city can stay for a week to learn about growing food and life outside London. So far, the trial has been a huge success. Tommy and Helen have helped Abby in the hothouse, climbed trees and pulled up lots of the pretty, albeit scraggly, plants Abby calls weeds. Though she wasn't quite so happy when Tommy proudly showed her the thorny plant he'd dug up using the big spade. Apparently, the rose wasn't a weed.

Helen has blossomed over the past week, though Tommy still seems on edge. Like me, he is a child of the city, and this place, however new and exciting, doesn't feel like home.

Abby ruffles Tommy's curls and gently pushes him back toward the table. "I'll bring it over now."

She's going to miss them both, but perhaps, if the project does work out, she'll end up with part of the life she's dreamed of. A countryside home and plenty of children to fuss over. I think she'll be happy here.

As I sit down, I catch sight of the wooden box on the mantlepiece above the fire. Abby follows my gaze. "What do you think? Would he be bored stiff out here?"

"I think he'd have loved it," I reply, holding my bowl up to her ladle.

Tears glisten in her eyes. "I hope so. And, in a way, it feels like he is here." She sniffs. "That probably sounds weird."

I remember the amulet my mother had given me and how I'd carried it around for years. It had felt like I always had part of her close. I smile. "It doesn't sound weird at all."

Abby ladles the oats into the remaining bowls, then sits down. "Well, this is nice," she says brightly. "Like we're a real family."

Helen scowls at Tommy. "Why you kickin' me under the table?"

Tommy looks innocent. "Wasn't."

"You were so!"

Trey rolls his eyes. "Family, huh?"

But later, as our pod rises and I look down at her and Trey standing in the garden waving, Abby's words ring through my mind.

A real family.

It wasn't the family I thought I'd ever end up with, but I've realized family is not just the people you're born to or raised with. It's the people you choose to spend your life with.

These people – Trey, Abby and my Phoenixes – are my family.

And I wouldn't have it any other way.

Afterword

As a reader, finishing a series I love always fills me with mixed emotions. There's joy (and perhaps sadness) in reaching a happy or bittersweet ending and the satisfaction of seeing plot twists unravel and characters getting the endings they deserve. But there's also a vague sense of disappointment and loss at having to leave the world you love behind.

As an author, I feel similarly conflicted. Over the years it has taken me to write The Wall Series, I have grown to love my characters – even those who may not be particularly sympathetic. They've come to life in my mind, so much so, that I sometimes find myself in a situation wondering what Aleesha would do!

I hope very much that you've felt some of these emotions while reading this book and consider it a worthy end to the series.

If you have a spare five minutes, I'd really appreciate a short review explaining what you loved about the series on Amazon and Goodreads.

So what's next?

Well, if you're not ready to leave the world of The Wall Series yet, I have a couple of short stories set in this world, plus some exclusive deleted scenes from the first draft of Liberators (including the President's execution and a different twist on the final climax scene). You can get these for free, along with a copy of my standalone dystopian fantasy novella, Trial by Fire, when you sign up for my Readers' Club. This is also the best way to find out what I'm working on next and when my next series will be released.

Sign up here: https://www.subscribepage.com/thewallseries

I have many people to thank for helping me take Liberators from a scrawling mess of notes to the finished product you've read today. First, thanks to my beta reading team: Anni, Candy, Clare, Emma, Mum and Rhiannon. You always push me to improve my writing and force me to face those inconvenient plot problems I try to hide from!

In July 2019, I sat in an Edinburgh cafe bemoaning my struggles with plotting this book. The challenge felt overwhelming, and I wasn't sure I was up to it. My thanks to Derek, Kasia and Rhiannon for listing to my rambling plot, making suggestions and giving me faith that it would come good. And Derek – I know I spent the next six months refusing to follow your advice about the ending, but you were right all along.

Two wonderful editors have guided my hand and I owe a huge debt of thanks to Kim Young and Sophie Playle for their work on this and the previous books in the series. Thanks also to my cover designers, MoorBooks Design and Epic Fantasy Covers for making my books look so beautiful.

Finally, thank you to Sam. For always believing in me and never failing to doubt that I could finish what I started.

As Aleesha's and Trey's story draws to a close, another story begins. A new world with new characters, fighting for freedom, truth and love. I can't wait to discover what adventures they will take me on.

Alison xx

29 April 2020

P.S. Don't forget to sign up to my newsletter for updates on new

releases and free bonus content: https://www.subscribepage.com/
thewallseries

About the Author

Alison Ingleby is a USA Today bestselling author of sci-fi and fantasy fiction. She loves writing cross-genre books featuring complex characters, twisting plots and fast-paced action with a dash of romance.

When not writing, Alison enjoys reading, drinking tea and spending time outdoors. She lives in Yorkshire, England, but her heart loiters by the sea in north-west Scotland.

You can find out more about Alison on her website: https://alisoningleby.com/

Alison's Books

The Wall Series
Expendables (Book One)
Infiltrators (Book Two)
Defenders (Book Three)
Liberators (Book Four)
Outsider (prequel)

Short stories & novellas:

The Faerie Flag – a spellbinding retelling of the classic Scottish legend. For lovers of fantasy stories, fae and gentle romance.

Red Sun Rising: A Story from the Alteruvium Expanse – a short science fiction story about first contact, betrayal and a mother's love.

Made in the USA
Monee, IL
17 December 2022

22093469R00319